# Toward a
# Peaceable
# Future

D1601164

# Toward a
# Peaceable
# Future

Redefining Peace, Security, and *Kyosei*
from a Multidisciplinary Perspective

**Edited by Yoichiro Murakami,
Noriko Kawamura, and Shin Chiba**

The Thomas S. Foley Institute for
Public Policy and Public Service

WASHINGTON STATE UNIVERSITY

The Thomas S. Foley Institute for Public Policy and Public Service
PO Box 644840
Pullman, Washington 99164-4840

*Library of Congress Cataloging-in-Publication Data*

Toward a peaceable future : redefining peace, security, and *kyosei* from
a multidisciplinary perspective / edited by Yoichiro Murakami, Noriko
Kawamura, and Shin Chiba.
    p. cm.
  ISBN 0-615-12710-X
  1.  Peace--Study and teaching. 2.  Security, International--Study and
teaching.  I. Murakami, Yoichiro, 1936- II. Kawamura, Noriko, 1955- III.
Chiba, Shin, 1949-
  JZ5534.T69 2005
  303.6'6--dc22

                           2005000677

# Contents

# Foreword

The Thomas S. Foley Institute for Public Policy and Public Service was established in 1995 at Washington State University (WSU). The Institute, named in honor of Thomas S. Foley, former speaker of the U.S. House of Representatives and former U.S. Ambassador to Japan, was created to foster civic education, public service, and public policy research.

Located on the Pullman, Washington campus of Washington State University, the Institute supports programs in three general areas: Student and Educational Programs, Public Education and Public Service, and Public Policy Research.

**Student and Educational Programs.** The Foley Institute is a leader in efforts aimed at improving undergraduate and graduate educational opportunities. The Institute awards Scholarships and Fellowships to students who have demonstrated academic excellence and desire to pursue a public-service-oriented career. An Internship Coordinator is available to arrange student placements in legislative offices, public agencies, and non-profit organizations. Invited speakers from across the world regularly address WSU classes on topics of contemporary concern.

**Public Education and Public Service.** The nation is currently in the midst of a crisis in public confidence in the ability of our democratic institutions to work effectively. The Foley Institute makes an important contribution in fostering civic literacy, community involvement in public decisions, and a commitment to public service. Annual programs such as the Congressional and Presidential Scholar Lecture and the Civil Society and American Governance Lecture bring national, state, and local experts to campus to spark lively discussions and community awareness on a variety of topics.

**Public Policy Research.** The Foley Institute sponsors Public Policy Symposia featuring policy specialists, elected officials, and other experts on problems facing all levels of government. The Institute also supports public policy research conferences on a wide variety of domestic and international issues. Examples include events focusing on endangered salmon in the Pacific Northwest, the relationship between the decisions of the Rehnquist Supreme Court and congressional policymaking, the implications of globalization for international trade, the need for reform of the institutions and policies governing American public lands, the ramifications of deregulating the U.S.'s electric power supplies, and racial profiling, to name but a few. The Institute also maintains a competitive Summer Graduate Fellows program that assists WSU Ph.D. students with their research programs.

**The Foley Congressional Collection.** The Institute is the home of the Thomas S. Foley Congressional papers, library, artwork, photographs, and other memorabilia. The gift of the Foley collection means that Washington State University is the depository of over 60 years of state and federal congressional history. The complete inventory of Foley materials is available on the World Wide Web at www.wsulibs.wsu.edu/holland/masc/foley/page.htm.

The Foley Institute also works hard to honor the legacy of Thomas S. Foley by maintaining **a substantive policy focus on three chief areas of inquiry** that were defining elements during his more than 50 years of public service. The first area of inquiry is the study of **Congress,** congressional policymaking, and the relationship of Congress to the Presidential and Judicial branches of American government. The second is **International Affairs**, with special emphases on the issues of globalization, peace, and security. The third major area of inquiry involves a policy area of critical importance to Eastern Washington and the Pacific

Northwest region

Northwest region: **environment and natural resource policy**. One of the main avenues for exploring and understanding this area of focus is our Annual Science, Technology, Environment and Democracy lecture series.

This book fits squarely within the realm of International Affairs and is a product of Washington State University (WSU) and the Foley Institute's multi-disciplinary *Peace and Security Research Partnership* with International Christian University (ICU) of Japan. The partnership currently involves a total of 18 College of Liberal Arts faculty at WSU and 15 scholars from ICU. The purpose of the partnership is to deploy the significant scholarly resources of both universities in pursuit of a grand theory of "peace" that will ultimately help humankind foster the kinds of understanding, relationships and institutions most conducive to an enduring state of peace and security. Additional activities include research conferences, more book publications, graduate student conferences, a new *Peace and Security* Lecture Series at WSU, as well as annual student and scholar exchanges.

As we move further into the 21st century, our educational institutions must facilitate a better understanding of the social, political, historical, and economic dimensions of the challenges ahead. We believe that this book, *Toward a Peaceable Future: Redefining Peace, Security, and Kyosei*, is a step in this direction. As such, the book is a natural extension of the educational and research missions of the Foley Institute, and of the land-grant mission of Washington State University. As a result, we at the Foley Institute are proud to be the primary sponsor of this volume along with our partners from International Christian University, and, by extension, the Japanese Ministry of Education and Science, who through their generous Center of Excellence Grant on Peace and Security, provided a significant amount of the financial support for the joint WSU-ICU conference held in Pullman, Washington in September 2004. Without the conference, and the tremendous support given to this effort by the Presidents of WSU and ICU, Lane Rawlins and Norihiko Suzuki, respectively, this book would not have been possible. We think that readers will find it informative, thought provoking, and an invaluable asset contributing to civic literacy as regards the study of peace and security.

Edward P. Weber, Director
*The Thomas S. Foley Institute*
*for Public Policy and Public Service*
*January 2005*
*Pullman, Washington*

# Preface

## By the Editors

This is an outcome of a multi-year research collaboration between International Christian University (ICU) in Tokyo, Japan and Washington State University (WSU) in Pullman, Washington. ICU received a competitive grant from the 21$^{st}$ Century Center of Excellence (COE) Program of the Japanese Ministry of Education and Science under the title, "Research and Education for Peace, Security, and Conviviality." The goal of this program is to develop "comprehensive peace studies" and serve as a center of excellence or a hub for peace studies in Japan, East Asia, and the world.

Thanks to the good will, friendship and leadership provided by President Lane Rawlins of WSU, ICU's Former President Masakichi Kinukawa, and Current President Norihiko Suzuki, ICU entered into a collaboration agreement with WSU to develop joint research and education in the area of "comprehensive peace studies." As part of this program, both universities are now collaborating closely in diverse areas such as peace studies, sociological surveys and statistics, gender and environmental studies, international cooperation, and organizing graduate student conferences.

In conjunction with this overall research collaboration between ICU and WSU, we held an international conference entitled "Defining Peace, Security, and *Kyosei*" from September 18 to 21, 2004 in Pullman. The conference was co-sponsored both by the Thomas S. Foley Institute for Public Policy and Policy Service at WSU and by International Christian University's COE Program. It was a lively, thought-provoking conference, which brought about thirty researchers from both universities and resulted in the presentation of twenty papers. Moreover, the high point of the conference was a stimulating keynote address entitled "Struggles with Globalization: International NGOs in East Asia," presented by Dr. Susan Pharr, Edwin O. Reischauer Professor of Japanese Politics at Harvard University. The introduction and chapters in this book are the collaborative products which came out of this exciting international conference.

The editors of this volume would like to express deepest gratitude to Presidents Rawlins, Kinukawa, and Suzuki from both universities for their leadership and commitment to the ICU-WSU research and education partnership. We also would like to express our deep appreciation to Professor Edward Weber, Director of the Thomas S. Foley Institute for Public Policy and Public Service at WSU for his untiring, energetic support to make the conference and this publication possible. We also are grateful for the financial support provided by the Center of Excellence Grant Program of the Japanese Ministry of Education and Science, the Thomas S. Foley Institute, the Initiation of Collaboration Grant from the Office of Vice Provost for Research at WSU, and the Completion Grant from the College of Liberal Arts at WSU. In addition, this conference and book project would not have been possible without the advice and encouragement of Robert Harder, Director of International Programs at WSU, and Marina Tolmacheva, Associate Dean of the College of Liberal Arts at WSU. Finally, we would like to extend our heart-felt thanks to Alice Davenport, who assisted in the English editing, and to the director and editor-in-chief of WSU Press, Mary Read and Glen Lindeman, as well as to Margie Kimball (program coordinator of the Foley Institute), Christina Eder (conference manager for the Foley Institute), and Tomoko Nagaoka in the COE Office at ICU. It is our hope that this volume stimulates and induces the furthering of a collaborative and multi-disciplinary theoretical attempt on the subjects of peace, security, and *kyosei*.

Yoichiro Murakami
Noriko Kawamura
Shin Chiba

# Introduction
# Peace, Security, and *Kyosei*
## By the Editors

∗

A new start is pleasant and exciting. Especially when we have a sense that we are witnessing the birth of something new, we feel great excitement even if it is a small beginning. This book has had such a genesis. Certainly, there are plenty of works already written on peace, security, or *kyosei*—a Japanese word we are translating for the time being as "living together." Peace studies is an already well-established discipline of social sciences around the world. Safety management has been institutionalized for some time in public and private sector organizations throughout the world, if not "security management." The question of whether it is possible for different groups of people to live together peacefully has been an important part of the ethico-philosophical discussions among concerned scholars. However, scholars so far have seldom engaged themselves in an endeavor to discuss these concepts on peace, security, and *kyosei* in a holistic and multi-disciplinary manner. In this volume, scholars from various fields and disciplines, mostly American and Japanese, are trying to undertake this challenging task.

∗∗

Let us begin our discussion with a definition or redefinition of the three key concepts. We need to do so not only because defining the concepts that we are dealing with is a basic and indispensable process for research of this kind, but also because current situations in our latemodern age inevitably prompt us to redefine these concepts in a new light. Contrary to general expectation of the populace for the inauguration of a peaceful new century, the beginning of the twenty-first century turned out to be a horrifying, nightmarish experience of disaster. The terrorist attacks on the World Trade Center in the United States on September 11, 2001 shocked the world. Hannah Arendt's description of the twentieth century as "the century of war and revolution" might be equally applicable to the new century. September 11 was immediately followed by the United States' invasion of Afghanistan on October 7, 2001. Under the leadership of the neo-conservatives within the Bush administration, an "anti-terrorist war" was launched against Saddam Hussein's Iraq in March 2003. Brutal conflicts between the occupied forces and the opposing guerillas and militia forces still continue in the land of Iraq. These current turbulent situations are bound to call for the redefinition of such important concepts as peace, security, and *kyosei* against the latemodern reality of today's insecure world.

Fruitful and creative explorations and discussions of these terms began a few decades ago in the academic fields of peace studies, philosophy and ethics, sociology, political theory, and international relations. Practitioners, professionals, and specialists in the non-academic "real world" have also undertaken the task of redefining these terms. Although it is impossible to discuss all of the meaningful and constructive intellectual work which has been accomplished over the past few decades concerning these terms, it is necessary to provide a rough sketch of a few selected but significant intellectual endeavors to redefine the concepts of peace, security and *kyosei*.

✳✳✳

First of all, from an etymological viewpoint, the English word "peace" is derived from a Latin word, *pacem* or *pax*. Its original meaning points to something achieved by contract or agreement. In that sense, peace is a state of being free from conflicts or wars among human groups. Even today, in most cases the word "peace" is used to mean basically a warless state achieved by means of agreement or contract between groups or nations. However, the relations among groups and nations today are more complicated than ever. Even the types of war have dramatically changed. Consequently, the definitions of peace which were sufficient in the past are no longer adequate or appropriate today.

For instance, the Norwegian peace research scholar Johan Galtung has explored the concept of peace in an epoch-making manner over four decades. His celebrated conceptual framework produced several axioms, now well-known to specialists and students of peace research and its related disciplines. These axioms make the distinction between "negative peace" and "positive peace," and between "direct violence" and "structural violence."

According to Galtung, it is important to distinguish two concepts of peace: negative peace and positive peace. While the concept of negative peace is defined as "the absence of organized violence" between major human groups such as nations and racial and ethnic groups, the concept of positive peace is defined as "a pattern of cooperation and integration between major human groups."[1] He also refers to negative peace as the "absence of direct violence" and positive peace as "social justice."[2] Here, the conceptual distinction between direct violence and structural violence comes to play an important role. On the one hand, direct violence is the appearance of violence in an unambiguous and manifest way; structural violence, on the other hand, appears in an indirect and latent form. This indirect violence is generally built into the social structures regulating relations between individuals, groups, and nations.[3]

Galtung further elaborates on the concept of structural violence by introducing three new terms: "influence," "actual realizations," and "potential realizations." Thus he defines this type of latent or structural violence as follows: "Violence is present when human beings are being influenced so that their actual somatic and mental realizations are below their potential realizations."[4] Structural violence is juxtaposed to the narrow concept of violence, i.e., direct violence where "violence is somatic incapacitation, or deprivation of health alone (with killing as the extreme form), at the hands of an actor who intends this to be the consequence."[5] Galtung's premise is that if peace might singularly mean the absence of this sort of direct violence alone, then highly unacceptable orders would still be compatible with peace. This is nothing but defeatism on the part of peace research.

Therefore, Galtung maintains that a broader concept of violence (i.e., structural violence) is indispensable, and that an extended and affirmative concept of peace (i.e., positive peace) implies the actuality of cooperation among human groups; the integration of these groups; and social justice in societal dimensions of human relationships. Galtung's contribution to the deeper and fuller understanding of peace is paradoxically the result of his acute and probing analyses of the nature of violence. For him violence in either manifest or latent form, as already indicated, is "the cause of the difference between the potential and the actual, between what could have been and what is."[6]

We do not have space here to meticulously trace the manifold significance of Galtung's distinctions for theoretical studies and scholarly analyses of the central notions of peace research: peace, war, violence, conflict, and so on. Here it suffices to say that using these Galtungian distinctions and concepts, peace research, as well as research into war and violence, began to acquire an important theoretical basis for later developments. In current usage, the concept of positive peace, as opposed to negative peace, includes societal integration and cooperation, the realization of social justice and equity. More broadly, positive peace also encompasses economic and political stability, respect for fundamental human rights of the people, the rule of law, democratic organization of social and political life, a high quality of social welfare, ecological sustainability, and so forth.

Admittedly, however, the word "peace" can be applied to the state of mind. In the Old Testament the idea of peace is used frequently to express a mental state, although it should correspond to the Hebrew word, *shalom*. It is interesting to note that there is something in common between the word *shalom* and the English word "safety." The word *shalom* was, and still is, used to express the hope that someone else is peaceful and well. *Shalom* signifies an integral state of well-being that encompasses international peace, social welfare, and safety, and an individual's health, happiness, and inner peace.

The word "safety" has its origin in Latin words, such as *salus* (noun) and *salvus* (adjective), both of which are related to the idea of health or well-being. From these Latin words many English words besides "safety" were derived. The verb "to save" is one, and "to salute" is another. The latter originally meant to "wish somebody well and in good health."

It is said that "security" also stemmed from the Latin word *securus*. This word consists of two parts, *sed* and *curus*, which respectively mean "without," and "sorrow" or "worries." Thus, the original meaning of security was "being free from care and worries." This suggests that the meanings of the word "security" and "peace" partially overlapped in the past, because, as stated above, "peace" is used to designate a state of mind, which is free from concerns and sorrows. But, today the word "security," apart from its original meaning in classical Latin, is used to refer to the state of the relationship among groups, nations, and states both in domestic and international contexts. In recent years, some theorists have also been using this word to express "human security." But this last usage still seems to be closely linked with the concept of national security. For the notion of human security presupposes that the concept of national security should be applied to the security of individual humans.

With regard to the term "safety," it might be useful to consider a definition of "risk" here. For the notion "risk" is almost always discussed in conjunction with safety or security. The most probable explanation of the etymological origin of the word "risk" is a Greek word, *rhiza*. This Greek word originally meant cliff, and it evolved into vulgar Latin (non-classical Latin) as the verb *risicare*. The Latin word originally meant to navigate among cliffs and came to mean running into danger. This discussion shows several important points related to the idea of risk. The most important point is that risk is related to what is done, or more accurately, what is to be done by human will. In other words, a danger or a hazard comes to be a risk when it is considered to be controllable by human will and hands. Many of the dangers and hazards were perceived in the past as Acts of God, but today these same dangers are referred to as risks. In that sense, in the modern "civilized" world risks seem to be propagating themselves.

There is one more point to be added on the discussion of the word "risk." In Japanese, interestingly, there is no original word to correspond to the English term "risk." In order to express what risk means in their own language, Japanese people use the English word—although the word's pronunciation is converted in accordance with Japanese phonetic system to *risuku*. That seems to suggest that the Japanese may have traditionally developed a different way of dealing with natural disasters than English speakers: that is, Japanese tended to reconcile themselves to possible negative outcomes from natural disasters, and were unwilling to interfere with the course of nature in order to control or overcome potential disasters.

An additional point to note is that, in recent decades, a significant transformation took place in our understanding of the concepts of security and safety. This transformation is what we would call a shift from an early modern, Hobbesian paradigm of "state security" to a latemodern, post-nation state paradigm of "human security." This is a significant paradigm shift in the conception of security or safety. One of the contributors and editors of this volume, Yoichiro Murakami, made a proposal for founding a new discipline *Anzengaku* (safety or security studies) in the Japanese academic context of humanities and social sciences. In our judgment, Murakami's proposal both presupposes that this paradigm shift has taken place, and represents the shift itself.[7] Several chapters in this volume will directly or indirectly address this paradigm shift in more details.

✶✶✶✶

Next, let us ask the question: what does the Japanese word *kyosei* mean? At the beginning of this introduction we assigned it a provisional English translation, "living together." But as some of the Japanese contributors to this volume indicate, this Japanese word is employed in various ways. This word consists of two characters: *kyo* which literally means "together," and *sei* which means "to live." The Japanese word *kyosei* was introduced first as an academic term in biology, to refer to symbiosis. *Kyosei* in this sense is used in accordance with the standard definition established in the field of biology. In biology *kyosei* or "symbiosis" is divided into six different subcategories. These subcategories are based on different types of mutual influences of various populations which dwell side by side, namely [plus, plus], [plus, minus], [plus, null], [minus, minus], [minus, null], [null, null]. These categories are respectively called mutualism, antagonism, commensalism, competition, amensalism, and neutrality. This well-defined biological term "symbiosis," however, only partially implies a favorable and positive "living together." When we use the word *kyosei* in Japanese, we usually use it to express a hope that individuals, groups and countries could live in peaceful and convivial ways. Thus, in 2003 when International Christian University (ICU) in Tokyo proposed undertaking a comprehensive peace studies project for the 21st Century Center of Excellence (COE) Program in Japan, ICU's proposal was organized under the three fundamental concepts, and we initially translated the third concept *kyosei* as "conviviality." However, we later realized that this English translation tends to puzzle native English speakers. In the process of collaboration of this project between ICU and WSU, we have come to the tentative conclusion that the Japanese word *kyosei* should be used, as it is, even in English language discussions.

Among Japanese intellectuals, for about two decades now, the concept of *kyosei* has increasingly become a popular term in the context of humanities and social sciences, despite the fact that it originated in the field of biology. But the precise meaning of *kyosei* is not yet firmly established in Japan, and the concept of *kyosei* remains open to diverse interpretations among scholars. Because of this, at this point we would like to mention briefly three basic types of *kyosei* in current Japanese discussions.

First, the well-known architect Noriaki Kurokawa was one of the first to use the term *kyosei* in the milieu of the U.S.-Japan trade conflicts of the 1980s: his popular 1987 work was entitled *Kyosei no shiso: mirai eno raifu sutairu* (The Thought of *Kyosei*: The Lifestyle for the Future). This is a toleration model of *kyosei* which maintains one's own sacred cultural values and traditions in a somewhat essentialist manner, while recognizing others' cultural values and traditions as well. If, as Michael Walzer argues in his book *On Toleration* (1997), the gist of toleration is the peaceful coexistence of different traditions and cultural values, Kurokawa's *kyosei* idea belongs to this toleration model.[8] Kurokawa's idea of *kyosei* is based upon his commitment as a cultural essentialist, and he argues that "the idea of *kyosei* is the one which mutually recognizes each other's sanctuary."[9] The practical intent of his argument consists in the rigorous protection of Japanese values and cultural expressions *vis-à-vis* the forces of globalization including the United States' strong demands for the deregulation of Japanese markets, especially the rice market. According to Kurokawa, "the sanctuary of Japan is, among others, the emperor system, rice cultivation, *sumo* wrestling, *kabuki*, tea ceremony (Sukiya architecture)."[10] He maintains that "the condition by which the sanctuary is the sanctuary is that it shuns away from scientific analysis and internationally shared rules. Rather, it embodies an aspect which cannot be understood, which is an area of mystery, an origin of self identity, and an origin of cultural pride."[11] This *kyosei* model of Kurokawa is not interested at all in the transformation of, or even revision of, Japanese cultural values via negotiation, interaction or commingling with other cultural traditions. Therefore, Shuji Ozeki is right in characterizing Kurokawa's idea of *kyosei* as a premodern, sanctuary type of *kyosei* and in criticizing its static and essentialist nature. Though on the surface Kurokawa's concept is certainly a kind of *kyosei*, the real intent of Kurokawa's *kyosei* strategy is to keep Japanese values intact, pure, and undefiled. This is not only an expression of his cultural nationalism but also a manifestation of his cultural centralism or fundamentalism.

The second type of *kyosei* is a conversation model presented by a liberal theorist of law, Tatsuo Inoue. Inoue's 1986 work *Kyosei no saho: kaiwa toshiteno seigi* (Manner of *Kyosei*: Justice as Conversation) remains a stimulating work in the field of legal and political philosophy. The author was successful in articulating his vision of liberal philosophy by exploring the inner and necessary relationships between justice and liberalism. Inoue attempts to capture the essential moment of the liberal type of *kyosei* in the form of ordinary human conversation: "Conversation is the most fundamental human manner of *kyosei*."[12] By means of conversation, different persons enter into a common forum of interaction which is exemplified by an old notion of *societas*.[13] Inoue presents this conversation model of *kyosei* against a widely accepted communication model. According to him, the popular communication model tends to jeopardize the free and casual interaction of heterogeneous persons and their respective standing as independent and autonomous beings.[14] According to Inoue, the communication model often presupposes the mode of social union not in terms of a *societas* but rather in terms of a *universitas*. The old notion of *universitas* regards itself as a substantial and instrumental type of organization, which intends to realize a certain pre-determined, common goal.

Thus, Inoue's conception of *kyosei* seeks a formal union over a substantive union. It attempts to affirm a mode of social union, as exemplified by *societas*, while stressing the primary importance of individuals' respective independence and privacy. Inoue chose the English word "conviviality" to express this kind of liberal, autonomous and conversational conception of *kyosei*. This liberal notion of *kyosei*, like conversation, means the enjoyment of the natural and joyful process of interaction among heterogeneous persons or groups. It signifies the moments of agreement, opposition, controversy, competition—and above all fair play and the joy of interaction—without expecting to attain any particular result from *kyosei*.[15] In the 1992 study, *Kyosei no boken* (The Adventure of *Kyosei*), Inoue and his co-authors have defined *kyosei* as "a mode of social union open to the heterogeneous." For the author, "*Kyosei* is … a mode of social union where different individuals with different ways of life are not merely capable of acknowledging one another's free activity and opportunity for participation but also are able to build up positively their mutual relationships."[16]

The third type of *kyosei* is a commonality model, which has been the most prevalent model and has been used by many scholars, including Shuji Ozeki. Ozeki adopted his theoretical basis for *kyosei* from Karl Marx's notion of species being, *Gattungswesen*. In contrast to the formality stressed in Inoue's notion of *kyosei*, Ozeki's idea is a substantive one oriented toward the achievement of the commonly shared goals such as ecological sustainability and social equality. Ozeki and others define *kyosei* as follows:

> The concept of *kyosei* (symbiosis) has come to obtain a new positive significance in the field of thought and social sciences. It was originally an ecological concept that pointed to the cohabitation of different living creatures in the ecological context of physiological and life-maintaining activities. But today the concept of *kyosei* is being developed and elaborated, so that it signifies the mode of living together with the sense of equality and mutuality, transforming one another mutually while acknowledging one another's difference, opposition and diversity.[17]

This concept of *kyosei* has now been used and applied to multiple dimensions and relationships such as the relationship of humanity and nature and interaction among various human groups. In Japan some current slogans, for example, include not only "*kyosei* between humanity and the natural environment" and "*kyosei* among different nations or ethnic groups," but also "*kyosei* between male and female components of the society" and "*kyosei* between the people in good health and the handicapped people."[18]

This third type of commonality model, with minor variations, seems to be generally accepted as the meaning of *kyosei* in the current Japanese context.[19] Ozeki methodically analyzes the conversation model of *kyosei* developed by Inoue, for example. Since the latter model is congenial with, and even strongly supportive of, market competition, Ozeki argues, the conversation model cannot fully establish a needed commonality with weaker partners (such as socially vulnerable groups, racial and cultural minorities, exploited natural environment, and so forth).[20] At the same time, however, the ontological basis of Ozeki's notion of *kyosei* ultimately seems to reside in the Marxist idea of *Gattungswesen* of human nature; that is, the model's semi-essentialist formulation is not altogether immune from the static and fixated characterization with which Ozeki found fault in the first model of *kyosei* as developed by Kurokawa.[21]

From the viewpoint of education sociology, Hidenori Fujita, one of the contributors to this volume, has proposed categorizing the prevalent notion of *kyosei* (as discussed in the Japanese setting) into four different types: "embracive symbiosis," "segregated symbiosis," "civic symbiosis," and "market-oriented symbiosis."[22] There is no perfect match between the aforementioned three models of *kyosei* and Fujita's four modes of symbiosis. But, one might justifiably say that the toleration model of *kyosei* to a great extent overlaps with Fujita's idea of segregated symbiosis, the conversation model can be linked closely to his market-oriented model, and his civic symbiosis can be understood as a promising variation of the commonality model. At any rate, in Japan, the concept of *kyosei* is still fluid and thus remains open to further theoretical elaborations and diverse approaches.

✳✳✳✳✳

In conclusion, our position is that in order to develop truly comprehensive peace studies, the three concepts—peace, security, and *kyosei*—should be examined jointly. Our task undertaken here is to treat these concepts in a holistic way from a multidisciplinary perspective. For, as we have suggested earlier, although at times these three concepts may seem incompatible, they are inter-related and often inseparable both theoretically and in practice. This volume is simply a first attempt to explore new theories and open this new road. As the first step toward this endeavor, scholars from various disciplines in humanities and social sciences at ICU and WSU have contributed nineteen chapters. How do various disciplines define and/or redefine the concepts of peace, security, and *kyosei*? Through examination of possible linkages between their own disciplines and the three key concepts, the authors explore how their disciplines can contribute to the development of comprehensive peace and security studies in the twenty-first century. However, because of the vast scope of the topic and the limited space, each author was allowed broad flexibility in terms of focus—i.e., whether to deal with the three concepts equally or to concentrate on one concept or one pertinent aspect of the three. Furthermore, since this is our first collaborative attempt, the authors place varying emphasis on the question of how scholars may be able to integrate these three ideas into comprehensive peace studies in the future. Each author has written his/her chapter primarily with a view to encouraging the audience to engage in public dialogue in search of new ideas to shape a safer and more peaceable future.

✳✳✳✳✳✳

In the first two chapters, three scholars of international relations and international justice look at the most troubling issue of security in today's increasingly globalized, but at the same time fragmented, world. Martha Cottam and Otwin Marenin focus on "human security" as an integrating concept that ties together the three key concepts of peace, security, and *kyosei*. Tatsuro Kunugi addresses current global security problems at three levels—human security, state security, and "planetary security," and underscores the importance of international cooperation under the leadership of the United Nations.

Chapters three and four focus on psychological dimensions of peace, security, and *kyosei*. David W. Rackham uses biopsychosocial and social psychological approaches to examine the reactive impacts on individuals from the loss of peace, security, and *kyosei*, and suggests the significance of the field of "peace psychology." In chapter four, Craig D. Parks and Asako Stone compliment Rackham's study by focusing on psychological contributors to conflict development—person perception, ingroup-outgroup distinctions, and decision heuristics—with a view to finding psychological solutions to human conflicts.

Two well-established scholars in the discipline of sociology offer two stimulating and provocative essays in chapter five and six. Hidenori Fujita, an expert on education sociology, proposes new ways of defining *kyosei* in the general community and in education. Gregory Hooks, an expert on militarism, explores a possible path to what Galtung calls "positive peace" through critical examination of the perceived dangers of U.S. militarism.

Chapter seven was produced by a team of economists: William S. Hallagan, Yijun He, Frederick S. Inaba, Mudzivri Nziramasanga, and AKM Mahbub Morshed. They make the assumption that human social activities were driven by economic factors, and they look at the conflict end of the peace-war continuum and examine recent economic theories on how civil conflicts emerge.

In chapter eight Edward Weber, public administration expert, discusses the rise of subnational collaboratives and their potential contributions to maintaining peace and security. Another political scientist, Steven Stehr, an expert on U.S. homeland security, explores in chapter nine the lessons and problems the United States has experienced in its efforts to organize and coordinate homeland security.

In chapter ten and eleven, the two most senior and distinguished scholars among the IUC and WSU contributors examine questions surrounding the concepts and perceptions of "risk" and "safety." Eugene A. Rosa, in collaboration with Noriyuki Matsuda at Tsukuba University in Japan, offers a careful scientific comparison of risk perceptions between Americans and Japanese, which demonstrates the interactions of human capacity and culture in producing perceptual outcomes. Yoichiro Murakami, author of *Anzengaku* (safety or security studies), explores a new way of building a holistic safety theory that encompasses all three concepts of peace, security, and *kyosei*.

The next four chapters offer analyses from various disciplines of how ideas, perceptions, and beliefs play roles in promoting peace and *kyosei* among people. In chapter twelve, Yoshimichi Someya discusses various ideas of individual and public happiness from an anthropological perspective as a way to explore how best to maintain peace and *kyosei*. Mary M. Meares in chapter thirteen provides an overview of the concepts of peace, security, and *kyosei* from an intercultural communication perspective. In chapter fourteen, Michael W. Myers extends the discussion of *kyosei* among religions in his exploration of the philosophical and ethical implications of religious exclusivism vs. pluralism; and in the following chapter, Anri Morimoto further pursues the important question of whether *kyosei* is possible among different religions from a theological perspective.

The last four chapters mainly deal with the issues of peace, peace movements, and pacifism and their indivisible link with the concept of human security. T.V. Reed in chapter sixteen focuses on contemporary United States peace movements and develops a forward-looking argument for an active U.S. role in a transnational and global justice movement. Noël Sturgeon draws on her familiarity with gender and environmental studies in the United States, and she articulates a theoretical position on how to achieve peace and security from what she calls a transnational feminist environmentalist perspective. The last two chapters in the volume look at the unique challenges Japan is facing and explore possible lessons the world can draw from its particular experiences. Noriko Kawamura demonstrates a link between war memory and people's attitude toward peace through a critical examination of how Japan's public memory of the Asia-Pacific War shaped naïve pacifism in postwar Japan. Shin Chiba's chapter, on the other hand, sheds light on positive aspects of Japan's unique "constitutional pacifism," and offers a conclusion for this volume by proposing constructive concepts of the right to live in peace, which is closely connected with the concepts of human security and *kyosei*.

# Notes

1. Cf., Johan Galtung, *Peace: Research, Education, Action* [Essays in Peace Research, Volume One] (Copenhagen: Christian Ejlers, 1975), pp. 29, 76, 110-115. Galtung further argues as follows: "Absence of violence should not be confused with absence of conflict: violence may occur without conflict, and conflict may be solved by means of nonviolent mechanisms. The distinction between these two types of peace give rise to a fourfold classification of relations between two nations: war, which is organized group violence; negative peace, where there is no violence but no other form of interaction either and where the best characterization is 'peaceful coexistence'; positive peace, where there is some cooperation interspersed with occasional outbreaks of violence; and unqualified peace where absence of violence is combined with a pattern of cooperation." Ibid., p. 29.

2. Ibid., p. 76.

3. Ibid., p. 76.

4. Ibid., pp. 110-111. Cf., Mitsuo Okamoto, "Heiwagaku towa nanika" [What is Peace Studies], in Yasuhiko Yoshida, ed., *21 Seiki no heiwagaku* [Peace Studies in the 21st Century] (Tokyo: Akashi Shoten Publishers, 2004), pp. 18-21. Masaki Yokoyama, "Heiwa" [Peace], in Mitsuo Okamoto and Masaki Yokoyama, eds., *Heiwagaku no genzai* [The Present of Peace Studies](Kyoto: Horitsu Bunkasha Publishers, 1999), pp. 42-43. Masaki Yokoyama, "Kozoteki boryoku to sekkyokuteki heiwa" [Structural Violence and Positive Peace], in ibid., pp. 56-60.

5. Galtung, *Peace: Research, Education, Action*, p. 111.

6. Galtung explains this as follows: "Violence is that which increases the distance between the potential and the actual, and that which impedes the decrease of this difference. Thus, if a person died from tuberculosis in the eighteenth century, it would be hard to conceive of this as violence, since it might have been quite unavoidable. But if he died from it today, despite all the medical resources in the world, then violence is present according to our definition... A life expectancy of thirty years only, during the Neolithic period, was not an expression of violence. But the same life-expectancy today (whether due to wars, or social injustice, or both) would be seen as violence, according to our definition." Ibid., p. 111.

7. E.g., Yoichiro Murakami, *Anzengaku* [Safety/Security Studies] (Tokyo: Seidosha Publishers, 1998). Yoichiro Murakami, *Anzengaku no genzai* [The Presence of Safety/Security Studies] (Tokyo: Seidosha Publishers, 2003).

8. Walzer, for example, defines the idea of toleration as follows: "My subject is toleration—or, perhaps better, the peaceful coexistence of groups of people with different histories, cultures, and identities, which is what toleration makes possible." Michael Walzer, *On Toleration* (New Haven and London: Yale University Press, 1997), p. 2.

9. Noriaki Kurokawa, *Kyosei no shiso* [Thought of *Kyosei*] (Tokyo: Tokuma Shoten Publishers, 1987), p. 97.

10. Ibid., p. 98.

11. Ibid., p. 100.

12. Tatsuo Inoue, *Kyosei no saho* [The Manner of *Kyosei*] (Tokyo: Sobunsha Publishers, 1986), p. 256.

13. Ibid., pp. vii, x, 240-263.

14. Ibid., pp. vii, 240-263.

15. Ibid., pp. 232-6, 240-263. Inoue explains as follows: "Conversation is a fundamental mode of union in which different individuals enter into a formal union with respect paid for the heterogeneity of each individual. We can have conversation with others without sharing any of interest, concern, hobby, attachment, sensibility, belief, faith, view of life, worldview and so on... There can be a conversation even among the partners whose relationship is filled with as much tension as denying each other's *raison d'etre*. Even if their argument does not properly interact, here a kind of *kyosei* exists among the agents who oppose to one another by means of conversational activity itself." Ibid., p. 254.

16. T. Inoue, K. Nawada, T. Katsuragi, *Kyosei eno boken* [Adventure for *Kyosei*] (Tokyo: Mainichi Shinbunsha Publishers, 1992), p. 24.

17. M. Yoshida, S. Ozeki et al., eds., *Kyosei shiso no tankyu: ajia no shiten kara* [The Quest for Thought of *Kyosei*: From an Asian Perspective] (Tokyo: Aoki Shoten Publishers, 2002), p. 3.

18. Ibid., pp. 3, 12.

19. E.g., Sumiko Ueno, *Kyosei jidai no kenpo* [The Constitution in the Age of *Kyosei*] (Tokyo: Gakuyo Shobo Publishers, 1993). Sumiko Ueno, *Kenpo no kihon: jinken, heiwa, danjyo kyosei* [The Fundamentals of the Constitution: Human Rights, Peace, and *Kyosei* between Male and Female] (Tokyo: Gakuyo Shobo Publishers, 2000). Mitsuo Goto, *Kyosei shakai no sanseiken* [The Right to Vote in the *Kyosei* Society] (Tokyo: Seibundo Publishers, 1999).

20. Shuji Ozeki, "Kyosei shiso no tankyu to gendai" [The Quest for the Idea of *Kyosei* and the Present Age], in op. cit., M. Yoshida, S. Ozeki et al., eds. pp. 16-19.

21. E.g., ibid., pp. 20-26, 32-34.

22. E.g., Hidenori Fujita, "Education Reform and Education Politics in Japan," *The American Sociologist* (Fall 2000), pp. 42, 54-55. Fujita defines four types of symbiosis respectively as follows: "Embracive symbiosis is the mode of co-living that seems to be superior at traditional, pre-industrial communities where people live together with very limited social differentiation and are connected to strong social ties… Segregated symbiosis is one in which different groups of people are separated from each other socially, culturally, and sometimes, even spatially… Civic symbiosis is one that tends to be idealized in a democratic society. There all individuals are assumed as being equal, autonomous and independent, but at the same time, as having an orientation to accept different people, ideas and cultures, and to cooperate for improving their welfare… Market-oriented symbiosis is one that has spread along with the advancement of the capitalist, market economy and the expansion of cities. There, individuals tend to be self-oriented, concerned with personal benefits, indifferent toward others, and not willing to cooperate in order to improve social benefits." Ibid., p. 54.

**one**

# Human Security as an Integrating Concept in Peace, Security, and *Kyosei* (Conviviality) Studies

## Martha Cottam
## Otwin Marenin

### The Goals of Human Security

A commonly ignored reality central to the achievement of widespread peace, security and *kyosei* (social conviviality) is the basic need and right of people to be and to feel safe. We will argue that human security is a theoretical centerpiece for understanding the interconnectivity of peace, security and conviviality. Peace is assumed to be a condition in which people are free from violence in any form (war, civil strife, personal violence, etc.). Security is a condition in which people live in an environment that guarantees their safety from violence, which does not generate a pervasive sense of personal and group insecurity, and which operates in a manner perceived as fair and just. Social interactions are free of fears and concerns that a person's or a group's legitimate, everyday interactions with others will result in violence against that person or group. Finally, conviviality, in our view, points to the necessary balance between individual and collective identities and interests and, if thought of at the global level, points to the commonality of human hopes and fears which define the human condition, connect individuals and groups to larger notions of justice, and hold out the hope that peace, security and conviviality are not mere chimeras.

The idea of human security, broadly defined, helps integrate the concepts of peace, security and conviviality; translates these abstract notions into actions which have meaning in the lives of people; and suggests policies capable of addressing all stages along a continuum of security to insecurity. The relevance of human security as a goal, a justification and a standard for evaluating practical successes and failures will be examined in several ways: by suggesting a method of analyzing different objective and subjective stages in the escalation of insecurity in various societies; and by using concepts drawn from multiple theoretical perspectives and frameworks. The goal of this chapter is to assess the utility of human security as a mechanism for developing indicators and means for detecting and preventing the escalation of insecurity.

## The Production of Insecurity

Human security has emerged in recent years as a key concept—both as the basic goal to be achieved and as the standard for judging success or failure—in assessments of the unsettling impacts of globalization on people, communities and states; in discussions of political and economic development; and in analyzing the processes by which domestic order, stability and safety may be guaranteed to citizens, communities, and regimes. In addition, human security has become a key concept in considering a just global order; in seeking programs and policies to prevent the (re)occurrence of massive intercommunal violence; and in finding ways toward the peaceful resolution of fears, anger, resentment, revenge and hatreds which led to and accompanied intercommunal and genocidal violence. The failure of agencies and institutions to address and deal with these dilemmas allows the conditions which generate objective insecurity to flourish. The discussions of the impacts of globalization, or of a security sector architecture which works well and fairly, arise precisely because the risks, threats, and insecurity-generating conditions have not been adequately addressed.

We live in an insecure world, a world where individuals and societies are at risk, anxious about the present and the future, fearful of changes over which they will have little control, and resentful of that weakness. People are uneasy about their lives, which they see threatened not just by crime, violence, and wars, but by the general conditions in which they live—be these poverty, fears about their jobs, a sensed decline in the quality of life, rebellious children, the intrusion of technology into formerly private spaces, or a pervasive cynicism about the willingness or ability of political leaders to seek a common public good. Such fears and insecurities are engendered by objective changes in the world: chief among these are the forces and consequences of changes loosely categorized as globalization.

Globalization, the "dynamic process of change characterized by the growing cross border flows of trade, investments, finances, technology, ideas, cultures, values, and people" (Kugler and Frost, 2001: 4), has created new dilemmas from the local to the global levels for achieving peace and prosperity; and now provides the domestic and global contexts within which the search for human security is conducted. Public and private economic entities compete worldwide for control of resources and profits; the line between domestic and international politics has been blurred if not erased; borders do not provide national security since threats are global and fluid and changing; cultures clash; and people move—legally, illegally and as refugees and asylum seekers —to safer political and economic havens. Technological innovations enable progress but also may encourage terrorism. Peace and security require a global, coordinated response to the "new wars" which threaten the current age (Duffield, 2001; Kaldor, 1999, 2001; Worcester et al, 2002).

Development aid and assistance programs offered by international, regional and bilateral donors or through a large variety of programs delivered by NGOs (non-governmental organizations), frequently and specifically use the notion of human security as the criterion for what needs to be done (or what is the problem) and as the measure for progress (e.g., Human Security Center, 2004; UN, 2003).

The capacity of the Weberian state, through its putative monopoly of legitimate means of coercion (to provide safety, security and protection against crimes, disorders and deviance for its citizens and community) has weakened dramatically (Kaldor, 2001:4-5). This has led to a shift of the control and legitimacy of coercion to groups and agencies below the state level (communities, private corporations, vigilantes) and above the state level (regional security arrangements, international regimes). The reasons for the decline of the state can be debated, but the decentralization of the control of violence away from the state is a development that cannot be denied (Cawthra and Luckham, 2003; Johnson and Shearing, 2003).

The failure to achieve economic development and political stability for over four-fifths of the world's states and populations, the increasing interconnectedness of domestic and global concerns, and the emergence of power centers contesting state power and control, have all led to much disillusionment and uncertainty, in all societies, about the ultimate nature of the global system and the values enshrined in new institutions and in transnational regimes, practices and policies. Some bandy about the word "democracy" as the emergent victorious hegemonic value system and set of institutions and practices; while others argue for the superiority of cultural and religious belief systems; and yet others bow to the inevitability and utility of technological progress. What is missing among these contesting views is a sense that the new order is or will be a just one; and that a commonly held conception of justice can overcome the fragmenting impacts of interconnectedness and the increasing division of the world between post-modernizing states and those still seen as stuck in pre-technological cultures and politics. Kugler and Frost (2003) argue that societies which are "well suited for the global age" exhibit "political cultures" and "accountable and adaptive institutions based on some minimal level of trust" (p. 13).

Another consequence of the failures of development, globalization and justice has been an explosion of massive episodes of intercommunal violence, civil wars, warlordism, organized crime, transnational state-to-state aggression, and chaotic violence in the form of terrorist attacks on people and symbolic targets. The concept of security has little meaning in such conditions, beyond physical survival, until violence ebbs and minimal order is restored (Dziedzic, 2001; Oakley et al, 1998; Perito, 2004). Efforts at reconciliation and reassurance have been undertaken in some states following extended periods of state repression (e.g. South Africa, Guatemala, and Argentina), in societies experiencing intercommunal violence reaching genocidal levels, in failed states when the complete collapse of the state required international interventions to keep and build the peace, or in transitional/developing societies seeking a way forward (Stedman et al, 2002).

The concept of human security is central to all these discussions and to the reform and amelioration policies which are advocated and implemented. The standard of human security seems to provide a better understanding of the nature of the problems faced by people and groups—and of the ultimate and underlying goals to be achieved—than does a more narrow focus on economic development, political stability, the control of violence, or the promotion of human rights.

The core value of human security is quality of life, a standard which reaches far beyond minimal conceptions of physical security. Quality of life provides a broad set of criteria by which to judge why and how people and groups are secure, or insecure, why and how they feel insecure, or secure, and what objective and subjective conditions lead them to that state.

## Elements of Human Security

Human security has no easy definition, but consists of a bundle of cognate values and goals which, as a whole and when coherently linked, provide a broad framework for analyzing the sources of objective insecurity and the likely means to deal with them. Human security points to objective conditions in the current world which create insecurities, but also to the meaning such objective conditions have for subjective interpretations of threats, risks and opportunities. People may be objectively secure; but if they feel that they are insecure, then they are insecure. Both objective and subjective dimensions of security and insecurity are essential in assessing the prospects for human security.

Cognate values and processes incorporated into discussions of human security, or terms commonly mentioned, include the protection of vital first, second and third generation human rights (to which one can add the notion of generational rights or justice); the effective and roughly equal empowerment of all people and communities; the goal of good governance as a remedy to corruption, violence and inefficiency; a legitimate, effective and just security sector architecture; a vibrant civic society; a set of public and private mechanisms for conflict resolution, prevention and reconciliation; and an institutionalized system for promoting global governance which is sensitive to the variety of cultures and values across the globe.

Security means more than being protected against physical harm. The notion of human rights points to the importance of conditions of life which allow for the full development of an individual's potential, that is, it implies access to the minimal levels of resources, opportunities, and responsibilities which make for a meaningful life. Third generation rights assert, in similar fashion, the importance and value of autonomous cultural and social communities as counterpoint and balance to potentially excessive individualism and as a source of identity and support (or barrier against insecurity) for individuals.

The protection of vital rights will empower people and communities, objectively and subjectively; and will complicate or slow efforts by states and groups to create fears and insecurities. Civic rights (first generation rights), if effectively provided, protect individuals and groups against arbitrary state violence and exploitation. Rights to a meaningful life (second generation rights) provide people and groups with the resources and opportunities (education, employment, etc.) which allow them to participate effectively in societal life. Generational justice argues that current populations have an obligation to leave the world in as good or better a state (in terms of the possibilities of leading a meaningful life) as it was when they entered the world.

Good governance is the advocated remedy for the corruption, violence, inefficiencies and partisan performance seen as typical of many governments at the national and sub-national levels. Endemic corruption leads to violence by the state (normally the police, military and private armies of the powerful) against citizens (Chevigny (1995). Inefficiencies and waste lead to what Joseph (2003: 13) has called "catastrophic governance, [to] endemic practices that steadily undermine a country's capacity to increase the supply of public goods," sustain economic inequality and massive poverty, and enshrine private self interest as the governing principle for decision making in the state. Bad governance destroys the prospects and hopes for political and economic development.

The notion of the security sector, at the minimalist level, includes the police, military, intelligence services, border control agencies, and private and communal security providers. The provision of security is not just a government monopoly but is done by a mix of public, private and communal actors. To understand when and why the provision of security falters or fails requires an analysis which extends beyond the narrow conception that the police are the major domestic security agency. Minimal levels of security, so it is argued, are a necessary precondition for the creation of economic, political and social institutions which are crucial to any possibility for stability, order, development, and justice.

At the maximalist level, the concept of the security sector can be expanded to include supportive criminal justice institutions, a legal system which provides for fair and just dealings with allegations of deviance or criminality, a set of accountability institutions, and a political process providing for oversight and control (Ball, 2002; Chanaa, 2002; gfn website; Neild, 2002; OECD, 2000; UN, 2002; Winkler, 2003).

Yet the meaning of security, in both the minimalist and maximalist conceptions, includes the notion that the effective protection of safety and security of citizens be done in a fair and just manner and be subject to accountability and oversight by civic society and democratic political processes. A vibrant civic society acts as a balance to state and individual power, enables people and groups objectively and subjectively (they feel they can make a difference), and provides the fertile seedbed for individual and group self-awareness and development. That exercise of power requires, at the least, a political and economic system which values and legitimates the expression of individual and community preferences and seeks to include, in the production of public policies linked to human security, an equitable distribution of valued goods. Prevention before insecurity rises and violence occurs (e.g., restorative justice mechanisms) and reconciliation afterwards focus on preserving and reconstituting the minimal fabric of social life which allows people to live with some sense of well-being and safety, and with some certainty that the future will be peaceful and will enable them to engage in the routines of their daily lives without excessive fear and anxiety.

Human security offers one standard for reaching a minimal legitimate consensus that can transcend particularistic preferences—but only if effectively argued and advocated. The dimensions and cognate values and policy preference reflected in human security discourses are interconnected, of course. It will be unlikely that, unless the majority of values incorporated into the advocacy of human security as the goal are taken into account, that peace, security and conviviality will become a reality in the lives of most people of the globe.

Human security, hence, is a complex and multifaceted goal. One can arrange its complexity along three dimensions (creating a box of schemata). One dimension ranks the locus or target of security/insecurity from the individual, through family, community, state and global systems. A second dimension ranks the source of security/insecurity along the same continuum from the individual to the global system. A third ranks the severity of physical insecurity threatened or experienced from minor inconvenience; through criminal victimization, the production of fear by cultural and political processes, civil disorder, civil strife and turmoil, and intercommunal violence, to genocide and war.

## Psychological Origins of Insecurity

As noted earlier, human security is experienced objectively and subjectively. Human security also ranges along a continuum. For example, Bosnia, Rwanda, and the United States have experience with poverty, violations of rights, racism and ethnocentrism, and each has suffered violence as a consequence. But in 1944, human security was much higher in the United States than in Bosnia, then experiencing ethnic cleansing, or in Rwanda, then experiencing genocide. What factors help us understand where a society is located along that continuum, and why it occupies that space at a particular point in time? As the prior discussion has argued, security/insecurity reflect domestic, transnational and global conditions which are beyond the control and planning capacity of states, private corporations or populations. People are enmeshed in the conditions of their lives which have a specific structure and dynamic. But people still need to make sense of these conditions. In the section below, we discuss some of the psychological preconditions and origins for violence and insecurity which need to be understood in order to develop preventative and ameliorative policies and indicators of the actualities and probabilities of escalations in insecurity. Drawing from political psychology, a number of factors appear to be useful: patterns of group conflict, social identity and stereotyping, scapegoating and dehumanization, and perceptions of justice.

Studies of group conflict over real resources go back to the Sherif (1966) summer boys' camp studies where eleven-year-old boys were placed into competing summer camp groups and quickly became quite vicious in the battles against the other group. Studies based in Social Identity Theory demonstrate that groups engage in stereotyping and prejudice even in the absence of conflicting goals. Competition can occur even when the stakes are only psychological, and among groups that are arbitrarily formed by experimenters with no real interaction or conflicting goals (Allport, 1954; Tajfel, 1982; Brewer & Brown, 1998; Cottam et al, 2004). Indeed, both Social Identity Theory and general social cognition studies indicate that people naturally and inescapably place themselves and others into social groups. People then proceed to compare their group to other relevant comparison groups and are pleased with enhanced self esteem when those comparisons are positive. When the comparisons are negative, however, members of groups may switch groups (when possible), change the basis of comparison, or engage in competition to change their group's position *vis-à-vis* other groups. When attachment to a group is strong, and when the comparison with other groups is negative, particularly during difficult economic, social, and political circumstances, people engage in a search for a scapegoat (Staub, 1989; Waller, 2002; Cottam et al., 2004). Scapegoats are blamed for the perceiver's group's problems and are then often the brunt of violence. When the scapegoats are also dehumanized, that is, popularly described as less than human (often as insects, vermin, or rodents) the impulse arises to erase them from the face of the earth.

A common underlying perception in all of these psychological processes is that of threat. For example, our people are being, or are on the verge of being, deprived of what is rightfully ours; we are unjustly in an inferior position; some inferior group is trying to get ahead at our expense; or my personal position in the world is disintegrating. Such perceptions can be seen in defensive wars involving pre-emptive force, in ethnic cleansing, in racial conflicts, in gang warfare, and in spouse abuse. Alternatively, people may be motivated to commit acts of violence against others when they perceive an opportunity for their group to achieve something at the expense of another group. When others are seen as weak, or lacking in will, and when they are perceived as having caused suffering to one's own group, that may be seen as an opportunity for violence.

The exact nature of the perception of the other group is important in determining the kind of violence perpetrated. Image Theory maintains that there are a number of stereotypes or images that are commonly found in politics whether the arena be international or domestic (see Figure 1). Each image is associated with different behavioral predispositions. Enemies, for example, are equal in strength to the perceiver's group, and hence are best dealt with through indirect skirmishes and containment. A direct conflict could easily be lost by either side. Barbarians, on the other hand, are powerful and culturally inferior. Take them on and you lose, and the punishment will be horrible. Hence the inclination is to search for allies to address the asymmetry in power. A list of stereotypes, or images, in politics and the broader social milieu and the strategic preferences that are associated with them appears in Figure 1. These images can be found in domestic political situations, international political situations, and in non-political contexts such as urban gang warfare. As can be seen, they produce different kinds of violence with the worse violence being perpetrated on the rogue, particularly when the rogue is considered a scapegoat. When dehumanized, this stereotype leads to genocide.

The importance of differences in perceptions of other groups can be quickly illustrated with a comparison of the violence in South Africa and in Rwanda. In South Africa, so-called black on black violence between the Zulu Inkatha Freedom party and followers of the African National Congress reached the level of civil war in the late 1980s and early 1990s, yet it was resolved peacefully in 1996. In Rwanda, conflict between the Hutu and Tutsis resulted in genocide. There is a clear difference in images in these two cases. The Zulu IFP saw the ANC as an enemy and never dehumanized them. The Hutu, however, saw the Tutsis as rogues and scapegoats, and dehumanized them regularly as insects and cockroaches (Cottam & Infranco, 2004).

Therefore, particular stereotypes, combined with difficult political, economic and/or social contexts, produce a wide variety of non-peaceful behaviors—exploitation, violence by groups against groups, by state institutions against groups, by individuals against each other, discrimination, retribution, hostility and anger. People cannot be secure in such environments and often their insecurity is endemic. They are so accustomed to the situation that they do not even recognize that an alternative form of existence is possible. Sometimes hostilities reach a level where some entity intervenes (e.g., the international community, a neighboring country, community organizers seeking to end gang violence, the neighbors who call the police when a woman is being battered by her spouse). However, in such cases, recovery by the victims is little understood and is rarely complete. So the insecurity remains. Those who suffered less want those who suffered more to fix themselves, get over it, and get on with life.

Rwanda offers an important illustration of this. About 950,000 people were killed during the genocide, about 94 percent (893,000) of whom were Tutsi (Malvern, 2004: 251). Tutsis constituted 14 percent of Rwanda's eight million people before the genocide (1.12 million people). Doing the math, this means around 80 percent of the Tutsis were killed in the space of three months. What happened to the survivors? They did not receive massive shipments of aid. Instead, medical and survival aid poured into the refugee camps in Zaire where the killers had fled. Massive repatriation began in 1996, meaning that, despite the

## Figure 1. Political Stereotypes and Strategic Preferences

Image of other Political Actor→Threat/Opportunity→Strategic Preference

Enemy image→Threat high→Containment

Barbarian image→Threat high→Search for allies, augment power

Imperial image→Threat high→Submit/revolt when possible

Rogue image→Threat moderate/low→Crush

Degenerate image→Opportunity high/moderate→Challenge, take risks

Colonial Image→Opportunity high→Control, exploit

Ally Image (Will help in either context)→Threat/Opportunity→Negotiate agreements, Common strategy fact that 125,000 people were imprisoned for genocide, many survivors would still have to live next door to neighbors who had participated in the broad-based genocide. It is not difficult to imagine a profound lack of security for the survivors. In addition, Tutsis who had lived in exile before the genocide also returned but had difficulty feeling empathy with those Tutsis who survived (Gourevitch, 1998). If these Tutsis had relatives who died in the genocide, they typically had not known them personally, whereas the losses for survivors were so deep and personal that many reportedly wish that they too had perished in the genocide (Gourevitch, 1998).

Once conflict begins, differences between groups are augmented and similarities between the groups are minimized. Groups become increasingly distanced from each other and the possibility of violence accelerates. Identities become hardened and it becomes easier to see other groups as unidimensional caricatures, badly intentioned, harmful, and threatening. This contributes to an understanding of human security in a number of significant ways. First, it implies that social group distinctions that seem benign and even enjoyable can become sources of conflict very quickly when manipulated by effective leaders. Consequently, even though conflict between groups that have lived harmoniously for years seems unimaginable, it is still a potential source of insecurity. In Bosnia, for example, Serbs, Croats and Muslims had a history of ethnic coexistence. Bosnians could not identify which ethnic group a person belonged to through language or looks, and Bosnia was secular, with people enjoying religious holidays, but not politically motivated by religious differences. Last names alone could tell which group a person belonged to. This situation changed when Serb nationalism was mobilized by Slobodan Milosevic, and soon everyone had to "be" Muslim, Croatian, or Serb. As one Bosnian student stated, before the war his mother was ethnically a Catholic Croatian, and his father was a Muslim who smoked, drank liquor, and ate pork. This student did not consider himself anything other than Bosnian until the conflict started, at which point everyone had to be a member of one group. Neutrality or non-group membership was not an option. Then safety came through membership, and the other groups were demonized.

In war-torn societies, the cessation of hostilities does not automatically bring an end to the in-group/out-group dynamics that contribute so strongly to the initiation of violence. Suspicion, fear, anger, and hatred all remain—and most resolution and reconciliation efforts, such as the International Criminal Tribunals for Yugoslavia and Rwanda, leave many dissatisfied. Moreover, civilians in post-conflict societies are often victimized by criminals who have used instability to their advantage, such as vigilantes, and former combatants. Indeed, as Call and Stanley note, in "El Salvador and South Africa...civilians faced greater risk of violent death or serious injury after the end of the conflict than during it. Even where the end of civil wars has reduced the dangers to civilians, postwar crime waves and civil disturbances have been common" (2002: 303).

Many of the examples above have come from war-torn societies, but this should not lead to the false assumption that democracies are free of insecurity. Democracies have some structural characteristics that protect citizens from some forms of insecurity. Nonviolent power-sharing, civil society (wherein the control of the means of coercion shifts from individuals to the state thereby protecting people from the danger of violence at the hand of others), and accountability to a free and open press are considered to be important characteristics of democratic states that reduce human vulnerability to insecurity (Keane, 2002). But these characteristics cannot be absolute. Power sharing at home and control of the means of coercion by the state do not protect people from the possibility of war—an attack by another country. For power sharing to be fully effective all groups must be equal. Even if all groups are equal under the law, they may not be equal in each other's eyes, producing informal discrimination, feelings of vulnerability and inefficacy, and lack of equal access to the state's protective mechanisms. Civil society has its limits as well. People may be protected from the barbarities of a state of nature or a feudal society, but economic cycles, crime, lack of medical coverage, environmental degradation, and many other failures of civil society permit insecurity to fester. Civil society and democracy are no guarantee that normal human social cognitive patterns discussed above will not contribute to, or take advantage of, opportunities to express themselves, as the growth of hate crimes in newly democratic countries in Eastern Europe demonstrate (Hockenos, 1993; MacGinty, 2002). Finally, accountability can be limited through appeals to national security, denial, disinformation, and other common activities of political elites.

## Concluding Thoughts

In this chapter we have focused on the objective and subjective components of human security and insecurity. Human security is conceptualized as both a product of real objective threats and fears and those that are psychological in nature and that may be the result of objective conditions or fears of future conditions. Thus human security reflects realities that range from fundamental psychological patterns of group formation and competition, to local and immediate circumstances of meeting daily basic needs and safety, to global patterns of economic transformation and war. A central argument has been that a focus on human security automatically and necessarily forces one to construct a comprehensive scheme for assessing the objective and subjective realities and futures of peace, security and *kyosei*, or conviviality. Peace, security and conviviality are facts of life (which can be measured in a variety of ways, depending in their location in the three dimensional schemata), but they are also states of mind (which can also be measured), which are loosely contingent on the particular objective conditions in which people find themselves. Human security is a necessary condition for broad-based, local, national, and transnational peace, security and conviviality.

A second central argument in this chapter is that human security must be looked at in terms of multiple dimensions. We have proposed three such dimensions: a traditional dimension of the sources of insecurity ranging from individual→community→state→to the global system; a ranking of targets of insecurity ranging across the same individual to global system continuum; and a third dimension of real or perceived physical insecurity resulting from criminal victimization, fear caused by cultural or political trends, civil disorder, intercommunal violence, genocidal impulses, and war. Our hope is that future research will develop indicators along the three dimensions that will guide the collection of data that can be analyzed to gain a better sense of which conditions lead to the escalation of insecurity in all three dimensions. This, in turn, can lead to prescriptives to prevent, stop, de-escalate, and reduce human insecurity as well as recovering from past insecurities.

# References

Allport, G. (1954). *The nature of prejudice*. Cambridge, MA: Addison Wesley.

Brewer, M. B. & Brown, R.J. (1998). Intergroup relations. In D.T. Gilbert, S.T. Fiske, & G. Lindzey (Eds.), *The handbook of social psychology* (pp. 554-594), Vol. 2 4th edition. New York: McGraw-Hill.

Ball, N. (2002). Democratic governance of the security sector. Paper prepared for the UNDP Workshop on "Learning From Experience for Afghanistan," New York.

Bryden, A. & Fluri, P. (Eds.) (2003). *Security sector reform: Institutions, society, and good governance*. Baden-Baden: Nomos.

Call, C.T. & Stanley, W. (2002). Civilian security. In S.J. Stedman, D. Rothchild, & E. Cousens (Eds.), *Ending civil wars: The implementation of peace agreements*. Boulder: Lynne Rienner.

Cawthra, G. & Luckham, R. (Eds.) (2003). *Governing insecurity: Democratic control of military and security establishments in transitional democracies*. London: Zed Books.

Chanaa, J. (2002). *Security sector reform: Issues, challenges and prospects*, London: Institute for Strategic Studies, Adelphi Paper No. 344.

Chevigny, P. (1995). *Edge of the knife: Police violence in the Americas*. New York: The Free Press.

Cottam, M.L. & Cottam, R.W. (2001). *Nationalism and politics: The political behavior of nation states*. Boulder: Lynne Rienner.

Cottam, M.L. & Infranco, M.P. (2004). Crossing the threshold: An exploration of the escalation of violence in inter-communal conflict. Paper presented at the 27th meeting of the International Society of Political Psychology, Lund, Sweden, July 15, 2004.

DFID (Department for International Development, UK) (2002). *Understanding and supporting security sector reform*. London: DFID.

Duffield, M. (2001). *Global governance and the new wars: The merging of development and security*. London: Zed Press.

Dziedzic, M.J. (2001). Peace operations: Political-military coordination. In R.L. Kugler & E.L. Frost (Eds.), *The global century: Globalization and national security* (pp.315-334). Washington, D.C.: National Defense University Press.

Global Facilitation Network, at www.gfn-ssr.org/gfn_papers.cfm.

Gourevitch, P. (1998). *We wish to inform you that tomorrow we will be killed with our families: Stories from Rwanda*. New York: Picador.

Hockenos, P. (1993). *Free to hate: The rise of the right in post-communist Eastern Europe*. New York: Routledge.

Holm, T.T. & Eide, E.B. (Eds.) (2000). *Peacebuilding and police reform*. London: Franks Cass.

Johnston, L. D. & Shearing, C. (2003). *Governing Security: Explorations in Policing and Justice*, London: Routledge.

Joseph, R. (2003). State, governance and insecurity in Africa. *Democracy and Development*, 3, 2, 7-15.

Kaldor, M. (1999, 2001). *New and old wars: Organized violence in a global era*. Stanford: Stanford University Press.

Keane, J. (2002). Fear and democracy. In K. Worcester, S. Avery Bermanzohn, & M. Ungar (Eds.), *Violence and politics: Globalization's paradox* (pp. 226-243). New York: Routledge.

Kugler, R.L. & Frost, E.L. (2001). Introduction: Policies for a globalized world. In R.L. Kugler, & E.L. Frost (Eds.), *The global century: Globalization and national security* (pp. 3-5). Washington, D.C.: National Defense University Press.

Luckham, R. (2003). Democratic strategies for security in transition and conflict. In G. Cawthra & R. Luckham (Eds.), *Governing insecurity: Democratic control of military and security establishments in transitional democracies* (pp. 3-28). London: Zed Books.

MacGinty, R. (2002). Ethnonational conflicts, democratization, and hate crime. In K. Worcester, S. Avery Bermanzohn, & M. Ungar (Eds.), *Violence and politics: Globalization's paradox* (pp. 226-243). New York: Routledge.

Malvern, L. (2004). *Conspiracy to murder: The Rwandan genocide*. New York: Verso.

Sherif, M. (1966). *In common predicament: Social psychology of intergroup conflict and cooperation*. Boston: Houghton-Mifflin.

Neild, R. (October 2002). *Sustaining reform: Democratic policing in Central America.* Washington, D.C.: Washington Office on Latin America (WOLA), Citizen Security Monitor series.

Oakley, R.B., Dziedzic, M.J., & Goldberg, E.M. (Eds.) (1998). *Policing the new world order: Peace operations and public security.* Washington, D.C.: National Defense University Press.

OECD Development Assistance Committee, Informal Task Force on Conflict, Peace and Development Cooperation (2000). Security-Sector Reform and Development Co-Operation: A Conceptual Framework for Enhancing Policy Coherence. On oecd website.

Perito, R.M. (2004). *Where is the lone ranger when we need him? America's search for a postconflict stability force.* Washington, D. C.: United States Institute of Peace Press.

Stedman, S.J., Rothchild, D., & Cousens, E.M. (Eds.) (2002). *Ending civil wars. The implementation of peace agreements.* Boulder: Lynne Rienner.

Tajfel, H. (1982). *Human groups and social categories.* Cambridge: Cambridge University Press.

United Nations (2002). *Justice and security sector reform: A conceptual framework for BCPR.* (written by Nicole Ball), New York: United Nations. (BCPR stands for Bureau for Crisis Prevention and Recovery.) www.un-globalsecurity.org.

Vera Institute (2003). *Measuring progress toward safety and justice: A global guide to the design of performance indicators across the justice sector.* New York: Vera Institute.

Winkler, T. H. (2003). Keynote paper: Managing change, the reform and democratic control of the security sector and international order. In A. Bryden & P. Fluri (Eds.), *Security sector reform: Institutions, society and good governance* (pp. 13-40). Baden-Baden: Nomos.

## two

# Redressing Security Deficits in Our Fragmented World: UN Perspectives and Beyond

## Tatsuro Kunugi

### Introduction

During the last decade and a half, the global security situation has undergone extraordinary changes. While old threats have mostly faded away, new and daunting challenges to security have emerged. This has spurred new thinking about the very concept of security and the approach to security. On the occasion of the Millennium Summit of the United Nations, people around the world renewed and expanded their understanding of the formidable problems in the vast complex of socio-economic and environmental issues that the future concept of security will have to embrace.

Seen from this angle, security in our triad of "peace, security and *kyosei*" does not seem to be an end itself, on an equal footing with peace and *kyosei*. Security is, however, a necessary condition for peaceful and convivial existence. Absence of security or deficits in the provision of security–both real and perceived–create contexts and situations that undermine the trust and other conditions to sustain positive relationships among various actors. In other words, security is an intermediate global public good for assuring the other two goals in our triad.

The purpose of this study is threefold. First, it makes a brief review of the changing concept of security and the varying degrees of emphasis on dimensions and components of security. In appreciation of valuable work recently performed by three high-profile independent commissions, this review will mainly refer to the ideas underlying peace, security and human welfare as they appear in these commissions' reports.

Secondly, this chapter discusses the three dimensions of security, namely,
- State Security (inter-state security and intra-state security);
- Human Security (freedom from fear, freedom from want, and empowerment of people); and
- Planetary Security (conservation of nature and environmental integrity, and inter-generational equity).

In view of the current emphasis on human security, the other two dimensions, particularly planetary security, will be given due attention from a long-term perspective.

Thirdly, and in an exploratory manner, the study proposes to take a problem-solving approach by identifying possible ways to redress security deficits in our fragmented world. The term "redress" and not "address" is chosen, indicating the importance of specific actions to remedy, rectify or compensate specific verifiable or quantifiable security deficits. In other words, "redress" is preferred above "address" in much the same way as "redress wrongs and injustices" is in legal terms. The importance of synergistic partnerships and the legitimacy and leadership of the United Nations for promoting synergistic responses will also be emphasized.

## 1. The Changing Concept of Security

Until the early 1990s, the concept of security in international relations was narrowly defined as the security of the state from external aggression, from internal violence and subversive activities, as well as the protection of national interests in foreign policy. For a period of time, at the height of superpower rivalry and the nuclear arms build-up, the survival of humankind was itself the overarching security issue in military and strategic terms. In the South, developing countries were often preoccupied with ensuring the security of their newly-won independence and territorial integrity against external threats.

During this period, there was much human suffering as people were caught in dire economic, social and humanitarian situations often caused by their state's abject political failures. People's legitimate security concerns about their daily lives, however, seldom receive priority in high-level international political debate. For instance, the Security Council, at its first summit meeting on 31 January 1992, expressed only an understanding of broader threats to security in the following terms:[1]

> The absence of war and military conflicts amongst States does not in itself ensure international peace and security. The non-military sources of instability in the economic, social, humanitarian and ecological fields have become threats to peace and security. The United Nations membership as a whole, working through the appropriate bodies, needs to give the highest priority to the solution of these matters.

As will be recalled, around this time many violent conflicts had already arisen in various parts of the world within states rather than between states. The UNDP's *Human Development Report 1994*[2] introduced the innovative new concept of "human security" which equated security with people rather than territories, and with human development rather than military arms. The report noted that most threats to human security fall into one of seven categories, namely: Economic Security, Food Security, Health Security, Environmental Security, Personal Security, Community Security, and Political Security. The report proposed that these concerns be dealt with through a new people-centered paradigm of sustainable human development, arguing that it would capture the potential peace dividend.

Although other ambitious steps that the report recommended (e.g., the creation of a global human security fund, global taxes for resource mobilization and the restructuring of relevant global institutions, including the establishment of an Economic Security Council of the UN) have not yet been implemented, the rethinking of security it provoked has exerted considerable influence on international policy debates since its publication. A series of complex emergencies multiplying human miseries and disrupting development in various regions of the world have given added incentives to subsequent policy-oriented discussions, notably by the three "blue ribbon commissions": The Commission on Global Governance (1995);[3] The International Commission on Intervention and State Sovereignty (2001);[4] and The Commission on Human Security (2003).[5]

Each Commission's report had a different focus and proposed approach to a range of specific contemporary security issues. For the purpose of analysis and policy consideration, these security issues may appropriately be classified into three dimensions, namely, state security, human security and planetary security. The components of the three dimensions of security issues are, in reality, interlinked and partially overlapping, but they are also conceptually separable, requiring different responses in terms of planning, policy and management.

## 2. Three Dimensions of Security

### 2.1. State Security

The maintenance of inter-state security and intra-state security has traditionally been considered as one of the cardinal functions of the state. Along with a trend toward the general decline of state power in relation to non-state actors, the security function of states also seems increasingly challenged. The reasons for this are varied and include the following:

- Terrorism and other crimes defy conventional state control. These criminal activities may involve illicit traffic in small arms and technologies for weapons of mass destruction across increasingly porous borders.
- Humanitarian intervention has itself become a very controversial issue. As was seen in the former Yugoslavia and in Rwanda, the concept of state sovereignty is in the process of being reinterpreted as the state's responsibility to protect its people. A failure to do so would mean the forfeiture of sovereignty. In other words, a shift is emerging where human beings are recognized to matter more than state sovereignty.[6]
- The collective security system of the UN faces serious defiance by the one and only superpower's exceptionalism and its global unilateralism doctrine of the preemptive use of force.
- A much broader conception of human security is leading to an underappreciation of the centrality of the state's security function, even though a strong case can be made at the same time for the strengthening of the state's security function.[7]
- People are increasingly averse to the state of emergency prerogative which has often been abused in the past.

In light of these developments, which may or may not be temporary, it is useful to consider whether the following observation by Paul Streeten concerning the role of the state in socio-economic processes is equally applicable to the state's security function:[8]

> The state has become too big for the small things, and too small for the big things. The small things call for delegation downwards to the local level… The big things call for delegation upwards, for coordination between national policies, or for transnational institutions.

Streeten's comment is a useful starting point to consider whether, in addition to the security support activities of the UN, we also need greater utilization of regional organizations and wider participation of local communities and civil society organizations in the security functions of the state. It has to be emphasized that increased participation by non-state actors should be in accordance with the following two principles, namely, the subsidiary principle—the problem needs to be dealt with at the most appropriate level—and the principle of division of labor based on comparative advantage.

A great diversity in political cultures influences the understanding and application of security principles. Therefore, specific guidelines on the security functions of the state and the UN respectively need to be reinterpreted to allow effective response to the contemporary threats in various parts of the world. This important political question awaits extensive research both in theory and in practice.

### 2.2. Human Security

The UNDP's *Human Development Report 1994* defines human security as "safety from such chronic threats as hunger, disease and repression" and "protection from sudden and hurtful disruptions in the pattern of daily life–whether in homes, in jobs or in communities."[9]

The earlier mentioned seven categories of threats to human security, as identified and discussed in the above report, have been addressed by the Commission on Human Security. In addition to the seven categories, the Commission also emphasizes the importance of "knowledge, skills and values" for human security.[10] According to its report *Human Security Now*, the *first key* to human security is the protection of the "basic rights and freedoms of people" and the *second key* is "people's ability to act on their own behalf and on behalf of others."[11] As the Commission attaches great importance to the second key, i.e., empowerment, it underscores schooling, especially of girls, and the management of knowledge, skills and values for human security. The report argues that *people protected* can exercise many choices to develop their potentials as individuals and as communities. And *people empowered* can avoid risks and demand improvements in the system of protection. They can, for example, publicize food shortages early for the prevention of famines. An empowered people can also publicize and protest human rights violations by governments. The report also highlights economic and social gaps that increase fragmentation and hamper social integration, particularly of disadvantaged groups.

The expansive definition of human security, as exemplified by these two reports, has been criticized by some scholars for several reasons: that "securitizing" everything as a priority raises false hopes in the policy realm, preventing necessary trade-offs; and that the expansive definition may block deeper understanding of the issues both in conceptual and policy terms.[12]

On the other hand, Fen Osler Hampson notes with approval that the Human Security Commission report emphasizes that "different people, in different communities, face radically different risks to their own human security."[13] In this way he calls our attention to the fact that multiple risks jeopardize the security of individuals in particular communities. This insecurity stems from oppressive practices as felt by particular sections of society, for example through gender inequalities and unstable economic, social and environmental conditions. Hampson rightly urges us to develop a better understanding of these specific "communities at risk," and to reallocate resources to those who need them most.

## 2.3. Planetary Security

The Commission on Global Governance report, published in early 1995, emphasizes that "global security must be broadened from its traditional focus on security of states to include the security of people and the planet."[14] It notes that the increasing loss of biodiversity and forests, as well as growing environmental hazards are threatening the planet's capacity to support the human population. After discussing the actions needed to ensure *freedom from want* and *freedom from fear* (traditional expressions of the components of human security), Kofi Annan in his Millennium Report underscores a "third freedom"—the freedom of future generations to sustain their lives on this planet. He states, "we have been plundering our children's future heritage to pay for environmentally unsustainable practices in the present."[15]

Work toward securing environmentally sustainable development requires research into the linkages between several key factors, captured in the two equations below.

## Two Equations on Sustainable Development

$$^1 \quad I = P \times A \times T \qquad\qquad\qquad ^2 \quad S = \frac{R \times T}{P \times A}$$

**I**: Impact to Environment
**P**: Population
**A**: Affluence (i.e., per capita consumption)

**T**: Technology
**S**: Sustainability
**R**: Resource

[1] See Paul and Anne Ehrlich, *The Population Explosion* (1990), p. 58.
[2] See T. Kunugi, "The Roles of International Institutions Promoting Sustainable Development" in *Ambio—A Journal of the Human Environment* (1992), vol. 21, no. 1, p. 114.

The first equation shows that the product of the two factors—the number of people and their per capita consumption—is multiplied by an index of the environmental disruptiveness of the technologies that provide the goods consumed. On the other hand, the second equation shows that environmental sustainability is primarily a function of the intelligent use of natural resources. As natural resources diminish and the population increases, a greater impact is felt from technology (not only the technology and know-how that people apply to resource utilization, but also human ingenuity and management skills in terms of economic and social organization of action). Technology's importance to sustainable development practices is evident in examples such as resource-saving models and non-toxic green technologies.

These equations can serve not only as analytical tools to assess the specific issues pertaining to environmentally sustainable development, but also as prescriptive tools to help determine the direction and type of action that should be taken to restore and maintain the equilibrium in the population-resource-technology nexus in specific situations at the local, national, regional or global levels. When the equilibrium is upset at a particular level, focused planning and resource management at the global level should be utilized to restore and maintain the balance in the second equation. Likewise, it is important to note that environmentally sustainable development must serve the needs of the people, including those who have a lower standard of living and those who have no representation, such as future generations.

After presenting specific data on environmental degradation of land, freshwater sources, forests and their biodiversity, coastal and marine areas, and the atmosphere in the past 30 years (particularly across large parts of the developing world)—the *Global Environmental Outlook 3* (GEO-3) published by the United Nations Environment Program (UNEP) in May 2002 reports:[16]

> One of the key driving forces has been the growing gap between the rich and poor parts of the globe. Currently, one-fifth of the world's population enjoys high, some would say excessive, levels of affluence. It accounts for nearly 90 per cent of total personal consumption globally. In comparison, around 4 billion people are surviving on less than U.S. $1 to $2 a day.

The report also notes another key determining force, namely, the science and technology gap between the North and South. With regard to this point, I would argue it is highly desirable that much wider technological cooperation for sustainable development involving private and public partnerships is promoted not only as a part of North-South cooperation, but also more specifically through the new 'development round' of the WTO (World Trade Organization).[17]

The long-term dimension of planetary security for future generations is another important question that needs to be fundamentally repositioned in the global planning and resource management process. It should be articulated through the formulation of a theory of intergenerational equity: all members of each generation of humankind inherit a natural and cultural legacy from past generations, both as beneficiaries and as custodians, with a duty to pass on this heritage to future generations. This duty requires conservation and enhancement of the quality and diversity of the heritage.[18] During the 1980s increasing concerns over the depletion of natural resources and the degradation of environmental quality evoked responses at all levels—namely, national, regional and global—and on the part of leaders of civil society, international institutions and government bureaucracies. However, this ascendance of environmental consciousness and initiatives in various quarters has not been energetically pursued, given the mood of anti-climax that followed the 1992 Earth Summit in Rio.

National and international institutions concerned with the conservation and development of natural resources and cultural systems should be encouraged to integrate this intergenerational equity perspective into their activities. There is clearly a need for intensified efforts to study the earth's carrying capacity, and for the elaboration and wider application of principles and codes of conduct regarding the public management of our common heritage.[19] Internalizing the principles of intergenerational equity and the importance of the biosphere's equilibrium as base concerns for planetary security is imperative.[20] With much regret it has to be noted that neither the Rio Summit Declaration of 1992 nor the Johannesburg Summit Declaration of 2002 contains an express statement of the principle of intergenerational equity.

## 3. Redressing Security Deficits in Our Fragmented World

### 3.1. Holistic and Differentiated Approach

As seen in the previous section, security has three conceptually separable dimensions and each dimension has specific components. With the advance of science and technology accompanied by a marked increase in human activities on the globe, the nature, magnitude and interrelationships of these specific components are undergoing changes. In light of this, a holistic and integrative approach to security is necessary. "Redressing security deficits" rather than merely "addressing security deficits" is imperative for several reasons. First, the security components in all three dimensions are mutually inter-linked, although the components of the same dimension are more inter-connected with and interdependent on each other than with those in the other dimension. Successful intervention to alleviate and redress one of the components often helps alleviate other components. A holistic approach is therefore necessary with a focus on clusters of security issues rather than on a single issue.

Second, just like the quality of air we breathe, security can be more easily and appropriately defined and grasped by its absence or deficit than its presence. When security deficits are identified in relation to specific referents (and not merely as a common referent of high generality of concepts, values or ideals), these specific definitions will allow operationalization of action to redress concrete security deficits.

Third, assessing the nature and urgency of concrete security deficits will help determine an optimum allocation or reallocation of the limited resources available. It will also help strategic planning for the most effective response to security deficit situations depending on the different contexts with regard to time and space. Operational definitions with empirically verifiable and quantifiable referents can thus lead to much needed worldwide public policy debate regarding trade-offs.[21]

Fourth, experience gained over the past few decades in formulating and implementing international arrangements for redressing human rights violations and environmental harm or degradation may shed some light on the possibility for formulating appropriate codes of conduct and guidelines for providing effective remedies to operationally defined security deficits.[22]

### 3.2. Synergistic Partnership

It is widely accepted that globalization poses systemic challenges to the fabric of the contemporary world and that partnership among all actors, namely states and non-state actors, will be imperative to meet globalization-induced challenges. "Globalization" is the defining theme and "partnership" is the mantra of the moment. Indeed, calling for partnership that respects independence and differences among various actors appears uncontroversial. In reality, however, there are obstacles to building partnerships among actors of unequal power, influence and wealth, each of whom have different aims and operational styles.

World politics is undergoing a basic transformation (or what Jessica Tuchman Mathews calls "power shift"[23]) from a state-centric and hierarchical world toward a world with more democratic, inclusive and heterarchical forms of governance.[24] Therefore, it is necessary first to identify the main actors and their respective activities in relation to security issues, and second, to discuss what kind of partnerships are to be built in order to redress security deficits.

Among the four main categories of societal actors—namely, governmental organizations (GO), intergovernmental organizations (IGO), nongovernmental organizations (NGO) and for-profit organizations (FPO)—it is the IGOs, generally speaking (including the UN system and regional organizations), that in recent decades seem to have assumed an increasingly larger role in security issues, due to the influence of deepening interdependence and globalization. Except for current, and hopefully temporary, problems arising from the United States' unilateralism, earlier referred to, the general trend has been for the UN system to take a lead role in formulating shared visions, standard-setting for action to realize new visions, and coordinating concerted efforts for common goals of peace and security. This is in line with one of the main purposes of the UN as set forth in Article 1, paragraph 4 of the Charter: "To be a centre for harmonizing the actions of nations in the attainment of these common ends." The cooperative actions centering on the UN always encompassed a large number of NGOs. They include around 1,600 international NGOs today that have formal consultative status in the Economic Social Council of the UN under Article 71 of the Charter. Furthermore, a much larger number of additional NGOs contribute to the UN's operational activities in the environment, development and humanitarian fields.[25] In addition, around 1,200 FPOs are now participating in the Global Compact initiated by the UN Secretary-General in 2000. The Global Compact asks FPOs to embrace, support and enact, within their sphere of influence, a set of core values, stated in ten principles in the areas of human rights, labor standards and the environment.[26]

The role of business in conflict prevention, peace-keeping, and post conflict peace-building was taken up by the Security Council in an open debate held on 15 April 2004. Secretary-General Kofi Annan explained how private companies operate in many conflict zones or conflict-prone countries: the decisions of these companies on investment and employment, on relations with local communities, on protection of the local environment and on their own security arrangements can help the cessation of the conflict or can exacerbate the tensions. Furthermore the Secretary-General noted that private companies manufacture and sell the main hardware–from tanks to small arms and anti-personnel mines–and trade in natural resources, e.g., oil, "conflict diamonds," narcotics and timber.[27]

On 22 June 2004, the role of civil society in post-conflict peace-building was also discussed in an open debate in the Security Council with the participation of NGO representatives. Kofi Annan emphasized that civil society organizations, both local and international, had a role to play in the deliberative processes of the Security Council. Such organizations could help reduce the appeal of those trying to reignite conflict, could prepare local communities to receive demobilized soldiers and refugees, and could give a voice to the concerns of the marginalized.[28]

The role of regional organizations in security management and in building security communities has repeatedly been discussed since the end of the Cold War. In most cases, partnerships were formed or task-sharing arrangements were made between the UN and NATO, OAS (Organization of American States), OSCE (Organization for Security and Cooperation in Europe), and ECOWAS (Economic Community of West Africa). However, revolts against military regimes, ethnic cleansing and "the greed factor" sometimes made complex issues even more intractable, defying efforts to seek a suitable resolution.[29]

It is noted that the influence and role of other main actors are likewise important factors to be taken into account in specific situations. These actors can include the mass media, parliamentarians, local authorities, research institutions, academia and empowered people acting individually or in collectivity, and their partnerships working to redress security deficits. Generally speaking, however, it has to be recognized that synergistic partnerships between the four main societal organizations (namely, the UN system, governments, NGOs and FPOs) are by far the most important. The term "synergistic partnerships" is used here to mean that the effect obtained from the combined cooperative action of, or interaction between, two or more distinct actors is greater than that obtained from the sum of their independent actions. The effect obtained could be shared by other actors and by the public at large. It is therefore different from symbiotic mutualism, in which two or more actors derive mutual benefit from living together. Likewise, synergistic partnerships are different from business partnerships. The purpose of business partnerships, according to *Bouvier's Law Dictionary*, is the exclusive sharing of profits/benefits by partners alone, whereas the primary purpose of partnership for global governance should be the inclusive sharing of benefits for the well-being of humanity and other forms of global public goods.[30]

### 3.3. The Legitimacy and Leadership of the UN

A number of studies presented at the Millennium Symposium of the UN (2000) underline the UN's capacity to bring together disparate interest groups, and the UN's record as an agent of peaceful change. These studies also demonstrate the UN's potential for partnerships with other IGOs, government, FPOs and NGOs to collectively address the challenges of peace, governance, human development and the environment. In addition, other studies also reveal that transnational social movement networks have contributed to the evolution of a new form of synergistic partnership centering on the UN and its agencies.[31]

For the future evolution of the UN system, both the image and the reality of its work are important. Insofar as the troubled image of the UN's role in peace and security is concerned, the UN at present would appear to be at the nadir of its effectiveness. The fact remains, however, that thanks to enhanced participation of non-state actors, as well as concerted efforts of states in other sectors of the greater UN system (encompassing activities in economic and social development, environment, health, education and so forth), the image and the reality of the UN's performance in recent years has not suffered very much.

And all these activities, as recognized earlier in the present paper, are part of, or are closely linked to, the broadened concept of security. It can be argued that the relevance and effectiveness of the workings of the UN system could gradually be enhanced if the synergy-promotion function of the UN system were to be further nurtured. It is noted in this connection that the legitimacy of the UN system, to a large extent, hinges upon the enhancement of such a function in two ways.

First, it is important to recognize that today the concept of legitimate authority, as noted by James Rosenau, is undergoing a shift away from the traditional criteria of legitimacy, as derived from constitutional and other legal sources, to performance criteria of legitimacy. As such, the criteria share the core characteristics of democratic governance, e.g., respect for human rights, informed consent, popular participation, transparency, and accountability of the exercise of power.[32] It is relevant to note here that Max Weber conceived legitimacy to be a subjective disposition, namely, the willingness of people to subject themselves to a particular system of authority, and to accept its norms as binding. When these two ideas are applied to the UN system, its legitimacy depends on whether the world's people bestow authority and, therefore, legitimacy, on the UN system on the basis of an assessment of the UN's performance.

Second, there is no direct representative relationship between people around the world and the UN system, although civil society organizations acting on behalf of the world's people have become increasingly associated with the policy process, as well as operational activities, of the UN system. Given that it is an intergovernmental organization, the UN's formal constituency is its member governments. The UN, as it was established nearly sixty years ago, was and still is a "community of sovereign states" and it often fails to reflect a "community of humankind" in which individuals, civil society organizations and business entities are meaningful actors. Pressure to address the UN system's legitimacy gap by creating more explicit linkages to such actors (rather than only to states) has lately become stronger as these societal actors have become increasingly empowered on the international stage. If any move toward the representation system of non-state actors such as a Second General Assembly cannot be established soon in the intergovernmental structure of the UN, an important progressive step would be for the UN General Assembly to adopt a declaration on the principle that *the will of the people shall be the ultimate basis of the authority of global governance,* and that *the authority of the UN Charter, like the constitutions of all democratic nations, shall be construed as derived from the consensual will of the people.* Furthermore, in order to support this cardinal principle, a set of general rules of accountability applicable to actions of all partners in global governance should also be formulated and adopted by the General Assembly. It can be argued that these steps would conform with the broader trend toward human-centered democratic governance around the world, as well as with a shift to partnerships of all major actors in coping with global issues.[33]

The foregoing discussion points to the need for the UN system to take the role of synergizer so that positive benefits deriving from synergistic participation of multiple stakeholders can be used to work toward human welfare. The key question now is how to ensure that this synergy indeed does occur and is effectively used.

There is an absence of a central authority for value allocation through collective decision-making based on consensual knowledge of the community of humankind. Therefore, there is a need for proactive leadership of the UN system in global planning and resource management, and building and managing multi-actor partnerships should be a central focus of such leadership. Another question that has to be answered is what normative standards and procedures should the new partnerships meet to be deemed legitimate? Without delving into a detailed discussion of this question, reference is made to what Robert Keohane considers three essentials of governance, namely, accountability, participation, and persuasion.[34] For our consideration of the legitimacy of synergistic partnerships within the UN system, rational persuasion (rather than coercion) provides the strongest assurance of legitimacy for two reasons. First, with rational persuasion, people all over the world are increasingly better informed and more active, and, second, multi-actor partnerships in the realm of the emerging heterarchical "community of humankind" have to rely on persuasion relating to norms, principles and values when they deal with the existing hierarchical "community of states" that are primarily preoccupied with power and interests.

## Conclusion

The concept of security has recently become much broader to encompass a wide spectrum of issues. The expansive definition provides a more comprehensive, though not necessarily deeper, understanding of the threats to security. It also brings with it a problem of competing claims for priority in planning and resource management. For the purpose of analysis and policy response, security issues therefore need to be classified into the three dimensions of state, human and planetary security. The methodology advocated in the present paper is "redressing security deficits" since it enables weighing and balancing, in a disciplined way, the urgency and importance of the deficits with regard to different contexts in time and space.

The scope of this chapter is limited, as it does not cover problems related to security perception that may sometimes exert excessive impact, such as psychosomatic syndrome in the aftermath of 9/11 attacks. One may not deny altogether the influence of Samuel Hunting-ton's "Clash of Civilizations" hypothesis or the eminent British military historian Michael Howard's "Green Peril" ideas (a mythically united Islam attacking the West). But the study's primary focus has been with the manifestations of security deficits that can be empirically verified and quantified, in the manner urged by Anatol Rapoport's operational philosophy for integrating knowledge and action.[35] When such empirical referents can be identified and objectively assessed, this approach to security deficits should help global planning and resource management in a disciplined way. In the absence of a central world authority for value allocation through collective decision-making, the UN could perform a limited but important function to promote synergistic partnership of multiple stakeholders, a function crucial for global governance of security. This paper is meant to be exploratory in nature. It is hoped that the underlying principles evoked, and the focal points selected for scanning the vast security field will help in formulating norms and strategies for social engineering to structure appropriate responses to security threats and security deficits.

## Notes

1. Excerpted from a statement adopted by the Security Council at its meeting on 31 Jan. 1992.
2. UNDP, *Human Development Report 1994* (New York: Oxford Univ. Press 1994)
3. *Our Global Neighbourhood—The Report of the Commission on Global Governance* (New York: Oxford Univ. Press, 1995)
4. *The Responsibility to Protect—Report of the International Commission on Intervention and State Sover-eignty* (Ottawa: International Development Research Centre, 2001)
5. *Human Security Now: Protecting and Empowering People—Report of the Commission on Human Security* (New York: Commission on Human Security 2003)
6. *The Responsibility to Protect, op. cit.* Note 4, made a sterling contribution to worldwide policy discourse by recommending highly sensible and useful principles and guidelines for military intervention.
7. See interesting arguments on this question in Edward C. Luck, "Rediscovering the State," *Global Governance*, vol. 8, no. 1, 2002, pp. 7-11.
8. Silver Jubilee Papers on International Governance, Institute of Development Studies, University of Sussex, 1992, p. 2.
9. *Op. cit.* note 2 above, p. 23.
10. *Op. cit.* note 5 above, Chapter 7, pp. 114-128.
11. *Ibid.* p. 11.
12. See for example, Yuen Foong Khong, "Human Security: A Shotgun Approach to Alleviating Human Misery," *Global Governance*, vol. 7, no. 3, 2001, pp. 231-241.
13. Fen Osler Hampson "Human Security in the 21st Century: From Concept to Global Policy Response" (Notes for an address at Academic Council on the UN System, 17th Annual Meeting, Geneva, 30 June – 2 July 2004.) See also a sound critical review of the Commission's Report in Fen Osler Hamp-son and John B. Hay, "Viva Vox Populi," *Global Governance*, vol. 10, no. 2, 2004, pp. 247-264.
14. *Op. cit.*, note 3 above, p. 78.
15. Kofi Annan, '*We the Peoples': The Role of the UN in the 21st Century* (New York: UN, 2000), pp. 54-65. The report urges the following five sets of actions: coping with climate change; confronting the water crisis; defending the soil; preserving forests, fisheries and biodiversity; and building a new ethic of global stewardship.
16. GEO-3 Report and Data Compendium prepared by Division of Early Warning and Assessment, UNEP (in Adobe PDF format), 2002, Chapter 2: 'State of the Environment and Policy Perspective 1972-2002.'

17. This question is discussed in Gary Sampson and Bradnee Chambers (eds.) *Trade, Environment and the Millennium*, 2nd edition (Tokyo, New York: UN Univ. Press, 2002), Intro and Chapters 1-3.
18. See "Goa Guidelines on Intergenerational Equity" in Annex to Edith Brown Weiss, *In Fairness to Future Generations: International Law, Common Patrimony, and Intergenerational Equity* (Tokyo: UNU, 1989)
19. See Joel E. Cohen, *How Many People Can the Earth Support?* (New York, London: W.W. Norton Co., 1995) and studies cited therein. See also *State of the World* annually published since 1984 by the Worldwatch Institute in which its editor and chief author Lester R. Brown presents alarming forecasts of the earth's carrying capacity.
20. For discussion of the question, see Hans Küng and Helmut Schmidt (eds.), *A Global Ethic and Global Responsibilities: Two Declarations* (London: SCM Press, 1998); Hans Küng, *Global Responsibility: In Search of a New World Ethic* (London: SCM Press, 1991); William Leiss, *The Domination of Nature* (Boston: Beacon Press, 1974); Barry Commoner, *Making Peace with the Planet*, (New York: Pantheon Books, 1990)
21. Hampson (*op. cit.* note 13 above) urges a better understanding of different risks as the first step of resource reallocation. For instance, he refers to some $400 billion the U.S. has spent on the war against terrorism since 9/11, as compared to a fraction of that being spent on the human security needs of people and communities at risk in developing countries.
22. See discussions relevant to this question in: Lisa Newton, "Who Speaks for the Trees? Consideration for Any Transnational Code," and Robert K. Massie, "Effective Codes of Conduct; Lessons from the Sullivan and CERES Principles" in Oliver Williams (ed.), *Global Codes of Conduct: An Idea Whose Time Has Come* (Notre Dame Univ. Press, 2000), pp. 267-291; Dinah Shelton, *Remedies in International Human Rights Law* (Oxford Univ. Press, 1999), Part III where compensation, non-monetary remedies, e.g., truth commissions and international investigations, are discussed; and Samantha Power and Graham Allison (eds.), *Realizing Human Rights: Moving from Inspiration to Impact* (St. Martin's, 2000), part III.
23. *Foreign Affairs*, vol. 76, no. 1, Jan/Feb. 1997, pp. 50-67.
24. See Andy Knight, "State-Society Complexes and the New Multilateralism: Creating Space for Heterarchic Governance" in Kendall Stiles (ed.), *Global Institutions and Local Empowerment: Competing Theoretical Perspectives* (Palgrave Macmillan, 2000), pp. 30-46.
25. For discussion of NGOs in action with the UN agencies and NGO participation in UN policy process, see Thomas Weiss and Leon Gordenker (eds.), *NGOs, the UN and Global Governance* (Lynne Rienner, 1996).
26. To the original 9 principles, a principle dealing with anti-corruption was added at a one-day "Global Leaders Summit" on 24 June 2004. For the background and prospect of the Global Compact, see Jane Nelson, *Building Partnerships: Cooperation between the UN system and the private sector* (UNDPI, 2002), Chapts. III and VII.
27. UN Non-Governmental Liaison Service (NGLS), *Go Between*, no. 103, April-May-June 2004, p. 38.
28. *Ibid.*, p. 39.
29. See Thomas Weiss (ed.), *Beyond Subcontracting: Task-Sharing with Regional Security Arrangements and Service-Providing NGOs* (Macmillan, 1998) and Sorpong Peou, "Security community building for better global governance" in Volker Rittberger (ed.), *Global Governance and the UN System* (UN Univ. Press, 2001).
30. For discussion of synergy and a related theory that the incremental evolution of the UN system as a universal institution is being facilitated by the emergence of interactive synergy processes of the quadrilateral partnership centering around the UN, see Tatsuro Kunugi, "Challenges Posed by Globalization and Synergistic Responses: Multilateral Institutions in Transition," in A. Kiss, D. Shelton and K. Ishibashi (eds.) *Economic Globalization and Compliance with International Environmental Agreements* (Kluwer Law International, 2003), pp. 13-34.
31. See R. Thakur and E. Newman (eds.), *New Millennium, New Perspectives—The United Nations, Security and Governance* (Tokyo: UNU Press, 2000) and M. Keck and K. Sikkink, *Activities beyond Borders: Advocacy Networks in International Politics* (Ithaca: Cornell Univ. Press, 2001).

32. See James N. Rosenau, *The United Nations in a Turbulent World*, International Peace Academy Occasional Paper Series (Lynne Rienner, 1992), and *Distant Proximities: Dynamics beyond Globalization* (Princeton: Princeton Univ. Press, 2003).

33. See Robert O. Keohane, "Governance in a Partially Globalized World" in David Held and Anthony McGrew (eds.), *Governing Globalization: Power, Authority and Global Governance* (Cambridge: Polity Press, 2002).

34. See discussion of these points and the text of "Declaration of Accountability of Global Governance" adopted at the Citizens Conference on UN-NGO Relations, assembled in San Francisco on the fifieth anniversary of the signing of the UN Charter, see Tatsuro Kunugi, "Popular Sovereignty and Accountability for Global Governance," *Envisioning the United Nations in the 21st Century: Proceedings of the Inaugural Symposium on the UN 21 Project, 21-22 November 1995, UNU HQ, Tokyo* (First version issued by UNU, 1996), pp. 150-56; T. Kunugi and M. Schweitz, eds., *Codes of Conduct for Partnership in Governance—Texts and Commentaries* (UNU, 1999), pp. 302-305.

35. See Anatol Rapoport, *Operational Philosophy: Integrating Knowledge and Action* (Harper & Bros., 1953), Part III, where he discusses quantification of order, life and ethics, and the philosopher's job.

## Suggestions for further reading

Kofi Annan, '*We the Peoples*': *The Role of the UN in the 21st Century* (New York: UN, 2000).

Commission on Global Governance, *Our Global Neighbourhood—The Report of the Commission on Global Governance* (New York: Oxford Univ. Press, 1995).

Commission on Human Security, *Human Security Now: Protecting and Empowering People—Report of the Commission on Human Security* (New York: Commission on Human Security 2003).

International Commission on Intervention and State Sovereignty, *The Responsibility to Protect—Report of the International Commission on Intervention and State Sovereignty* (Ottawa: International Development Research Centre, 2001).

Hans Küng and Helmut Schmidt (eds.), *A Global Ethic and Global Responsibilities: Two Declarations* (London: SCM Press, 1998).

T. Kunugi and M. Schweitz (eds.), *Codes of Conduct for Partnership in Governance—Texts and Commentaries* (UNU, 1999).

James N. Rosenau, *The United Nations in a Turbulent World*, International Peace Academy Occasional Paper Series (Lynne Rienner, 1992).

R. Thakur and E. Newman (eds.), *New Millennium, New Perspectives—The United Nations, Security and Governance* (UNU, 2000).

UNEP, GEO-3 Report on 'State of the Environment and Policy Perspective 1972-2002,' and Data Compendium prepared by Division of Early Warning and Assessment (in Adobe PDF format), 2002.

Thomas Weiss (ed.), *Beyond Subcontracting: Task-Sharing with Regional Security Arrangements and Service-Providing NGOs* (Macmillan, 1998).UNDP, *Human Development Report 1994* (New York: Oxford Univ. Press 1994).

### three

# Reflections on Peace, Security, and *Kyosei* (Conviviality) from Several Psychological Perspectives

## David W. Rackham

*Peace is not a relationship of nations. It is a condition of mind brought about by a serenity of soul. Peace is not merely an absence of war. It is also a state of mind. Lasting peace can come only to peaceful people.* (Jawaharlal Nehru)

*Peace is not an absence of war, it is a virtue, a state of mind, a disposition for benevolence, confidence, justice.* (Baruch Spinoza)

## The General Context

The purpose of this paper is to present a psychological perspective on issues of peace, security and *kyosei* (conviviality) as part of a wider effort to develop a more global multidisciplinary theoretical perspective on these issues. While these three phenomena can be differentiated conceptually, they are closely intertwined from a psychological perspective. Within a community, or between communities, a sense of conviviality (*kyosei*) encourages a sense of security which, in turn, fosters a peaceful dynamic within or between particular communities. The converse is also true in the sense that a peaceful context is likely to induce a sense of security and, hence, a spirit of *kyosei*.

## The Nature of Contemporary Psychology

The relevance of psychology as a discipline and professional practice to issues of peace, security and conviviality relates to its complex, multidisciplinary history and its many cognate disciplines past and present. The formal history of psychology as an independent discipline began in the latter part of the nineteenth century. This advent was followed by attempts over the first seventy-five years to define the overall content and methodology of the new scientific psychology in terms of grand systems or theories. Given the complexity of the subject matter (the human mind and behavior), it was inevitable that many of these approaches would fail. While some approaches persist to the present day, others are recognizable now only in terms of the legacy they have left to smaller scale modeling and theorizing. Today, psychology is a very diverse enterprise from the point of view of its subject matter.

In terms of level or unit of analysis for a given phenomenon, psychology tends to sit somewhere toward the middle of the dimension illustrated in Figure 1. However, psychologists may work at any level of analysis on this dimension depending on their particular interest. One feature that characterizes psychology in general is that the focus of inquiry is ultimately on the individual and his/her unique characteristics and experiences. This is true even when the environmental context is given special emphasis as in social psychology, community psychology, cross-cultural psychology and clinical psychology. It is these characteristics of psychology that confer a special trans-disciplinary relevance to the discipline in both the theoretical and practical spheres. In fact, psychology could be considered to be the prototypical liberal arts discipline by virtue of the diversity of its multidisciplinary origins, subject matter, methodologies, and wide array of contemporary cognate disciplines (McGovern, Furomoto, Halpern, Kimble, & McKeachie, 1991).

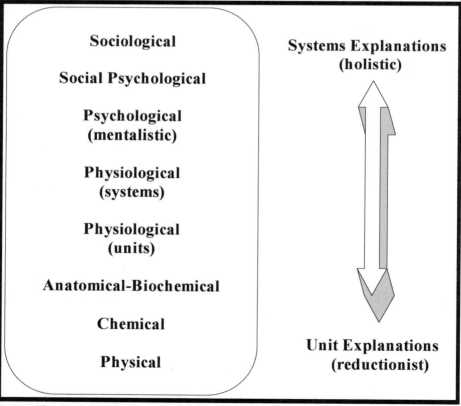

*Figure 1. The relative positioning of psychology as a discipline in terms of the level of explanation.*

## Psychology as a Discipline with Societal Implications and Responsibilities

As there is a psychological dimension to almost every human feature and activity (Lundin, 1991), it can be argued that psychologists have a great deal to contribute in theory and practice to issues of widespread public concern. Miller (1969) and Bevan (1982, cited by Bevan, 1991), for example, were firm in their belief that scientific psychology could have profound social and personal implications, akin to a psychological revolution in society at large. It is psychologists who have developed an expertise to help people change their behaviour, both individually and collectively, in ways conducive to solving many of the world's major problems.

Fowler (1990) has described psychology as a "core discipline" because (1) psychological methodologies are widely used by other disciplines, and (2) the major problems afflicting society today are problems related to behavior and lifestyle. These are precisely the areas in which psychologists are best prepared to contribute to solutions. Many issues of public concern transcend traditional academic or disciplinary boundaries. Psychology is inherently inter-disciplinary in practice and origin. As such, psychologists may have an advantage in being able to see issues, including issues of peace, security and *kyosei,* from a variety of perspectives.

In short, psychology, in its claim to be both a science and a profession, has a vested interest in contributing to the public welfare in many domains (See also Coon & Sprenger, 1998; DeLeon, 1986; DeLeon, 1993, Howitt, 1991; Johnson, 1992; Kiesler & Morton, 1988; Louttit, 1992; Hodgkinson & Stewart, 1991; Sloan, 1992; Smith, 1990; Rackham, 1996).

## Positing A Role for Psychology in Issues of Peace, Security, and *Kyosei*

When it comes to issues of peace, security and *kyosei* from a psychological perspective, the bottom line is that it is individuals who have attitudes, beliefs and values which are often shared with other individuals in community or national settings. Ultimately, it is individuals who act, albeit in frequent concert with others. It is individual psychological beings who create the conditions for a loss of *kyosei*. It is individuals who perceive a decline in their sense of personal or collective security. And it is individuals who suffer the physical/medical and psychological/behavioral consequences of a loss of *kyosei* and security when peace gives way to conflict.

Psychologists are increasingly involved in crisis intervention and amelioration around the world as the serious psychological consequences of terror, war and deprivation in general come to be better appreciated. Psychologists can make significant contributions to understanding the dynamics that predispose individuals to violence and conflict, or conversely, predispose individuals to engage others in a spirit of cooperation and peace. A major aspect of the conflict resolution process is psychological in nature, for resolving a conflict requires protagonists to adjust their attitudes and behavior in ways conducive to peaceful engagement with one another. Complex social psychological principles are at work determining whether individuals, or groups of individuals, including nation states, are able to engage one another in a positive and peaceful way or in a negative and destructive manner.

In short, psychology has much to contribute to the understanding and management of issues of peace, security and *kyosei*. The diversity of contemporary psychology, both in terms of content and methodology, enables a wide range of possible theoretical perspectives on these issues. In due course, two of the many possible psychological perspectives on these issues will be considered here—a biopsychosocial perspective and a social psychological perspective—with greater emphasis by far on the former.

## Basic Human Needs as Posited by the Humanistic Psychologist Abraham Maslow

The humanistic psychologist Abraham Maslow posited a hierarchy of human needs often illustrated in the form of a triangle as shown in Figure 2. At the base of the triangle, we find essential physiological needs—food, water, shelter, security—which, if not met, can, at the very least, severely compromise the quality of life an individual can enjoy.

The need for safety or security is fundamental to human welfare. The lack of security can compromise the ability to meet basic physiological needs, not to mention the higher-level needs identified by Maslow. The need to belong, and the need to love and be loved are critical for the psychological well-being of the individual. The classic work of Harry Harlow with monkeys raised with surrogate mothers pointed to the very real possibility that similar pathological consequences may await susceptible human beings who are deprived of love and general psychological support or comfort (Harlow 1959a,b; Harlow, 1960, Harlow, 1965).

The social psychological literature confirms the importance of self-esteem for the psychological well-being of the individual. While the nature of self-esteem and its origins may vary from culture to culture, it seems clear that the loss of self-esteem is likely to promote

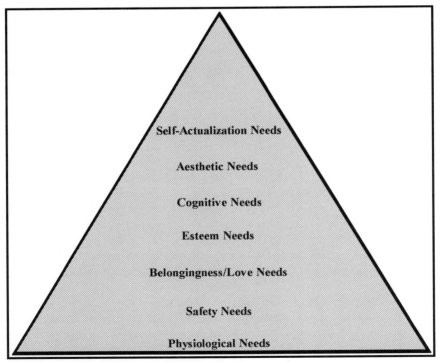

Figure 2 . A representation of Maslow's (1968) hierarchy of human needs.

certain forms of psychopathology and physical pathology in susceptible individuals. The inability to meet cognitive and esthetic needs can result, at the very least, in an individual falling short of his/her potential.

At the apex of the triangle sits the need for self-actualization. The need to become truly one's self, to fulfill one's potential, to transcend the limits of self-awareness and self-service, is met by a relatively small proportion of the population according to Maslow. It should also be noted that cultural prerogatives modulate the extent to which this is a significant need in a given society

## When Basic Needs Are Compromised or Unmet: The Stress Reaction— Acute and Chronic

Hans Selye is known as the father of modern stress theory (Selye, 1955; Selye, 1956; Selye, 1973; Selye, 1978). Subsequently, Lazarus and Folkman (1984) proposed a transactional model of stress which incorporated an appraisal dimension for the determination of whether or not an event would be perceived as stressful.

Stress may be defined as a state of bodily arousal provoked by specific external or internal events. The stress reaction may be construed as a kind of transaction between the individual and his/her external and internal environments (Lazarus & Folkman, 1984). External envi-

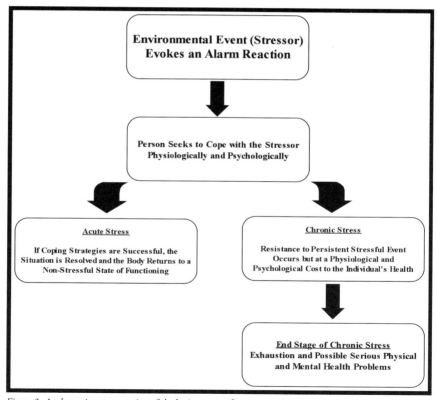

*Figure 3. A schematic representation of the basic aspects of a stress reaction, acute or chronic.*

ronmental events that qualify as stressors can include degraded or impoverished physical or social environments. Such stressors range from the daily annoyances (hassles) of life to major cataclysmic events produced by natural or human-caused disasters, including warfare. Internal stressors are typically psychological in nature and relate to issues of self-esteem, personality characteristics and traits, memory of past trauma, etc.

A general overview of the stress reaction is shown in Figure 3. In response to a situation perceived as stressful, the body prepares to deal with the emergency. This is often referred to as a "fight or flight" response. Should the situation resolve itself quickly, then the individual experiences an acute stress reaction and the system functions adaptively. Should the stressful situation be prolonged and coping strategies are not fully successful, the person may enter a state of chronic stress which can exact significant physiological, psychological and medical costs for the individual in the longer term.

Figure 4 incorporates the appraisal dimension of the bodily reaction to an environmental event. Whether the body is mobilized to cope with an emergency depends on whether the situation is, in fact, perceived as threatening. Primary appraisal determines if, in fact, a threatening situation exists. If a threat is perceived to exist, secondary appraisal determines whether adequate coping strategies are available to the individual. These include physiological and psychological resilience as a result of past experience, personality characteristics, and genetic predispositions to respond to stress in particular ways.

The stress reaction involves a complex cascade of physiological and biochemical reactions (Carola, Harley, and Noback, 1990). Through what is known as the hypothalamic-adrenal-pituitary (HPA) axis, the body is prepared for a fight or flight response. Bodily changes include an increase in cardiac rate (pulse) and blood pressure, a faster respiration rate, a tensing of the skeletal muscles, and increased blood flow to the brain resulting in a

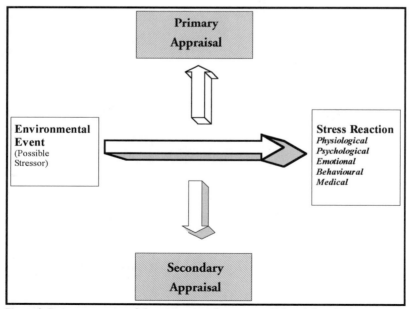

Figure 4. Basic components of the acute stress phenomenon (Adapted from Taylor, 1999, p. 171).

heightened state of vigilance. Blood supply to the skin, digestive tract, kidneys and liver is reduced and there is a corresponding increase in blood sugar, fats and cholesterol and a rise in platelets and blood clotting factors to prevent serious blood loss. This is a perfectly adaptive reaction as long as the crisis situation abates after a reasonable period of time.

Should an acute stress reaction metamorphose into a chronic stress reaction, then the longer-term physiological and psychological consequences may well be negative and even life-threatening for certain individuals, depending on a complex interplay of biological, psychological and environmental factors. For those who react negatively, common symptoms of stress include a variety of physical complaints such as fatigue, headache, insomnia, gastrointestinal discomfort, sympathetic hyperactivity, etc. Psychological symptoms include a decline or distortion in memory and thinking processes, increased or decreased emotional reactivity, anxiety, and depression. Behavioral manifestations may include an increase in nervous habits, alterations in eating behavior, and enhanced irritability and aggressiveness. All these contribute to a decline in the quality of life experienced by the individual as the ability to meet basic needs is compromised.

In susceptible individuals, chronic stress may lead to, or exacerbate, the process of a disease, physical or mental. Chronic stress may produce direct physiological changes, produce changes in behaviour that lead to negative physiological consequences, or produce changes in behavior that exacerbate existing physiological and behavioral patterns through a lack of compliance with appropriate restorative strategies.

Clay (2001a,b) outlines for the lay reader the role of psychosocial factors in cardiovascular disease. These factors, which include frustration, hostility, and personality type, may precipitate cardiovascular and/or cerebrovascular disorders directly or indirectly through changes in the individual's lifestyle. It is well known that endocrine disorders such as diabetes are also adversely affected by elevated levels of stress.

Lehrer, Sargunaraj, and Hochron (1992) point to the psychological dimensions of bronchial asthma and other respiratory disorders which are aggravated by elevated stress levels. Cohen and Williamson (1991) have reviewed the evidence related to the role of stress in the course of infectious disease in humans. Gastrointestinal disorders such as ulcerative colitis and irritable bowel syndrome (IBS) are known to be modulated by stress reactions (Whitehead, 1992) and Andersen, Kiecolt-Glaser, and Glaser (1994) have addressed the importance of psychological/behavioral factors in their biobehavioral model of cancer stress and disease course.

A newly emerging discipline known as psychoneuroimmunology (PNI) focuses on the bi-directional links between the individual's psychological state, his/her nervous system, and the immune system. Kiecolt-Glaser and Glaser (1992) and Maier, Watkins, and Flesher (1994) have outlined the possible routes by which the individual's psychological state can modulate the reactivity of the immune system, and vice versa. Evidence suggests that a state of chronic stress can suppress the activity of the immune system, making the individual more susceptible to disease, or making it more difficult for the individual to recover from an ongoing disease process. This complex interplay between an individual's psychological state, the nervous system, and the immune system determines overall how adaptive an individual's transactions with the environment prove to be.

While stress is inherent to the human condition, the ability to enjoy a reasonable quality of life is likely to be enhanced if the individual experiences a sense of *kyosei*, a sense of security or a safe place, and a state of peace. The loss of a sense of security, the loss of a sense of *kyosei*, and the influence of strife in a person's life are likely to increase stress levels in ways detrimental to the individual's long-term prospects. The evidence is sufficiently strong to suggest that poorly managed responses to stressful situations have biological, psychological/emotional and behavioral implications for the long-term well-being of the individual. Maladaptive coping strategies may lead to interpersonal problems, including mistrust and denigration of others and the need to dominate or control others. Inability to cope with chronic stress may then feed back to undermine the individual's ability to meet even the most basic needs for food, shelter, and a sense of security. The end result for some individuals is the loss of a sense of hope that life is meaningful or even possible.

## A Biopsychosocial Perspective on Issues of Peace, Security, and *Kyosei*

Psychology is becoming increasingly biological as technology has allowed greater insights into the mind-brain relationship and ever-increasing knowledge of the human genome contributes to greater understanding of how genetic predispositions interact with the environment to produce an individual's psychological profile and his/her behavior (See Rosenzweig, Leiman, & Breedlove, 1996; Pinel, 2003).

The term "biopsychosocial" implies that each individual is a complex biological and psychological entity existing in, and conditioned by, the environments in which that individual has lived, is living, and will live. The term "environment" can be construed in a broad sense to include the multiple physical and socio-cultural contexts in which each individual is situated in a state of mutual and reciprocal interaction during the course of his/her lifetime. As a biological, psychological and sociocultural entity, each individual is successful to greater or lesser extents in meeting the basic human needs outlined by Maslow (1968). Internal physiological and psychological factors and external environmental factors, such as socioeconomic deprivation as a result of natural disasters or human conflict, can inflict a severe toll on individuals in the form of maladaptive chronic stress reactions with profound health consequences for susceptible individuals. The existential psychologist, Viktor Frankl, puzzled as to why some could survive while so many others perished in the Nazi concentration camps of World War II, and concluded that those who had a reason to live, who still found meaning in their lives, stood a significantly greater prospect of survival than those who had lost hope, and who thus, in the end, lost their lives (Frankl, 1962).

The biological aspect of this perspective is rooted in the evolutionary history of the species, the particular genetic legacy of each individual, and the brain as the physical/chemical basis of mind. Bereczkei (2000) documents the relevance of a new, integrated approach to human behavior known as evolutionary psychology. According to this perspective, cognitive and emotional phenomena emerge through a process of evolutionary selection and it is these phenomena that guide our social behavior, rendering each individual more or less adapted to solving the essential challenges of everyday existence. Stressors are often encountered under conditions of deprivation of basic resources required for life (e.g., food deprivation and its attendant consequences for brain development as considered by Tanner & Finn-Stevenson, 2002). Chronic stress may develop if the psychological integrity of the individual is threatened as a result of social isolation, family breakdown, loss of status and self-esteem, or community conflict and strife. For Plomin and Colledge (2001), the ultimate challenge is to understand how genetic tendencies and predispositions engage the particular environments encountered by an individual during the course of his/her lifespan development.

The psychological aspect of the biopsychosocial perspective is the individual's mental representation (knowledge) of the environment emerging from his/her transaction with that environment and the sense of whether the demands imposed by that environment can be met in an adaptive manner.

Shapiro, Schwartz, and Astin (1996) point to the importance for individual well-being of perceiving a sense of control over one's destiny. In susceptible individuals, the lack of a sense of control may exacerbate stress and anxiety-related disorders, depression, substance abuse disorders, and eating disorders. Control also seems to be a critical factor in the prognosis for disorders of a primarily physical nature. The effect of control on physical and psychological health and illness is likely to be the result of a complex interplay of factors that Shapiro et al. (1996) seek to understand in terms of a biopsychosocial model of control. In this model, the biological component includes genetic predispositions to exercise behavioral self-control and/or factors related to the degree to which people feel in control of their internal and external environments. Among the social factors in this model are stressors which arise through interaction with the environment. Psychological factors relate to the extent to which a sense of control matches what is real and possible for the individual in a particular context. Psychological mismatches may engender stress, leading to a compromised functioning of the immune system.

The social component of the biopsychosocial perspective is the environmental context (social, cultural) in which the person exists. Biologically determined predispositions engaging a continually changing environment produce the psychological profile of the individual. The individual is always in a mutual and reciprocal interaction with the environment such that changes in the environment produce changes in the psychological and behavioral state of the individual. Over time, people develop adaptive or maladaptive responses to the demands of life. An adaptive state exists when the individual feels a sense of security and a state of *kyosei* with his/her fellow beings. This constitutes a state of peace, both internal and external.

Sperry (1993) has argued that values (psychological phenomena) can exert a powerful influence on biological functioning and, hence, can play a powerful role in shaping the individual and the world for better or worse. Shapiro, Schwartz, and Astin (1996) suggest that many of the global problems people face today are related to the psychological phenomenon of control, especially in terms of the perceived right to exercise control and how that control is exercised. It should be noted that cultural prerogatives determine to a great extent when and how the opportunity for control will be exercised. As Maslow (1968), Fowler (1991) and others have argued, the time must come when the exercise of control moves beyond control for personal gain to control exercised for the purpose of the collective well-being of our planet.

In short, a biopsychosocial perspective may be most useful in pointing to the physiological, psychological and medical consequences of individuals confronting environments in which a sense of *kyosei* is lost, a sense of insecurity becomes pervasive, and peace gives way to conflict. Strife and warfare affect the psychological and physiological well-being of all individuals in ways unique to those individuals' biopsychosocial profiles. Short of death as an immediate and direct result of conflict, the long-term impact of warfare on the individual is found in the effects warfare has on the individual's physiological and psychological state as a result of a diminution or loss of basic resources (food, water, shelter), a loss of social support accruing from disrupted family and community relationships, the stigma and discrimination that may emerge as a result of such deprivation, and a loss of hope for the future. Economic and political realities associated with insecurity and conflict ultimately have their impact on the lives of individuals, a reality that may be acknowledged implicitly but not always explicitly. Understanding the profound physiological and psychological impact of insecurity and conflict on individual lives may help to provide a perspective that encourages a more considered analysis of the alternatives to conflict as a means of resolving disputes between individuals and groups of individuals, up to and including the level of nation states.

## A Social Psychological Perspective

A social psychological perspective on issues of peace, security, and *kyosei* is inherent in the biopsychosocial perspective outlined above. The social psychological perspective emphasizes the reciprocal relationship between individuals and the social groupings to which they belong.

Social groups form for many reasons and at many levels of integration, up to and including the modern nation state. Any standard textbook in social psychology (e.g., Myers, 1996) will include a section on the dynamics of groups. Groups typically have norms or rules that apply to all members and each member has a particular role to play in the group. Groups often demand evidence of loyalty to the group and can apply pressure on individuals to comply with group norms (Asch, 1955). The classic studies of Stanley Milgram on obedience to authority revealed how difficult it is for an individual to resist the expectations and demands of group leaders (Milgram, 1974).

Social groups can provide the individual with a strong sense of security and *kyosei* if the individual is generally accepting of the group's goals and expectations. Many goals cannot be achieved unless individuals work in concert so group behavior often produces adaptive and desired consequences.

Also inherent in the social dynamics of the group is the potential for highly maladaptive behavior for the individual and society at large. The phenomenon of deindividuation encourages a sense of anonymity and a diminution of a sense of personal responsibility for one's behavior. Group decision processes may produce less than optimal consequences for the individual and for the group as a whole. A tendency toward group polarization can strengthen both positive and negative tendencies within the group while groupthink may produce a consensus in decision-making that is detrimental to the individual, to the group, and to other groups.

Attribution is the process by which inferences are drawn about what motivates the behavior of other individuals and other groups. When these attributions are accurate and fair-minded, adaptive consequences often follow for the individual and the group. But when prejudice (See Gaines & Reed, 1995), stereotyping, and discriminatory attitudes and behavior color the attribution process, individuals and groups are more likely to come into conflict with one another. Prejudice may arise for many reasons, including perceived inequality of status between individuals or groups, different religious affiliations, an enhanced sense of differences between the in-group and the out-group, and frustration due to a thwarting of goals. As differences between individuals or groups are exaggerated and similarities are muted or ignored, conflict becomes more likely.

The role of group leadership in promoting peace or conflict cannot be underestimated. A leader can make or break an organization. Levinson (1994) explored the psychological roots of corporate failure and noted that leadership played a critical role in the success or failure of an organization. Hogan, Curphy, and Hogan (1994) demonstrated, in the American context at least, what leaders do and how effectively or ineffectively they do it. The authors claim that many flawed leaders emerge because leaders are rarely selected on the basis of the criteria essential to success in the job.

Clearly, a social psychological perspective should be incorporated in any higher level integrative and multi-disciplinary account of issues related to peace, security, and *kyosei*. Each individual is rooted in one or more groups during his/her lifetime. Psychological and behavioral dispositions are strongly influenced by group processes and group leaders play a major role in shaping the attitudes and behavior of the group. An understanding of these social psychological dynamics can be deployed not only in the interests of maintaining peace, security and *kyosei* but also in the process of conflict resolution when attitudinal and behavioral change are essential to restoring a more peaceful environment.

## Concluding Observations

In his recent volume, *Shaking Hands with the Devil: The Failure of Humanity in Rwanda*, Lieutenant-General Roméo Dallaire, the commander of the ill-fated United Nations Assistance Mission in Rwanda in 1994, illustrates the importance of a psychological perspective in issues of peace, security, and *kyosei*. Himself a prominent victim of post-traumatic stress disorder (PTSD) following his experience in Rwanda, Dallaire describes the potential consequences—for peacekeepers, peacemakers, and their families—of a descent into insecurity and chaos such as occurred in Rwanda. The biopsychosocial and social psychological perspectives outlined above provide ways of understanding the tremendous human cost incurred when peace, security, and *kyosei* are compromised or lost.

Dallaire points to the social psychological climate created by extremists which allowed Hutus to engage in massive genocide against their countrymen, the Tutsis. He points to the rage engendered in those who have no rights, no security, no hope, and no future and who are thereby predisposed to see violence as the only reasonable solution to their terrible dilemma. Dallaire counsels the world, and particularly the developed world, to engage in the promotion of what he calls a new century of humanity.

The importance of a psychological perspective in issues of peace, security and *kyosei* has been argued in this paper. Many psychological perspectives are possible, but this paper has focused primary on a biopsychosocial perspective, emphasizing the physiological, psychological and medical costs which may accrue to susceptible individuals who find themselves in situations where a sense of *kyosei* is lost, security gives way to a state of insecurity, and peace gives way to conflict. Psychologists are becoming more and more interested in bringing their expertise to bear on issues of peace, security, and *kyosei*. The American Psychological Association (APA) has a Division of Peace Psychology (Division 48) and a journal of Peace Psychology is now being published on a quarterly basis. Psychologists such as Deutsch (1993) are interested in educating young people in methods to develop a more peaceful world by incorporating psychological principles and methods known to encourage cooperative interactions between individuals and groups. The Internet is becoming an increasingly important forum for sharing psychological insights on issues of peace and security.

In short, psychology and psychologists have an important contribution to make toward a more global understanding of issues related to peace, security, and *kyosei*. In particular, the biopsychosocial perspective outlined in this paper is trans-disciplinary and multidisciplinary in nature and addresses the complex nature of human experience in its biological, psychological, and social domains. It is hoped that in the years to come psychologists will play an ever greater role in helping to promote peace, security, and *kyosei* (conviviality) in our troubled world.

## References

Andersen, B. L., Kiecolt-Glaser, J. K., and Glaser, R. (1994). A biobehavioral model of cancer stress and disease course. *American Psychologist, 49*(5), 389-404.

Asch, S. E. (November 1955). Opinions and social pressure. *Scientific American*, 31-35.

Bereczkei, T. (2000). Evolutionary psychology: A new perspective in the behavioral sciences. *European Psychologist, 5*, 175-190.

Bevan, W. (1991). Contemporary psychology: A tour inside the onion. *American Psychologist, 46*, 475-483.

Carola, R., Harley, J. P., & Noback, C. R. (1990). *Human anatomy and physiology*. New York: McGraw-Hill Publishing Company.

Clay, R. A. (2001). Research to the heart of the matter. *Monitor on Psychology*, Volume 32, No. 1 January.

Clay, R. A. (2001). Bringing psychology to cardiac care. *Monitor on Psychology*, Volume 32, No. 1 January.

Cohen, S., & Williamson, G. N. (1991). Stress and infectious disease in humans. *Psychological Bulletin*, 109, 5-24.

Coon, D. J., & Sprenger, H. A. (1998). Psychologists in service to science: The American Psychological Association and the American Association for the Advancement of Science. *American Psychologist, 53*, 1253-1269.

Dallaire, R. A. (2003). *Shake hands with the devil: The failure of humanity in Rwanda*. Toronto: Random House Canada.

DeLeon, P. H. (1986). Increasing the societal contribution of organized psychology. *American Psychologist*, 41, 466-474.

DeLeon, P. H. (1993). Psychology and the public policy/political process: new roles for "old" psychologists, revisited. *The General Psychologist, 29*(1), 6-8.

Deutsch, M. (1993). Educating for a peaceful world. *American Psychologist, 48*, 510-517.

Fowler, R. D. (1990). Psychology: The core discipline. *American Psychologist, 45*, 1-6.

Frankl, V. E. (1962). *Man's search for meaning*. Boston: Beacon Press.

Gaines, S. O. Jr., & Reed, E. S. (1995). Prejudice: from Allport to DuBois. *American Psychologist, 50*, 96-103.

Harlow, H. F. (1959a). Basic social capacity of primates. *Human Biology, 31*, 40-53.

Harlow, H. F. (1959b). Love in infant monkeys. *Scientific American*, 200(6), 68-74.

Harlow, H. F. (1960). Primary affectional patterns in primates. *American Journal of Orthopsychiatry, 30*, 676-684.

Harlow, H. F. (1965). Total social isolation: Effects on Macaque monkey behavior. *Science*, 148, 666.

Hodgkinson, P. E., & Stewart, M. (1991). *Coping with catastrophe: A handbook of disaster management*. London: Routledge.

Hogan, R., Curphy, G. J., & Hogan, J. (1994). What we know about leadership: Effectiveness and personality. *American Psychologist, 49*, 493-504.

Howitt, D. (1991). *Concerning psychology: Psychology applied to social issues*. Philadelphia: Open University Press.

Johnson, D. (1992). Why are behavioral scientists out of the room when policies that regulate human behavior are formed? *The General Psychologist, 28*(2), 24-27.

Kiecolt-Glaser, J. K., & Glaser, R. (1992). Psychoneuroimmunology: Can psychological interventions modulate immunity? *Journal of Consulting & Clinical Psychology*, 60(4), 569-575.

Kiesler, C. A., & Morton, T. L. (1988). Psychology and public policy in the "health care revolution." *American Psychologist*, 43, 993-1003.

Lazarus, R. S., & Folkman, S. (1984). *Stress, appraisal, and coping*. New York: Springer-Verlag.

Lehrer, P. M., Sargunaraj, D., & Hochron, S. (1992). Psychological approaches to the treatment of asthma. *Journal of Consulting and Clinical Psychology*, 60, 639-643.

Levinson, H. (1994). Why the behemoths fell: Psychological roots of corporate failure. *American Psychologist*, 49, 428-436.

Louttit, R. T. (1992). Psychology and public policy. *The General Psychologist*, 28(2), 27-29.

Lundin, R. W. (1991). *Theories and systems of psychology* (4th ed.). Lexington, Mass.: D.C. Heath & Co.

Maier, S. F., Watkins, L. R., & Flesher, M. (1994). Psychoneuroimmunology: The interface between behavior, brain, and immunity. *American Psychologist*, 49, 1004-1017.

Maslow, A. (1968). *Toward a psychology of being*. Princeton, NJ: Van Nostrand.

McGovern, T. V., Furomoto, L., Halpern, D. F., Kimble, G. A., & McKeachie, W. J. (1991). Liberal education, study in depth, and the arts and sciences major—psychology. *American Psychologist*, 46, 598-605.

Milgram, S. (1974). *Obedience to authority*. New York: Harper and Row.

Miller, G. A. (1969). Psychology as a means of promoting human welfare. *American Psychologist*, 24, 1063-1075.

Myers, D. G. (1996). *Social psychology* (5th ed.). New York: The McGraw-Hill Companies, Inc.

Pinel, J. P. (2003). *Biopsychology* (5th ed.). Boston: Allyn & Bacon.

Plomin, R., & Colledge, E. (2001). Genetics and psychology: Beyond heritability. *European Psychologist*, 6, 229-240.

Rackham, D. W. (1996). Psychology in the public forum—unity in service? *Educational Studies*, 38, 81-107.

Rosenzweig, M. R., Leiman, A. L., & Breedlove, S. M. (1996). *Biological psychology*. Sunderland, Massachusetts: Sinauer Associates, Inc., Publishers.

Selye, H. (1955). Stress and disease. *Science*, 122, 625-631.

Selye, H. (1956). Stress and psychobiology. *Journal of Clinical and Experimental Psychopathology*, 17, 370-375.

Selye, H. (1973). The evolution of the stress concept. *American Scientist*, 61, 692-699.

Selye, H. (1978). *The stress of life* (rev. ed.). Oxford: McGraw-Hill.

Shapiro, D. H., Schwartz, C.E., & Astin, J. A. (1996). Controlling ourselves, controlling our world: Psychology's role in understanding positive and negative consequences of seeking and gaining control. *American Psychologist*, 51, 1213-1230.

Sloan, T. (1992). Psychologists challenged to grapple with global issues. *Psychology International*, 3(4), 1-7.

Smith, M. B. (1990). Psychology in the public interest: What have we done? What can we do? *American Psychologist*, 45, 530-536.

Sperry, R. W. (1993). The impact and promise of the cognitive revolution. *American Psychologist*, 48, 878—885.

Taylor, S. E. (1999). *Health psychology* (4th ed.). Boston: McGraw-Hill.

Tanner & Finn-Stevenson (2002). Nutrition and brain development. *American Journal of Orthopsychiatry*, 72, 182-193.

Whitehead, W. E. (1992). Behavioral medicine approaches to gastrointestinal disorders. *Journal of Consulting and Clinical Psychology*, 60, 605-612.

**four**

# Psychological Dimensions of Conflict

## Craig D. Parks and Asako Stone

Psychologists have been interested in the study of conflict for almost as long as psychology has existed as a discipline. A computer search of the psychology journals back to 1896 turns up almost 4,000 articles that address conflict in some fashion. Indeed, by the mid-1920s the study of the psychology of conflict was sufficiently well-engrained that models of general behavior began to appear that included conflict as a predictive element. Further, some of psychology's most heavily debated issues center around conflict; for example, the efficacy of interactive problem-solving at reducing ethnic tensions (e.g., Kelman, 1998).

Psychological research on the causes and consequences of conflict has generally confined itself to small groups, often as small as two persons. This is partially because of the discipline's traditional emphasis on micro-level processes, partially because there is evidence that people cannot accurately conceive of the magnitude of large-scale conflicts (Kahneman, Ritov, Jacowitz, & Grant, 1993), and partially because large-scale conflict cannot easily be simulated in the laboratory, the research venue of choice for most psychologists. The sub-specialty of political psychology, however, has made inroads into understanding the dynamics of large-scale conflict.

The purpose of this chapter is to introduce some of the primary psychological contributors to the development of a conflict. We shall focus on general social conflict, and not address conflict in close relationships, though that research tradition has identified some principles that may well have application to the understanding of more global conflict. The bulk of the essay will focus on three major psychological contributors to conflict development: person perception, ingroup-outgroup distinctions, and decision heuristics. After discussing the essential features of these phenomena, we will consider how their impact might potentially be minimized, and conclude with some thoughts on how this psychological research might be linked to works in other disciplines.

## Person Perception

One of the greatest causes of conflict has its roots in misperceptions of others. The psychological literature is rife with examples of such person-perception errors. If these erroneous perceptions in turn influence our behaviors, as they almost always do, some type of conflict episode may well result, because the target of our actions will likely see our behavior as unjustified, and react adversely. As such, much psychological research into conflict addresses how and why we perceive others as we do. In this section, we will summarize some of the major principles of person perception as they relate to conflict.

## Stereotypes

We encounter many people in daily social life. Every person presents to us a considerable amount of information that must be processed and stored in order for us to determine how to interact with the person. To simplify this task, people create *social categories,* or groupings of people with like characteristics. These groupings contain information about what members of the category are typically like, and help us anticipate how an upcoming interaction with a member of that category might go. For example, if your social category "policeman" contains the information that police officers are humorless when on duty, should you have to interact with a policeman you will know to be serious and direct. Social categories have been shown to exert a powerful influence on how we perceive and interact with others, and all else being equal, people prefer to base their perception of another person on category information rather than collect information about that person (Pendry & Macrae, 1994).

While these categories are useful in helping us process large amounts of social information, it is also the case that we can come to rely too heavily on them when perceiving others, and in particular we can come to believe that all members of a category possess all of the features of that category, even though there is evidence to the contrary. Such a belief is referred to as *stereotyping.* In particular, people who maintain stereotypic beliefs tend to emphasize either very negative or very positive features associated with the category, and underemphasize the degree of variability within the category (Fiske, 1998). For example, research has shown that people tend to stereotype African-American men as being athletic, but also criminal-minded (Niemann, Jennings, Rozelle, Baxter, & Sullivan, 1994). Being the target of a stereotype has been shown to have both psychological (Steele & Aronson, 1995) and physiological (Blascovich, Spencer, Quinn, & Steele, 2001) consequences, and it is perhaps not surprising that advocation of stereotypic beliefs is often a precursor of intergroup conflict.

While stereotypes are beliefs about particular groups of people, *prejudice* is an affective reaction to a group, and unlike stereotypes is always negative. Thus, maintaining a stereotype for homosexual men would indicate that one has a set of characteristics that one expects to see in all gay men; being prejudiced against homosexual men would indicate that encountering gay men causes one to have a negative emotional reaction. A particularly insidious type of prejudice, termed "ethnocentrism," is the belief that one's own group is superior to all other groups, and by extension, that all members of one's own group are superior to all members of all other groups. Thus, an ethnocentric white might believe that even the least skilled white is nonetheless more talented than the most skilled Mexican-American.

Prejudice is destructive to social relations and is a major cause of conflict. For example, it has been shown that prejudiced individuals will willingly endorse very derogatory statements about the target group (Munro & Ditto, 1997) and will support extreme policies directed toward controlling the target group (e.g., Sears, Citrin, Cheleden, & van Laar, 1999). As has been shown innumerable times in world history, those who are the target of prejudice do not long tolerate such treatment, and conflict is the inevitable result.

## Attributions

We have seen that stereotypes lead us to form certain expectations about the behavior of others. An *attribution* is an inference about the personal traits of others. Thus, we saw that people typically believe African-American men play basketball very well, which is a behavioral inference, but are also supportive of law-breaking, which is a trait inference. Attributions are a common part of social life and occur because it is psychologically uncomfortable to not know why something occurred. We make attributions even when we possess less-than-complete information about the situation being observed. For example, we may see a man kick a dog and conclude that the man is cruel. This may be a correct conclusion, or it may be that the dog attacked the man before we arrived on the scene, making the man's actions justified. People generally assume that their attributions are accurate, even after freely admitting that they could be lacking important situational information. Perhaps not surprisingly, attributions are often inaccurate.

*Attributional Errors.* One particularly problematic type of error is the *fundamental attribution error*. This error refers to the general belief that others' behaviors always reflect their disposition. For example, a driver who runs a red light would be assumed by most observers to be a careless driver, even though the person might instead be hurrying to the hospital. The fundamental attribution error contributes to the development of conflict because it can lead us to assume hostile intent for a negative behavior when in truth no such intent exists.

A variety of attributional errors manifest themselves when we consider perception of people of other nations. For example, the *group-serving bias* is the assumption that our group's actions are motivated by positive goals, but the positive actions of hostile groups are motivated by negative goals. Thus, we send aid to a needy country because we are humanitarian, but our enemies aid needy countries because they are trying to win converts. In a similar vein, the *blacktop illusion* occurs when people infer that the motivation of the enemy's leaders differs from that of their people (Burn & Oskamp, 1989). This would lead to the conclusion, for example, that the Iraqi people would like to be friendly with the U.S., but the Iraqi leaders refuse to pursue such a policy.

## Ingroups and Outgroups

The process of categorization has an impact not only on how we see particular people, but also on how we see groups as a whole. In general, the creation of categories leads to the identification of groups to which we belong (known as *ingroups*) and groups to which we do not belong (*outgroups*). Any one person can belong to both an ingroup and an outgroup. For example, while your best friend likely shares many features with you, it is likely that you and your friend differ on some primary features–perhaps gender, race/ethnicity, age, occupation, or some personality traits.

We noted earlier that categorization is useful for daily social functioning. However, categorization can also enhance dissimilarities among different categories (Brewer & Miller, 1996). Most notably, people tend to favorably distinguish ingroup members from outgroup members—an ingroup member is seen as more credible, more deserving of rewards, and as an overall more desirable person than a comparable outgroup member. This *intergroup bias*, which typically serves to help maintain self-esteem, often induces hostile attitudes toward outgroup members. As such, the study of ingroup-outgroup processes receives considerable attention from conflict researchers.

## Social Identity Theory

One of the explanations for intergroup bias is social identity theory (Tajfel & Turner, 1986). This theory argues that individuals have a fundamental desire to positively evaluate themselves to maintain or heighten their self-esteem. This can be accomplished by presenting ingroups in a positive light, and outgroups in a negative light, and thinking of intergroup relations as "us versus them" situations (Brewer, 1999; Hogg, Abrams, Otten, & Hinkle, 2004). Such a perception leads to less openness to outgroups, attention only to information that favorably presents the ingroup, and stronger commitment to the view that the outgroup is unattractive. This selective attention to information makes it difficult for mediators to highlight the good qualities of the outgroup, and thus minimize the conflict.

Compounding the problem is the fact that members of an ingroup selectively compare themselves to a particular outgroup that is relevant to their group identity and is inferior to themselves. In other words, ingroup members are strategic in their selection of both the ingroup and the comparison group, looking for the most desirable ingroup, and inferior relevant outgroup, available. Sometimes the selected ingroup is objectively quite tangential, like a sports team, but the assumption is nonetheless made that the person is talented because his/her favored group is talented. The difficulty this principle poses for the resolution of conflict is that it can often be difficult to determine exactly which ingroup the person is claiming membership with, and which outgroup is serving as the object of comparison.

### Ingroup Bias versus Outgroup Bias

The general notion of intergroup bias actually consists of two components: a positive attitude toward one's ingroups (ingroup bias), and a negative attitude toward outgroups (outgroup bias) (see Brewer & Miller, 1996). It is possible for an individual to be ingroup- and outgroup-biased, or to be just ingroup-biased. In this latter situation, the person will not necessarily be hostile toward the outgroup, but will probably not be especially supportive either. The former situation is more problematic because a person who is outgroup-biased will typically not be open to attempts to foster positive relations among different groups, and if anything will desire to accentuate the differences among the various groups. Outgroup bias, then, seems to be a major barrier to the reduction of conflict.

The roots of outgroup bias seem to be in an overemphasis on the differences between the ingroup and outgroup, coupled with a general expectation that outgroup members possess largely negative characteristics. This fosters maintenance of stereotypes about outgroup members, and lessens the motivation to acquire new and correct information about others. Consequently, it discourages people to collaborate with members of the outgroup, and can lead to a phenomenon known as "scapegoating," which occurs when one blames members of the outgroup for their own misfortune. Scapegoating seems to occur when the boundaries between the ingroup and outgroup begin to blur, and may be a technique for re-enhancing the distinctiveness between the groups (Mummendey & Wenzel, 1999). Scapegoating can thus be seen as an attempt by ingroup members to discourage conflict resolution—rather than focusing on the similarities between ingroup and outgroup, those who scapegoat are emphasizing how the groups differ.

## Decision-Making Heuristics

Heuristics are rules of thumb or mental shortcut strategies that help us balance the demands for information processing presented to us by daily life with our cognitive abilities. They are useful in decision-making because they allow us to gather information regarding alternatives and consequences with less effort than would be expended if we conducted a full information search. Heuristics enable us to process incoming information quickly and make fairly good estimations and decisions. However, use of heuristics can also lead to biased and inaccurate judgments. As such, they often play a role in the development of conflict. Many heuristics have been documented (see Gilovich, Griffin, & Kahneman, 2002)—here we will introduce just those that to seem play the most central role in conflict development and maintenance.

### *The Availability Heuristic*

The availability heuristic helps us process information about, and make decisions that relate to, causality, frequency, and probability. Under this heuristic, judgment about the causality, probability of, or frequency of an event occurring is based on how cognitively available and accessible examples are in memory (Tversky & Kahneman, 1974). When using this heuristic, people search their memories for examples of the events in question. Judgment of the base rate of the event is a function of how easily examples are recalled, and how many different examples can be recalled. Events that are easily remembered, or for which one can recall many examples, are assumed to occur more frequently than events that are difficult to remember, or for which we have few concrete examples.

It is the case that, on the whole, frequently occurring events *are* more easily remembered and more plentiful in memory. Thus, the availability heuristic often does lead us to make acceptably accurate decisions. However, there are many situations in which use of this heuristic can produce serious decision errors. For example, our personal experiences may not be representative of the population as a whole. Perhaps we have had unusually few, or unusually many, encounters with the event in question (e.g., I have never been pulled over for speeding and don't know anyone who has, so I conclude that police officers rarely stop anyone who is breaking the speed limit). When this occurs, the inferences drawn on our own experiences will produce an inaccurate percept of the world at large.

Another instance in which availability heuristics distort decision-making processes is called *imaginability*. Having personal experience with the event in question can often lead us to imagine unusually vivid scenarios associated with that event, and this in turn leads us to overestimate the frequency and severity of the event. For example, it has been shown that people who know someone who died of skin cancer perceive more risks associated with suntanning than do people who do not know anyone who died of skin cancer. Having had personal experience with skin cancer leads one to mentally simulate many ways in which the disease can be contracted.

From a conflict standpoint, the availability heuristic is problematic because it can cause over- or underestimation of the frequency or probability of an event. Hence, one may undertake an action that is correct given the estimated frequency, but incorrect for the actual frequency, and misunderstandings and hard feelings may result. For example, if Country A, which has a history of armed conflict with other nations, imagines from that history that newly-hostile Country B is building its arsenal more quickly than it actually is, Country A may respond with its own accelerated weapons program, causing Country B to see it as an aggressor.

### The Representativeness Heuristic

The representativeness heuristic is a strategy under which judgments of an event or object are based on the event/object's similarity to other stimuli or categories (Kunda, 1999). It operates much like stereotyping. Thus, we might observe a man who is large, muscular, has dirty fingernails, and talks about an old car he is restoring, and use these pieces of information to infer that he is an auto mechanic, because these features are similar to those which are contained in our category of "auto mechanic." Importantly, none of these features are exclusive to auto mechanics—the person could just as easily be an attorney who restores cars for a hobby, for example. Therein lies the potential for the representativeness heuristic to induce conflict—the inferences that we make about someone or something could make it seem as if our perceptions are guided by stereotypes. The representativeness heuristic has associated with it a host of specific errors.

*Base Rate Ignorance.* A key aspect of the error potential of the representativeness heuristic is ignorance of base rates. Much research shows that people will often ignore base rates in favor of seemingly diagnostic, category-based information (Gilovich et al., 2002). Imagine that the person described above is part of a group of ten people, nine of whom are known to be accountants and one an auto mechanic. If the person above is chosen at random, the chances are 9/10 that he is an accountant, but people will typically ignore this base rate and infer, based on the physical features, that he is the auto mechanic. It is certainly possible that he is (in fact, there is a 10 percent probability that he is), but the more reasonable conclusion is that he is an accountant.

Related to base-rate ignorance is the problem of sample-size ignorance. A small sample size seldom represents the population as a whole; as such, inferences drawn from such samples tend to be skewed and inaccurate. Concluding that an event is "frequent" because it happens two out of three times is very different from that conclusion being based on the fact that the event occurred twenty out of thirty times.

*Regression Effects.* Another representativeness-related problem is the failure to account for regression effects, or the fact that an extreme event is often followed by a more normal event, because events typically regress to the mean or the norm. Problems arise when people ignore the regression and instead assume that the extreme event is the norm, which in turn leads to overestimation of the frequency of the unusual event.

*The Gambler's Fallacy and the Hot Hand.* The gambler's fallacy and the hot hand both arise when one treats independent events as dependent (Burns & Corpus, 2004). The gambler's fallacy is the belief that an unusual sequence of independent events can be disrupted, while the hot hand is the belief that the unusual run will continue. Examples are the belief that a slot machine that has not paid off for a long time is "due to win" (the gambler's fallacy) or the belief that a basketball player will make his next shot because he has made eight in a row (the hot hand). In both cases, the decision-maker is failing to understand the random nature of events.

*The Conjunction Fallacy.* The conjunction fallacy refers to the belief that conjunct events are more probable than a single event, when from a probabilistic standpoint the reverse is typically true (Tversky & Kahneman, 2002). Put more formally, the conjunction fallacy occurs when people assume that $P(pq) > P(p)$. Often these conjunct events are components of more general stereotypes. For example, with Tversky and Kahneman's (1982) "Linda problem" people tend to see a woman who has stereotypically feminist qualities as more probably being a feminist bank teller than simply a bank teller, when from a probability standpoint the opposite should be true.

The representativeness heuristic, then, has many facets. The key point to understand is that all of these facets lead one to misestimate the likelihood that some event or characteristic will manifest itself. Such a misestimate can create further misunderstandings, which can easily spiral into a deeper conflict.

### Anchoring and Adjustment

Anchoring and adjustment is the third major heuristic we want to discuss. With this heuristic, people derive an estimate by starting with, or "anchoring on," some easily-accessible base value, and then adjust (often inadequately) away from that base. For example, students who are asked to estimate the mean grade-point-average (GPA) for all students at their university will typically produce a value that is very close to their own GPA. Their GPA serves as the anchor, from which they adjust a trivial amount. Research has shown that people will anchor on even unrealistically extreme values—for example, people who are first asked if a famous person died at age twelve will say "no," but then estimate that the person died quite young; those who are asked if the person died at age 200 will also disagree, but then estimate that the person died at an advanced age (e.g., Chapman & Johnson, 1994; Mussweiler & Strack, 2000). The respondents are anchoring on the ridiculous values, and adjusting away from them. Importantly, even experts demonstrate problematic anchoring-and-adjustment strategies (Northcraft & Neale, 1987).

The important point that one should take from this introductory discussion of heuristics is that it is easy for decision-makers to commit rather innocently some serious errors in estimation. These errors can cause misunderstandings, and in turn escalation of hostility.

### How Can We Combat These Psychological Miss-Steps?

We have identified a number of psychological influences on the development of conflict. What can the practitioner do to minimize the impact of these influences, or perhaps even prevent them from occurring? Unfortunately, prevention has proven to be quite difficult. There is some evidence that people can be taught about heuristic-based errors and how to avoid them (e.g., Baron, 1990; Hansen & Helgesen, 1996), though the best evidence suggests that such training is rather involved and needs to include some discussion of the logic of hypothesis testing. Such an approach may not be especially practical in real settings of potential conflict. Minimizing the impact of ingroup-outgroup differences seems to be heavily influenced by culture, in that such differences are more important in some, typically collectivist, cultures (e.g., South Korea) than other, more individualist cultures (e.g., the United States) (e.g., Rhee, Uleman, & Lee, 1996). This cultural influence presents an important barrier to attempts to foster inclusion rather than exclusion; in fact, researchers who have attempted to address minimization of ingroup-outgroup conflict in collectivist cultures have succeeded primarily in demonstrating how complicated an undertaking it is (e.g., Bond & Venus, 1991). Happily, similar attempts within individualist cultures have on the whole been more successful (e.g., Pearson & Stephan, 1998).

Correcting false impressions and stereotypes has received a considerable amount of attention among research psychologists. Some degree of success can be achieved if a large amount of evidence in support of the new perceptions is presented (Weber & Crocker, 1983) or if the stereotyped person can be fitted into a new social category that includes the perceiver (Dovidio, Gaertner, Isen, & Lowrance 1995). However, common stereotypes can become part of a social fabric—some researchers estimate that such stereotypes can be known by as much as 80 percent of the general population (Devine & Elliot, 1995)—and such pervasiveness makes them very hard to alter. Theorists currently emphasize early education of children on acceptance of difference in others—stereotypic thinking and prejudicial behavior can appear as early as five years of age (Aboud, 1988). Altering stereotypes in teens and adults is more of a challenge, as there is currently no method that has proven to be universally effective. Some have emphasized the need to target and change social norms regarding prejudice, a process termed "delegitimization" (Kelman, 2001). In the shorter term, a growing emphasis is on creation of situations of interdependence among the stereotypers and their targets, because there is evidence that people avoid use of stereotypes, and are open to processing individuating information, when their fate is partially dependent upon the stereotype target (e.g., Kelman, 1999). Whether the interdependent approach truly alters stereotypes, or is a more temporary effect, is not clear, however.

## Psychology and History

Particular conflicts are often discussed in terms of their psychological or historical antecedents, but it is rare to see a joint consideration of the two domains. We understand historically why Israelis and Palestinians dislike each other; our preceding discussion gives some clues as to how the two groups might psychologically see the situation; but might the history and the psychology also be interactive? Real-world intergroup relations exist across time, so the history of interactions between the groups may well affect the ways in which individuals perceive and behave toward the outgroup. Indeed, psychologists who study conflict and interdependence argue that psychology needs to integrate historical factors into their theorizing in order to develop truly descriptive models of conflict resolution (Messick & Liebrand, 1997). In this final section, then, we wish to argue for the value of collaboration between psychologists and historians. Consider the following example.

### *China-Japan Relations: Recent History and Psychology*

Sino-Japanese relations during World War II have had an enduring influence on Chinese perceptions of the Japanese, and have contributed to escalation of conflict between the two countries. While the Sino-Japanese conflict during WWII and the current Sino-Japanese conflict regarding employment of Theater Missile Defense (TMD) are far removed from each other, psychological models of intergroup conflict suggest a connection between the two events, and can offer an explanation for the perceptions and behaviors of the representatives from both countries.

The occupation of Manchuria in 1931 was immediately followed by the second Sino-Japanese War (1937-1945) and the 1937-1938 Nanjing Massacre (Chang, 1997; Honda, 1999). Objectively these events were very destructive to the Chinese, but to this day Japan does not recognize them as such. In the wake of these events, the Chinese government made two demands of the Japanese government: officially apologize for starting the Sino-Japanese War and demilitarize. The Chinese have never received an official apology. Japanese demilitarization did occur via Article 9 of the Japanese constitution, but China perceives a planned deployment of TMD in Japan as a first step to the revision of Article 9, and ultimately to the remilitarization of Japan. Adding to the tension, current Japanese Prime Minister Junichiro Koizumi has made repeated visits to the Yasukuni Shrine, which includes among the enshrined those who fought the Chinese and South Koreans. On April 7, 2004, a Japanese court ruled that Koizumi's visits to the shrine were illegal, though Koizumi does not agree with the judgment.

Let us now consider the psychological impact, and possible antecedents, of these events. Consider first that Japan claimed its superiority over other Asian nations after it became an imperialist country (Chang, 1997). This is a classic example of a downward comparison of an outgroup. We have seen that ingroup members desire to differentiate from outgroups in order to enhance self-esteem, and it may be that, because of ethnic similarities between the Chinese and the Japanese, the Japanese wanted to differentiate from the Chinese. This also suggests that the Japanese perceived the Chinese as an undesirable group from which they wanted to be distinguished.

As noted above, even after the surrender, the Japanese government did not offer a formal apology to the Chinese government. Psychologically, this could have been the result of the Japanese seeing the Chinese as inferior to themselves—research has shown that people tend not to feel the need to explain their actions to perceived-inferior others (see Fiske, 2001). And in fact, this is historical evidence that the Japanese despised the Chinese for being less modernized than Japan. Since the Japanese and Chinese are ethnically similar, China's lack of modernity could have reflected badly on Japan, in that someone who is an ethnic outgroup to both countries (e.g., someone whose origins lie in the Western hemisphere) might well infer that the two countries are more similar than they actually are—thus, China's lack of progress leads to the conclusion that Japan is also not very progressive (see Tversky, 1977). The Japanese believed that it was their obligation to educate the Chinese by coercing China into acting favorably toward Japanese interests. Because of the failure to alleviate anti-Chinese sentiment in Japanese culture, many Japanese did not perceive a need to apologize for the Nanjing Massacre. Instead, many, in particular those on the right of the political spectrum, accused the Chinese government of fabrication of the incident (Honda, 1999), and some high-ranking Japanese officials made public pronouncements questioning the need for an apology.

It is also noteworthy that at present, Japan's similar pattern of imperialism toward South Korea has enhanced the alliance between China and South Korea, in that each sees Japan as a common enemy. In general, the sharing of a common problem acts to blur the distinction between one's own group and another group (Gaertner & Dovidio, 2000). In this situation, the "common problem" for China and South Korea is the dominating behavior of the Japanese—thus, the fact that Japan dislikes both China and South Korea should act to bring the Chinese and South Koreans closer together, and this is indeed what has happened.

Finally, it is interesting that, in the war's aftermath, many Japanese citizens came to deny having personally supported the war effort, and to see themselves as having been victimized by their own militaristic leaders. (This perception is referred to as *higaisha ishiki*.) Boen and colleagues (2002) have recently shown that supporters of a political party tend to deny party affiliation after an election loss, in order to improve their self-image by avoiding association with a defeated group. *Higaisha ishiki* may well be an example of such self-enhancement.

## Conclusion

The history and essence of continuing China-Japan tensions are far more detailed than we have presented. Our goal is simply to demonstrate that one can fruitfully draw upon psychological principles to help explain hostile behavior between nations, and that one can use historical analyses to modify and refine psychological models. Connections between psychology and history are not unknown (for example, models of groupthink—see Raven, 1998, for an example), but we believe that such connections can and should be strengthened.

## Final Thoughts

The overarching goal of this paper was to highlight the major psychological factors that contribute to the development and maintenance of conflict; discuss some techniques for potentially overcoming these factors; and illustrate how this research work can fit into larger analyses of real conflict episodes. The brief nature of this chapter required that we limit our illustration to integration with just one other discipline, but a true interdisciplinary approach would involve a number of other disciplines as well—sociology, political science, economics, and anthropology, to name just a few. It is our hope that our chapter will stimulate interest in such collaboration, at both the empirical and applied levels.

## References

Aboud, R. (1988). *Children and prejudice*. New York: Basil Blackwell.

Baron, J. (1990). Harmful heuristics and the improvement of thinking. *Contributions to Human Development, 21,* 28-47.

Blascovich, J., Spencer, S. J., Quinn, D., & Steele, C. (2001). African-Americans and high blood pressure: The role of stereotype threat. *Psychological Science, 12,* 225-229.

Boen, F., Vanbeselaere, N., Pandelaere, M., Dewitte, S., Duriez, B., Snauwaert, B., Feys, J., Dierckx, V., & Van Avermaet, E. (2002). Politics and basking-in-reflected-glory: A field study in Flanders. *Basic and Applied Social Psychology, 24,* 205-214.

Bond, M. H., & Venus, C. K. (1991). Resistance to group or personal insults in an ingroup or outgroup context. *International Journal of Psychology, 26,* 83-94.

Brewer, M. B., & Miller, N. (1996). *Intergroup relations*. Pacific Grove, CA: Brooks/Cole.

Burn, S. M., & Oskamp, S. (1989). Ingroup biases and the U.S.-Soviet conflict. *Journal of Social Issues, 45,* 73-89.

Burns, B. D., & Corpus, B. (2004). Randomness and inductions from streaks: "Gambler's fallacy" versus "hot hand." *Psychonomic Bulletin and Review, 11,* 179-184.

Chang, I. (1997). *The rape of Nanking*. New York: Basic Books.

Chapman, G. B., & Johnson, E. J. (1994). The limits of anchoring. *Journal of Behavioral Decision Making, 7,* 223-242.

Devine, P. G., & Elliot, A. J. (1995). Are racial stereotypes really fading? The Princeton trilogy revisited. *Personality and Social Psychology Bulletin, 21,* 1139-1150.

Dovidio, J. F., Gaertner, S. L., Isen, A. M., & Lowrance, R. (1995). Group representations and intergroup bias: Positive affect, similarity, and group size. *Personality and Social Psychology Bulletin, 21,* 856-865.

Fiske, S. T. (1998). Stereotyping, prejudice, and discrimination. In D. T. Gilbert, S. T. Fiske, & G. Lindzey (Eds.), *Handbook of social psychology* (vol. 2, pp. 915-981). Boston: McGraw-Hill.

Fiske, S. T. (2001). Effects of power on bias: Power explains and maintains individual, group, and societal disparities. In A. Y. Lee-Chai & J. A. Bargh (Eds.), *The use and abuse of power* (pp. 181-193). New York: Psychology Press.

Gaertner, S. L., & Dovidio, J. F. (2000). *Reducing intergroup bias: The common ingroup identity model.* New York: Psychology Press.

Gilovich, T., Griffin, D., & Kahneman, D. (2002). *Heuristics and biases.* New York: Cambridge University Press.

Hansen, D. E., & Helgesen, J. G. (1996). The effects of statistical training on choice heuristics in choice under uncertainty. *Journal of Behavioral Decision Making, 9,* 41-57.

Hogg, M. A., Abrams, D., Otten, S., & Hinkle, S. (2004). The social identity perspective: Intergroup relations, self-conception, and small groups. *Small Group Research, 35,* 246-276.

Honda, K. (1999). *The Nanjing massacre* (K. Sandness, Trans.). Armonk, NY: M. E. Sharpe.

Kahneman, D., Ritov, I., Jacowitz, K. E., & Grant, P. (1993). Stated willingness to pay for public goods: A psychological perspective. *Psychological Science, 4,* 310-315.

Kelman, H. C. (1998). Social-psychological contributions to peacemaking and peacebuilding in the Middle East. *Applied Psychology: An International Review, 47,* 5-28.

Kelman, H. C. (1999). The interdependence of Israeli and Palestinian national identities: The role of the other in existential conflicts. *Journal of Social Issues, 55,* 581-600.

Kelman, H. C. (2001). Reflections on social and psychological processes of legitimization and delegitimization. In J. T. Jost & B. Major (Eds.), *The psychology of legitimacy* (pp. 54-73). New York: Cambridge University Press.

Kunda, Z. (1999). *Social cognition: Making sense of people.* Cambridge, MA: MIT Press.

Messick, D. M., & Liebrand, W. B. G. (1997). Levels of analysis and the explanation of the costs and benefits of cooperation. *Personality and Social Psychology Review, 1,* 129-139.

Mummendey, A., & Wenzel, M. (1999). Social discrimination and tolerance in intergroup relations: Reactions to intergroup difference. *Personality and Social Psychology Review, 3,* 158-174.

Munro, G. D., & Ditto, P. H. (1997). Biased assimilation, attitude polarization, and affect in reactions to stereotype-relevant scientific information. *Personality and Social Psychology Bulletin, 23,* 636-653.

Mussweiler, T., & Strack, F. (2000). Considering the impossible: Explaining the effects of implausible anchors. *Social Cognition, 19,* 145-160.

Niemann, Y. F., Jennings, L., Rozelle, R. M., Baxter, J. C., & Sullivan, E. (1994). Use of free responses and cluster analysis to determine stereotypes of eight groups. *Personality and Social Psychology Bulletin, 20,* 379-390.

Northcraft, G. B., & Neale, M. A. (1987). Experts, amateurs, and real estate: An anchoring-and-adjustment perspective on property pricing decisions. *Organizational Behavior and Human Decision Processes, 39,* 84-97.

Pearson, V. M. S., & Stephan, W. G. (1998). Preferences for styles of negotiation: A comparison of Brazil and the U.S.. *International Journal of Intercultural Relations, 22,* 67-83.

Pendry, L. F., & Macrae, C. N. (1994). Stereotypes and mental life: The case of the motivated but thwarted tactician. *Journal of Experimental Social Psychology, 30,* 303-325.

Raven, B. H. (1998). Groupthink, Bay of Pigs, and Watergate reconsidered. *Organizational Behavior and Human Decision Processes, 73,* 352-361.

Rhee, E., Uleman, J. S., & Lee, H. K. (1996). Variations in collectivism and individualism by ingroup and culture: Confirmatory factor analysis. *Journal of Personality and Social Psychology, 71,* 1037-1054.

Sears, D. O., Citrin, J., Cheleden, S. V., & van Laar, C. (1999). Cultural diversity and Multicultural politics: Is ethnic balkanization psychologically inevitable? In D. A. Prentice & D. T. Miller (Eds.), *Cultural divides* (pp. 35-79). New York: Russell Sage Foundation.

Steele, C. M., & Aronson, J. (1995). Stereotype threat and the intellectual test performance of African-Americans. *Journal of Personality and Social Psychology, 69,* 797-811.

Tajfel, H., & Turner, J. C. (1986). The social identity theory of intergroup behavior. In S. Worchel & W. G. Austin (Eds.), *Psychology of intergroup relations* (2nd ed., pp. 7-24). Chicago: Nelson-Hall.

Tversky, A. (1977). Features of similarity. *Psychological Review, 84,* 327-352.

Tversky, A., & Kahneman, D. (1974). Judgment under uncertainty: Heuristics and biases. *Science, 185,* 1124-1131.

Tversky, A., & Kahneman, D. (1982). Judgments of and by representativeness. In D. Kahneman, P. Slovic, & A. Tversky (Eds.), *Judgment under uncertainty* (pp. 84-98). New York: Cambridge University Press.

Tversky, A., & Kahneman, D. (2002). Extensional versus intuitive reasoning: The conjunction fallacy in probability judgment. In T. Gilovich, D. Griffin, & D. Kahneman (Eds.), *Heuristics and Biases* (pp. 19-48). New York: Cambridge University Press.

## five

# *Kyosei:* A Vision for Education and Society in the 21st Century

## Hidenori Fujita

### 1. Kyosei as a guiding principle of social reform and reorganization

#### Kyosei *in Japanese*

*Kyosei* is now the most popular keyword for organizing/reorganizing various social projects and activities in Japan (Fujita 1997). Accordingly, it is adopted as one of the three key terms composing the Japanese title of the 21st Century Center of Excellence Program of International Christian University (hereafter, ICU/COE or COE).

In Japanese, *kyo* stands for "co-," "syn-" or "together," and *sei* for "life," "live," "living" or "vivid." Accordingly, *kyosei* literally means "co-living, living together or symbiosis," which presupposes the co-existence of more than two units such as persons, races, ethnic groups, classes, organizations, organisms or species. It also presupposes or expects some kinds of relation, interaction or interdependence among these various units.

In the English title of the ICU/COE program, the term "conviviality" is adopted for *kyosei*. This term refers to a particular mode of *kyosei*: an interactive relationship among human beings that is peaceful, friendly and pleasantly cheerful. This is because some core members of the ICU/COE program specialize in international relations and world peace, and expect peaceful, trustful and friendly relationships among countries, racial/ethnic groups, organizations/associations and individuals.

This usage of "conviviality" is not unique to the ICU/COE program. Ivan Illich, probably for the first time, used this term in a similar but broader sense. In his books, *Deschooling Society* (1970) and *Tools for Conviviality* (1973), Illich proposed "convivial society" as a vision of ideal society and "conviviality" as an organizing principle of human relations and social networks, in contrast with modern industrialized and schooled society where people's actions, attitudes and relations to others and environments are exploitative and alienated.

The term *kyosei* is much broader than conviviality and is not limited to human relations among human beings. It is also used to refer to the relations between human beings and various non-human species, materials, industrial products and environments, as well as between various species. Accordingly, *kyosei* is rather close to the English term "symbiosis" that refers to a relationship between people or two different living things. More correctly, *kyosei* is much broader than "symbiosis," because the former includes even the relations between human beings and non-living things such as industrial goods and natural environments.

But there is a critical difference between *kyosei* and "symbiosis" in terms of their connotations. *Kyosei* connotes and expects some form of positive, idealistic relationships: that is, peaceful, trustful, permissive, mutually supportive, cooperative/collaborative and sustainable relationships. However, "symbiosis" does not necessarily have this connotation. In this respect, *kyosei* is rather similar to "conviviality."

Based on the above clarification of the terms, this chapter, in principle, uses "symbiosis" as a descriptive or analytical term and *kyosei* as a normative or idealistic term, and examines the forms, structures and functions in relation to education and citizenship.

### Kyosei *as a vogue word and a guiding principle of daily practices, businesses, policies and social reforms/reorganizations*

Since the 1990s, *kyosei* has become a vogue word in various discourse circles, not only in academics but also in politics, business, social movements and mass media. Following are some examples of such usage:

*kyosei-no-jidai* (age of symbiosis)

*taminzoku-kyosei* (multi-racial/ethnic symbiosis)

*tabunka-kyosei* (multi-cultural symbiosis)

*danjo-kyosei* (gender symbiosis or symbiosis between men and women)

*kyosei-teki kankei* (symbiotic relationship or convivial relationship)

*kyosei-shakai* (symbiotic society)

*kyosei-kyoiku* (symbiotic education)

*shizen tono kyosei* (symbiosis with nature, plants and animals)

*kyosei-teki kankyo* (symbiotic environments)

*kyosei-teki seihin* (symbiotic products)

This list, particularly the last three phrases, suggest how widely *kyosei* is used in Japan. With growing concerns about environmental destruction and sustainability, the last three phrases have become widely used. Government, organizations and mass media are now concerned with so-called green politics, and both national and local governments are developing various green policies and measures. Many manufacturing companies are putting significant effort into developing environmental technology and products that are non-destructive to the natural environment, including animals, plants and human beings. Such companies also advertise commodities that are kind to human bodies and natural environments. An increasing number of people have become conscious about their own health, environmental sustainability, and a life style compatible with such concerns. Such individuals prefer to buy and use products that are kind to their bodies and to the natural environment.

In similar contexts, many other terms are also used in social, cultural and political discourse, including "peace," "international understanding," "international cooperation," "inter-cultural understanding," "global citizen," "welfare," "well-being," "mutual development and transformation," "eco-system," "eco-life," "security," "safety," "healthy," "amenity" and "liveliness," in addition to "environmental technology," "green politics," "sustainability" and "sustainable growth."

The widespread use of these terms does not necessarily mean that Japan is more advanced in green politics and policies, environmental technology or people's attitudes and daily practices, in comparison with many other developed countries. The point to be acknowledged here is how fascinated the Japanese are now with the term *kyosei* and how widely it is used in Japan. It has become a vogue word for a guiding principle of reframing and reorganizing value orientations, attitudes and activities of people, businesses, social institutions and policies. In reality, the word is also widely used as one of the key perspectives in various academic disciplines and in social/environmental planning: for example, in biology, ecology, physiology, earth science, biochemistry, medical science, social planning, architecture, urban engineering, environmental planning, welfare economics, human ecology, urban ecology, urban studies, sociology, psychology, cultural anthropology, political science and philosophy.

## 2. Origins and Perspectives of Symbiosis in Biology and Sociology

### Biological perspectives

The term "symbiosis" was first used as an academic term in biology or bio-ecology in the late nineteenth century. Simon Schwendener (1869), van Benedén (1879), Heinrich Anton de Bary (1879) and Albert Bernard Frank (1885) are the first generation scholars who used and developed this term (*Mushroom the Journal* 2002). From this first generation onward, "symbiosis" has become one of the key perspectives in biology, referring to the state and mode of living together or to the relationship/association between two different organisms or species in the biological and ecological world (Margulis 1981, 2$^{nd}$ ed. 1993).

In the writings of these scholars, the following three forms of symbiosis were identified: "parasitism," the association that is disadvantageous or destructive to one of the two organisms; "commensalism," the association that is beneficial to either one of the two organisms and not beneficial nor harmful to the other; and "mutualism," the association that is beneficial or dependent to both of the two organisms, though Lynn Margulis considers these terms to be problematic due to their cost-benefit, economic connotation (Margulis 1993: 167).

Margulis, who is famous for the symbiotic theory of cell evolution, considers Darwin's notion of evolution driven by competition as incomplete, and contends that symbiosis is a major driving force behind evolution. "Life did not take over the globe by combat, but by networking" (Margulis and Sagan 1986: 15, quoted from *Wikipedia* 2004). This claim is important for our thinking about the meaning and function of symbiosis in human and social enterprises, because it suggests that social development and *kyosei* should be enabled and promoted not only by competition but also by cooperation, interaction and networking.

### Sociological Perspectives

In sociology, it is the Chicago School that introduced the term "symbiosis" in the 1920s as one of the key terms of human ecology and urban sociology (Park 1925, 1936a, 1936b, 1939, 1952; Park and Burgess, 1921; Hawley 1986). According to R. E. Park (1939, reprinted in 1952), symbiosis is conceptualized as follows: "there are forms of association in which human beings live upon society as predators or parasites upon a host; or they live together in a relation in which they perform, directly or indirectly, some obscure function of mutual benefit but which neither they nor their symbionts are conscious" (Park 1952: 242).

Here, symbiosis is conceptualized mainly as a functional association that is obscure and not noticed by both parties. This seems to be influenced by the biological perspective mentioned above. What is important here is that the symbiotic relation designates not only social relations and interactions but also the functional association embedded in the social relations and interactions. Moreover, the symbiotic relation/association has several other dimensions in addition to a functional dimension, which will be discussed in the next section.

Park distinguished two types of human society: "There is a symbiotic society based on competition and a cultural society based on communication and consensus" (Park 1936, reprinted in 1952: 157). The symbiotic type of society/organization based on competition "takes the form, ordinarily, of a division of labor among competing organisms or groups of organisms." On the other hand, the social type of society/organization "is based on communication and consensus, which implies a kind of solidarity based on participation in a common enterprise"(1939, reprinted in 1952: 244). He continues, these "two types of organization, the symbiotic and the social, interact and combine to bring about the specific types of association—ecological, economic, political, or customary and cultural—which distinguish the institutions of society or the types of social organizations" (1952: 244).

As seen in these quotations, Park used "symbiotic" and "social/cultural" as two dimensionally different and contrasting terms, and distinguished a symbiotic society from a cultural society. A. H. Hawley (1986: 30) made a similar type of distinction.

It seems more appropriate, however, to see any society as symbiotic. Accordingly, our task is to investigate society in terms of the forms and functions of symbiosis: that is, how a society is organized and institutionalized in terms of symbiotic relations, and how the different forms of symbiosis function in education and in social life.

## 3. Analytical Framework of Symbiosis as a Social System

### *Definition of Symbiosis and Units of Symbiotic System*
Any society or community is symbiotic, because it is composed of many individuals who live together and interact with each other in various ways. Symbiosis is defined as the state of living together in one way or another. Any society or community exists as a symbiotic system. Needless to say, symbiosis is not limited to a human society. It is also applicable to the ecosystem that includes the relationships of human beings with the other organisms and with inanimate material. But this study focuses mainly on human relations or human society.

The units of a social system are individuals and various social entities such as class, gender, ethnic group, organizations and associations/networks. Local communities, nation states and various international organizations and associations/networks are also considered as units at one level or another. In the modern world, symbiotic relations extend around the world, due to globalization and the expansion of information technology.

### *Dimensions of Symbiotic System or Relations*
The units of a symbiotic system are interrelated and interdependent in various ways. The following six dimensions can be distinguished as important: spatial, structural, cultural/symbolical, institutional/organizational, practical and functional. The first four dimensions relate to the system's apparatus or foundations, while the functional dimension refers to how the apparatus and its elements function, and the practical dimension refers to how the units act and interact with each other on the basis of foundations.

In the spatial dimension, individuals and groups cohabit in a certain area or space, such as neighborhoods, localities, countries or the entire globe. Natural environments and physical constructs may also be included in this dimension. Within each space, the units are interdependent and interact with each other in various ways. The interdependence and interaction can be either direct or indirect, but tends to be more indirect as the physical space becomes larger, or as the distance between the units becomes wider. In any case, it can be said that cohabitation leads to coexistence and brings the units into a symbiosis as a social system.

At the structural dimension, the units are allocated to various statuses/roles and divided into various social groups and categories. The statuses, groups and categories are differentiated in various ways, and they are often hierarchically or unequally structured in terms of power, property, prestige and various life chances. This differentiation and structuration is often based on the division of labor and the specialization of statuses/roles, but various historical, political and cultural factors have also caused various antagonistic forms of differentiation such as domination/subordination, discrimination/segregation and social closure/exclusion.

At the cultural and symbolic dimension, cultures, norms and customs define, regulate, signify and legitimize various social differentiations, activities and enterprises, and daily actions and interactions. These cultures, as well as social differentiations, activities and actions contain, evoke and convey symbolical meanings among the units as actors. These cultures are diverse, multi-faceted, stratified and often conflictual, and the significance and functioning of these cultures and symbolical meanings depend on their situations and relationships. Furthermore, there are dominant/majority cultures and peripheral/minority cultures. This results in cultural conflicts and cultural politics and also causes the differentiation of life chances and cultural reproduction (Bernstein 1973, 1975; Bourdieu & Passeron 1970, Bourdieu 1979).

Regarding the institutional and organizational dimension, societies have developed various institutional rules as well as specific institutions and organizations. The term "institution" is variably used, but three usages or dimensions can be distinguished. First, it is used as more or less a synonym for an organizational entity, such as school, university and hospital. Second, the term refers to a social system or apparatus, which is called "institutional system" in this chapter, such as a monetary system, electoral system or education system. This institutional system is composed of and based on prescribed rules, regulations and laws that specify and regulate organizational arrangements and activities, and brings about the "patterning of social structure and activities" around those rules, regulations and laws (Meyer et al. 1994: 10).

The third usage is the one proposed by some institutional sociologists. They define institutions as "cultural rules giving collective meaning and value to particular entities and activities, integrating them into the larger schemes" (Meyer et al. 1994: 10). An institution in this usage is called "institutional rules" in this study. Although these rules may be better considered as a part of the cultural dimension, it is important to note here that institutional systems and their associated institutional rules combine to bring about and more or less legitimize certain patterns of social structure, activities and interactions. John Meyer and co-authors (1994:10) said, "Institutionalization, in this usage, is the process by which a given set of units and a pattern of activities come to be normatively and cognitively held in place, and practically taken for granted as lawful (whether as a matter of formal law, customs, or knowledge)." In this respect, how the institutional systems and rules are organized is critically important to think about a more preferable mode of symbiosis and *kyosei*.

These institutional and organizational arrangements have been developed, accumulated and historically restructured within the boundary of a space or circle, in relation to the functional, structural and cultural features of the system, as well as constructing/reconstructing and vitalizing those features of the system. These arrangements provide for and limit the chances of daily experience; and by regulating daily experience, function to socialize actors (units).

The practical dimension refers to the daily actions and interactions of the units, or to their experiences in their "life-world" or "world of everyday life" (A. Schutz 1973). Their experiences and life-world are more or less framed and structured differentially by the forms of spatial, structural, cultural and institutional arrangements mentioned above. This is important especially for children, because it is in this life-world, and through the experiences there, that children develop their abilities and personalities, including attitudes to others and the society, friendship, value orientations, sense of justice, self-dignity, self-efficacy and so forth.

Finally, the functional dimension refers to the functional relationships/interdependences among the units and among the spatial, structural, cultural, institutional and practical dimensions (sub-systems), as well as between those dimensions and the social system as a whole. A typical example of this dimension is the interdependence in a division of labor. But there are many other functional relationships. In the spatial dimension, for example, if a town is cohabited by two antagonistic social groups, inhabitants' daily lives in such an area will be influenced in various ways. In the cultural dimension, a shared culture that is taken for granted or appreciated by members of the social group or society tends to contribute to maintaining order and solidarity within the social entity. But solidarity in the in-group "is always more or less an effect of conflict with an out-group" (Park 1952: 261). Furthermore, if there is a dominant culture with peripheral cultures, the former tends to discriminate and to oppress the latter, intentionally or unintentionally.

### *Modes of Symbiotic Relationship*

Daily life, actions and experiences of individuals are more or less influenced and framed by the forms of a symbiotic system or symbiotic relations. This form varies from society to society, depending on how its symbiotic system is organized in the dimensions mentioned above, and depending on which modes of relationship are predominant.

Eight modes of relationship, four major ones and four derivative ones, are paired as follows: isolation and indifference, competition and domination, utilization and parasitism, and communication and collaboration. Violence and destruction could be distinguished as an additional mode, but here we see it as a special case of competition, utilization or communication, because violence is an alternative way of communication when verbal communication is abandoned.

Where the distance between the units is large, those units tend to be isolated from each other and indifference to the other tends to be the norm. But in a modern globalized world or in a modern urbanized society, the mode of isolation has decreased significantly. Yet, this does not mean that the mode of indifference has also declined along with the decrease of isolation. In fact, people's indifference to others, to community affairs and to the issues of the society has expanded, particularly in metropolitan areas, even though these people are interdependent among others in the spatial, structural, institutional and functional dimensions. In this context, participation, commitment and involvement has been valued in contrast with indifference.

Secondly, regarding the mode of competition, a typical example is market competition. But there are many other types of competition—for example, in schools, in political parties and among countries. Competition itself as a mode of relationship is not necessarily denied. Rather it is considered as legitimate, if it includes the conditions of openness and fairness. However, too excessive or violent competition is seen as inappropriate or destructive. A rampaging financial market is one general example of excessive competition, and the stringent entrance examinations of Japanese universities is another specific example. War is an extreme case of violent competition, which is destructive and often brings about the domination of the loser by the winner. Although competition is generally seen as legitimate, its derivative mode, domination, has been normatively denied. Here, the term "domination" is used to represent many other terms that designate similar phenomena, such as oppression, exploitation, segregation, discrimination and exclusion. Over the years, all of these unequal relationships have been gradually seen as unjust, and reform actions and policies have been taken to increase equality and equity in the institutional and organizational entities and in society at large.

Thirdly, utilization is another major mode of relationship. The relationship between the providers of goods and services and their customers or clients is a typical case of this mode. But there are many other cases. Human beings always utilize natural resources and environments. Actors, both individuals and entities, consciously or unconsciously utilize various resources of social networks in everyday life (for example, to obtain information, favors, support and so forth). In many cases, this utilization is mutual, or is conceived as mutual. In some cases, however, utilization is not mutual but one-sided. In cases where this one-sidedness is constant and/or excessive, its relationship is parasitism. Parasitism is advantageous to one of the two parties, but not necessarily disadvantageous or destructive to the other. If the parasitic relation is recognized and considered as burdensome by the disadvantaged party, some kind of negotiation, adjustments or revolt will likely occur sooner or later. If the parasitism is destructive or excessively exploitative in nature, the parasitic party needs to become aware of the problem, and to change its parasitic style to a non-destructive one for sustainability. It is this destructive parasitism that has become widely recognized as a serious problem in the relations between human beings and the natural environment.

The fourth major mode is communication, through which individuals (and entities) interact with each other, exchange ideas and opinions, and develop shared norms and cultures as well as mutual understanding, trust and respect. Needless to say, communication may bring about distrust, hostility and contempt. But it is a way by which conflicts, antagonism and domination are modified and by which parties can move toward peaceful co-existence or peaceful symbiosis. The derivative mode of communication is collaboration and cooperation, which presupposes communication among those participating in a collaborative or cooperative enterprise.

## 4. Four forms of Symbiosis and Organizing Principles of Education and Society

Societies vary in terms of the form of symbiosis that is developed by the modes of relations in the spatial, structural, cultural and institutional dimensions mentioned above. This form is important, because it tends to condition the functioning of the system, and the system elements, as well as to influence the ways of living, actions, experiences, life chances, attitudes and value orientations of the members of the society. We could examine all societies or compare several societies by investigating how each society is organized in these dimensions of symbiosis and examining which modes of relation are predominant. In the following pages, however, we propose four major forms of symbiosis, taking the above-mentioned analytical framework into account, and discuss some general tendencies of symbiosis and the significance of *kyosei* in the modern globalizing world.

## *Four Forms of Symbiosis as Ideal Types*

Four forms of symbiosis, or four types of symbiotic society, can be identified: embracive symbiosis, segmented/segregated symbiosis, market-oriented symbiosis and civic symbiosis (Fujita 1999, 2000b).

Embracive symbiosis is one in which there are common values and beliefs shared among the members of the society. Norms are inclusive and work to bind members' actions and daily life, members are connected to strong social ties, status structure is generally not much differentiated, the organizational and institutional system is not complicated, knowledge is shared by most of the members, the socialization function is largely embedded in the daily life, and learning for the job takes place largely through on-the-job training. Furthermore, in a society of this type, members' lives are mutually supportive to various extents, and daily interactions are generally numerous and often convivial—though some members may have negative feelings, for example, that the norms and customs are too restrictive or that they themselves are always watched and oppressed. In terms of modes of relationship, a community or a society may be isolated from other communities or societies, but individuals within the community are connected by strong social ties and by daily interaction and communication. This form of symbiosis seems to exist in traditional, pre-industrial communities where people live together with very limited social differentiation.

Segmented/segregated symbiosis is one in which division of labor has developed, the status structure is hierarchically differentiated, knowledge is specialized and appropriated differentially by individuals, and different groups of people are more or less distinguished and separated from each other socially, culturally, and sometimes even spatially. This institutional and organizational system is not only complicated but also discriminatory to a significant extent; the labor market is segmented and stratified, and there is a significant expansion of the practice of segregating individuals—not only by ability but also by social categories (or ascribed statuses) like gender, ethnicity and family background—in school education, the labor market and social life. In a society of this type, social ties and solidarity could be strong within each social group, but there might be antagonistic relations between the oppressors and the oppressed. Such feelings as dissatisfaction, anger, antagonism or resignation tend to exist among those discriminated against and segregated, and may be expressed in anti-social behaviors or rebellion.

Market-oriented symbiosis is one that has spread along with the advancement of the capitalist market economy and with urbanization. The basic structure of society is similar to that of a segmented/segregated society: the division of labor has developed further than in a segregated society; the labor market is segmented and stratified; the status structure is hierarchically differentiated; the institutional and organizational system is complicated; and knowledge is specialized and appropriated differentially by individuals. The uniqueness of this type lies in the following: in this system individuals tend to be self-oriented, concerned with personal benefits, indifferent to others, to common values and to community affairs, and not willing to cooperate in order to improve community life and social benefits. They may cooperate for some common benefits, but mostly for those limited to a special interest group to which they belong, or only when it is necessary for their own sake.

Civic symbiosis is one that tends to be idealized in a modern democratic society. Although the basic structure of society is similar to that of a segmented/segregated or market-oriented society, the major difference from them lies in the following: in this system all individuals are assumed to be autonomous, independent, equal in basic human rights and worthy of human dignity and respect, and at the same time, are assumed to have an orientation to accept different people, ideas and cultures, to participate in various community affairs and social activities as responsible citizens, and to cooperate for improving common benefits and social welfare.

### Current Stage of Symbiosis

It is probably right to say that in the pre-modern world, embracive symbiosis was more or less predominant. But since industrialization, urbanization and the expansion of cross-boundary interaction and interdependence among different regions took place, segmented/segregated symbiosis has emerged and become more or less observed in many societies. Since the middle nineteenth century, this type of symbiosis has emerged in many urban cities like London and Chicago. It is indeed based on the observations of this type of society that Karl Marx developed his ideas of class struggle in the capitalist society, and that R. E. Park and other Chicago School sociologists introduced the term symbiosis in their writings on urban ecology and community. Then, as the modern capitalist market economy has expanded and urbanization marches on, market-oriented symbiosis has also gradually become noticeable; at the same time, civic symbiosis began to be proposed and pursued as an ideal form of the society. Thus, we are now in the stage where these four types of symbiosis are overlapping in varying degrees and modes.

More specifically, in developed countries and urbanized cities, the segmented/segregated and market-oriented types of symbiosis tend to be predominant. On the other hand, less developed countries and less urbanized localities still retain embracive symbiosis, which tends to be cherished among many members there. In addition, in many advanced countries and localities, various ideas and schemes of civic symbiosis have been considered as desirable and partially institutionalized for transforming their society from segmented/segregated symbiosis toward civic symbiosis, or for eliminating and ameliorating various social maladies, pains, and inequalities that are associated with segmented/segregated and/or market-oriented symbiosis, as well as the restrictive and oppressive features of embracive symbiosis.

It is in this context that civic symbiosis or *kyosei* is proposed and pursued not only as an ideal for future society, but also as a guiding principle to reorganize and restructure the society. But this is not an easy task. War, terrorism, antagonism, domination, oppression, exploitation, discrimination, segregation, crime, violence, abuse and cruelty, which are largely associated with or caused by the contradictions of segmented/segregated symbiosis, seem to be stubborn realities of the human world and are threatening peace, security and welfare. Environmental pollution and degradation, largely associated with and caused by the actions and objectives of market-oriented symbiosis, are also factors that threaten peace, security, welfare and sustainable development.

All of these problematic phenomena are to be solved or overcome. But there is another critical tendency which could undermine the foundations of and possibilities for civic symbiosis and *kyosei*. It is the recent neo-conservative and consumer-oriented reform trends and their associated value and attitudinal orientations that emphasize freedom of choice, market efficiency and self-responsibility. These reforms tend to devalue equality and mutual support; instead they attempt to restructure the institutional and organizational system into one that expands and legitimizes new forms of separation, social closure and social exclusion in the names of meritocracy, self-determination and self-responsibility, and to make people oblivious and indifferent to unjust inequality, discrimination, segregation, exclusion and poverty that surround them. These reforms also tend to promote privatization at the expense of social life and public enterprises. In other words, they further promote market-oriented symbiosis, and increase the contradictions of segmented/segregated symbiosis. This reform tendency is noticeable especially in school education.

### Current Education Reform in Relation to Civic Symbiosis

In Japan, like in the United States, United Kingdom and other countries, educational reforms by the "logic of the strong" have been implemented and expanded since the 1990s. Here, the "logic of the strong" means the ideological principles and slogans that put the strong, likely smarter and wealthier children, before the weak and poor children (Fujita 1997, 2000a, 2000b). Among the many reforms, the following three are particularly relevant to the issue here: (1) the introduction of combined junior and senior high school education (six-year secondary schools) and combined primary and junior high school education, both of which will inevitably lead to the transformation of the existing single-track 6-3-3 school system into a partially multi-tracked one; (2) the introduction of the "school choice" scheme of various kinds at elementary and secondary education levels, by relaxing the neighborhood "assigned" school system, by allowing local education boards to establish schools similar to "charter schools" in the United States, and by allowing profit-seeking companies to manage schools; and (3) the introduction of school assessments and the public release of these assessment results, through which some local educational boards began assessing their schools based on the results of common achievement tests.

All of these reforms place schools into a quasi-market situation, making them compete amongst themselves for more and smarter students; which, in turn, bring about the problems of school ranking, educational tracking and early selection. There are many theoretical reasons and empirical evidence to show that these reforms would deteriorate school education, students' learning and the society as a whole (Fujita 1995, 1997, 2000a; Whitty 2002). Because of limited space, only the following two points will be discussed.

First, school choice schemes of any kind may bring about discriminatory differentiation among schools in terms of popularity and quality because both the popularity and quality evaluation of schools depends not only on the quality of educational programs and services provided by each school, but also on the quality or quality evaluation of students at each school. This is particularly important in elementary and lower secondary schools, because their essential role is to provide a basic and uniform education to all students; therefore, any functional differentiation among them can neither be rationalized nor legitimated.

Second, the educational system is an institutionalized system which conditions, regulates and influences students' learning, intellectual development, character building, career perspectives and life choices in various ways. Accordingly, if this system is unfairly, unjustly and inequitably organized and structured, students' learning and socialization can become alienated and distorted in various respects. It is because students learn and socialize themselves not only through the formal curriculum, such as subjects, content, lesson materials and publicly conveyed educational goals and value messages, but also through the hidden curriculum, including the basic structure of the educational system, its institutional and organizational arrangements, and their associated actions, norms and cultures.

### Civic Symbiosis and Kyosei as Guiding Principle to Reorganize Education and Society

If we seek to realize a society of civic symbiosis and *kyosei*, not a society of segmented/segregated symbiosis and market-oriented symbiosis, then we need to organize our educational systems based on principles that promote civic symbiosis and *kyosei*. If contradiction exists between the formal and hidden curriculums, those students who are unsuccessful in schools will sooner or later recognize this contradiction; and they are likely to condemn schools, teachers and society for treating them unfairly, and form negative attitudes and values that are filled with distrust, antagonism, destructive impulses and low self-esteem.

As H. Levin noted (1990: 248), "choice is one of the major tenets of both a market economy and democratic society." Choice is something good in and of itself both in a market economy and democratic society, and constitutes the core value of the modern definition of freedom. But, unlike the market economy, co-existence and open public discussion are also core tenets of a democratic society. In such a democratic society, a wide variety of individuals and groups live together, make commitments to others and to their common values, and keep order and maintain their identity over generations. Accordingly, civic symbiosis or *kyosei* is crucial for the development and maintenance of a democratic society. This value of civic symbiosis or *kyosei* cannot be realized by choice, but may be realized through acceptance, participation, commitment and cooperation. If education is the foundation for a democratic society, organizing it along the lines of choice will undermine this foundation. It is critical to make public schools open to everyone, and for all people in a region to accept and to participate in it. In this sense, civic symbiosis or *kyosei* should become a guiding principle to reorganize education and society.

Finally, it is important to discuss the distinctions between civic symbiosis and *kyosei*. In this chapter, "symbiosis" has been used as a descriptive or analytical term, while *kyosei* has been identified as a normative or idealistic term. As discussed above, however, civic symbiosis contains both ideas. Accordingly, both terms can be used interchangeably. In fact, symbiosis and civic symbiosis are used as English translations of *kyosei* and *shimin-teki kyosei* in my earlier study (Fujita 2000b). The Japanese word *shimin* means citizen or civilian, and *teki* is a suffix used to make a noun become an adjective.

However, there are some differences between *kyosei* and civic symbiosis. Among them, the following two might be important. First, *kyosei* refers not only to human relations, including the relationships among social entities, but also to the relationships between human beings and environments, including buildings and industrial products. Civic symbiosis, however, refers mainly to the former. Second, symbiosis, including civic symbiosis, indicates the state and mode of co-existence and therefore conveys the static nuance, while *kyosei* implies not only a specific state and mode of co-existence but also the orientation and action to realize and maintain peaceful, trustful, permissive, mutually supportive, and cooperative/collaborative relationships.

As discussed in previous sections, it is important to create an "institutional system" congruent with civic symbiosis, because this system influences daily actions and experiences of individuals and entities, and will transform "institutional rules," and the structure and functioning of symbiotic relations. Accordingly, public schools, especially at basic education levels, are expected to have the following features as a part of the institutional system: (1) no exclusion and no isolation—all children should be accepted and their differences should be admitted as equal and autonomous citizens; (2) learning and caring community—a safe, peaceful and convivial space for living, learning and mutual development; (3) rich and appropriate basic education that promotes learning and development of common basic knowledge, mutual trust, self-dignity and a "we" feeling (Fujita 1997, 2000a).

This study does not suggest that the formal curriculum or curriculum content is unimportant. For example, the UNESCO report, "Learning: A Treasure Within," suggests that to develop the following four life skills as an interrelated combination of psychosocial and interpersonal skills is critical in the modern globalizing and multi-cultural world: critical thinking skills for learning to know, practical skills for learning to do, interpersonal skills for learning to live together and personal skills for learning to be (UNESCO, 1996). By the same token, we could say the following four components of learning are important for promoting civic symbiosis and *kyosei*: learning to be sovereign; learning public ethics for participation, commitment and taking responsibility; learning mutual trust, mutual understanding, mutual development, and conflict resolution; and learning identity formation and self-dignity.

These learning experiences, and the institutional system that promotes these experiences, are important for developing a *kyosei-teki* social capital that includes trust, security and peace, and developing a *kyosei-teki* self that has trust, ontological security and cathectic peace (Giddens 1991: 38- 44).

## References

Bernstein, B. 1973. *Class, Code and Control*, Vol. 1. London: Routledge & Kegan Paul.
Bernstein, B. 1975. *Class, Code and Control*, Vol. 3. London: Routledge & Kegan Paul.
Bourdieu, P. 1979. *Distinction* (Tr. by Nice, R.). Harvard University Press, 1984.
Bourdieu, P. & Passeron, J. C. 1970. *Reproduction in Education, Society and Culture* (Tr. by Nice, R.). Sage Publications, 1977.
Fujita, H. 1993. "Kyoiku no Koukyosei to Kyodousei" (Publicness and Commonness of Education). Morita, H. et al. eds. *Kyoikugaku Nenpou* (Annals of Educational Research), Vol. 4, pp. 85-119. Tokyo: Seori Shobou.
Fujita, H. 1997. *Kyoiku Kaikaku: Kyosei-jidai no Gakkou-zukuri* (Education Reform: Schooling in a age of *Kyosei*). Tokyo: Iwanami-shoten.
Fujita, H. 1999. "Shimin-teki Kyosei to Kyoiku-kaikakku no Kdai" (Civic *Kyosei* and the Prospects for Education Reform). Fujita, H. et al. eds. *Kyoikugaku Nenpou* (Annals of Educational Research), Vol. 7, pp. 409-455. Tokyo: Seori-shobou.
Fujita, H. 2000a. *Shimin-shakai to Kyoiku: Shin-jidai no Kyoiku-kaikaku Shian* (Civic Soceity and Education: A Proposal for Education Reform in a New Age). Tokyo: Seori-shobou.
Fujita, H. 2000b. "Education Reform and Education Politics in Japan." *The American Sociologist*, Vol. 31, No. 3 (Fall), pp. 42-57.
Giddens, A. 1991. *Modernity and Self-Identity: Self and Society in the Late Modern Age*. Calif.: Stanford University Press.
Hawley, A. H. 1986. *Human Ecology: A Theoretical Essay*. Chicago: The University of Chicago Press.
Illich, I. 1970. *Deschooling Society*. N.Y.: Harper & Row.
Illich, I. 1973. *Tools for Conviviality*. N.Y.: Harper & Row.

Margulis, L. 1981. *Symbiosis in Cell Evolution: Microbial Communities in the Archean and Proterozoic Econs.* N.Y.: W. H. Freeman and Co. (2$^{nd}$ edition, 1993)

Margullis, L. & D. Sagan 1986. *Micorcosmos: Four Billion Years of Evolution from Our Microbail Ancestors.* NY: Summit Books.

Meyer, W. J., J. Boli & G. M. Thomas 1994. "Ontology and Rationalization in the Western Cultural Account." Scott, W. R. & J. W. Meyer, eds. *Institutional Environments and Organizations: Structural Complexity and Individualism.* Calif.: Sage Publications, pp. 9-27.

*Mushroom the Journal* 2003. "The Origins of Symbiosis: An Anthology of the Fundamental Writings of the Field." www.mushroomthejournal.com/symbiosisflier.html.

Park, R. E. 1915. "The City: Suggestions for the investigation of human behavior in the city environment," *AJS*, Vol. 20, No. 5, pp. 577-612.

Park, R. E., E. W. Burgess & R. D. Mckenzie 1925. *The City.* Chicago: The University of Chicago Press.

Park, R. E. 1952. *Human Communities: the city and human ecology.* The Free Press, Glencoe.

Whitty, G. 2002. *Making Sense of Education Policy.* London: Sage Publications.

*Wikipedia, The Free Encyclopedia* 2004. "Symbiosis." en.wikipedia.org/wiki/Symbiosis

# six

# The Path to Positive Peace: On the Creative Destruction of U.S. Militarism*

## Gregory Hooks

This chapter examines U.S. militarism—a topic that has received too little attention. Militarism is a frequent focus when scholars examine non-democratic nations. But it is often assumed that democratic nations do not go to war as a result of a militarist tradition; that is, they wage defensive wars that are forced upon them. But this assumption is misplaced. It is not only the case that democracies wage wars of choice (e.g., the U.S. invasion of Iraq), but democracies such as the United States have been the victors in wars among the great powers of the twentieth century. Thus, the assumption that democracies are inherently pacific diverts attention from the militarist traditions that have molded U.S. history and impedes understanding of the actions—and dangers posed—by the world's preeminent military power.

Although studied too little, U.S. militarism has not been ignored, and I draw on insightful works by C. Wright Mills, Michael Mann and Randall Collins to better understand U.S. militarism and the dangers that it poses. C. Wright Mills (1956) reminds us that the military is on one of the three pillars of the American "power elite." Whereas critical scholars cite Mills and laud his insights, these same scholars often dismiss the importance of the military—arguing that military is subservient to economic elites and institutions. I take Mills' s view quite seriously and share his insistence that the military must be examined in its own right. Mann (1988) focused on the militarism of democracies and, in so doing, develops the notion of "spectator sport wars." United States' military doctrine places a primary emphasis on reducing U.S. casualties while allowing the citizenry to vicariously experience the excitement of war. But this does not mean that the United States has been committed to peace. On the contrary, it merely channels the United States toward wars in which it enjoys a decisive advantage by depending on technologies that allow U.S. troops to fight from a distance. Complementing the above insights, Randall Collins (1974) discusses cruelty at the societal level. For example, ferocious cruelty, common in preindustrial societies, is cruelty in which violent assaults on others was condoned. In fact, the cathartic release may have helped to reinforce the cohesion of society. In industrialized societies, especially in an era of human rights treaties and non-governmental organizational monitoring, ferocious cruelty is rare. But cruelty has not disappeared; it has just become colder and more calculated.

This modern callous cruelty is highlighted in two case studies: 1) the environment damage and looming threat of even greater danger of weapons of mass destruction; and 2) the abuse of war prisoners. The Japanese and American contributors to this volume are striving to better understand war, peace and positive peace. The term "positive peace" is very close to the Japanese term *kyosei*, or conviviality, in the title of this volume. This examination of U.S. militarism points to the importance of settling on a definition of peace that is *not* merely the absence of a war. Rather, positive peace (Galtung 1988, pp. 220-24)—or conviviality—refers to an interdependence among people and institutions that not only diverts war but nurtures an interdependent agenda to promote democratic institutions, environmental stewardship and the quality of life. At present U.S. militarism impedes positive peace—at home and throughout the world. Schumpeter (1942) coined the term "creative destruction" to capture the dynamism of market forces in remaking the economic landscape. A creative and democratic movement inside and outside the U.S. offers the greatest promise for remaking the United States and the world—a movement that would creatively destroy U.S. militarism, and in its place build institutions that promote national and international security by actively nurturing interdependence and an enduring positive peace.

## American Militarism

Throughout its history, the United States has pursued geopolitical objectives—and this pursuit led to armed conflict. When states "encountered no one with comparable control of coercion, they conquered; when they met rivals, they made war" (Tilly 1990, p. 14). The editors of *Fortune* observed that between 1776 and 1935, the U.S. "filched more square miles of the earth by sheer military conquest than any army in the world, except only that of Great Britain. And as between Great Britain and the U.S. it has been a close race, Britain having conquered something over 3,500,000 square miles since that date, and the U.S. (if one includes wresting the Louisiana Purchase from the Indians) something over 3,100,000" (in Mills 1956, p. 177n). The United States destroyed a number of Native American civilizations and ruled the surviving Native Americans with despotism. To a large extent the conquest of North America was decentralized and implemented by amateurs. The "technical and numerical superiority of the American frontiersman who confronted the American Indian made it unnecessary for a true warrior stratum and a large, disciplined administration of violence to emerge" (Mills 1956, p. 178).

Nineteenth century militarism focused on North America—for example, the Indian Wars and expropriations of land, the Mexican-American War, and the Civil War. In the twentieth century, the United States emerged as the world's leading power, and asserted its national security interests in various ways across Eurasia and the Western Hemisphere (Leffler 1992). Given the United States' record of conquest and its emergence as the global leader in the twentieth century, the primary task should be to specify the nature of U.S. militarism (not to ignore the militarism that has been important throughout the nation's history). The failure to focus on the issues of U.S. militarism is part of a more general tendency to view democratic states as inherently more pacific than their authoritarian counterparts (see for example, Lasswell 1941). But democracies—not authoritarian regimes—were the leading military powers of the nineteenth century, and democracies emerged victorious from World War I, World War II and the Cold War. Reiter and Stam (2002) explain the military success of democracies is not solely due to the greater economic resources or battlefield advantages (e.g., cohesion of troops) associated with liberty and freedom. Rather, because elected leaders are ultimately held accountable to voters, democracies are less likely to go to war than authoritarian regimes—they enter wars when the likelihood of success is relatively high (Reiter and Stam 2002). Like many other present day democracies, the United States has a tendency to fight wars against foes that are far weaker and to rely on dramatically superior technological advantage to keep casualties to a minimum.

The responsiveness of democracies to the electorate takes on a cynical cast in Michael Mann's (1988) discussion of "spectator sport militarism." Mann says that democracies not only wage wars against enemies that tend to be much weaker, but there is an effort to dramatize the bravery and military accomplishments. From popular accounts of Indian Wars in the nineteenth century to the videos of missile strikes in contemporary wars, the United States has provided vicarious participation to spectators far from the frontlines. The differences in casualty rates are also striking. Whereas the population of Native Americans declined precipitously (only a portion of this decline was a direct result of military campaigns), the United States military and general civilian population suffered relatively few casualties in the Indian Wars of the eighteenth and nineteenth centuries. The United States did suffer significant casualties in World War I and World War II—but these pale in comparison to the casualties suffered by the USSR, China, Germany and Japan. Similarly the United States experienced significant casualties (tens of thousands) in the Korean and Vietnam Wars, but Korean and Vietnamese casualties are counted in the hundreds of thousands and millions. Since the Vietnam War and widespread resistance to the draft (Davis 1974), the United States has been even more committed to keeping American casualties to a minimum. So far, U.S. military actions in Afghanistan and Iraq have cost relatively few American lives. Even with American casualties exceeding 1,000 in Iraq by late 2004 (Iraq Coalition Casualty Count 2004), this is far lower than conservative estimates of casualties of Iraqi civilians (Iraq Body Count 2004), many of whom died as a direct result of U.S. military actions.

Cruelty has long been an element of militarism. But the manifestation of cruelty differs according to the historical era and the structural foundation of society. Pre-industrial societies often displayed ferocious cruelty—a public and cathartic assault on prisoners (for a vivid depiction of ferocious cruelty, see the opening passages of Foucault 1977). But industrialized societies, especially democracies, are more likely to display a callous cruelty. In this sort of cruelty, damage to ecosystems and the death of civilians are recognized and accepted collateral damage that goes with warfare: that is, "cruelty without passion, the kind of hardship or violence people may inflict on others without special intent to hurt … [this type of violence] arises from structures that cut off the possibility of personal empathy" (Collins, 1974, p. 431). By fighting wars as spectator sports and placing a primary emphasis on keeping U.S. casualties to a minimum, the United States has developed a military posture that imposes horrific hardships on enemy forces and on civilian populations caught in the crossfire.

## Case Studies of Callous Cruelty: Environmental Threats and Abuse of Prisoners

### *Environmental Threats Posed by U.S. Militarism*

War emerged with civilization. That is, settled agricultural societies gave rise to population growth, social surplus, structured inequality and the centralized state—and these are the preconditions for the organized and sustained violence we refer to as war. From the dawn of civilization, through the middle of the twentieth century, weapons killed people by piercing or crushing their bodies. In the industrial era (and when relying on conventional weapons), the environmental impact of militarism has been profound—but indirect. Mass industrial warfare has scarred the environment: modern military forces voraciously consume natural resources (especially petroleum) to clothe, feed and transport troops. Moreover, the modern chemicals used to propel projectiles have frequently been toxic, and the projectiles have consisted of heavy metals (iron, copper, steel, and depleted uranium). Military forces leave a trail of environmental degradation under most circumstances—and especially in the twentieth century the concentration of chemicals and metal debris has left battlefields uninhabitable for generations (Webster 1996). In the latter half of the twentieth century—with the bombings of Hiroshima and Nagasaki dramatically ushering in this era—the environmental damage of warmaking and militarism became qualitatively more dangerous. Armaments referred to as "weapons of mass destruction" (hereafter WMD) are designed to poison the environment. That is, WMD are distinct because they do not kill by piercing and crushing human bodies; they kill and disable opposing military forces by making the environment uninhabitable. This can be accomplished by chemical weapons that poison the air and water, biological weapons that cause infection, and nuclear weapons that create superheated air and radiation.

This is *not* to suggest that chemical and biological weapons first appeared in the twentieth century:

- The ancient Athenians (probably because the Greeks were among the first to leave a written record) offer one of the first well-documented cases of chemical weapons (poisoning the drinking water). During the Peloponnesian War, Sparta subjected Athens to toxic levels of sulfur dioxide by burning clouds of sulfur and pitch.

- Medieval and Renaissance forces used catapults to send diseased carcasses (horse and cattle) into besieged cities in order to spread infection.

- Europeans sold or gave to Native Americans blankets infected with small pox (see Barnaby 2000; Van Creveld 1989; McCarthy 1969).

Despite the long history of chemical and biological weapons, the most devastating environmental scars of the past were the indirect consequence of efforts of military forces to pierce or crush the bodies of enemies. The weapons and military organizations of the present and future pose an unprecedented threat to humans and the environment. To adapt Erickson (1994), we confront a "new species of trouble." To come to terms with these emergent threats environmental sociology must come to terms with treadmill dynamics driven by arms races and geopolitics. Weapons are now being designed to poison the air and water, infect human populations, and to destroy the environment. The manufacture and use of these weapons scar the land, air and water to a degree and in ways that are unprecedented.

The Industrial Revolution transformed warfare. Chemical energy (i.e., gunpowder) was harnessed to hurl heavier projectiles, at greater distance and with greater accuracy. Moreover, industrial societies generated and diverted a much larger social surplus to warmaking. As a consequence, the battles of the nineteenth and twentieth centuries left a stark and enduring legacy. In northern France, the major battlefields of World War I—i.e., Verdun, the Marne and the Somme—continue to be dangerous, despite the return of trees, grasses and fauna. Unexploded shells from World War I continue to surface nearly a century later. While some of these areas have now returned to agriculture (after hundreds of farmers had been killed due to contact with unexploded ordnance, including mustard gas), other areas still remain uninhabitable (Webster 1996). Because World War I deteriorated into trench warfare along a well-established front, the hostilities resulted in a relatively small number of places with extraordinarily high amounts of contamination. During World War II—and most of the wars in the ensuing decades—battles and military formations were more fluid. The debris of war is distributed more broadly across a wider area (besieged cities such as Stalingrad offer obvious exceptions, see Webster 1996). For decades following World War II, people have been killed and injured by unexploded ordnance strewn across the land and water of Europe and Asia.

While World War II was the last "major" war, it did not usher in a period of peace. Moreover, the mass production of mortars, artillery, and landmines coupled with aerial bombardment made the wars of the late-twentieth century exceptionally dangerous for non-combatants. Throughout Southeast Asia, landmines and unexploded bombs continue to kill and maim decades after the American withdrawal from Vietnam (see United Nations 2004a). In recent years, long after peace was declared, thousands of mines have remained in the ground and have continued to victimize the civilian populations of many countries. A current controversy centers on the use of depleted uranium by U.S. forces in Kosovo, Kuwait and Iraq. Shells tipped with depleted uranium are especially effective in piercing tanks and other armored vehicles, and critics condemn the use of these shells because they become dangerous when the uranium is pulverized on contact. The use of such shells threatens the health of those breathing or coming into contact with dust containing uranium. Depleted uranium thus represents another in the long list of environmental threats that is a side effect of war (United Nations 2004b).

The development and deployment of weapons of mass destruction must be placed in a larger institutional and social context (see Hooks and McLauchlan 1992; McLauchlan and Hooks 1995). Capitalism yielded an unprecedented social surplus that states diverted to warmaking on an unprecedented scale—it also gave rise to the invention of invention: "A transition took place from a situation in which inventions were for the most part not only exceptional but accidental and unexpected, to one in which technological change—and the anticipation of technological change—became the normal state of affairs" (Van Creveld 1989, pp. 218-19). As a consequence, in the century following the industrial revolution (1840-1940), the lethality of warfare for soldiers and civilians multiplied many times over (McNeill 1982). In the nineteenth and early twentieth centuries, the focus of this systematic harnessing of science and industry was the "rationalization of slaughter" using conventional weapons (Pick 1993). In many respects, World War I and World War II were the culmination of efforts to harness chemical energy to create deadlier and more accurate explosives deployed by a wide range of armored vehicles (powered by steam and internal combustion engines).

With a focus on nuclear weapons, E.P. Thompson discusses the ironies of the late twentieth century. Although the Pentagon does not "occupy a vast social space" (Thompson 1982 [1980]: 66), the U.S. deploys weapons of unprecedented destructiveness. Where earlier technologies required mass mobilization and overt sacrifice, now a relatively small and insulated group of U.S. military decision makers can wage wars against smaller nations as a "spectator sport" (Mann 1988). The U.S. now has weapons at its disposal that are capable of destroying much of the world in a matter of hours, using an insignificant share of the gross national product to do so. Although its arsenal of weapons puts the world at risk, the entire U.S. has not become a military-industrial complex.

The arms race is best conceived of as an arch over society, its twin pillars, in the military and military-industrial sectors, stand on the edge of society. Most members of society live for the majority of the time without being aware that the arch is there, above them, although in fact it is constantly being enlarged, with jagged edges pointing down on them as well as up at 'the enemy'. The arch requires many of the best building materials in society, but most people do not see these being diverted from ordinary social uses (Shaw 1988, p. 104).

It is counterintuitive to think of the military as posing a greater threat to the environment as its "social space" shrinks. Nevertheless, this contradiction is at the heart of science-intensive weapons of mass destruction. That is, the U.S. military is not shrinking because the pressures of geopolitics and arms races have abated. Rather, the declining social space of the U.S. military, and its increasing insulation from democratic oversight, have both been driven by strategic planning and efforts to stay ahead of military rivals. But this smaller military force wields weapons that are increasingly horrific; and military researchers are still working to make even deadlier weapons.

Although these weapons pose unprecedented dangers, it is important to recognize that they have so far been deployed—to date and with rare exceptions—in the context of conventional warfare. Atomic bombs were dropped on Hiroshima and Nagasaki. In this case, the United States did not wage nuclear war with Japan; it concluded a conventional war by making an unprecedented and widely condemned use of WMD. The United States defended this decision on the grounds that displaying the awesome power of these horrific weapons prevented far greater casualties that would have surely resulted from a conventional invasion of Japan.

Germany is credited (condemned) for the first large-scale use of chemical weapons—and Germany's argument for deploying such weapons ran parallel to the argument advanced by the United States when dropping the first atomic bombs. For example, in 1915, near the village of Ypres (Belgium), German forces released chlorine gas and allowed the wind to carry the poisonous gas to the trenches in which enemy troops were massed (Cole 1997, pp. 1-2). On a tactical level, these chemical weapons worked—the Allies abandoned these poisoned trenches, and German casualties were minimal. However, by the end of World War I, both Allied and Axis troops were using ever more deadly chemical agents, crippling and killing millions of soldiers and civilians in horrific fashion (Cole 1997; McCarthy 1969; Murphy, Hay and Rose 1984).

In the Vietnam War, the United States dropped "agent orange" and other defoliants on vast areas of Vietnam. One purpose of defoliation was to make enemy troops more visible and exposed to U.S. conventional weapons; but a second purpose was to simultaneously poison the flora, fauna, and human population of Vietnam. In similar fashion, the United

States used tear gas and other more toxic chemicals to force enemy troops in Vietnam to abandon bunkers—and entire villages. Again, the use of these chemical agents made conventional weapons more deadly (see McCarthy 1969; Murphy, Hay and Rose 1984; Webster 1996). There is strong evidence that accidental (and possibly deliberate) releases of biological weapons have killed unsuspecting citizens and soldiers (Barnaby 2000; Cole 1996; McCarthy 1969). However, to date, despite allegations and rumors, there have been no documented cases of biological weapons deployed in battle. One reason may be the inefficiency and danger of using such weapons. In contrast to nuclear and chemical weapons, biological weapons act relatively slowly (i.e., it takes days for the deadly infection to occur), and these weapons are extraordinarily dangerous for the soldiers deploying them.

Even if nuclear, chemical and biological weapons remain secondary in warfare, their threat to the environment is daunting. In place of a labor-intensive, and mass military force, leading military powers (with the United States possessing unrivalled stocks of chemical, biological and nuclear weapons) are investing heavily in dangerous WMD. Even as the U.S. military has conquered and is occupying two nations (Afghanistan and Iraq), total active duty military personnel is down twenty-five percent from 1990 and is now slightly more than half the size of the Armed Forces in the 1950s and 1960s (see U.S. Department of Defense 2004). The shrinking size of the U.S. military is not an unmixed blessing—it comes with the growth of WMD and associated ecological costs. Chemical and biological agents that are designed to kill humans and poison the environment are stored, tested and deployed on army bases around the world, but the United States has the largest and most elaborate complex in the world devoted to WMD. Put simply, military installations that store, test and deploy WMD—whether nuclear, chemical or biological—as well as the area surrounding them are now poisoned and will remain so for the foreseeable future. Technologies to clean up these places do not yet exist—and it may prove impossible to develop them. But the treadmill of destruction drives military organizations to continue to develop these weapons, and pressure mounts to deploy them on battlefields (for an elaboration of the treadmill of production, see Hooks and Smith 2004).

## Violating the Human Rights of Detainees

By maintaining technological superiority (especially in the realm of air power), the United States inflicts staggering casualties on enemy forces while minimizing casualties. This approach to warfare places a primary emphasis on information—knowing the location of critical military assets (human and physical) is essential. Reflecting the growing importance of intelligence, the United States has steadily refined its techniques to extract information from prisoners.

At the height of the Cold War, the Central Intelligence Agency prepared the top-secret report: *KUBARK Counterintelligence Interrogation—July 1963* (U.S. Central Intelligence Agency 1963). Chapter IX of this report, "The Coercive Counterintelligence Interrogation of Resistant Sources," provides guidance of when and how to use coercion. This decision hinges on utilitarian—not human rights—considerations. That is, interrogation, including coercion, is "simply a method for obtaining correct and useful information" (U.S. Central Intelligence Agency 1963, p. 85). In a similar vein, this report suggests that beating or direct physical abuse of prisoners be used as a last resort because these techniques are less likely to yield reliable information. Instead, this report showed that, relying on prior research, the

CIA favored sensory deprivation and forcing prisoners to hold uncomfortable positions for extended periods (U.S. Central Intelligence Agency 1963, p. 94). Thus, isolation, humiliation and forcing prisoners to hold uncomfortable positions for hours—techniques that were used systematically from Guantanamo Bay to Abu Ghraib—were not "invented" by guards. These techniques had been laid out in manuals prepared decades earlier.

Over the course of the Cold War, this approach to interrogation was refined (see for example, U.S. Central Intelligence Agency 1983):

> [This manual] drew heavily on the language of the earlier [KUBARK] manual, as well as on Army Intelligence field manuals from the mid 1960s generated by "Project X"—a military effort to create training guides drawn from counterinsurgency experience in Vietnam. Recommendations on prisoner interrogation included the threat of violence and deprivation and noted that no threat should be made unless the questioner "has approval to carry out the threat." The interrogator "is able to manipulate the subject's environment," the 1983 manual states, "to create unpleasant or intolerable situations, to disrupt patterns of time, space, and sensory perception" (National Security Archives 2004).

Taken together, these documents reflect a cumulative record in both the social scientific evidence considered and in the apparent cynicism they embrace.

The utilitarian justification for harsh treatment of detainees suggests a strong element of continuity in U.S. treatment of detainees. Prisoner abuse motivated by revenge or catharsis is condemned—but comparable treatment that extracts information is justified. The United States is and has been well aware that these techniques violate international norms. In a prologue to the 1983 report, the CIA acknowledged that the "use of force, mental torture, threats, insults or exposure to inhumane treatment of any kind as an aid to interrogation is prohibited by law, both international and domestic; it is neither authorized nor condoned" (U.S. Central Intelligence Agency 1983). Although policy makers in the intelligence and military establishment "were well aware these abusive practices were illegal and immoral" (National Security Archives 2004), these materials were subsequently translated into Spanish and used to train American and allied military officers (National Security Archives 2004).

The callous treatment of prisoners has intensified since the attacks of September 11, 2001, and in the wars waged in Afghanistan and Iraq. In the wake of public reports of horrific abuse at Abu Ghraib and elsewhere, the United States government has conducted several investigations. Ironically, one of these public reports concludes with a defense of callous cruelty: the Schlesinger Report insists that techniques used at Abu Ghraib were needed in the war on terror and expresses concern that the abandonment of such techniques would have a "chilling effect" on interrogations. In this regard, the Schlesinger report criticized the International Committee of the Red Cross (ICRC) as follows: "If we were to follow the ICRC's interpretations, interrogation operations would not be allowed. This would deprive us of an indispensable source of intelligence in the war on terror" (Schlesinger et al. 2004, p.85). The report also criticized the ICRC for not being in tune with current geo-political realities, arguing: "The panel also believes the ICRC, no less than the Defense Department, needs to adapt itself to the new realities of conflict, which are far different from the Western European environment from which the ICRC's interpretation of the Geneva Conventions was drawn" (Schlesinger et al. 2004, p.88).

The Bush Administration did more than dust off interrogation manuals drafted decades ago. The Guantanamo Bay detention facility was used to detain (nominally) dangerous prisoners in the war on terror and to systematically extract intelligence. As the Iraqi insurgency gathered momentum in 2002 and 2003, these techniques were applied to tens of thousands of detainees in Iraq. Although relatively few of the detainees at Abu Ghraib were being held for specific crimes, the United States saw them as a rich source of intelligence information. In addition to the coercive techniques developed and refined by the CIA over the preceding half-century, the Bush Administration hoped to exploit Arab modesty over sexuality. The well-documented sexual humiliation—forced to stand naked, to masturbate and to perform sexual acts—was only the beginning of the torture. These acts were photographed in order to blackmail detainees—while detained the threat of publicizing these photos was used to extract information. And the threat of releasing the photos was thought to ensure continued cooperation after detainees were released. "It was thought that some prisoners would do anything—including spying on their associates—to avoid dissemination of the shameful photos to family and friends" (Hersh 2004). The sexual abuse that shocked the world—and for which the lowest ranking military personnel are being punished—is not an aberration. Rather, it is the logical result of the callous cruelty that guides U.S. military doctrine—as extended by the Bush Administration.

## Conclusion: Creative Destruction

The preceding examination of U.S. militarism provides a context for reflecting on definitions of war and peace. The interdisciplinary peace literature offers a useful starting point for defining these terms.

- *Violence:* This term refers to direct assaults on human beings. This definition is expansive; it includes actions intended to kill or maim, but it also includes a "structure of violence" that systematically deprives humans of basic needs. Ultimately, the absence of violence draws attention to larger issues, notably a concern for human rights and meeting human needs (Galtung 1988, pp. 220-22, see also Galtung 1975).
- *Peace:* Peace is defined as the absence of violence. Too often, the official "peace" established between states at the end of a war would not meet the definition of peace established in this literature. For example, the cessation of hostilities between armed states at the end of the Korean War or Vietnam War did not bring an end to violence in these regions. The stringent definition of peace advanced by Galtung and the peace literature more generally, is especially valuable for research that stakes out a position based on values (i.e., opposition to violence) (Galtung 1988, pp. 216-20).
- *Positive Peace:* Even the stringent definition of "peace" presented above does not fully capture the positive interaction among states and peoples of the world. Thus, positive peace (a term that is very close to *kyosei*, or conviviality, that is employed in several essays in this volume) involves far more than the cessation or avoidance of hostilities. Positive peace demands more than that people or nations avoid harming one another. Rather, people or nations must cooperate and help one another meet human needs. This active interdependence contributes to a reduction in human suffering and helps impede a downward spiral toward violence (Galtung 1988).

The definitions provide a lens to evaluate contemporary U.S. militarism. Given that the manufacture and storage of weapons of mass destruction pose enormous dangers to people and ecosystems, their very existence constitutes "structured violence." Similarly, in Afghanistan and Iraq, the United States' handling of prisoners in the war on terror has not complied with contemporary human rights protocols. The system of gulags maintained by the United States around the world is itself a structure of violence. Because the United States is far and away the most powerful nation on earth—and because it controls a disproportionate share of the weapons of mass destruction—the actions and policies of the United States play a pivotal role at the global level.

Joseph Schumpeter (1942) coined the term "creative destruction" to capture the dynamism—especially technological dynamism—inherent in capitalism. I adopt this term to consider a reduction of U.S. militarism (see also Hooks 1991). For Schumpeter, creative destruction highlighted the manner in which technological innovation often transformed social institutions and firms—new firms rose to prominence while older and seemingly omnipotent firms failed to embrace technological change and crumbled. Schumpeter's phrasing also captures a sense of optimism even as sweeping changes unfold. It is this sense of optimism and embrace of transformation that makes creative destruction an apt phrase when charting a different course for U.S. national security doctrine. If the U.S. is to turn away from the structured violence—as witnessed by callous treatment of prisoners and reliance on WMDs—sweeping institutional changes will be necessary. President Dwight Eisenhower recognized these dangers decades ago, and his recommendations continue to be insightful:

> This conjunction of an immense military establishment and a large arms industry is new in the American experience. The total influence—economic, political, even spiritual—is felt in every city, every Statehouse, every office of the Federal government. We recognize the imperative need for this development. Yet we must not fail to comprehend its grave implications. Our toil, resources and livelihood are all involved; so is the very structure of our society. In the councils of government, we must guard against the acquisition of unwarranted influence, whether sought or unsought, by the military-industrial complex. The potential for the disastrous rise of misplaced power exists and will persist....Disarmament, with mutual honor and confidence, is a continuing imperative. Together we must learn how to compose differences, not with arms, but with intellect and decent purpose. Because this need is so sharp and apparent I confess that I lay down my official responsibilities in this field with a definite sense of disappointment. As one who has witnessed the horror and the lingering sadness of war—as one who knows that another war could utterly destroy this civilization which has been so slowly and painfully built over thousands of years—I wish I could say tonight that a lasting peace is in sight (Eisenhower [1961] 1992, pp. 363-64, 365).

In the decades since Eisenhower's farewell, the U.S. military has grown stronger, its operations and decisions remain secret and its power (over prisoners and WMDs) continues unchecked. Or in Eisenhower's words, the "potential for the disastrous rise of misplaced power exists and will persist." For Eisenhower's goal to be met, disarmament (not the capacity to overwhelm enemies and callously extract information from detainees) must be the overarching goal of U.S. military policy. Pursuing this goal would entail a sweeping overhaul of power in the United States government and military institutions. It is extraordinarily unlikely that such a sharp redirection of U.S. policy will come from those ensconced in the military-industrial complex. Instead, the creative destruction of the current military establishment must come from below. Citizens of the United States and the peoples of the world must exercise vigilance, demand accountability and help chart a course for the United States and the world to enjoy the fruits of positive peace. Thus, creative destruction is at the same time a daunting task and our best hope of avoiding the horrors that loom in the structured violence of U.S. militarism.

* I am indebted to Chad L. Smith (Texas State University-San Marcos) for discussion of the environmental threats posed by U.S. militarism and to Chad Mosher (Washington State University) for the discussion of human rights abuses.

## References

Barnaby, Wendy. 2000. *The Plague Makers: The Secret World of Biological Warfare*. New York: Continuum.

Cole, Leonard. 1997. *The 11th Plague: The Politics of Biological and Chemical Warfare*. New York: W.H. Freeman.

Collins, Randall. 1974. "Three Faces of Cruelty: Towards a Comparative Sociology of Violence." *Theory and Society* 1: 415-440.

Davis, Vincent. 1974. "Levee en Masse, C'est Fini: The Deterioration of Popular Willingness to Serve," Pp. 89-208 in J. Lovell and P. Kronenberg (eds.), *New Civil-Military Relations*. New Brunswick, NJ: Transaction Books.

Eisenhower, Dwight. [1961] 1992. "President Dwight D. Eisenhower's Farewell Speech to the Nation." Pp. 361-67 in *The Military-Industrial Complex: Eisenhower's Warning Three Decades Later*, edited by G. Walker, D. Bella, and S. Sprecher. New York: Peter Lang.

Erickson, Kai. 1994. *A New Species of Trouble*, New York: W.W. Norton & Co.

Foucault, Michel. 1977. *Discipline and Punish: The Birth of the Prison*. New York: Vintage.

Galtung, Johan. 1975. "Violence, Peace, and Peace Research." Pp. 109-34 in J. Galtung (ed.) *Peace: Research, Education, Action: Essays in Peace Research, Volume I*. Copenhagen: Christian Eljers.

———. 1988. "Twenty-five Years of Peace Research: Ten Challenges and Some Responses." Pp. 213-43 in J. Galtung (ed.) *Transarmament and the Cold War: Essays in Peace Research, Volume VI*. Copenhagen: Christian Eljers.

Hersh, Seymour. 2004. "The Gray Zone." *The New Yorker* (May 24, 2004). Available online at: http://www.newyorker.com/fact/content/?040524fa_fact, accessed October 17, 2004.

Hooks, Gregory. 1991. *Forging the Military-Industrial Complex*. Champaign: University of Illinois Press.

Hooks, Gregory and Gregory McLauchlan. 1992. "The Institutional Foundation of Warmaking: Three Eras of U.S. Warmaking, 1939-1989." *Theory and Society* 21: 757-788.

Hooks, Gregory, and Chad L. Smith. 2004. "The Treadmill of Destruction: National Sacrifice Areas and Native Americans."*American Sociological Review* 69: 558-575.

Iraq Body Count. 2004. "Civilians Reported Killed by Military Intervention in Iraq." Available online at: http://www.iraqbodycount.net/, accessed November 11, 2004.

Iraq Coalition Casualty Count. 2004. "Military Fatalities: By Month." Available online at: http://icasualties.org/oif/, accessed November 11, 2004.

Lasswell, Harold. 1941. "The Garrison State." *American Journal of Sociology* 46: 555-68.

Leffler, Melvyn. 1992. *A Preponderance of Power: National Security, the Truman Administration, and the Cold War*. Stanford, CA: Stanford University Press.

Mann, Michael. 1988. *States, War, and Capitalism*. New York: Basil Blackwell.

McCarthy, Richard. 1969. *The Ultimate Folly: War by Pestilence, Asphyxiation and Defoliation*. New York: Alfred A. Knopf.

McLauchlan, Gregory, and Gregory Hooks. 1995. "Last of the Dinosaurs? Big Weapons, Big Science, and the American State from Hiroshima to the End of the Cold War." *Sociological Quarterly* 36:749-76.

McNeill, William. 1982. *The Pursuit of Power*. Chicago: University of Chicago Press.

Mills, C. Wright. 1956. *The Power Elite*. New York: Oxford University Press.

Murphy, Sean, Alastair Hay, and Steven Rose. 1984. *No Fire, No Thunder: The Threat of Chemical and Biological Weapons*. London: Pluto Press.

National Security Archives. 2004. *Prisoner Abuse: Patterns from the Past: National Security Archive Electronic Briefing Book No. 122*. Washington, DC: National Security Archives (George Washington University). Available online at: http://www.gwu.edu/~nsarchiv/NSAEBB/NSAEBB122/, accessed October 17, 2004.

Pick, Daniel. 1993. *War Machine: The Rationalisation of Slaughter in the Modern Era*. New Haven: Yale University Press.

Reiter, Dan, and Allan C. Stam. 2002. *Democracies at War*. Princeton: Princeton University Press.

Schlesinger, James, et al. 2004. *Final Report of the Independent Panel to Review DOD Detention Operations*. Washington, DC: U.S. Department of Defense. Available online at: http://www.globalsecurity.org/military/library/report/2004/d20040824finalreport.pdf, accessed November 11, 2004.

Schumpeter, Joseph A. 1942. *Capitalism, Socialism, and Democracy*. New York: Harper and Brothers.

Shaw, Martin. 1988. *The Dialectics of War*. London: Pluto.

Thompson, E.P. [1980] 1982. "Notes on Exterminism, the Last Stage of Civilisation." Pp. 41-80 in *Beyond the Cold War: A New Approach to the Arms Race and Nuclear Annihilation*, edited by E.P. Thompson. New York: Merlin Press.

Tilly, Charles. 1990. *Coercion, Capital and European States, A.D. 990-1990*. Oxford: Blackwell.

United Nations. 2004a. "E-Mine: The Electronic Mine Information Network." Available online at: http://www.mineaction.org/, accessed January 14, 2004.

———. 2004b. "Depleted Uranium Fact Sheet." Available online at: http://postconflict.unep.ch/dufact.html, accessed January 14, 2004.

U.S. Central Intelligence Agency. 1963. *KUBARK Counterintelligence Interrogation—July 1963*. Available on-line at: http://www.gwu.edu/~nsarchiv/NSAEBB/NSAEBB122/CIA%20Kubark%201-60.pdf, accessed October 17, 2004.

———. 1983. *Human Resource Exploitation Training Manual (Part 1)*. Available on-line at: http://www2.gwu.edu/~nsarchiv/NSAEBB/NSAEBB122/CIA%20Human%20Res%20Exploit%20A1-G11.pdf, accessed October 17, 2004.

U.S. Department of Defense. 2004. "Military Personnel Statistics." Available online at: http://web1.whs.osd.mil/mmid/military/miltop.htm, accessed on January 14, 2004.

Van Creveld, Martin. 1989. *Technology and War: From 2000 BC to the Present*. New York: Free Press.

Webster, Donovan. 1996. *Aftermath: The Remnants of War*. New York: Pantheon Book.

## seven

# An Examination of the Economic Theory of Civil Conflict

## William S. Hallagan, Yijun He, Frederick S. Inaba, Mudzivri Nziramasanga, and AKM Mahbub Morshed

## 1. Introduction

The purpose of the project, "Defining Peace, Security, and *Kyosei*" seems to us to be a very difficult task. To us, the concept of "peace, security, and *kyosei*" is abstract, relative, and difficult to pin down to universal specifics. Any proposed definition of "peace, security, and *kyosei*" will depend upon the proposer's specific worldview, which is itself a product of a complex interplay of specific cultural, social, religious, philosophical and disciplinary backgrounds. Thus, rather than a unanimous consensus of the definitions the best we could hope for are different perspectives on this concept in order to help us understand it. In other words, we regard various definitions as pieces of a puzzle that taken as a whole will provide the final understanding of just what is meant by the phrase "peace, security, and *kyosei*."

This is certainly true of the many contributions to this project. But this approach brings its own challenges. In addition to the sheer variety of studies contributed to the project, a very wide spectrum of issues is presented. For example, this study addresses the issues concerned with one end of the spectrum, where peace, security, and *kyosei* is radically and violently absent from civil life. In particular we look at economic theories that try to explain how civil conflicts emerge. At the opposite end of the spectrum are issues dealing with the complete fulfillment of peace, security, and *kyosei*. A study representative of this end of the spectrum would probably be one with a Buddhistic worldview, although no such study was done for this project. In between these two benchmarks we find the majority of the studies contributed to this volume.

The chapter offers perspectives on the absence of peace, security, and *kyosei*. Why are some societies consumed with civil strife and conflict, while others experience long periods of peace, security, and *kyosei*? Why is peace, security, and *kyosei* so transitory in those societies in which peace and civil war alternate from one period to the next? Since economists view economic benefits and costs as cornerstones to social activity, civil conflict is viewed as the outcome of the failure of rival factions in a society to reach an agreement on specific issues in which economic factors are fundamental. Most of what this chapter has to say about civil conflict comes from the recent economics literature that takes this view.

We believe that a thorough understanding of existing economic theories and models of civil conflict is necessary: (a) in order to gain an understanding of the role of both peace and civil conflict in economic development; and (b) in order to articulate economic policies that encourage peace. Economic models have been constructed to study a wide variety of contests. Some models explain the behavior of firms that are intent on driving rival firms out of business. Others explain why workers threaten to strike in order to gain wage concessions from management, while yet other models explain the process whereby political parties vie for the votes of a populace. Finally, there have been economic models that explain the behavior of policy-makers who formulate policies to discourage criminal behavior. Because this has been such a wide range of studies in this area, we anticipated that we would find a variety of economic models of civil conflict. However, we were somewhat surprised to discover that the studies had a fairly consistent and uniform structure.

The general structure of these models of civil conflict can be summarized as follows:

- Two parties compete over the control of assets. These assets can be wealth or something that generates income and wealth. Control confers the right to use the assets and to secure the benefits derived from them.
- Initially, one of the parties has control of these assets.
- Conflict is one way that control can be altered. In conflict, one party wins while the other party loses, with the winner gaining complete control over the contested assets. Once conflict has been initiated, it is resolved according to a theoretical construct, the "conflict function," that specifies the probability of each party winning, depending upon the resources each commits to the conflict.
- The alternative to conflict is peace or "no conflict." In some models peace implies that the initial assignment of control is retained. In other models peace must be negotiated whereby control over the assets is determined by peaceful agreement.

Under this structure, conflicts are inherently non-cooperative and involve strategic contests between the parties. Hence, it is understandable that all the models use game theory, which allows the application of a powerful set of tools to analyze the models and to derive testable hypotheses.

Although this essay focuses on theoretical issues, there are other issues that warrant some passing mention. For example a large body of empirical research has searched for plausible economic causes of wars. These studies ask several questions: in countries and regions that have gone through wars, is it more likely that the levels of wealth and income were low versus high? Was an unequal distribution of wealth and income more likely to be observed? Another significant area of economic research has been in measuring the cost of civil conflict. In addition, the World Bank has made a major effort to develop policy tools which help deal with such issues as preventing civil wars and reducing their duration when they occur, or to help eliminate the factors that impede the peaceful resolution of disagreements before they erupt into conflict.

In the following section, the commonalities of the various models we reviewed are identified in order to construct what we argue is the basic methodology used in these papers. Also identified are important differences between the models, for often these differences are important in deriving new theoretical insights into why and how conflicts occur. The rest of this essay discusses the models in five selected studies.

## 2. Basic Methodology: Common and contrasting elements of economic models of civil conflict

Economic models of civil conflict are based on the assumption that conflict can be explained, in large part, by the behavior of rational agents who use scarce resources in situations in which some of the outcomes are determined by conflict. From here economic models vary with respect to the way in which they treat the following aspects:

a) The way in which the outcome of conflict depends upon agents' choices;
b) The way in which rationality is defined and takes into account the agent-interactions that result in conflict as one of the possible alternatives;
c) The way in which agents and resources are aligned with the respective sides of a conflict; and
d) The resource costs of conflict.

*How economic models treat these aspects forms the foundations of a basic methodology.*

Suppose that a civil conflict involves two factions, each of which commits resources to the conflict. Then, without exception, the relevant models cited in the bibliography assume that the resolution of the conflict is uncertain and the probability with which each faction wins depends upon the resources committed by each faction. The resulting probability relationship is called a "conflict function," because this relationship is analogous to the production function of neoclassical price theory. A "standard" conflict function is one that specifies the probability of winning in accordance with the relative amounts of resources that a faction commits to the conflict (Hirshleifer, 1988, 1989, and 2000).

Depicting the outcome of conflict in terms of a conflict function clearly shows one way in which conflict involves the interaction between the parties. Consequently, the standard approach to deal with rational behavior under such conditions is to use game theory. As will be shown below, non-cooperative game theory has been used to model agents' behavior for both actual conflict events and for the decision processes that lead up to conflicts. All of the papers reviewed use this approach.

Garfinkel and Skaperdas (2000) use both non-cooperative and cooperative game theory. They employ bargaining theory from cooperative games to model the process of negotiating a peaceful settlement as an alternative to conflict. That the Garfinkel and Skaperdas paper explicitly models an alternative to war, i.e., peace, sets it apart from the other papers in the list.

In game theory, rationality is defined as acting in one's self-interest, taking into account how the actions of others might affect one's self-interest and how one's action might influence the actions taken by the others. In the models of civil conflict, the self-interest of each faction is directly correlated with specific resources. For example, Garfinkel and Skaperdas (2000) use a consumable good, butter, as the resource desired by each faction. In their quest to acquire butter, the factions can either divide up this resource peacefully or go to war to obtain it. Grossman (1999) assumes that each faction uses its army to either retain or seize the power of government to tax the output produced by the citizenry. Thus, the appropriation of the wealth of the citizenry guides the self-interest of each faction. Similar to Grossman, Roemer (1985) and Gershenson and Grossman (2000) use the retention and acquisition of the power of government to appropriate a given amount of wealth to guide the self-interest of each faction. In Collier (2000), the rebel faction is motivated to loot the country's income on a continuing basis, rather than capturing, once and for all, the resources from which that income is derived. That is, in this case the rebels' motivation is similar to that of criminals rather than revolutionaries who seek a permanent replacement of the existing government.

Most of the papers surveyed here assume that the rival factions are an a priori condition. However, two notable models, Grossman (1999) and Roemer (1985) require that faction leaders recruit members for their respective coalitions. Grossman's faction leaders recruit members from the peasant labor market by offering to hire them for a wage, just like workers. Roemer's rebel leader, whom he calls "Lenin," promises to share with fellow insurgents the wealth that is confiscated by winning the civil war. Thus, finding the desired distribution of shares is a precondition for recruiting the desired insurgent coalition. As for the incumbent faction leader currently in power, called the "Tsar," the government army's size is not restricted, presumably because the Tsar has conscription power over the working class.

The papers surveyed, here, generally recognize that civil conflict channels resources away from their most efficient use. That is, civil conflict results in a loss of economic efficiency. For example, in Garfinkel and Skaperdas (2000), a faction allocates butter (a consumable good) and guns (a non-consumable good) that is not desired, but is needed in order to resist defeat in the event of conflict. Similarly, in Grossman (1999), and in Gershenson and Grossman (2000), resources channeled into war become costs that reduce the faction's wealth. However, only Garfinkel and Skaperdas (2000) treat the direct destruction of wealth as a consequence of violent conflict, irrespective of the resources used to wage war.

## 3. Economic models of civil conflict

In this section, five papers are briefly reviewed and discussed.

### *Grossman (1999), "Kleptocracy and Revolutions."*

In Grossman (1999), civil conflict is modeled as a confrontation between two rival factions. It is initially assumed that one faction is the government with the power to tax the output of peasant farmers, whereas the other faction, the rebel faction, seeks to forcefully seize that power from the government. If the rebel faction succeeds in seizing power, then it becomes the ruling government and the deposed government faction becomes the rebel coalition. Thus, civil conflict is about the retention and seizure of the power to appropriate wealth from the peasant class.

Each faction recruits its army from the peasant labor market by offering to pay each soldier for his/her allegiance. The incentive to assemble an army increases with the wealth the faction expects to appropriate, via taxes, after it wins the conflict and seizes power. In Grossmans' model, the rebel leader will engage in battle against the government army only if the rebel soldiers are sufficiently effective fighters. Otherwise the rebel leader will quit, thereby averting conflict. Grossman assumes that the rebel forces' fighting effectiveness is uncertain and depends upon such factors as ideological values, troop morale, and the well-being of family back home. In Grossman's theory, the likelihood of civil conflict increases as the rebel forces' fighting effectiveness improves.

Grossman defines the social cost of civil war (social waste) as the value of the resources diverted away from the production of output. That is, all resources diverted by both factions from production into civil conflict and into deterrence when conflict is absent comprise social waste.

### Gershenson and Grossman (2000), "Civil conflict: Ended or never ended?"

Using a model that is almost identical to Grossman (1999), Gershenson and Grossman examine why some conflicts terminate with a clear and permanent victor, as in the Communist defeat of the Nationalist Chinese, whereas other conflicts go through repeated cycles in which hostilities subside and re-emerge first with one faction defeating a second one, then with the second faction defeating the first, and so on. Examples of these conflicts occur between rival tribes in Africa. In the Gershenson-Grossman model, each faction commits resources generally to the conflict rather than specifically to hire soldiers. Furthermore, it is not specifically assumed that the ruling faction taxes the output of the peasant farmers to appropriate wealth. Rather, it is assumed that the ruling faction appropriates the country's wealth, but that the amount of the appropriation varies between factions.

In deciding whether or not to force a conflict to challenge the ruling faction, the insurgent faction (the one that is not in power) compares the expected benefit from winning the conflict with the cost of committing resources to the conflict. The benefit from winning the conflict varies with the amount of the country's wealth which a given faction can appropriate after seizing power. The cost of committing resources to the conflict depends upon the faction's effectiveness in using its resources in the conflict. The insurgent faction's willingness to force a conflict thus depends on the effectiveness with which it can appropriate the country's wealth and on the faction's effectiveness in using its resources in the conflict. From this, Gershenson and Grossman derive three conclusions:

1) There are conditions under which no attempt will be made by the rebel insurgents to seize power. There is no civil war.

2) There are conditions under which the rebel faction will attempt to seize power, and will continue to do so until it succeeds. But once the faction seizes power and establishes itself as the ruling faction, the other faction will make no attempt to regain power. So there will be civil war that terminates once the incumbent ruler is deposed.

3) There are conditions under which either faction will attempt to seize power whenever it is not in power. Here there will be never-ending civil conflict as each faction will attempt to seize power whenever the rival faction rules.

### Garfinkel and Skaperdas (2000), "Conflict without misconceptions or incomplete information."

The Garfinkel and Skaperdas study introduces three new and important factors into the models of civil conflict. First, the paper explicitly accounts for the fact that conflict destroys resources and wealth. Furthermore, if wealth can be passed on from one period to the next, then the social cost of destroying wealth via conflict will be felt by future generations. Second, this study makes peace an explicit alternative to war. Third, within the peace alternative, it includes a separate process that determines the terms of peace. In accounting for the destructive consequences of war, the authors have developed a particularly interesting insight: in the short run, rival factions will tend to avoid conflict and will prefer to opt for peace. However, in the long run, the costs of having peace (that is the cost of deterring war) might accumulate to the point where war is the desired alternative. Having war and peace as explicit alternatives requires that decision makers know the outcomes of each. The outcome of war is clear: the winner will end up taking everything. That leaves the conditions for peace to be determined. In this regard, Garfinkel and Skaperdas use bargaining theory (from the cooperative theory of games) to model how the outcomes of peace are determined. In negotiating a peaceful settlement, the factions bargain to determine the division of wealth under peace. But if the factions fail to agree on a settlement, then war is the default alternative. It follows from bargaining theory that a party can improve upon its settlement if it can increase its advantage in the default alternative. That is, a stronger position if war were to occur will improve the terms of the peace settlement. Hence, the price for peace increases as additional resources are committed to planning for the contingency of war—an implication which is clearly seen in the Garfinkel/Skaperdas model.

The Garfinkel/Skaperdas model provides two interesting suggestions regarding the prospects for peace. First, if wars are sufficiently destructive, conflict is less likely and peace is more likely. This suggestion agrees with the deterrence argument made during the nuclear arms race. The authors' second suggestion is that when war is destructive, peace is more likely; and that when the future returns on wealth is sufficiently high, peace is also likely. In other words, the fact that wealth can be passed on to future generations raises the cost to society of destroying wealth via war; and this provides a greater incentive for society to avoid war and opt for peace. The Garfinkel/Skaperdas framework suggests that the occurrence of wars might be due to concrete, materialistic factors and not necessarily to vague, uncertain, and irrational ideology.

In a model much in the spirit of Garfinkel and Skaperdas (2000), but without an explicit consideration of a peaceful settlement or a reckoning of the destructiveness of war, Neary (1997) identifies the conditions that can give rise to four different equilibrium outcomes of the model. Neary concludes that wealth distribution is a key factor in explaining peace and conflict. He shows that peace is more likely, when total initial wealth is relatively small and evenly distributed to each faction, or if most wealth is initially owned by one faction. Either war or peace is equally likely when each faction has initial amounts of wealth, with one side having only a little more. On the other hand, war is very likely when one faction is very rich and the other faction is very poor. In this equilibrium, the poor faction devotes all of its wealth towards conflict.

### Roemer (1985), "Rationalizing revolutionary ideology."

Roemer's model is unique among those surveyed for this paper. First, the authors explicitly specifies the process by which the actions of the factions affect the outcome of conflict; the process is not simply assumed to be part of the standard conflict function. Second, in this model, agents are motivated to join the revolution by the promise of a better life under a new regime, rather than by being hired in labor markets. This makes it possible to describe the attributes of the rebel group in terms of their income or wealth. In order to better appreciate the place of Roemer's work relative to other models, it will be useful to explain the conceptual basis for the model.

In this paper, Roemer defines "revolution" as a movement by a group of individuals within a population, a "coalition," which seeks to overthrow the ruling regime in order to redistribute wealth. The leader of the coalition, called "Lenin" as in Grossman's study, guides the movement and recruits members to the coalition by designing the reforms for wealth distribution. These proposed reforms not only define the revolution's objectives, thereby serving as a guide for the movement, but the reforms also serve to recruit members. People who favor the reforms and who are willing to commit to these changes join the movement. The leader of the ruling regime, called the "Tsar," is responsible for defending the regime by designing policies that would hinder the formation of a revolutionary coalition, if one were to form, to ensure that the coalition is not successful. For example, punishing those who attempt to overthrow the regime might serve as an effective deterrent for revolution. Intuitively, the success of a revolution depends both upon the coalition that supports it and upon the actions of the Tsar to hinder it.

Roemer proposes a mathematical model of the processes described above defining its equilibrium and deriving logical conclusions from this model. These conclusions shed light on several interesting issues:

- The composition of the equilibrium coalition can be described in terms of the coalition's mix of rich and poor people.
- The equilibrium revolution can alter the distribution of wealth: i.e., the distribution can be made more equitable.
- Certain regimes with higher inequalities of wealth are more likely to confront successful revolutions.
- Regimes exist that threaten to punish the rich more harshly than the poor in order to deter revolution.

### Collier (2000), "Rebellion as a quasi-criminal activity."

Collier argues that some rebellions have much in common with criminal activity. He characterizes these rebellions as ones in which the goal is not the overthrow of the incumbent regime (to change the ownership of wealth and property), but rather to repeatedly appropriate the revenues of specific segments of the economy. For example, Collier discusses cases where insurgents battle against government troops to seize the revenues derived from the export of a natural resource. Such activities provide good targets for looting—because of the high profits that make looting lucrative, and because of the fixed and non-movable nature of the resources.

Collier's basic model is a conflict game between a rebel leader and a decision maker for control of the government. The rebel's income from looting is assumed to be determined by the size of the rebel army and by the size of the opposing government army. The rebel's objective is to maximize his/her income, subject to a *financial viability constraint* and a *survivability constraint*. The financial viability constraint simply ensures that the rebel's looting activity adequately feeds and houses the rebel army. The survivability constraint reflects Collier's assumption that the rebel knows the number of fighters he/she needs in order to be minimally successful against the government forces. A rebel force that fails to meet this constraint is sure to be annihilated by the government force, so that looting is sure to be fruitless. In this case, the rebel will cease his/her activity.

As for the government, it budgets a share of its tax revenues for military expenditures. This allows the government to deploy an army to deter the rebels' looting activity, so long as the cost of training and supporting this army does not exceed the military's budget.

The theoretical solution to Collier's conflict game provides implications regarding conditions in which insurgents are likely to emerge in order to loot the rents from a country's natural resources. The model also permits inferences regarding the characteristics one can expect of potential insurgent looters and the characteristics of countries that may be likely targets of rebel looters. Collier and his co-authors follow this approach in conducting empirical studies of civil conflict, albeit with somewhat different models.

## 4. Concluding Remarks

Our examination of some of the recent theoretical literature on the economics of civil conflict has revealed a number of interesting perspectives on situations in which peace, security, and *kyosei* are absent. From the perspective of economics, civil conflict can be viewed in the context of rational choice about how resources are employed. In fact an important conclusion from these studies is that contention over the control and allocation of scarce and valuable resources might increase the likelihood of civil conflict and the breakdown of peace, security, and *kyosei*. Furthermore, although peace, security, and *kyosei* is a public concern (in the sense that everyone in the society is affected by it), decisions regarding civil conflict might be in the hands of only a few. Specifically, civil conflict can be the chosen by only a few faction leaders, who are guided by private interests and benefits. Therefore, in some cases, the presence or absence of peace, security, and *kyosei* in a society might also depend on the control by a few, as is the case with civil conflict.

This chapter has provided a different perspective for understanding peace, security, and *kyosei* by examining the circumstances that contribute to its absence, namely civil conflict. The approach that economics takes is to understand how rival factions fail to settle their differences with regard to the control and ownership of economic resources. Understanding these circumstances will hopefully suggest actions that a society might take in order to avoid civil conflict and to usher in a period of peace, security, and *kyosei*.

## References

Collier, Paul and Anke Hoeffler (1998), "On economic causes of civil war," *Oxford Economic Papers* 50, 563-573.

Collier, Paul (2000), "Rebellion as a quasi-criminal activity," *Journal of Conflict Resolution* 44(6), 839-853.

Collier, Paul and Anke Hoeffler (2001), "On the incidence of civil war in Africa," *Journal of Conflict Resolution* 46, 13-28.

Collier, Paul and Anke Hoeffler (2002), "Aid, policy and peace: Reducing the risks of civil conflict," unpublished working paper, May 2002, World Bank.

Garfinkel, Michelle R. and Stergio Skaperdas (2000), "Conflict without misperceptions or incomplete information," *Journal of Conflict Resolution* 44(6), 793-807.

Garfinkel, Michelle R. (1990), "Arming as a strategic investment in a cooperative equilibrium," *American Economic Review* 80(1), 50-68.

Gershenson, Dmitriy and Herschel I. Grossman (2000), "Civil conflict: Ended or never ending?" *Journal of Conflict Resolution* 44(6), 808-822.

Grossman, Herschel I. (1991), "A general equilibrium model of insurrections," *American Economic Review* 81, 912-921.

Grossman, Herschel I. (1999), "Kleptocracy and revolutions," *Oxford Economic Papers* 51, 267- 283.

Hirshleifer, Jack (1988), "The analytics of continuing conflict," *Synthese* 76, 201-233.

Hirshleifer, Jack (1989), "Conflict and rent-seeking success functions: Ratio vs difference models of relative success," *Public Choice* 63, 101-112.

Hirshleifer, Jack (2000), "The macrotechnology of conflict," *Journal of Conflict Resolution* 44(6), 773-792.

Neary, Hugh M. (1997), "Equilibrium structure in an economic model of conflict," *Economic Inquiry* 35, 480-494.

Roemer, John E. (1985), "Rationalizing revolutionary ideology," *Econometrica* 53, 85-108.

Skaperdas, Stergios (1991), "Conflict and attitudes toward risk," *American Economic Review* 81, 160-164.

# eight

# Scaling Down the Search for Peace and Security: Lessons Learned from the Emergence of Subnational Collaboratives

## Edward P. Weber

In the political science literature much effort has been expended on the interaction between nation states, and on nation states as the primary or dominant players when it comes to discussions over how best to provide peace and security. There are good reasons for this, not the least of which is that nation states are legally recognized political entities with the authority to write and negotiate the terms of international agreements, and, perhaps most importantly, to enforce such agreements using sanctions, whether economic, military, or otherwise. In recent times, however, it has become increasingly clear that the achievement of peace and security on a day-to-day basis for many people requires more than traditional nation state-based efforts in the economic and military realms; the achievement of peace also requires the harnessing of institutions at the sub-national level. This is so because such regional and/or local institutions are easier for ordinary citizens to comprehend given their direct connection to everyday lives and decisions, and, hence, their direct connection to citizens' overall feelings of security and well being. It is also the case because institutions, or sets of roles, rules, norms, decision making procedures, and programs that serve to define social practices, and to guide interactions of those participating in these practices, matter to behavior, and behavior directly affects whether peace and security obtain, or are possible (Young 1997).

Given these factors, not all sub-national institutions are created equal in their ability to affect the desired outcomes of peace and security. Of particular interest to this study is the growing use of sub-national *collaborative* institutions over the past several decades. Policymakers, bureaucratic practitioners and citizens in dozens of countries and thousands of communities across the globe have been choosing collaboratives as a more effective way to resolve difficult public problems, to resolve policy conflicts among groups and individuals with differing values and interests, and to craft positive, trust-based relationships that strengthen a community's ability to act collectively, among other things (Agranoff and McGuire 2003, 25; Kemmis 2001; Pretty 2003; Putnam 2000; Weber 2003; Western and Wright 1994). More specific to the ideas of peace and security, we can say that these collaborative arrangements, if designed properly, hold the potential for lessening or eliminating conflict and antagonism, for promoting harmonious interactions among groups and individuals, and for resolving difficult public policy problems that, to the extent they are left unresolved, contribute to a sense of distress and insecurity among the general populace (Miller 1992; Sirianni and Friedland 2001; Weber 1998; Young 1997, 4).

This study explores collaboratives and the connections between collaborative institutions and the goals of peace and security.[1] The discussion starts with the practical rationale for the importance of sub-national institutions in the larger quest for peace and security, before turning to a brief consideration of the collaborative phenomenon and the development of the kinds of peace and security outcomes likely to be produced by collaboratives. Two final sections examine the broader literature on collaboratives in order to elicit the institutional design conditions under which such outcomes are most likely to be produced and to suggest future directions for research in this area.

## Why Focus on the Sub–national Level?

In recent years there has been a growing literature in political science that recognizes the increasing importance of sub-national institutional efforts for resolving conflict and maintaining peaceable adjustments of disputes among parties pursing differing interests and goals. In fact, a plausible argument can be made that for *most* citizens, when it comes to resolving public problems, sub-national efforts have a more direct, important and enduring impact than national efforts on whether the citizens' lives are peaceable and secure on a day-to-day basis. This is so for several practical reasons.

First, there is a more direct connection of regional and local issues and disputes to citizens' daily lives; therefore it is easier for people to understand the connection between efforts to resolve local and regional conflicts and their own overall well being. Second, in advanced industrial countries that have experienced many decades of peace and security within their own homelands, a certain complacency exists. People tend to take for granted that national peace and security is and always will be provided, because peace and security have been the norm for so long. Therefore, disputes and concerns over domestically based public problems (such as environmental protection, the levels of local crime and violence, natural disasters, economic issues, and so on) loom much larger vis-à-vis international affairs as problems needing effective and immediate attention. Third, although the increase in the incidence and severity of international terrorism in the past few years does place added emphasis on the efforts of nation states in any "war on terror," the decentralized, intermittent, and clandestine character of terrorism, especially as it affects open democratic societies, also means that enduring success against terrorism ultimately requires healthy, functioning sub-national institutions with appropriate resources, personnel, and robust connectivity to national institutions. Fourth, in countries that are experiencing conflict and strife, especially in weak states with limited national institutional (governmental) capacity, sub-national efforts are likely to supplement and, to the extent they are successful, buffer people from the larger turmoil and offer people an alternative method for resolving conflict and staying secure. Therefore, sub-national institutions loom larger in the minds of many people as "a" or "the" key mechanism for resolving conflict and securing peace.

## Sub-national Collaboratives

The sub-national collaboratives under discussion here are ongoing governance arrangements in which inclusive coalitions of the unalike come together in a deliberative, consensus-based format to resolve public policy problems affecting their region or community. Such efforts are governance arrangements, as opposed to government-based, because the act of governing involves

> the establishment and operation of social institutions or, in other words, sets of roles, rules, decision making procedures, and programs that serve to define social practices and to guide interactions of those participating in these practices.... [P]olitically significant institutions or governance systems are arrangements designed to resolve social conflicts, enhance social welfare, and, more generally, alleviate collective action problems in a world of interdependent actors. Governance, on this account, does not presuppose the need to create material entities or organizations—"governments"—to administer the social practices that arise to handle the function of governance (Young 1996, 247; Ellickson 1991; North 1990).

As such, these collaboratives necessarily involve institutional arrangements that engage a multiplicity of diverse actors spanning the public, private and civic sectors, and including multiple levels of government, across the political spectrum, and across policy arenas and government agencies where appropriate. Collaboratives thus involve active citizen participation and shared power arrangements grounded in deliberation, consultation and negotiation, through which private citizens and stakeholders often take on leadership roles and are involved directly in decision-making, implementation, and enforcement processes along with government officials, especially when it comes to how goals are to be achieved.

Successful, enduring reform of a public school system, for example, is not just a question of education policy, but of community strength, health, public safety, and widespread public involvement in the governance and improvement of school performance. The successful transformation of communities and ecosystems into environmentally sustainable entities is not just a matter of strengthening environmental policies: it also involves bringing society back into the decision-making mix; giving citizens ownership of the problem so that they will actively support the sustainability goal; and coordinating and integrating such policy with economic, education, social, and transportation policy. Perhaps nowhere is the example of a difficult public problem requiring extensive and continual collaboration more harshly exhibited than in the United States' response to the attacks on the World Trade Center in September 2001. However, other examples can be found in catastrophic natural disasters (e.g., earthquakes, floods, etc.) that strike communities. The need to integrate across interests, governments and established response systems in a seamless manner is essential to pull off successfully the rescue, relief and recovery efforts, as well as the prevention and mitigation efforts to prepare for and reduce the impact of future disasters. In each of these cases, successful problem solving entails a collaborative capable of integrating the many specialized functions of existing government organizations and programs with the multiple and diverse resources and interests found among the cross-sections of society affected by such problems.

Such collaboratives differ from more traditional voluntary associations often found at local levels of governance and from interest groups. These collaboratives involve coalitions of the unalike that tend to span a full (or fuller) spectrum of political interests and socio-economic strata, to focus specifically on public problems, to approach public problems in a more comprehensive, integrated fashion, to link interests and officials across levels of government and policy areas (as opposed to having a narrow focus), and to span traditional boundaries, whether geographical/ecological, political, or administrative in nature.

However, such a basic description and comparison does not tell us a great deal about the potential benefits, risks, and institutional elements required to catalyze and sustain such initiatives to the point where the promise of a collaborative is realized.

## Connecting the Dots: Collaboratives, Peace, and Security

The collaboratives under discussion here engender a variety of outcomes that promote greater harmony and collective problem-solving capacity in the communities adopting such arrangements.

### Engendering a Unified, Integrated, Trust-Based Community Network

The institutional arrangements employed by collaboratives help to create new community networks, while also expanding and strengthening existing community networks that can be called upon for communication, informal decision-making, and public action. The new dynamic connects a series of individual, separate organizations and networks (representing narrow, often self-contained segments of a particular community) to produce a more unified, integrated, trust-based community network. This transformation is analogous to the difference between the weakness and fragmentation evident in a shattered piece of glass lying on the ground and the strong integration of a multi-colored, multi-shaped glass mosaic that has been welded together for a purpose. In short, the new network strengthens the capacity of the community to act collectively in several ways.

First, the process of working together helps diverse elements of the community construct a common community history. For example, this can involve old timers and newcomers, or business interests and environmental activists. The common history becomes a way of defining the community by articulating the issues that matter to the community, and it provides a starting point for building new relationships and for constructing a shared vision of what the community wants to become (Priester 1994, 121).

Second, the unified, integrated network strengthens the capacity for collective action by facilitating the creation of informal decision-making institutions and catalyzing the creation of new integrally related "spin off" organizations, both of which complement existing formalized arrangements (see Weber 2003, 197-98, for several examples).

Third, deliberating together and cooperating with others on efforts which provide community-wide benefits tends to break down negative stereotypes, and can lead to new, more positive working relationships grounded in trust. The newly-minted trust encourages people to view others as partners and neighbors rather than adversaries, and to communicate with others in a direct, open and honest manner instead of hiding information for strategic advantage. According to a growing number of social capital scholars, building such a web of horizontal, cooperative relationships grounded in trust makes it more likely that a community will demonstrate an enhanced capacity for effective self-governance and the peaceable resolution of disputes (Fukuyama 1995; Putnam 2000). In addition, the growth in positive, trust-based relationships means that as the circle of trust expands, citizens' feelings of security and safety will also expand.

### Better Information, Improved Outcomes

The collaborative dynamic, if designed properly, includes the idea of revealing closely held information and working together to create higher quality scientific and implementation data bases from which emerge program design, compliance and enforcement decisions (as opposed to the conflict process where the rule is to conceal political stakes and other types of information). The cross-fertilization resulting from information sharing means that more citizens are educated and, in some cases, more minds are changed regarding the positive value of public programs. It also makes more likely the creation of more fully specified policy data bases (better information), which allow authorities to develop new solutions for problems. Put differently, the better information creates opportunities for innovation and for the transformation of governance policies and programs. In the area of environmental policy, for example, risk assessment reviews, and integrated pollution control or holistic ecosystem-based approaches—as opposed to single-media (e.g., air, water, land) or fragmented problem-specific approaches—become more of a possibility as more data bases are created (e.g., extensive chemical-specific data bases, whole-facility risk profiles, and comprehensive data bases needed to make them work). One-size-fits-all rules designed for national or regional application give way to customized, more effective solutions better able to "fit" with the geographic, economic and social realities of the locale under scrutiny. Greater rigor in program monitoring arrangements becomes possible, and rules focusing on measurable indicators (more closely resembling the real world results intended by decision makers) begin to replace proxy-based enforcement regimes.

### Empowerment and Ownership through Shared Power, Flexibility and Choice.

Collaboratives engage a full range of participants by sharing power and by increasing opportunities for innovative policy programs which emphasize a greater degree of discretion and flexibility for government decision-makers, for private sector organizations, and for citizens. In almost all cases, the government retains the authority to decide policy goals, allocate property rights, enforce decisions, and so on. But in this model with respect to *how* public goals are implemented and achieved, the authority relationship is relaxed and power is shared.

Authority and responsibility are also shared, and the principle of flexibility honored, by granting participants relative freedom of choice regarding a range of different pathways to the agreed-upon goal. In many cases, decision-makers develop a menu of alternative (equivalent or better) compliance paths, each of which is designed to achieve the goal in question, but at the same time allow those closest to the problem (i.e., those ultimately responsible for program results) to decide which alternative works best for them in terms of cost, technical feasibility, etc.

The idea is that with credible stakes in policy outcomes, participants will claim ownership of collaboratively produced results, and are thus more inclined to target and mobilize resources in support of those results. The enhanced willingness of citizens to invest in the work of governance (e.g., in terms of program design, voluntary compliance with rules, or program implementation and monitoring) not only improves governance effectiveness, but also lessens conflict and antagonism, and promotes more harmonious interactions among groups and individuals (Bieirle and Cayford 2002; Ostrom 1990; Weber 1998, 24; 2003).

### *The Development of Certain Skills and Character Traits.*

Moreover, given the emphasis on bringing a society and its citizens into the public policy decision-making framework, the character and competence of citizens plays a more prominent role in the problem solving and conflict resolution equation. More specifically, *communitarians* argue that successful inclusion of citizens in a governance arrangement requires certain skills and character traits (virtues) from the citizen-participants (Glendon 1995). From this perspective, "[t]he challenge of social policy is not just the manipulation of incentives but also the formation of character: 'In almost every area of important public concern, we are seeking to induce persons to act virtuously.... In the long run, the public interest depends on private virtue" (Galston 1995, 38; inset quote from JQ Wilson 1985). The *communitarian* literature goes on to suggest (1) that not all citizens possess the necessary bundle of skills and character traits required to promote a healthy and peaceable system of democratic governance; and (2) that some institutional arrangements are better than others at inculcating the kinds of skills (e.g., deliberation, compromise, consensus-building) and virtues (e.g., civility, honesty, law-abidingness) demanded by such citizen-based democratic arrangements.

### *Taming Selfish Passions and Transforming Individuals' Worldviews.*

Such collaborative, deliberative, participative elements increase opportunities for citizens to engage in the primary political art of deliberating, or reasoning together. This active involvement can connect citizens to government in a positive way by giving them a stake in governing and helping tame selfish passions through deliberation, information sharing, and a better understanding of the "big" policy picture affecting the community (Sandel 1996, 5-6). As part of this, the new governance arrangements remind citizens of the need for a new attitude toward the responsibilities of citizenship. The new attitude recognizes and accepts the connection between civic responsibility, active engagement in public life, and a community's quality of life.

As part of this process, the collaborative format can enhance the potential for individual transformation through participation at the individual and community levels. The work of Michael Piore (1995), and others (e.g., Barber 1984) suggest that individuals regularly engaged in community deliberation, or in deliberative communication processes, no longer see their preferences and priorities in strictly individual terms, but rather in the context of broader community norms, values or structures. Their changing views of themselves as individual members of a community, and their changing preference for various policies, unfold in the context of their collaboration with others in the process of governance. Transformations are likely to occur on two levels. Participation in governing efforts might help individuals to better see their relationship to others including differences and similarities of ideas (Warren 1992), or to identify primarily with part of a larger group (Dawes, van de Kragt, and Orbell 1990). This is because participants learn many different sides of an issue, which may well translate into greater willingness to take others' opposing views into account and to tolerate others who are different from themselves. Participants thus might begin to better understand themselves in the context of community, rather than to identify themselves only as autonomous individuals. Moreover, when individuals begin to see their own preferences in a broader community context there are likely to be positive consequences for the overall capacity of a community to address *collective* problems (a performance benefit), including those associated with peace and security.

### *Mutual Gain Outcomes*

Instead of imposing zero-sum outcomes of benefit to only a few interests, the collaborative dynamic focuses on producing the kinds of "win-win" mutual gain solutions necessary for building and maintaining consensus among all the stakeholding interests. Mutual gains are achieved when participants reap greater benefits through a collaborative format than they are currently receiving under existing institutional arrangements. Participants do not need to harvest the same kinds of benefits to meet the mutual gain criteria; rather they can experience benefits in the areas of most importance to them individually. In a case involving environmental policy, for example, an environmentalist might "win" faster environmental clean up or more stringent pollution control standards. Business stakeholders, on the other hand, might benefit from lower regulatory compliance costs, or from greater flexibility in how they achieve pollution reduction. This, in turn, can lead to cost savings from an improved responsiveness to changing market conditions. Government regulators might encounter benefits such as less litigation and improved rulemaking timeliness, and fewer costs associated with oversight activities by political superiors. The important thing is that each participant is "winning," or garnering benefits simultaneously within the same transaction.

## Conflict and Collaboration in the Public Policy Arena: The Question of Institutional Design

With few exceptions, conflicts over the content and direction of public policy are the norm in democratic societies, whether at the national, regional or local level. Multi-party systems, interest group systems with many voices, diverse communities with varied interests, systems of government which allow multiple opportunities to stop political initiatives, and, in some cases such as the United States, adversarial political cultures, militate against collaboration. Collaboration is further deterred by its requirement that neighbors and adversaries (potential, imagined, or real) share privately gathered information. The revelation of private information increases participants' vulnerability and makes uncertain the achievement of promised benefits. Because information sharing creates opportunities for the development of a more robust set of implementation mechanisms, the realm of possible outcomes is greater, and the shape of final agreements is less predictable. There is also the chance that participants' requisite commitment to good faith bargaining will be tenuous. Some may be advancing hidden agendas to the detriment of other participants. The risk is that once certain information is revealed, participants may renege on their commitment, withdraw from the process, and use the information to advance their own interests at the expense of their fellow collaborators. And, even after a consensus conclusion is reached, there is always the possibility that some participants will revert back to former patterns of conflict, perhaps through a different venue (e.g., litigation), or through an appeal to political officials with the power to nullify or substantially modify the agreement.

These barriers to collective action suggest that not all institutional designs will be equally successful in producing the desired outcomes described above. Some institutional components will be needed to initiate and sustain collaboration, so that the process moves from the point where participants and community members simply *recognize* the positive potential of collaboration to the endpoint, or outcome, where an improved flow of benefits is realized for each interest or set of participants, and where improved conditions for future cooperation and conflict resolution are in place.

Catalyzing collaboration and moving it forward to a successful endpoint requires an assurance mechanism. The assurance mechanism is an institutional arrangement—a set of rules—governing interaction, which reduces the uncertainty and risks associated with the collaborative effort by selectively promoting collaboration, by structuring participant behavior to minimize the likelihood of defections, and by giving each participant a meaningful stake in outcomes. By reducing uncertainty, the framework of "rules" will engender the trust necessary for collaboration to take hold and for peaceable "win-win" problem resolutions, acceptable to a broad, cross-cutting coalition of interests to be produced and implemented (Agranoff and McGuire 2003, 182; Fukuyama 1995; Ostrom 1990). Specifically, the assurance mechanism introduces greater certainty and trust using nine constituent parts—rules for managing conflict and for guiding a unified interaction of participants toward the collective goal.

The nine elements of the assurance mechanism are (1) certain transaction-specific conditions; (2) a credible commitment to collaboration by entrepreneurial leaders; (3) social capital; (4) formal binding agreements to govern negotiations and their aftermath; (5) a reputation for commitment to collaborative processes by the organization(s) in charge of the problem resolution exercise; (6) participant norms governing interaction, deliberation, and *ex post* behavior; (7) adherence to the principle of inclusivity; (8) the need for participants with long-term interests in the public problem under discussion; and (9) the presence of a third-party intervenor.

*Transaction-Specific Conditions.* Transaction-specific conditions identify the subset of public problems conducive to collaboration by offering information on the manageability of potential collaborative endeavors as well as information on whether such endeavors are possible (opportunity) (Susskind 1999). The more conditions met, the lower the degree of

---

## Table 1. Transaction–specific conditions

- The opportunity exists to develop creative compromises

- Policy implications of issues to be resolved are more or less limited either programmatically, geographically, or to common practices in a specific industrial sector

- Affected interests are identifiable, cohesive, and possessive of the authority needed to deliver group support for collectively decided agreements

- Does not involve issues of fundamental values that cannot be compromised

- There is a well-developed factual data base to frame the discussion and resolution of pertinent issues

- Firm deadlines, either statutory, judicial, or programmatic

objective difficulty encountered during the collaborative process. For example, opportunity must exist for the kinds of creative compromises critical to bargaining success. Important here are ambiguous laws which grant public officials and citizens discretion in decision-making, or the endorsement of the collaborative endeavor by key officials, or endorsement by community members in the case of a local effort. Transaction-specific conditions might also include the limiting of collaborative processes to questions of "how" (implementation), rather than "what" (substantive policy goals) *unless* the new goal addresses a problem that falls outside the jurisdictional prerogatives of existing government initiatives. (See Table 1 for all the conditions.)

*Entrepreneurial Leadership.* Leaders of collaborative efforts, whether government officials, interest group representatives, or private citizens, have primary responsibility for convincing the full range of affected interests to credibly commit to collaborative arrangements and to their eventual results. Such leaders must be skillful enough to bring the efforts of self-interested individuals and organizations in line with the needs and interests of collective public goals. This can be accomplished by continually championing the benefits of collaboration to participants, while simultaneously assuring them that their interests will be protected during the collaborative process. The challenge of establishing a credible commitment to collaborative strategies takes the entrepreneurial leader beyond mechanical, incentive-based solutions into the realm of the "organic," where the leader must build trust, must reduce information asymmetries among participants by forging open lines of communication, and must share the eventual success in a meaningful way with stakeholders (Miller 1992, 217-23). Firm evidence of the leadership's own credible commitment to collaboration and fairness, a function of past performance (reputation), and a willingness to use authority and the resources at their disposal to promote, enforce and protect consensus deals, is needed as well.

*Organizational Reputation.* Collaboration is also facilitated by the extent that the public agency or agencies participating in a collaborative effort have a reputation for credible commitment to collaborative processes and their subsequent outcomes and a reputation for fairness when dealing with unforeseen contingencies as they arise (Kreps 1992). If such conditions do not exist, affected private sector entities, public interest groups, citizens, and state-level interests will be more likely to discount the possible gains from collaboration, and they will be less likely to join in, much less promote a collaborative effort, even when the expected gains are substantial. Thus an entrepreneurial leader's task of persuading affected interests to work together in good faith is easier if an organization has established a trustworthy reputation in support of collaboration.

*Social Capital.* Social capital is central to a community's collective public problem solving capacity. To the extent a community has a web of horizontal, cooperative relationships built on trust, its capacity for effective governance and peaceable dispute resolution is enhanced (Putnam 2000; Fukuyama 1995). In this sense, collaboration is organic, not mechanical; collaboration involves building and expanding these trust-based relationships so that information is shared, agreements are implemented willingly, and so on. As such, collaboratives must involve community-building processes that help people recognize how much they share in common. The processes can be as simple as getting people together on a regular basis in non-threatening social settings, such as potluck meals, breakfast meetings, or tea ceremonies. Alternatively, community-building processes can be integrated into the collaborative proceedings at the start of every session so as to remind everyone of the collective, community-based aspects of their joint endeavor.

*Formal Binding Rules.* In the collective problem solving setting, collaborative strategies based on leadership, reputation, and social capital are necessary, but not sufficient, to induce affected interests to trust others with the information that enables the group to make enduring collective decisions. Improving the likelihood that participants' good faith bargaining efforts will not be wasted requires a set of formal binding rules governing the collaborative negotiation process and its aftermath. Such rules restrict the ability of both public sector leaders and stakeholders to pursue self-interested behavior at the expense of long-term cooperation (Miller 1992). Examples include:

- bargaining arrangements granting participants a direct role in crafting public programs;
- agreements not to litigate or otherwise intervene once decisions have been finalized; and
- the adoption of a consensus decision-rule (because broad agreement increases legitimacy, lowers implementation resistance, engenders self-enforcement, and respects minority rights).

It is also important to build explicit written consideration of participants' interests into the mission statement and into programmatic language (or legislative and regulatory language if the case involves that level of action). Relevant examples here include a broad, cross-cutting, balanced mission statement (e.g., considering the environment, economy and community), appropriate monitoring and data reporting requirements, automatic penalties for non-compliance, and agreement on a standard decision-making procedure that forces decision makers to consider a broad cross-section of interests and values before the decision is made. Table 2 provides an example of just such a procedural framework taken from a col-

---

### Table 2. Watershed Integrity Review and Evaluation (WIRE)

1. **Watershed Perspective:** Does the project employ or reflect a total watershed perspective?
2. **Credibility:** Is the project based upon credible research or scientific data?
3. **Problem and Solution:** Does the project clearly identify the resource problems and propose workable solutions that consider the relevant resources?
4. **Water Supply:** Does the project demonstrate an understanding of water supply?
5. **Project Management:** Does project management employ accepted or innovative practices, set realistic time frames for their implementation and employ an effective monitoring plan?
6. **Sustainability:** Does the project emphasize sustainable ecosystems?
7. **Social and Cultural:** Does the project sufficiently address the watershed's social and cultural concerns?
8. **Economy:** Does the project promote economic diversity within the watershed and help sustain a healthy economic base?
9. **Cooperation and Coordination:** Does the project maximize cooperation among all parties and demonstrate sufficient coordination among appropriate groups or agencies?
10. **Legality**: Is the project lawful and respectful of agencies' legal responsibilities?

laborative, the Henry's Fork Watershed Council in the state of Idaho, which focuses on protecting and preserving the environment, the economy and the community. The ten-point framework also serves as a scoping device that helps increase the probability of program success, by screening and ultimately limiting the number of programs, according to general principles of broad-based benefits (hence broad buy-in from a wide range of participants), information credibility, feasibility, and cultural sensitivity (Weber 2003).

*Participant Norms.* Participant norms are critical for achieving and sustaining governance performance, whether in a collaborative or otherwise. This is because norms create a specific set of behavioral expectations for members of a community, employees in an organization, practitioners of a profession, or participants in a particular institutional arrangement (Etzioni 1996; March and Olson 1989; North 1990; Weber 2003). As Gormley suggests, "if [norms are] well-crafted and well-diffused, [they] can substitute for formal structural controls" (Gormley, 1995). Success here requires that group leaders and individual participants readily and regularly enforce norms if violations occur during deliberations, and that individual members regularly observe the norms as a part of their lives outside the collaborative problem solving process. Table 3 lists critical norms and explains how each works.

*Inclusiveness.* The importance of the principle of inclusiveness, in all its many aspects, cannot be overstated. In terms of political representation, participants with the power to

## Table 3. Participant Norms

| Participant Norm | How each works |
|---|---|
| **Inclusiveness** | —all have a right to participate once they accept the norms governing participant behavior<br>—reinforced by asking questions considering the preferences of "absent" interests |
| **Civility/respect for others** | —each participant has equal worth and is afforded equal opportunity to influence decisions<br>—civil debate<br>—shared deliberation (no monopoly of the discussion)<br>—violence, or the threat of, is out of bounds |
| **Integrity/ honesty in communication and action** | —necessary for success of community-building goal and good faith bargaining required to solve problems |
| **Dual role (as community member and representative of particular interest)** | —obligates participants to take a broader view of problems<br>—commits participants to help their neighbors solve community-based problems |
| **Commitment to balanced mission and holistic approach** | —intolerance for pattern of decisions benefiting only one segment of the community, or one element of the mission |
| **Trust as obligation** | —participants obligated to follow through on public commitments<br>—essential to program performance and self-enforcement dynamic |

block or undermine outcomes must be included, and given a credible stake in the collaborative process. Otherwise, the coalition of participants seeking peaceable, collective problem resolutions will encounter added uncertainty, and will face a greater likelihood of failure, as those left out in the cold mobilize resources in opposition, or withhold critical information in defense of their stakes (Weber 1998). Inclusiveness also involves transparency. This means ensuring an open-access design and open, public information systems (i.e., do not hide anything). The elements of representativeness and transparency are reinforced to the extent that a collaborative closely follow a balanced mission statement, an "inclusive," standardized decision process, and participant norms (as described above).

*Repeat Games.* A final measure of credible commitment helping to reduce uncertainty is whether stakeholders' involvement in the policy arena, or in the problem at issue, is of a long-term, iterative nature. Viable, ongoing entities that interact regularly on a number of issues and have repeat interactions (e.g., in the regulatory arena, or because participants live in the community affected by the problem targeted by the collaborative process) are more likely to perceive collaboration from a long-term perspective rather than as a one-time opportunity to advance their own self-interest.

*The Role of Third-Party Intervenors.* It is generally agreed that the presence of a professional facilitator, or mediator, is an important factor in nurturing collaborative efforts to win-win conclusions. Mediators help to coordinate bargaining activities and to facilitate the flow of information among parties, summarizing and organizing information, identifying prospective tradeoffs among the participants, and offering additional perspectives in terms of possible choices and alternative outcomes. Despite the near consensus on the importance of third-party intervenors, there is still considerable disagreement over their proper role, the need for them to stay involved for the duration of collaborative processes, or even whether participants with some modicum of facilitation training can successfully undertake the same role.

## Conclusion

The puzzle of how to achieve peace and security is multi-faceted and is likely to involve explication and understanding of multiple levels of analysis and scales of application. The institutional dimension involving subnational collaboratives, as outlined here, is an integral part of the puzzle. This chapter has explored the connections between specific types of institutions and desired outcomes, as well as the conditions under which collaborative institutions are most likely to produce such outcomes. Thus, we have taken steps toward solving a portion, however small, of the larger peace and security puzzle.

The scholarly effort to study institutions and decipher their relationship to outcomes, of course, is never ending, as is the challenge of achieving peace and security for statesmen, nations, communities, and citizens alike. This realization leads to the consideration of next steps for a research agenda into the institutional component of the peace and security puzzle. At the present time, an adequate framework for assessing collaborative capacity does not exist, although there are a few nascent efforts in this area of inquiry (Ebrahim 2004; Provan and Milward 2001; Weber, Lovrich and Gaffney 2004). To the extent that such an assessment tool can be developed, decision-makers and community members will be in a better position to know how well a particular effort is working, and whether community problem solving capacity is being enhanced, maintained or diminished. There is also a need for larger, more systematic tests of the propositions outlined above, particularly in regards to the necessary conditions for collaborative success. The data to date are largely drawn from case studies and journalistic accounts. The time is ripe for either a meta-analysis of existing data, or a large "n" research design, or both.

## Note

1. The lessons are drawn from literature that focuses primarily on the United States, with limited attention to Europe. As such, it is not clear that the institutions under discussion apply in countries beset with ongoing military-based hostilities and/or impoverished conditions. Although see *Science* (2003), in which roughly 500,000 collaboratives in the natural resource arena alone are noted across the globe regardless of the condition of particular countries.

## References

Agranoff, Robert, and Michael McGuire. 2003. *Collaborative public management: New strategies for local governments.* Cambridge, MA: The MIT Press.

Barber, Benjamin R. 1984. *Strong Democracy: Participatory Politics for a New Age.* Berkeley, CA: University of California Press.

Beierle, Thomas C., and Jerry Cayford. 2001. *Public Participation in Environmental Decisions: Lessons from the Case Study Record.* Report for *Resources for the Future,* (Summer), Washington, D.C.

Dawes, Robyn M., Alphons J. C. van de Kragt, and John M. Orbell. 1990. "Cooperation For the Benefit of Us—Not Me, or My Conscience." In J. Mansbridge. ed. *Beyond Self Interest.* Chicago, IL: The University of Chicago Press: 97-110.

Ebrahim, Alnoor. 2004. "Institutional Preconditions to Collaboration: Indian Forest and Irrigation Policy in Historical Perspective," *Administration & Society* 36(2): 208-242.

Ellickson, Robert. 1991. *Order Without Law: How Neighbors Settle Disputes.* Cambridge, MA: Harvard University Press.

Etzioni, Amitai. 1996. *The New Golden Rule: Community and Morality in a Democratic Society.* New York, NY: Basic Books.

Fukuyama, Francis. 1996. *Trust: Social Virtue and the Creation of Posterity.* Touchstone Books.

Galston, William A. 1995. "Liberal Virtues and the Formation of Civic Character." In M. A. Glendon and D. Blankenhorn. eds. *Seedbeds of Virtue: Sources of Competence, Character, and Citizenship in American Society.* Lanham, MD: Madison Books: 35-60.

Glendon, Mary Ann. 1995. "Introduction: Forgotten Questions." In M. A. Glendon and D. Blankenhorn. eds. *Seedbeds of Virtue: Sources of Competence, Character, and Citizenship in American Society.* Lanham, MD: Madison Books: 1-16.

Gormley, William T., Jr. 1995. *Everybody's Children: Child Care as a Public Problem.* Washington, D.C.: The Brookings Institution.

Kemmis, Daniel. 2001. *This Sovereign Land: A New Vision for Governing the West.* Washington, D.C.: Island Press.

Kreps, David M. 1992. Corporate Culture and Economic Theory. eds. J. A. Alt and K. A. Shepsle. *Perspectives on Positive Political Economy.* Cambridge: Cambridge University Press, 90- 143.

March, James, and Johan Olsen. 1989. *Rediscovering Institutions: The Organizational Basis of Politics.* New York, NY: The Free Press.

Miller, Gary J. 1992. *Managerial Dilemmas: The Political Economy of Hierarchy.* Cambridge: Cambridge University Press.

North, Douglass C. 1990. *Institutions, Institutional Change, and Economic Performance.* Cambridge: Cambridge University Press.

Ostrom, Elinor. 1990. *Governing the Commons: The Evolution of Institutions for Collective Action.* Cambridge: Cambridge University Press.

Piore, Michael J. 1995. *Beyond Individualism.* Cambridge, MA: Harvard University Press.

Pretty, Jules. 2003. "Social Capital and the Collective Management of Resources," *Science* 302 (December): 1912-1914.

Priester, Kevin. 1994. *Words into Action: A Community Assessment of the Applegate Valley.* Ashland, OR: The Rogue Institute of Ecology and Economy (May).

Pritzker, David. M., and Deborah Dalton. 1990. "EPA Regulatory Negotiation Candidate Selection Criteria," in D. M. Pritzker and D. Dalton (eds.), *Negotiated Rulemaking Sourcebook.* Washington, D.C.: Administrative Conference of the United States; 42

Provan, Keith G., and H. Brinton Milward. 2001. Do networks really work? A framework for evaluating public-sector organizational networks. *Public Administration Review* 61(4):414-23.

Putnam Robert. 2000. *Bowling Alone: The Collapse and Revival of American Community.* New York, NY: Simon and Schuster.

Sandel, Michael J. 1996. *Democracy's Dscontent: America in Search of a Public Philosophy.* Cambridge, MA: The Belknap Press of Harvard University Press.

Sirianni, Carmen, and Lewis Friedland. 2001. *Civic Innovation in America: Community Empowerment, Public Policy, and the Movement for Civic Renewal.* Berkeley, CA: University of California Press.

Susskind, Lawrence. 1999. *The Consensus Building Handbook.* London: SAGE Publications.

Warren, Mark. 1992. "Democratic Theory and Self Transformation." *American Political Science Review,* 86 (1) (March): 8-23.

Weber, Edward P. 2003. *Bringing Society Back In: Grassroots Ecosystem Management, Accountability, and Sustainable Communities.* Cambridge, MA: The MIT Press.

Weber, Edward P. 1998. *Pluralism by the Rules: Conflict and Cooperation in Environmental Regulation.* Washington, D.C.: Georgetown University Press.

Weber, Edward P., Nicholas P. Lovrich, and Michaal Gaffney. Forthcominig. "Collaboration, Enforcement, and Endangered Species: A Framework for Assessing Collaborative Problem Solving Capacity," *Society and Natural Resources.*

Western, David, and R. Michael Wright. 1994. *Natural Connections: Perspectives in Community-based Conservation.* Washington, D.C.: Island Press.

Wilson, James Q. 1985. "The Rediscovery of Character: Private Virtue and Public Policy." *The Public Interest,* 81: 15-16.

Young, Oran R. 1996. "Rights, Rules, and Resources in International Society." In S. Hanna, C. Folke, and K. G. Maler, eds. *Rights to Nature: Ecological, Economic, Cultural, and Political Principles of Institutions for the Environment.* Washington, D. C.: Island Press: 245-64.

Young, Oran R. 1997. "Rights, Rules, and Resources in World Affairs." In O. R. Young. ed. *Global Governance: Drawing Insights From the Environmental Experience.* Cambridge, MA: The MIT Press: 1-23.

## nine

# Coordinating Homeland Security in the United States: Problems and Prospects

## Steven Stehr

*"There is a fascination in Washington with bureaucratic solutions—rearranging the wiring diagrams, creating new organizations. Some of the saddest aspects of the 9/11 story are the outstanding efforts of so many individual officials straining, often without success, against the boundaries of the possible. Good people can overcome bad structures. They should not have to. We have the resources and the people. We need to combine them more effectively, to achieve unity of effort."*

—Testimony of 9/11 Commission Chairman Thomas H. Kean
and Vice-Chairman Lee H. Hamilton
before the United States Senate
Governmental Affairs Committee, July 30, 2004.

## Introduction

After the terrorist attacks of September 11, 2001 against the World Trade Center, the Pentagon quickly elevated the issue of homeland security to the top of the nation's policy agenda. Traditionally, the task of maintaining national security in the United States has been primarily the responsibility of the federal government. But because of the nature of the contemporary terrorist threat, which involves the potential of a wide variety of attacks anywhere in the country, federal, state, and local governments have a shared responsibility in preventing further attacks and in preparing for and responding to terrorist events should they occur. A number of highly respected institutions including the U.S. General Accounting Office, the Brookings Institution, the RAND Corporation, the National Academy of Public Administration, the Century Foundation, the National Governor's Association, the U.S. Conference of Mayors, and the National League of Cities, all have issued reports on the state of homeland security in the United States. A common conclusion of these reports is that the coordination of efforts between and among the multiple agencies and governmental jurisdictions responsible for keeping America safe is the primary problem facing the nation as we attempt to protect ourselves from future terrorist attacks. Although there is widespread agreement that coordination of efforts is the problem, the recommendations found in these and other reports issued since September 11 do not offer many practical suggestions about how to deal with coordination problems in homeland security. This chapter attempts to identify the key coordination problems in implementing homeland security policy and offers some modest suggestions for improving the domestic security delivery system.

There are several what might be termed "first principles" under-girding this chapter. First, implementing homeland security policy involves all levels of government (federal, state, and local), organizations and groups in the private and not-for-profit sectors, and individual citizens. Complicating matters is the fact that the United States has a highly decentralized political system. There are approximately 88,000 separate government entities in the U.S., when school districts, special districts, counties, cities and municipalities are included. Coordination between levels of government, between governments in the same region, and between governmental agencies and the private and non-profit sectors is often problematic.

Second, many functional domains—such as intelligence, law enforcement, fire services, emergency medical services, public health, emergency management, and the military—play an important role in implementing domestic security policy. Owing to differing professional perspectives, competing organizational cultures and missions, and the desire for bureaucratic autonomy, coordination of effort is difficult to achieve among the agencies and organizations charged with protecting the public.

Third, homeland security is only one of many public problems competing for scarce resources. Citizens continue to expect high quality schools, good environmental quality, adequate health care, and all of the other goods and services delivered through public programs.

Fourth, the structure of homeland security in the United States is a work in progress. There is still considerable uncertainty regarding the appropriate roles and responsibilities of federal, state, and local governmental entities, the best way to create effective partnerships, the proper mix of policy tools to enhance domestic security, and the way to develop performance indicators for measuring progress toward objectives.

This chapter proceeds as follows. It first will briefly summarize the current organizational structure of homeland security in the United States, highlighting the inter-governmental and multi-disciplinary nature of the task. The argument advanced here is that the coordination of multi-organizational, multi-jurisdictional networks through all phases of the cycle of homeland security activities (prevention, preparedness, response and recovery) is the primary problem facing the designers of domestic security policy. Second, this chapter discusses some of the primary impediments to effective coordination and implementation of homeland security policy. Third, it examines some lessons gleaned from the social science research literature that can be applied to the organizational problems associated with domestic security policy. The primary focus here will be on the literatures concerned with disaster preparedness and response, complex system reliability, and organizational network theory. Finally, this chapter discusses several issues where theory has not yet caught up with practice and suggests some potentially useful avenues for future research.

## The Organization of Homeland Security in the United States

At the federal level, the Department of Homeland Security (DHS) has the primary responsibility for administering domestic security policy. Created on March 1, 2003, DHS merged the functions of twenty-two separate agencies into one cabinet-level department. DHS is organized around four collections of related programs called directorates: Border and Transportation Security (BTS); Emergency Preparedness and Response (ERP); Science and Technology (S&T); and Information Analysis and Infrastructure Protection (IAIP). The Coast Guard, the Bureau of Citizenship and Immigration Services, the Secret Service, and the Office of State and Local Coordination (which administers grants) all report directly to the Secretary of Homeland Security.[1] Of the directorates, BTS has the largest budget and administers programs with the highest public profile. BTS includes the Transportation Security Administration (TSA), Immigration and Customs Enforcement (ICE) (which enforces immigration policy primarily by apprehending those in the country illegally), and Customs and Border Protection (which protects the borders themselves). The proposed DHS budget for fiscal year 2005 is approximately $40 billion (an increase of approximately 10 percent over 2004), or about 2 percent of the entire federal budget. As of March 1, 2004, DHS had 160,000 full time employees. More than half of all DHS employees work for the BTS directorate, and over 70 percent of these work as baggage screeners at airports for TSA.

Despite the wide-ranging activities of DHS, many of the tasks associated with homeland security take place elsewhere, either in the agencies of state and local governments, in other federal agencies, or in the private or not-for-profit sectors. Fewer than 15 percent of all law enforcement personnel in the United States work for the federal government, and less than half of these work for DHS (Lehrer, 2004). Besides being the main locus of first responders, state and local governments are the primary administrators of disaster mitigation policies, and emergency preparedness and response plans. Although FEMA personnel help coordinate activities following most major disasters (primarily through disaster assistance programs), it only has about 1,700 employees. Compared to state and local governments, the reach of DHS is relatively limited. DHS employees are highly concentrated in and around major cities, and in border and coastal regions. In fact, DHS employees are present in only 625 of the nation's 3,146 counties (or 20 percent). Many other functions related to homeland security such as intelligence gathering (FBI), tracking terrorist financing (the Drug Enforcement Agency), and investigating bombings (the Bureau of Alcohol, Tobacco, Firearms, and Explosives) are also conducted outside of DHS. Finally, homeland security is also the responsibility of private companies and non-profit agencies. According to a White House Homeland Security Presidential Directive issued on December 17, 2003, 85 percent of the critical security infrastructure in the United States is held in private hands. Finally, as the case of the philanthropic response following the attacks of September 11 demonstrates, government-funded victim assistance was only a very small part of the total aid rendered to those who suffered economic or psychological harm. Historically, insurance companies and the not-for-profit sectors have provided significant portions of disaster recovery resources.

This brief review highlights several important aspects of the structure of homeland security in the United States. First, protecting the nation from acts of terrorism involves the activities of people with multiple functional specializations. Decades of research on organizations has consistently shown that collective action is more difficult when specialized training and role-based incentives focus on discrete parts of the overall task.[2] In addition, although DHS receives much of the media and the public's attention, it is clear that implementing homeland security is a complex undertaking involving many agencies, organizations, and levels of government. As Charles Wise puts it, "the organizational issue of homeland security implicates the organizations of various venues, including the organization of individual federal departments and agencies, state and local governmental organizations, and private-sector organizations, as well as their relationships with each other" (2002: 131).

## Problems in Coordination

Developing and implementing a national homeland security is primarily an organizational design problem. In his recent book, which examines the impact of the September 11 attacks on the American political system, Don Kettl puts the matter starkly when he writes that "Homeland Security, at its core, is about coordination" (2004: 28). For students of organizations and public management, this is not a new concern. However, given the potential for mass casualties and fatalities resulting from terrorist attacks, the issue has added importance in this policy arena.

There are at least three areas where coordination problems arise in homeland security. First, large-scale formal organizations often find it difficult to coordinate the efforts of their sub-units. This coordination problem is typically not the result of people intentionally acting in dysfunctional ways, but rather results from individual units (usually staffed by specialized experts in a single field) following incentives to focus on only a small part of the big picture.[3] This problem is exacerbated when a number of agencies with pre-existing missions and organizational cultures are merged, as in the case of DHS. Some of the recent criticisms of DHS focus on this very point (Crowley, 2004). Eli Lehrer points out that nearly all of the agencies that became part of DHS have long-standing missions that are only tangentially related to homeland security and, as a consequence, "homeland security remains for many of them a second-level priority" (2004: 76). The existence of pre-existing goals and objectives in FEMA (natural disaster mitigation and victim assistance), the Secret Service (dignitary protection and counterfeiting), Immigration and Customs Enforcement (undocumented workers), Customs and Border Protection (border management and drug smuggling), and the Coast Guard (national maritime police force) makes it much more difficult for DHS to coordinate its activities and to focus on terrorism. This problem is also present in the local government context and is exacerbated by the fact that public safety agencies at these levels of government have many responsibilities in addition to homeland security.

A second coordination problem arises when multiple organizations in a given policy arena have overlapping responsibilities and must work together to address public problems. Most public problems are not neatly subdivided so that individual agencies can work on them in isolation. Instead, complex inter-organizational networks develop or emerge. Networks are "structures of interdependence involving multiple organizations or parts thereof, where one unit is not merely the formal subordinate of the others in some larger hierarchical arrangement" (O'Toole, 1997: 45). Networks composed of multiple organizations do not rely solely on formal authority to guide their activities; they also involve exchange relations and coalitions built around common interests. Under certain conditions—such as when network goals are relatively clear, responsibilities are neatly divided among member organizations, and there exist high levels of support for the purposes of the network arrangement—multi-organizational systems can be quite successful as coordinating mechanisms.

In the context of the terrorist threat, there are many examples of the necessity of inter-organizational coordination. At the federal level, gathering and analyzing intelligence, at a minimum, requires the coordinated action of the CIA, FBI, DHS—and, depending on the type of threat, will require coordination of state and local law enforcement officers, border security personnel, and others. The breakdowns in this area, detailed in the *9/11 Commission Report,* demonstrate the difficulties inherent in such an undertaking. Even though FBI agents in Arizona, Florida, and Minnesota each separately were concerned that young Arab men were learning to fly large commercial airliners, no connection between them was made.[4] At the local government level, disaster planning and response requires joint action from emergency management officials, from law enforcement, fire, emergency medical technicians, public health professionals, and, again depending on the type of disaster, from building inspectors, engineers, food safety experts, and transportation and utility officials. Although many of the so-called "first responders" acted with extreme bravery following the attacks on the World Trade Center towers, coordination problems between the New York Police Department and Fire Department ultimately contributed to the loss of life of many firefighters and police officers (National Commission, 2004, chapter 9).

The third coordination problem is caused by the highly decentralized nature of the American political system and the necessity for various units of government to work together. A common misconception about the American political system is that cities, counties, school districts, and the states have a legal obligation to the federal government or to each other. Instead, each governmental jurisdiction is legally and politically autonomous, though they are highly interdependent. Since each governmental unit is responsible to a different constituency and sees national problems from a localized perspective, tensions are bound to surface.

A number of organizations have weighed in on the importance of the intergovernmental relations component in homeland security. For example, the National Academy of Public Administration (NAPA, 2004) recently issued a report in which it identified some of the challenges of managing intergovernmental relations for homeland security. Among them are:

1. City and state officials lack common understanding of the functions, mandates, goals, outcomes, and their roles for homeland security.
2. Trust, necessary to make homeland security intergovernmental partnerships work, is lacking among many city and state officials.
3. Networks of governmental and quasi-governmental agencies are highly complex.
4. Limited authority—legal or political—prevents top-down command and control.
5. Some cities, states, and federal agencies lack capacity to be effective partners.

Besides the tensions between the federal government and state and local governments, coordination is also difficult between and among sub-national governments. In October 2002, the Century Foundation (formerly the 20th Century Fund) commissioned reports on the homeland security activities in four states (Pennsylvania, Texas, Washington, and Wisconsin).[5] The reports are remarkably similar in their central findings with regard to the challenges of coordination. For example, although much progress has been made in homeland security preparedness in the state of Washington, officials interviewed for the report admitted that coordination within the state was problematic (Stehr, 2003). Among their concerns:

- Regionally based planning is problematic due to resistance by locally elected officials, lack of trust between officials in different jurisdictions or disciplines, and competition over resources.
- Disparities between large and small jurisdictions in the areas of resources and consequence management capacity have widened.
- Concerns have been expressed by local governments that state and federal officials are insufficiently knowledgeable about resource needs in cities and counties to make effective decisions about what initiatives to undertake.

It is unrealistic to expect these and other coordination problems to magically disappear. There are honest differences in opinion regarding what the term homeland security means, what a national strategy to address domestic security strategy should look like, and which threats should be taken most seriously. This does not mean, however, that we cannot take steps to improve the organizational design of homeland security. Social scientists have a long-standing interest in how to make large-scale, complex organizational systems more reliable in their performance under extreme conditions (Baker and Chapman, 1962; Perrow, 1999; Sagan, 1993). We will now turn our attention to some of the lessons learned from this line of inquiry.

## Lessons From Social Science Research

*Lesson Number One: Do not assume that a centralized organizational structure is appropriate for all types of homeland security problems.*

As a starting point, discussions about the appropriate organizational design for homeland security should avoid making simplistic assumptions about the type of organizational structure required. As March and Cohen (1984) point out, government reform efforts are typically based on political considerations and not on a clear understanding of how best to match processes to goals. In a similar vein, Knott and Miller (1987) make a compelling case that the selection of the standard, hierarchical design, based on specialization and rules, satisfies the political needs of the main stakeholders in the federal administrative apparatus, and thus is widely adopted even when conditions may not warrant this organizational form. The reorganization of homeland security activities and the creation of DHS appears to follow the pattern of designing structures based on the familiar hierarchical approach. So too does the recommendation of the 9/11 Commission that intelligence gathering and dissemination be placed in the hands of a national terrorist information center headed by an intelligence "czar" (National Commission, 2004). But the adoption of hierarchical designs and processes is likely to be particularly unsuitable for organizations that operate in complex, dynamic, and unstable environments. Complex organizational environments create the need for greater decentralization of authority and less emphasis on formal structures (Rainey, 1997; Thompson, 1967).

Charles Wise asks, "Which approach to organizing homeland security: hierarchy or network" (Wise, 2002:141)? He points out that many of the problems of coordination in the area of homeland security are probably not amendable to hierarchical solutions. To be effective, top-down coordination requires an understanding of which organizations need to be coordinated and what their relationships should be, and an agreement on what objectives each unit needs to accomplish to reach the overall goal. None of these requirements are currently met in the area of homeland security. We are, according to Wise, in the process of discovering the appropriate network (or more accurately, the *networks*) of organizations, and determining what their relationships should be. Thus, a workable organizational design for homeland security will require a better understanding of the operational qualities of this policy arena.

The lesson that should be drawn from this discussion is not that hierarchical approaches to organizing for homeland security are necessarily ineffectual. Instead, the lesson is that the creation of an appropriate organizational design for implementing national security policy should be treated as a hypothesis and that, presumably, a suitable mix of hierarchy, informal coordination, and self-organization can be discovered.

### *Lesson Number Two*: *Strike a balance between anticipation and resilience.*

In *Searching for Safety* (1988), Aaron Wildavsky develops a theory that accounts for the considerable degree of safety present in contemporary societies even in the face of increasing technological risks. In this study, he contrasts a strategy of anticipation (which assumes the ability to plan for catastrophic events as a way of eliminating or reducing their effects before they occur) with a strategy of resilience (which assumes a capacity to reorganize resources and engage in adaptive behaviors after an event has occurred). According to Wildavsky, "anticipation is a mode of control by a central mind; efforts are made to predict and prevent potential dangers before damage is done" (1988: 77). Resilience, in contrast, is the "capacity to cope with unanticipated dangers after they have become manifest, learning to bounce back" (1988:77). Whereas anticipation involves "predicting hazards, specialized protections, centralization, and detailed standards," resilience is developed by "trial and error, general capacities, and decentralization" (1988: 224). Wildavsky concluded that seeking a balance between anticipation and resilience is the most beneficial strategy for coping with potential risks.

Although difficult to quantify, a case can be made that the current homeland security structure favors anticipation over resilience. As noted above, the resources of DHS are largely committed to border and transportation security, and to intelligence gathering. But community resilience should also be an important component of a national homeland security policy. As a recent RAND Corporation report puts it, "All terrorism is local" (RAND, 2004:4). Although there has been a dramatic increase in federal spending for homeland security, it is not clear that many American citizens can count on an adequate level of security in their communities.

Ashton Carter recommends that governments in the United States embark on a multi-year, multi-agency effort to combat catastrophic terrorism (Carter, 2001/2002). His analogy for this task is the Cold War. Following the detonation of an atomic bomb by the Soviet Union in 1949, Americans confronted the fact that a distant enemy could visit unimaginable damage on the U.S. Carter writes "the nation mobilized over time a response that was multi-faceted, multi-agency, and inventive" (p. 13). The response included aspects of deterrence and retaliation (nuclear bombers, missiles, submarines), warning (spy satellites), civil defense (to minimize casualties), and research and development (e.g., the creation of think tanks like the RAND corporation). A similar approach could be adopted for current homeland security challenges.

***Lesson Number Three: Build Community and Organizational Network Capacity.***
One way to increase community resilience is to enhance organizational network capacity. H. Brinton Milward and Keith Provan have been among the leaders in evaluating the determinants of success in public sector inter-organizational networks. They argue that there are three levels of network analysis: community, network, and organization/participant levels (Provan and Milward, 2001; cf. Provan and Milward, 1995). This scheme allows for a relatively inclusive approach to identifying key stakeholder groups and network effectiveness criteria at each level. While Provan and Milward have focused their work on the delivery of health and human service programs, others have applied this reasoning to large-scale disasters. For example, a number of researchers have found that the degree of integration among organizations that comprise the emergency response network *prior to* disasters is a reliable predictor of readiness and response effectiveness (Carley and Harrald, 1997; Gillespie, et al., 1993; Drabek, 1986; cf. Stehr, 1999). In their major study of community preparedness, Gillespie and his colleagues concluded that disaster preparedness predicts response effectiveness, and that the structure of inter-organizational relations predicts disaster preparedness (1993, p. 97-98).

The application of these research findings to homeland security policy should be evident. Efforts should be undertaken to find existing gaps in collaborative capacity and, where possible, to provide incentives for network participation such as reciprocation agreements, shared training and educational experiences, mutual response assurances, and network budget allocations. As for network centralization, Bardach (2001) suggests that inter-organizational coordination requires "managerial craftsmanship." The components of managerial craftsmanship include acceptance of leadership, an effective communication network, trust, and continuous learning. At the local level, the logical locus of craftsmanship for homeland security is the community emergency management director. One positive outcome of the attacks of September 11 is the elevation in stature of the emergency manager. Once relegated to a more peripheral role in policy making, emergency managers are now an increasingly important player in developing and maintaining local homeland security policies.

***Lesson Number Four: Assume That Homeland Security Systems Will Sometimes Fail.***

In a sobering assessment of the final report of the 9/11 Commission, Richard Posner writes that "the tale of how we were surprised by the 9/11 attacks is a product of hindsight; it could not be otherwise. And with the aid of hindsight it is easy to identify missed opportunities (though fewer than had been suspected) to have prevented the attacks, and tempting to leap from that observation to the conclusion that the failure to prevent them was the result of not of bad luck, the enemy's skill and ingenuity or the difficulty of defending against suicide attacks or protecting an almost infinite array of potential targets, but of systematic failures in the nation's intelligence and security apparatus that can be corrected by changing the apparatus" (Posner, 2004). Posner's view, elaborated more fully in the essay, is that no amount of planning or structural changes in our homeland security system will make us completely safe. This sentiment nicely summarizes the final lesson presented in this paper: the organization of homeland security should incorporate an assumption that sometimes systems will fail.

Posner's viewpoint has its adherents among some organizational theorists. Martin Landau and Donald Chisholm believe we should begin from the standpoint that "the most important fact that can be known about organization, any organization, is that it is error-prone" (Landau and Chisholm, 1994). They counsel that we should embrace what they term "failure-avoidance management" as opposed to the more typical, optimistic "success-oriented management," and that norms of organizational efficiency should be replaced with norms of organizational reliability. In a similar vein, Charles Perrow (1999) developed a theory of "normal accidents" that advances the argument that systems that are interactively complex and tightly-coupled will be struck by accidents that cannot be predicted. Because of the complexity, independent failures will interact in ways that can neither be foreseen by system designers nor comprehended by system operators. If the system is tightly-coupled (that is, if what happens in one part of the system has a direct impact on the other parts of the system), the failures will rapidly escalate out of control. Finally, Lee Clarke (1999) argues that we should not have too much faith in disaster planning and management. In Clarke's view, planning for catastrophic events is primarily an exercise in symbolism. The aim of preparation is not to develop realistic assumptions and scenarios about what is likely to happen, but rather is focused on convincing key stakeholders that risks can be controlled.

Why Americans and the designers of American public policies are loathe to admit that system failure is possible—even when these failures are conspicuous—is a complex story. Part of this story surely rests on Americans' faith in technological fixes combined with a "can do" attitude that makes admitting the potential for error unthinkable. In homeland security planning, however, the costs of not preparing for system error could be catastrophic. But what can be done to prepare for "institutional disappointment"? One suggestion is to employ some well-known fault analysis techniques that are used in the field of engineering. These could include identifying experts who, in a disinterested manner, approach a design or plan with the expressed purpose of uncovering failure and to estimate the consequences of such failure for the system (Landau and Chisholm, 1994). Another approach might involve adopting a standard method from military organizations: competing red and blue teams (Carter, 2001/2002). In these exercises, the red team tries to devise attack tactics, and the blue team tries to devise countermeasures. A number of other system evaluation techniques such as pre-audits and post-audits might be employed to detect, identify, and isolate potential for organizational error in homeland security systems.

## Conclusion

This paper has identified some of the important coordination and organizational challenges associated with designing and implementing homeland security policy. It also offers some tentative lessons mined from the social science research literature regarding what can be done to develop a more effective approach to domestic security. In closing, I would like to emphasize that it is crucial that the structures of homeland security in the United States be developed based on the foundations of accumulated knowledge and on empirical research that will be conducted in the future. The security of the nation hinges on the ability of policy makers to cast aside old assumptions and stereotypes about organizational design and to embrace innovative ways of thinking about homeland security.

## Notes

1. For more in-depth discussions of the creation and activities of DHS see Kettl, 2004 and Lehrer, 2004.
2. See Wilson (2000) for a discussion of this research.
3. See Knott and Miller (1987) discuss what they call "trained incapacity."
4. As part of his study of serial killers, Steven Egger (1984) coined the term "linkage blindness" to describe the failure to note connections between seemingly discrete events that later are shown to have been highly interdependent.
5. These reports may be accessed at the Century Foundation's website (www.tcf.org) under the Homeland Security Project.

## References

Baker, George W. and Dwight W. Chapman, 1962. *Man and Society in Disaster*. New York, Basic Books.

Bardach, Eugene, 2001. "Developmental Dynamics: Interagency Collaboration as an Emergent Phenomenon." *Journal of Public Administration Research and Theory*. 11: 149-164.

Carley, K.M. and Harrald, J.R., 1997. "Organizational Learning Under Fire: Theory and Practice." *American Behavioral Scientist*. (January), 40:310-332.

Carter, Ashton, B., 2001/2002. "The Architecture of Government in the Face of Terrorism." *International Security*, Winter, 26:5-23.

Clarke, Lee, 1999. *Mission Improbable: Using Fantasy Documents to Tame Disaster*. Chicago: University of Chicago Press.

Crowly, Michael, 2004. "Playing Defense: Bush's Disastrous Homeland Security Department." *The New Republic*, (March 15) issue 4,652: 17-21.

Drabek, Tom E., 2003. *Strategies for Coordinating Disaster Responses*. Institute of Behavioral Science, Natural Hazards Research and Application Information Center, University of Colorado, Monograph #61.

Drabek, Tom E. 1986. *Human System Responses to Disaster: An Inventory of Sociological Findings*. New York: Springer-Verlag.

Egger, Steven A., 1984. "A Working Definition of Serial Murder and the Reduction of Linkage Blindness." *Journal of Police Science and Administration*. 12:348-357.

Gillespie, D. et al.,1993. *Partnerships for Community Preparedness*. Institute of Behavioral Science, University of Colorado, Boulder.

Kettl, Donald F., 2002. "Promoting State and Local Government Performance for Homeland Security." The Century Foundation Homeland Security Project. Available at www.tcf.org.

Kettl, Donald F., 2004. *System Under Stress: Homeland Security and American Politics*. Washington, D.C.: CQ Press.

Knott, Jack and Gary Miller, 1987. *Reforming Bureaucracy: The Politics of Institutional Choice*. Englewood Cliffs, NJ: Prentice-Hall.

Landau, Martin and Donald Chisholm, 1994. "The Arrogance of Optimism." *Journal of Contingencies and Crisis Management*. (March) 2:37-45.

Lehrer, Eli, 2004. "The Homeland Security Bureaucracy." *The Public Interest*, (Summer) Number 156, pp. 71-85.

May, Peter, 1988. "Disaster Recovery and Reconstruction." In Louise Comfort (editor) *Managing Disasters: Strategies and Policy Perspectives*. Durham, NC: Duke University Press, pp. 236-251.

National Commission, 2004. *The 9/11 Commission Report*. The Final Report of the National Commission on Terrorist Attacks Upon the United States. New York: W.W. Norton & Company.

NAPA, 2004. "Advancing the Management of Homeland Security: Managing Intergovernmental Relations for Homeland Security." Washington, D.C.: National Academy of Public Administration.

O'Toole, Laurence J., 1997. "Treating Networks Seriously: Practical and Research-based Agendas in Public Administration." *Public Administration Review*, volume 57 number 1: 45-52.

Perrow, Charles C., 1999. *Normal Accidents: Living With High Risk Technologies.* (second edition) Princeton, NJ: Princeton University Press.

Posner, Richard A., 2004. "The 9/11 Report: A Dissent." *The New York Times*, August 29, Sunday Book Review, p. 1.

Provan, Keith G. and H. Brinton Milward, 2001. "Do Networks Really Work? A Framework For Evaluating Public-Sector Organizational Networks." *Pubic Administration Review* (July/August), 61: 414-423.

Provan, Keith G. and H. Brinton Milward, 1995. "A Preliminary Theory of Interorganizational Network Effectiveness: A Comparative Study of Four Community Mental Health Systems." *Administrative Science Quarterly*. 40:1-33.

RAND Corporation, 2004. "Empowering State and Local Emergency Preparedness: Recommendations of the Advisory Panel to Assess Domestic Response Capabilities for Terrorism Involving Weapons of Mass Destruction." Available at www.rand.org.

Sagan, Scott. 1993. *The Limits of Safety: Organizations, Accidents, and Nuclear Weapons.* Princeton, NJ: Princeton University Press.

Stehr, Steven D., 2003. "Homeland Security in the State of Washington: A Baseline Report on the Activities of State and Local Governments." A report for the Century Foundation's Homeland Security Project. Available at www.tcf.org.

Stehr, Steven D., 1999. "Community Recovery and Reconstruction Following Disasters." Ali Farazmand (editor), *Handbook of Crisis and Emergency Management*, New York: Marcel Dekker.

Thompson, James D., 1967. *Organizations in Action.* New York: McGraw-Hill.

Wildavsky, Aaron, 1988. *Searching For Safety.* London: Transaction Books.

Wilson, James Q., 2000. *Bureaucracy: What Government Agencies Do and Why They Do It.* (new edition), New York: Basic Books.

Wise, Charles, 2002. "Organizing For Homeland Security." *Public Administration Review*, volume 62, number 2: 131-144.

# ten

# Risk Perceptions in the Risk Society: The Cognitive Architecture of Risk of Japanese and Americans

## Eugene A. Rosa and Noriyuki Matsuda

## Introduction

The dropping of atomic bombs on Japan in 1945 brought World War II to an abrupt end. But nuclear technology not only ended a war, it also launched an entirely new phase in history—the nuclear age, an age textured with technologies of increasing complexity. Nuclear weapons and nuclear power plants present unavoidable risks. But these are not the only technological risks of a post-modern world. Other complicated, risky technologies—such as newer chemicals that are more complex and toxic, or genetic engineering—have also contributed to the growing world matrix of technological risks.

The apparent, unprecedented growth in complex, risky technologies has attracted the lens of sociologists, and neologisms have been created for sociological theory. German theorist Ulrich Beck (1986) has defined the contemporary era as the "Risk Society," Anthony Giddens (1990) situates risk as the key consequence of a post-modern world, and Nico Stehr (2001) defines the contemporary era as the "Fragile Society." Insofar as these theoretical characterizations are accurate we can ask: How do the citizens of the post-modern era understand the risks they face? And in particular: How do citizens in two of the most technologically advanced nations, Japan and the United States, consider risks? These questions frame the research reported here.

A context of cultural variability, such as a comparison between Japan and the U.S., provides the ideal setting for uncovering fundamental human processes—perceptual, analytic, emotional, and behavioral—that may overpower the deep and pervasive influence of culture. Assessing and responding to risk is an unavoidable and universal feature of human existence—from the distant past to the present the very survival of the species depends upon it. Hence, because they are all members of a single species, *homo sapien sapien,* it is reasonable to expect commonality for certain fundamental cognitive processes in all humans, irrespective of cultural context. Risk may be one stimulus that activates this commonality. And a cross-cultural orientation is especially applicable to an understanding of risk perceptions. The idea of risk taps into one of the most universal of human experiences: uncertainty. Humans have always lived and will always live in a world of both knowledge and uncertainty. In addition, risk, itself, embeds uncertainty. One of the most explicit recognitions of the role of uncertainty, embedded in the idea of risk, is the definition by Rosa (1998): "Risk is a situation or event where something of human value (including humans themselves) is at *stake* and where the outcome is *uncertain*."

To summarize, on the one hand, uncertainty is a condition of ubiquity across time and place, and on the other hand, an indispensable defining feature of risk. Risk, it follows, is also a universal human condition across time and place. This ontological foundation leads to a pair of competing hypothesis to guide research: (i) risks are expected to be perceived in the same basic way across cultures because humans—as a single species—have a common cognitive architecture that filters perceptions in the same basic way; or, (ii) human perceptions (including perceptions of risk or uncertainty) are so embedded within cultural meanings that they are expected to exhibit the same variability as for other aspects of human experience.

Hypothesis (i) derives from recognition of the unique qualities of the human species, especially qualities that reveal the complex cognitive structures common to humans everywhere. As a single species it is assumed that humans (*homo sapien sapiens*) have a common cognitive means for processing complex inputs along multiple channels. Hence, we would expect humans everywhere to process perceptions, thoughts, and memories and to make judgments and decisions using a common set of neurological algorithms. As aptly expressed by Nyland, "These aspects of our experiences will be stored in our memories, in a kind of structure, or a cognitive map of reality. A cognitive map is understood as a kind of structure, that is, an abstract representation of events, objects, and relationships in the real world" (1993:2).

Hence, with proper stimuli and with proper techniques it should be possible to tap into the cognitive architecture and represent its stored structures as cognitive maps. Cognitive psychology has studied such stimuli and has developed techniques for the mapping of perceptions, including risk perceptions. Examples are legion in that literature. Because of the common cognitive architecture underlying all human thought, hypothesis predicts cognitive maps that are culturally invariant.

Hypothesis (ii), derived from cultural theory, challenges the expectation that risk perceptions are invariable across cultures. While it may be true that the human species is partly defined by a common cognitive architecture, it does not necessarily follow that that architecture will process the multitude of environmental inputs in one way or in similar ways. Instead, this architecture—basically a raw, pre-programmed structure—may be *tabula rasa,* i.e., little more than a neurological readiness for complex reasoning. Cultural theorists such as Douglas and Wildavsky (1982) and Thompson, Ellis, and Wildavsky (1990) would argue that this structure requires programmed meaning to function—the very meaning that is provided by culture.

## Cross-cultural Studies

With few exceptions cross-cultural studies of risk perceptions have adopted the psychometric paradigm developed by Paul Slovic and his colleagues at Decision Research in Eugene,

Oregon (Lichtenstein, Slovic, Layman & Combs, 1978; Slovic, Fischhoff & Lichtenstein, 1985; Slovic, 1987). The psychometric paradigm emphasizes the use of psychophysical scaling and multivariate techniques (especially factor analysis) to create quantified cognitive risk maps. The research within this paradigm has shown that risk perceptions can be mapped via factor analysis with a relatively simple structure. In particular, a two-factor structure typically accounts for a clear majority (roughly 70 percent to nearly 90 percent) of the variance in risk perceptions. The first factor is labeled dread risk and the second is labeled unknown risk.

Using psychometric techniques comparable to those applied to U.S. samples, risk perception data, to date, have been collected in Hungary (Englander, Farago, Slovic, & Fischhoff, 1986), Norway (Teigen, Brun, & Slovic, 1988), Hong Kong (Keown, 1989), Poland (Goszczynzka, Tyszka, and Slovic, 1991), France (Karpowicz-Lazreg and Mullet 1993), and Sweden and Brazil (Nyland, 1993). Most striking is the general finding that for each of the sampled cultures, just as for the U.S., a two-part structure emerges. Moreover, almost without exception, the two factors are most aptly labeled "dread" and "unknown," again displaying consistency with the U.S. findings. In very general terms, then, people in diverse cultures apparently characterize their risk environments in similar ways.

As favorable as this evidence may be for claims of universal cognitive processing of risk stimuli—support for hypothesis (i)—there are good reasons to exercise caution before cementing such a conclusion. First, despite the apparent similarity in the overall cognitive maps, there were a number of differences in the perception of individual risks. For example, while Americans in these studies were often most concerned with unknown risks, members of the other cultures were often most concerned with known risks. Second, a common methodological flaw weakens virtually all cross-cultural studies where the United States is one of the comparative cultures: the failure to collect U.S. data concurrently with the collection of the other comparative cultural data. Instead, recent data from the other cultures are usually compared to U.S. data that are typically over two decades old. This practice is questionable because it assumes that the risk perceptions of Americans are stable and, therefore, always appropriate for comparative analysis. Available evidence, however, suggests that American risk perceptions have been changing (Kraus and Slovic, 1988; Keown, 1989). Finally, a third methodological flaw is that all comparisons are with societies that are either relatively small (geographically and in population size), such as Hong Kong and Hungary, or are part of a Western cultural tradition. These methodological practices raise further questions about the true comparability of the samples examined.

## Japan: Paradigm Comparative Culture

There are three conditions which should be met before we can appropriately test for cultural differences: (i) the societies considered should have modern, complex technologies; (ii) the societies should share many common risks; and (iii) the societies considered should have cultures which are distinctly different. All of these conditions, we argue, are optimally met with a comparison between Japan and virtually any large, advanced Western society, such as the United States.

That Japanese history and culture is different from Western history and culture is a fact that virtually no one would dispute. Japan has a large population (at 127 million, the seventh largest in the world), and, like many societies in the West, Japan has clearly reached a stage of advanced industrialization—again like many societies in the West, its citizens are exposed to many of the same risks. A comparison between cultures with such distinct cultural traditions (between West and East) is a more reliable test of the universality hypothesis than, for example, a comparison between two Western cultures. For the substantive and methodological reasons outlined above, we focused on comparisons between Japanese and Americans. We refer to this as the Japan-US Research Program, or J-US.

## The J–US Research Program

The J-US Research Program comprises three distinct phases: Phase I, a pre-test phase, Phase II, an execution stage, and Phase III, a latent variable modeling stage.

*Samples*: College student samples were used in all phases of the research program. It is appropriate to note that college student samples, often viewed as a methodological shortcoming in research, can be viewed here as a special strength for several reasons. First, because the central concept under investigation is culture, by definition this means that any group sampled within the culture should bear its influence. Second, many of the risks being assessed are the result of recent developments in science or advanced technology. Proper assessment of these risks, then, requires some awareness on the part of respondents, and this is more assured with college students who are often well-informed on such matters. Third, college students are expected to have cognitive strategies focusing on perception, memory and thinking (Sears, 1986). Fourth, and most importantly, sociologists (Form, 1979) have identified a major concomitant of advanced industrialization (and the internationalization of economies) to be a "convergence" in the overall structure of societies, accompanied by growing similarities in attitudes and values. Colleges and universities are likely one setting where the impacts of changing values and attitudes are first experienced. This means, in turn, we would expect college student samples from two advanced societies, *ceteris paribus*, to be more similar than samples drawn from other settings. The net effect of this expectation is a more conservative, and therefore more rigorous, test of cultural differences.

*Phase I: Pre-test:* The principal objectives of this phase were to create a Japanese language version of the standard psychometric instrument used in previous studies, and to refine the research protocols for administering the instrument.

*Instrument Development*: Instrument development was accomplished in several steps. We began with the taxonomy of eighty-one risks and hazards, employing nine dimensions of risk evaluation that had been standardized and tested rigorously by Slovic and Lichtenstein (1985). We believed that a refined version of this instrument would permit valid, direct comparisons of risk perceptions between Japanese and Americans and would provide a baseline for future comparisons. Slovic and Lichtenstein (1985) later increased the number of dimensions to eighteen, but the added dimensions are far less empirically established. Next, the standard list of eighty-one risks and nine dimensions were modified to this cross-cultural context. Risks that did not exist in both cultures (e.g., high school football) or that did not have comparable rates of incidence or familiarity to both cultures (e.g. coal tar hair dyes) were removed. To preserve the factor space characteristics of the Slovic and Lichtenstein cognitive maps, approximately six risks were removed from each of the four quadrants of that factor space. In addition to the three nuclear issues included in the typical Slovic and Lichtenstein instrument, four additional nuclear risks (radioactive waste disposal, transportation of nuclear waste, nuclear power plant operation, and food irradiation) were included. Finally, newer cross-cultural risks (upper atmosphere ozone depletion, the greenhouse effect, dioxins, crime, pesticides, herbicides and AIDS), which had never before been examined, were added to the list. These modifications produced a final list of seventy risks. Table 1 is a complete list of the seventy risks.

## TABLE 1.
## LIST OF 70 RISKS AND HAZARDS FOR CROSS–CULTURAL RESEARCH

**Consumer Products**
1. Microwave Ovens
2. Food Preservatives
3. Saccharin
4. Caffeine
5. Chemical Cleaners
6. Electrical Appliances
7. Food Irradiation
8. Home Space Heaters

**Social and Medical Risks**
1. Prescription Drugs
2. Oral Contraceptives
3. X-rays
4. IUDs
5. Antibiotics
6. Aspirin
7. Vaccinations
8. DNA Research
9. Crime
10. Surgery
11. Alcoholic Diseases
12. Radiation Therapy
13. Alcohol Related Accidents
14. Motor Vehicle Accidents
15. AIDS
16. Handguns

**Voluntary Risks**
1. Skateboards
2. Smoking Tobacco
3. Trampolines
4. Downhill Skiing
5. Bicycles
6. Motorcycles
7. Fireworks
8. Hang Gliding
9. Railroad Accidents
10. Commercial Aviation

**Environmental Risks**
1. Fluoridated Water
2. Lead Paint
3. Leaded Gasoline
4. Electric Fields
5. Nitrogen Fertilizers
6. 2,4,5-T (Dioxins)
7. Pesticides
8. Asbestos
9. Mercury
10. Greenhouse Effect
11. Auto Exhaust Fumes
12. LNG Transport
13. Herbicides
14. Upper Ozone Depletion

**Non-nuclear Technologies**
1. Hydroelectric Power
2. Plastics (manufacture/disposal)
3. Synthetic Rubber Manufacture
4. Solar Electric
5. Fossil Fuel Electric Power
6. Heavy Farm Machinery
7. Elevators
8. Bridges (construction/use)
9. Coal Mining Diseases
10. Dams (construction/use)
11. Skyscraper Fires
12. Coal Mining Accidents
13. Non-nuclear Electric Power
14. Skyscrapers (build/maintain)
15. Dynamite

**Nuclear Technologies**
1. Transport Nuclear Materials
2. Nuclear Power Routine Radiation
3. Radioactive Waste Disposal
4. Nuclear Reactor Accidents
5. Nuclear Weapons Testing
6. Nuclear Power Production
7. Nuclear Weapons (war)

*Administration Protocol:* The completion of a risk questionnaire is a somewhat tedious and demanding task, susceptible to effects of fatigue and inattention. To reduce this susceptibility we sought to keep the amount of time necessary to complete the survey to less than sixty minutes. To accomplish this, only seven of the nine standard dimensions of risk evaluation were retained for this survey. Four of the risk dimensions retained (*controllable-uncontrollable, calm-dread, not catastrophic-catastrophic, and voluntary-involuntary*) were associated with the Dread-risk Factor in the typical Slovic and Lichtenstein study, and the other three risk dimensions (*known-unknown to the individual, old-new, and known-unknown to science*) were associated with the Unknown-risk Factor. These seven dimensions of risk perception have been identified by Slovic (1987, 1988) as having high factor loadings in previous research. The risk dimensions were described in a short question format and seven-point Likert-type scales were anchored by the descriptive bi-polar adjectives (e.g., dread-calm, new-old). The dimensions and response formats can be found in Rosa et al., 2000.

*Japanese Translations:* After constructing the English language version of the questionnaire, two Japanese native language translators were employed to translate the survey into standard Japanese language usage. Working independently, one translator provided a Japanese translation. The second translator back-translated this version into English. This procedure was followed until the back-translated version provided the same common meaning as the initial English version. As a further check two additional native-speaker Japanese translators revised and confirmed the accuracy of the translations. The translations were subject to further review and corroboration in Tokyo by native Japanese speakers at the Institute of Applied Energy and by risk experts at the National Institute of Police Science. A final confirmation of the accuracy of the translations and of the usefulness of the instrument was its adoption by the Institute of Applied Energy in Tokyo in surveys it conducted.

*Pre-test:* Two samples of college students were chosen for the initial evaluation of the revised psychometric instrument. The first sample of sixty-two (thirty-seven female and twenty-five male) U.S. college students (enrolled in upper-division social science classes at Washington State University, Pullman and Vancouver campuses), completed the survey during the summer term. The comparable sample of sixty-nine (twenty-one female and forty-seven male) Japanese college students also completed the survey during the same period. This second sample consisted of two separate groups, approximately equal in size, of Japanese students from a variety of Japanese universities temporarily located in the U.S. One group was enrolled in an intensive English language course at Washington State University. This group had recently arrived from Japan, had no previous exposure to American culture, and had low mastery of the English language. The other group consisted of Japanese veterinary students, who, as part of their training, attended clinical workshops in the U.S.: one week at the University of California-Davis and one week at Washington State University. Upon completion of the survey virtually every Japanese participant, with the aid of native speaking Japanese translators, was debriefed about their comprehension of the survey instrument. Of the sixty-nine Japanese participants, only four raised any questions about the meaning of survey items, and even here the discrepancies were too slight to seriously vitiate the substantive interpretations of these items. All Japanese participants received $10 in remuneration for completing the survey, while U. S. participants received additional points toward their course grade.

This pre-test confirmed our two key expectations. We were able to administer the instrument well within the hour time limit we had imposed: that is, the vast majority of students from both cultures completed the instrument in well under an hour, and none required over an hour. And based upon the feedback from primary translators and the native language reviewers, and upon the debriefing of subjects after the instrument had been completed, we were confident that we had created a common instrument (in two languages) that would produce valid results in both cultures.

*Results*: We performed a variety of analyses on this pre-test data. Since the results of those analyses have already appeared elsewhere (Kleinhesselink and Rosa, 1991) we will not reproduce them in detail here. Instead, we will summarize the key findings.

Frequency distributions, including means and standard deviations, were computed for each of the seventy risks and for each of the seven dimensions of risk. The Japanese sample tended to view the seventy risks and hazards as *older* (thirty-three vs. sixteen significant t-tests) and risks for which they had *more individual knowledge* (thirty-two vs. twelve significant t-tests). In contrast, the U.S. sample tended to view the seventy risks as *more controllable* (twenty-one vs. thirteen significant t-tests) *less dreaded* (twenty-two vs. seven significant t-tests) and *less catastrophic* (twenty-two vs. nine significant t-tests).

Following the procedures of Slovic and Lichtenstsin (1985) a correlation matrix of the responses on the seven dimensions of risk was obtained. These dimensions were factor-analyzed with a principal components method. For both samples a two-factor solution emerged, similar and consistent with all previous studies which use the procedures of the psychometric paradigm. And for both samples, the new-old, individual knowledge, and scientific knowledge dimensions had factor loadings that ranged from .73 to .84 while none of the other four dimensions had a loading higher than .44. This factor, previously identified as the Known-Unknown risk factor, explained 26 percent of the averaged variance. The catastrophic potential, controllability, voluntariness and dread dimensions had factor loadings ranging from .52 to .76 while none of the other three dimensions had loadings higher than .26. This factor has previously been identified as the Dread risk factor, and explained 33% of the averaged variance.

Taken together, the Dread factor and the Unknown factor, explained 60 percent of the variance in the American sample and 56 percent of the variance in the Japanese sample. While the amount of explained variance is somewhat lower than in previous studies, it is substantively consistent with those studies.

Following the procedures of Slovic and Lichtenstein (1985) two factor scores, a dread score and an unknown score, were computed for each of the seventy risks by weighting the ratings on each risk dimension proportionately to the importance of the dimension for the factor and summing over all dimensions. This weighted summation assigned high or low scores to individual risk items, depending upon whether the ratings were high or low on the dimensions most closely associated with each of the two factors. The results were plotted in a two-dimension factor space, producing a cognitive map for each sampled culture. The overall contours of the cognitive maps were quite similar for both cultures, suggesting that the "cognitive map" of risk perceptions has the same coordinates for both cultures. Furthermore, the Japanese and American contours were quite similar to the cognitive maps produced in previous studies in the United States and in other cultures studied so far.

While there were striking similarities between the two cultures—a common two-factor solution, and similar cognitive maps—there were also striking differences. The two cultures were most similar in the way in which *dread* was assigned to their perceptions of technological hazards. For example, the most dreaded activity in both cultures was nuclear war.

Additionally, in both cultures all seven nuclear issues (nuclear power production, nuclear weapons (war), transportation of radioactive materials, nuclear waste disposal, reactor accidents, nuclear weapons tests, and routine emissions of radioactive gases) were closely clustered together and highly dreaded.

However, while the clustering of nuclear issues at the extreme end of the dread dimension was similar between the two cultures, the clustering on the Known-Unknown risk dimension was quite different. To further explore these differences we computed the mean nuclear risk scores for both cultural samples on the three dimensions associated with the unknown risk factor. In the U.S. sample, nuclear risks were viewed as somewhat new, and as generally unknown both to the individual and to science. In contrast, these same nuclear risks were viewed as some of the most well known risks to the Japanese sample, i.e., older and better known to the individual and to science. For example, the average individual knowledge score of the seven nuclear risks was 3.07 for the Japanese sample and 5.84 for the U.S. sample on the 1-7 Likert scale. Likewise, the scientific knowledge average score was 3.84 for the Japanese sample and 6.31 for the U.S. sample. (For the knowledge dimension a high score means "unknown.") The old-new average score for the Japanese sample was 6.24 vs. 3.63 for the U.S. sample. (For the old-new dimension a high score means "old.") All twenty-one of the t-test comparisons for the three dimensions were significant. Furthermore, on a 7-point Likert scale, a score of four is neutral. Thus, in both a relative comparison between the two cultures and in the Likert scale comparison, Japanese citizens viewed nuclear issues as somewhat known while U.S. citizens viewed them as very much unknown.

Similarly, the Japanese students rated many of the medical and chemical risks as significantly older and more known than did the American students. At the same time, the Japanese students perceived a variety of voluntary risks (bicycles, downhill skiing, hang gliding, fireworks, skateboards, trampolines, electric appliances, etc.) as less known than did their American counterparts.

*Discussion*: The principal objectives of Phase I of the J-US Research Program—to create a Japanese language version of the standard psychometric instrument used in previous studies, and to refine the research protocols for administering the instrument—were effectively achieved. The final, refined instrument passed several levels of scrutiny regarding the validity of translation, including the scrutiny of the Japanese subjects who, during their debriefing, raised few questions about the meaning of the instrument's instructions or of its components. The protocols for administering the instrument were, likewise, refined and ultimately proved to be effective and practical. The pre-test results, especially for the American sample that could be compared directly to prior studies, also attested to the effectiveness of the refined instrument; the fact that the results were comparable to prior findings suggests that the instrument was tapping the same perceptual structure as the original instrument from which it was derived.

**Phase II: Execution of Data Collection:** The first objective of this stage was to collect samples of sufficient size in both cultures simultaneously for a variety of multivariate analyses. The second objective was to subject the data to analyses typical of the psychometric tradition. The key output of these analyses would be cognitive maps for the Japanese and American samples that could be compared to the pre-test results for consistency, and to prior American and other cross-cultural findings.

*Data Collection*: The risk instrument developed in Phase I was used to collect all subsequent data collected in the J-US Research Program. It was administered concurrently to samples of Japanese and American university students. A total of 152 U.S. male and female university students enrolled in psychology or sociology courses at Washington State University completed the risk instrument during the fall semester. During the same semester, 273 Japanese male and female university students, enrolled in psychology or social science courses at either Nihon University or the University of Tsukuba, also completed the risk instrument. Concurrently collected data, absent from nearly all prior cross-cultural studies, was an important element of this data-collection phase. This was an important step because mishaps, accidents, and disasters—and the media attention they attract—could contaminate differences found between cultures measured at two different points in time. Found differences might not be due to the shaping of culture, but, instead, might be an artifact of historical events.

*Results*: The data were first subjected to a straightforward comparison. The population means and standard deviations were computed for each of the seventy risks and for each of the seven dimensions of risk. Table 2 presents these means and standard deviations for the two samples on each of the seven dimensions after averaging respondent responses on all seventy risks and hazards.

## TABLE 2.

## COMPARISON OF MEANS AND STANDARD DEVIATIONS FOR THE SEVEN RISK DIMENSIONS AND PROPORTION OF SIGNIFICANT T–TEST COMPARISONS: JAPAN AND THE UNITED STATES

| Dimension[c] | Means and Standard Deviations[a] | | Number of Significant t-Test Comparisons[b] | |
|---|---|---|---|---|
| | Japan | U.S. | Japan>U.S. | U.S.>Japan |
| New/Old | 2.23 (1.92) | 2.54 (1.89) | 14 | 33[d] |
| Unknown to science | 3.21 (1.91) | 2.85 (1.66) | 35 | 21[d] |
| Unknown to individual | 3.77 (2.04) | 3.84 (1.83) | 29 | 29[d] |
| Involuntary | 4.39 (2.06) | 3.79 (2.16) | 38 | 10 |
| Uncontrollable | 3.46 (1.99) | 2.74 (2.00) | 51 | 2 |
| Dread/Calm | 4.35 (2.06) | 3.81 (1.92) | 43 | 5 |
| Catastrophic | 4.22 (2.18) | 3.99 (2.06) | 26 | 9 |

a Standard deviations in parentheses.
b Out of 70; p>.05.
c For each dimension, higher scores mean, respectively, newer, unknown to science, unknown to exposed individuals, involuntary, controllable, dread, and catastrophic.
d All seven nuclear risks included.

Table 2 also presents the number of significant t-tests (P<. 05) between the Japanese and American samples for each of the seventy risks and hazards evaluated within each of the seven dimensions of risk perception.

Patterns in this data resemble those found in the analyses of the pre-test data of Phase I. In general, the Japanese sample tended to view the seventy risks as *older* (thirty-three vs. fourteen significant t-tests) and as risks for which there were *less scientific knowledge* (thirty-five vs. twenty-one significant t-tests). There was no overall difference in individual knowledge (twenty-nine vs. twenty significant t-tests). A closer examination of the seven nuclear technology-related hazards (transporting nuclear materials, nuclear power-routine emissions, radioactive waste disposal, nuclear reactor accidents, nuclear weapons testing, nuclear power production, and nuclear weapons (war)), revealed a striking pattern of cultural differences; namely, that nuclear risks were perceived as *well-known* risks to the Japanese, but as moderately *unknown* risks to the Americans.

To further explore these differences, we computed the mean nuclear risk scores for each cultural sample on the three dimensions constituting the *unknown risk* factor. In the U.S. sample, nuclear risks generally fell on the neutral to unknown side of the scale both for individuals and for science. These risks were intermediate on the new-old dimension. In sharp contrast, the same seven nuclear risks were perceived to be some of the most well known risks to the Japanese: nuclear risks were perceived as older and more well known to individuals and to science. The average individual knowledge score for the seven nuclear risks was 2.39 for the Japanese sample and 4.50 for the American sample (here, a larger number means "newer," more "unknown to the individual," and more "unknown to science"). The old-new average score for the Japanese sample was 1.96, while for the U.S. sample it was 3.9. Likewise, the average scientific knowledge score was 2.05 for the Japanese and 4.01 for the Americans. All twenty-one t-test comparisons for the three dimensions were significant.

A score of four is the neutral point on a 7-point Likert scale. Thus, in all cases the average Japanese score was well below four, while the average American score was either very close to or above four. Thus, both in the relative comparison between the two cultures and in the Likert-type scale meaning comparison, Japanese students perceived nuclear risks as quite well known, while their American counterparts perceived them as slightly unknown or in between.

Examination of the dimensions—dread, controllability, voluntariness, catastrophic— associated with the *dread* risk factor revealed a mixed pattern of results for the seven nuclear items. On the dread dimension, literally all nuclear risks were more dreaded in Japan than in the United States. However, the overall relative difference was small (United States = 6.2 and Japan = 6.5). The 6+ scores for both cultures (on a 7-point Likert scale where the neutral point is 4) means that nuclear risks are highly dreaded in both cultures. On the other three dimensions constituting the dread factor—controllability, voluntariness, catastrophic—only a small fraction of t-test comparisons between the two samples was significant. Again, in both cultures the seven nuclear risks were viewed as highly uncontrollable, highly involuntary, and highly catastrophic.

As with the pre-test and as with other studies within the psychometric paradigm, we followed the factor analytic procedures of Slovic and Lichtenstein (1985). The factor analysis, consistent with all previous research, resulted in two factors: *dread* and *knowledge*. The two factors explain between 60 and 65 percent of the variance. Then, again consistent with established procedures, factor scores were computed for each of the seventy risks, first by weighting the numerical ratings on each risk dimension proportionately to the importance of the dimension for the factor, and by then summing over all dimensions. This weighted summation gives each of the individual seventy risks either a high or low score depending on whether the ratings are high or low on the dimensions most closely associated with each of the two factors. These results were then mapped for each sample separately into a two dimensional space. These cognitive maps are presented as Figures 1 and 2.

The *dread* risk axis comprises the four dimensions that loaded on this factor: dread-calm, uncontrollable-controllable, involuntary-voluntary, and catastrophic-not catastrophic. The *unknown* axis comprises the three dimensions that loaded on this factor: new-old, unknown-known to science, and unknown-known to individuals.

## Figure 1. Cognitive Map—United States Data

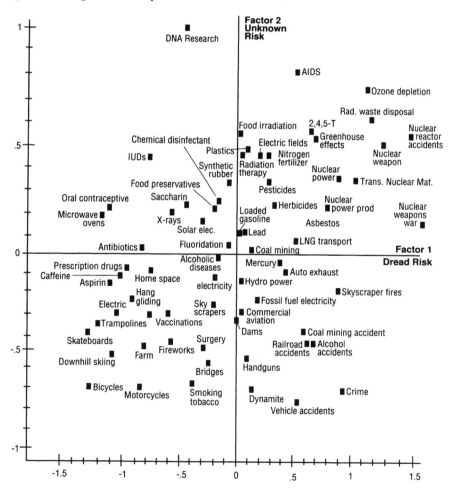

Perhaps the most compelling feature of the data for both samples is the clustering of the seven items related to nuclear technology. All nuclear items cluster together at the high dread end of the horizontal, dread axis. For Americans, nuclear war is particularly dreaded, a finding consistent with previous research (Slovic, Fischhoff, and Lichtenstein, 1985). The Japanese most dread a nuclear reactor accident. What is unmistakably clear is that nuclear risks evoke strong perceptions of dread in both cultures. At the same time, the cultures differ on the *unknown* risk factor—the vertical axis. All seven nuclear items are located on the upper section of that axis (the upper right quadrant) for the American sample, but on the lower section of that axis (the lower right quadrant) for the Japanese sample. As we found in the comparisons of means and in the t-tests performed above, the nuclear risks were perceived as somewhat unknown to Americans, but from somewhat to quite well known to Japanese.

## Figure 2. Cognitive Map—Japan Data

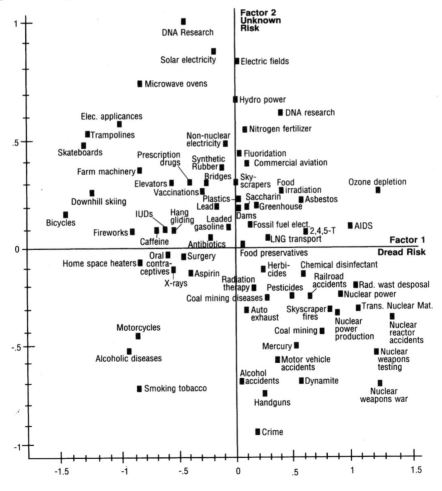

This finding warrants elaboration. That the Japanese perceived nuclear risks as old and better known and that Americans perceived them as newer and more unknown makes sense in a historical context. Japan is the only society ever to have had nuclear weapons used against it in war and is, therefore, the only society to have direct experience with the explosive destruction of nuclear weapons as well as the massive doses of radiation these weapons produced. The Nagasaki and Hiroshima bombings of August 1945 are a remembered wartime legacy in Japan. It is likely that this memory inclined the Japanese students to view all nuclear risks as older and better known than the American students.

*Discussion*: The chief objectives of Phase II of the WSU Research Program were to administer concurrently, to samples of Japanese and Americans, the instrument developed in Phase I, according to the protocols refined in Phase I. Both objectives were successfully attained. This resulted in a putatively valid and rich data set which could be used to subject the hypotheses underlying the entire research program to stringent tests.

The first set of tests using this data set yielded results that are interesting, on the one hand, and challenging on the other hand. With respect to the cognitive maps, we found it quite interesting that they were dimensionally equivalent: the maps represented a two-factor solution for both Japanese and Americans and explained similar amounts of variance for both. This provides some basis for arguing that the structure of risk perceptions in both cultures is, if not the same, at least quite similar. At the same time, we found differences in the positioning of certain clusters of risk items within the maps—the nuclear technology items being the most obvious of these.

The cognitive maps produced by our analyses can be viewed as analogous to geographic maps. In the latter case, if we asked individuals to draw a map of their own country, we would expect that most people could produce some version of their country. We would further expect variability in the accuracy of the elicited maps, but most people should be capable of providing some pictorial representation of their own country. Presumably, the representation would reflect the picture of their country's geography stored in their memory. Similarly, we would expect that the cognitive maps produced by individuals in our analyses, with the aid of the mathematics of scaling procedures, would be representative of the cognitive landscapes of those individuals. Maps created from specific elements within those landscapes, such as risk perceptions, should likewise be pictorial representations of that domain of the landscape.

In tying the cognitive maps produced by our data to the original analogy, we saw that geographical maps could provide a framework for interpreting our results. We found that the contours of the cognitive maps between Japanese and Americans were similar, but with discrepancies in content. This resembles a situation where, after being asked to draw a map of their own country, individuals produced general shapes that were more or less correct, but where specific landmarks—rivers, mountains, boundaries, etc.—were misplaced. Perhaps this is what we are observing in the cognitive maps of Japanese and Americans; they cognitively organize the collection of risks to which they are exposed within a space whose contours are similar, but the placement of items in each cognitive space is quite different.

These findings return us to the hypotheses underlying the research program. Because of the similarity in the contours of the Japanese and American cognitive maps, can we now conclude that the risk perceptions of Japanese and Americans are sufficiently similar to support the pancultural continuity expectation? Or, is the distribution of the individual risk items within the maps sufficiently different for us to conclude that culture exercises a significant shaping influence on risk perceptions? The results presented do not permit an un-equivocal answer to these questions. The analytic techniques used here, as elsewhere in the psychometric paradigm, are insufficiently refined to permit an answer to such a fine-tuned question. However, the more refined tool of multivariate causal modeling is sufficiently refined to use for such purposes.

*Phase III: Modeling:* The specific tool suited to the task at hand is the latent variable model. Phase III of the J-US Research Program comprised the development and testing of a variety of latent variable models with the Phase II data.

*Analytic Strategy:* We began by first modeling the sub-set of seven nuclear items (See Table 1) because of the interesting patterns they displayed the cognitive maps between Japanese and Americans, because they were the most dreaded items for both samples, and because they were where the most pronounced differences were found.

*Basic Model:* In a typical factor analysis within the psychometric tradition, factor scores (as above) are typically obtained by computing weighted averages for each risk dimension. This is done to reduce the data structure from three to two dimensions so that factor analyses can be performed. In our modeling efforts we took a slightly different approach. In particular we performed a factor analysis, for the nuclear technology items, on the individual risk items, and found that they loaded on certain risk dimensions. In other words, the measured perceptions of the individual risk items are the indicators of the risk dimensions—which in modeling language are called "latent constructs."

The factor loadings (343 in total) are not shown here to conserve space. The pattern of loadings first revealed that the seven risk dimensions in our data set were independent

## Figure 3. Basic Latent Variable Model

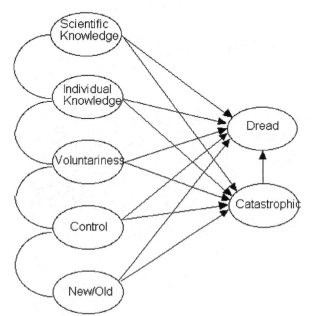

constructs. For example, the *dread* and *catastrophic* dimensions were not part of a common construct, dread, as is the interpretation in the psychometric tradition, but were separate constructs. Furthermore, the results suggested that these dimensions affect each other and, in turn, are affected by the other dimensions, or constructs. The path diagram of these results is presented as Figure 3, which we label the "Basic Model."

We performed goodness-of-fit tests for this model using the EQS program (Bentler, 1989). In particular, we subjected the data to the Likelihood Ratio $\chi^2$, the GFI and AGFI goodness-of-fit tests. We found that the basic model performed poorly for all indexes, regardless of sample. We, therefore, sought to refine the basic model.

*Refined Models*: We accomplished our refinement by iteratively fitting a number of alternative models, with a reduced number of constructs, to the data. Small factor loadings or small path coefficients were the bases for dropping constructs. The result of this iterative process was a refined model for each data set, Japanese and American, that we have labeled "Best-fit" model. Figure 4 presents the Best-fit path model for each data set. The model coefficients are standardized path coefficients.

The Likelihood-Ratio $\chi^2$ provided a poor fit for each sample: Japan $\chi^2$ (448) = 822.629, p< 0.001; United States $\chi^2$ (158) = 222.395, p < 0.001. However, the GFI and AGFI provided acceptable fits for both samples: Japan GFI = .807, AGFI = .772; United States GFI = .844, AGFI = .793. The GRI and AGFI indices indicate that the models perform fairly well in reproducing the original data matrices. On this statistical basis we did not reject these two refined models.

Descriptively, the structure of the models displays similarity and differences. The key similarity, corroborating the factor analyses with the basic model, is that the *dread* and *catastrophic* dimensions are separate constructs and that the catastrophic has a recursive influ-

## Figure 4. Best-fit Models

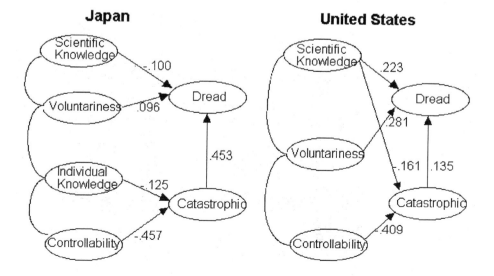

ence on dread. Another similarity is that both of these constructs are recursively influenced by the other constructs in the model. The key difference is that the individual knowledge construct is retained in the Japan model but not in the American model.

Within a similarity of structure, the models represent a fundamentally different set of processes. For the Japanese, catastrophic images are a function of lack of individual knowledge about risks and of having little control over them. In turn, dreaded images are a function of catastrophic images (and indirectly, individual knowledge and controllability), lack of scientific knowledge, and involuntariness. In contrast, the catastrophic images of Americans are a function of lack of scientific knowledge about the risks and, like the Japanese, lack of control over them. The dreaded images of Americans are, then, a function of catastrophic images (and indirectly scientific knowledge and controllability), the availability of scientific knowledge, and involuntariness.

## Conclusions

Here we have provided a description of the steps and results of the J-US Research Program. The program was designed to better understand how the cognitive architecture of citizens in two of the leading technological societies, Japan and the United States, frame perceptions of risk. At a more fundamental level it was designed to make systematic progress in understanding some of the basic human processes underlying perceptions of a wide variety of risks. In particular, the goal of the research program was to demarcate between pancultural and culturally variant features of the cognitive processes of risks.

Phase II of the research program produced a rich data set with which to test not only the specified hypothesis, but also to perform sub-analyses and other refinements. This data set was first analyzed using the standard factor-analytic techniques of the standard psychometric paradigm. In general, the findings from the United States-Japan comparison replicated previous results produced within this paradigm—including the cross-cultural results. The cognitive maps produced by this analysis indicated common contours between the Japanese and Americans, but different cognitive content. Without a formal basis for judging whether contour or content should be the criterion for determining which of our hypotheses were supported, the fundamental questions generating the research program remained unresolved.

To resolve them we turned to latent variable modeling in Phase III of the research program. This phase produced results on only the sub-set of seven nuclear technology risks contained in the data set. We developed a refined, best-fitting model for each culture based upon the nuclear items. What these models seem to be telling us is that Japanese and Americans form similar perceptions of the dread and catastrophic potential underlying their perceptions of nuclear risks. But, importantly, the cognitive routes they use to arrive at those images are fundamentally different. This finding is particularly challenging, leaving us with several alternative interpretations.

One interpretation would favor hypothesis (i) by emphasizing the similarity between the perceptions of Japanese and Americans, ignoring the different pathways leading to their common perceptions. A second interpretation would favor hypothesis (ii) by arguing that the differences in the pathways of reaching common perceptions is *prima facie* evidence of deep cultural influences. A third, more nuanced interpretation would support both hypotheses, in a linked sequence of interaction. One could reason that biology provides the basic cognitive equipment for apprehending the world, but that equipment is ineffectual without a program to run it. That program is culture. Hence, perception outcomes are prefigured by a unique species capacity, but realizing that capacity requires culture.

Because the latter interpretation is complex and subtle, but also rich and promising, it merits elaboration. An analogy between computer hardware and software is apt here. The cognitive architecture of the human species may be likened to a computer (i.e., hardware); it has a readiness to perform complex tasks, but is totally incapable of performing those tasks without instructions—a program, or software. "Software," in the world of ordinary human experience, is culture. Culture imposes an organized structure on the individual's highly capable, program-ready but *tabula rasa* mind. It imposes a template (software) consisting of a cultural map shared by other members of a given culture. Culture, or software, filters environmental inputs in systematic ways so that members of the same culture process information in similar ways. And since cultures vary widely we would expect parallel variability in risk perceptions. Nevertheless, since the preconditions for all variations in processing reside in the original architecture (cognitive hardware) there will be similar outcomes from the culturally variable processing of fundamental perceptions, such as risk. This complex process can be summarized with another computer analogy. Apprehensions of fundamental ontological features of the world should result in common outcomes regardless of the specific approach. For example, two very distinct processes accomplished a mapping of the human genome in the United States: a laborious bottom-up laboratory research approach versus a high-speed parallel computer processing approach. Nevertheless, both approaches arrived at the same solution. Similarly, with a common hardware at their disposal, the societies of Japan and the United States process risk information differently but, nevertheless, result in similar perceptions among their members.

In sum, we believe we have made considerable progress in developing a richer understanding of the structure and processes by which humans form their perceptions of risks. We also believe that we now have a considerably deeper understanding of how cognitive architecture, interacting with culture, shapes the processing of risk perceptions by Japanese and Americans. We are especially intrigued by the possibility that the dominant hypotheses in the perception literature (pan-cultural unity versus cultural shaping), which we set out to test, have proven to be a false dichotomy.

## References

Beck, Ulrich. 1992 [1986]. *The Risk Society: Toward a New Modernity.* London: Sage.

Bentler, P. 1989. *EQS: Structural Equations Program Manual.* Los Angeles, CA: BMDP Statistical Software, Inc.

Douglas, M. and Wildavsky, A. 1982. *Risk and Culture.* Berkeley: University of California Press.

Englander, T., Farago, K., Slovic, P, and Fischhoff, B. 1986. "A comparative analysis of risk perception in Hungary and the United States." *Social Behaviour* 1:55-66.

Form, W. 1979. "Comparative industrial sociology and the convergence hypothesis." *Annual Review of Sociology* 5:1-25.

Giddens, Anthony. 1990. *The Consequences of Modernity.* Stanford, CA: Stanford University Press.

Goszczynzka, M., Tyszka, T. and Slovic, P. 1991. "Risk perception in Poland: A comparison with three other countries." *Journal of Behavioral Decision Making* 4:179-193.

Hinman, G. W., Rosa, E. A., Kleinhesselink, R.R. and Lowinger, T.C. 1993. "Perceptions of Nuclear and Other Risks in Japan and the United States." *Risk Analysis* 13:449-455.

Karpowicz-Lazreg, C. and Mullet, E. 1993. "Societal risk as seen by the French public." *Risk Analysis* 13:253-258.

Keown, C. F. (1989). "Risk perceptions of Hong Kongese vs. Americans." *Risk Analysis* 9:401-405.

Kleinhesselink, R. R. and Rosa, E. A. 1994. "Nuclear Trees in a Forest of Hazards: A Comparison of Risk Perceptions between American and Japanese University Students. Pp. 101-119 in Thomas C. Lowinger and George W. Hinman (eds.), *Nuclear Power at the Crossroads: Challenges and Prospects for the Twenty-First Century*. Boulder, CO: International Research Center for Energy and Economic Development, University of Colorado.

——. 1991. "Cognitive Representation of Risk Perceptions: A Comparison of Japan and the United States." *Journal of Cross-Cultural Psychology* 22:11-28.

Kraus, N.H. and Slovic, P. 1988. "Taxonomic Analysis of Perceived Risk: Modeling Individual and Group Perceptions Within Homogeneous Hazard Domains." *Risk Analysis* 8:435-455.

Lichtenstein, S., Slovic, P., Fischhoff, B., Layman, M. and Combs, B. 1978. "Judged frequency of lethal events." *Journal of Experimental Psychology: Human Learning and Memory* 4:551-578.

Nyland, L. G. 1993 "Risk Perception in Brazil and Sweden." *Rhizikon Risk Research Reports* No. 15, Stockholm: Center for Risk Research, Stockholm School of Economics.

Renn, O. and Rohrmann, B (eds.). 2000. *Cross-Cultural Risk Perception: A Survey of Empirical Studies.* Dordrecht: Kluwer Academic Publishers.

Renn, O. and Swaton, E. 1984. "Psychological and Sociological Approaches to the Study of Risk Perception." *Environment International* 10:557-575.

Rosa, Eugene A., Noriyuki Matsuda, and Randall Kleinhesslink. 2000. "The Cognitive Architecture of Risk: Pancultural Unity or Cultural Shaping?" Pp. 185-210 in Ortwin Renn and Bernd Rohrmann, (eds.), *Cross-Cultural Risk Perception: A Survey of Empirical Results.* Dordrecht: Kluwer Academic Publishers.

Rosa, E. A. 1998. "Metatheoretical Foundations for Post-Normal Risk." *Journal of Risk Research* 1:15-44.

Sears, D. O. 1986. "College sophomores in the laboratory: Influences of a narrow data base on social psychology's view of human nature." *Journal of Personality and Social Psychology* 51:515-530.

Slovic, P. 1987. "Perception of risk." *Science* 236:280-285.

Slovic, P., Fischhoff, B. and Lichtenstein, S., 1985. "Characterizing perceived risk," Pp. 91-125 in R. Kates, C. Hohenemser, and R. Kasperson (Eds.), *Perilous Progress: Managing the Hazards of Technology*. Boulder CO: Westview Press.

Stehr, Nico. 2001. *The Fragility of Modern Societies: Knowledge and Risk in the Information Age.* London: Sage.

Teigen, K. II, Brun, W. and Slovic, P. 1988. "Societal risks as seen by a Norwegian public." *Journal of Behavioral Decision Making* 1:111-130.

Thompson, M., Ellis, R. and Wildavsky, A. 1990. *Cultural Theory.* Boulder, CO: Westview Press.

### eleven

# An Introduction to Safety Theory

## Yoichiro Murakami

## 1. Security, Safety, and *Anzen*

The English words "safety" or "security" are usually translated into *anzen* in Japanese and vice versa, and the semantic space of the one is almost the same or identical to that of the other, but it cannot be overlooked that these words reflect their own culture respectively, and that as a consequence there are some differences in connotation between them. The fact that *anzen* can be translated as both "safety" and "security" is evidence to show that *anzen* and "safety" (or "security") are not identical to each other. The Japanese word *anzen* consists of two ideas, *an* and *zen*. *An* means to be "peaceful, pacific, smooth, satisfied and without hindrance." *Zen* means to be "whole, fulfilled, perfect and completed." Thus the semantic space of *anzen* overlaps with that of "security" and "safety," but it covers something more too. Psychological or even spiritual connotations such as fulfillment and satisfaction can be conveyed by the word *anzen*.

In that sense, dealing with the issues of safety and security is not completely the same as dealing with those of *anzen*. In the present discussion we are in a context where we cannot overlook this difference. Yet, given that this paper is written in English, we will use, for the time being, the word "safety," neglecting the larger meaning implicit in the Japanese concept.

## 2. System for Safety Management

The idea of safety is often discussed in conjunction with a consideration of risk. For instance, we can distinguish between two phrases, "safety management" and "risk management." Of course "safety" is the opposite of "risk," but in this context, the use of these words shows us that they are closely related to each other. As stated in the introduction of this book, the concept of risk implies human will to control hazards and danger. In other words, the final goal of human efforts to control hazards is safety. That is, the goal is to minimize the probability of risk and to minimize losses if the minimized probability should actually be realized. The way to accomplish these goals is called "safety management" or "risk management." Safety management consists of several stages which together comprise a regular system. In this section, we will examine these stages.

The first stage of safety management is risk perception. While the rest of the risk management process mostly uses quantitative methods, this stage inevitably makes use of qualitative valuation, since risk is perceived mainly by subjective feelings and senses.

Let us refer to a typical example to illustrate this. Once I was invited to talk on food safety by a non-governmental organization (NGO). The NGO's activities were related to the negative effects of generically modified organisms (GMO) and food additives. In other words, NGO members had a highly developed perception of risk from GMO and food additives. However, when I entered the hall where I was supposed to deliver my speech, I was astonished to find that the room was filled with tobacco fumes. The NGO's risk perception sensitivity to the dangers of tobacco smoke seemed to be far less than its perception of the danger of GMO foods! This example clearly shows that the extent to which one identifies the risk of a particular matter depends on one's subjective sensitivity. In other words, we cannot deny such kinds of bias in risk perception. This point is often expressed in the form of a question: how safe is safe enough? Some people would answer "to this degree," while other people would answer "to that degree."

There seems to be a principle of distance in the degree of risk sensitivity: both in terms of spatio-temporal distance and psychological distance. Our sensitivity to a risk is roughly proportional to the spatial, temporal and psychological distance between the risk and ourselves. We are able to be quite sensitive to a risk which might take place within the area of our daily life. We are less able, however, to be sensitive to a risk which our remote descendants might meet. This is the issue usually called "generational ethics" or "generational value conflicts" in environmental problems. In any case, it is, in principle, impossible to develop a universally accepted standard. The degree of risk sensitivity differs from person to person, depending on his or her knowledge, experience, and sense of values.

Another factor contributing to risk perception is how we should estimate benefits vs. risks. In other words, risk perception necessarily involves a judgment on the risk-benefit balance. If one puts the emphasis on benefits, the degree of risk perception will go down, and vice versa. To put a greater priority on one factor results in a smaller weight being given to the other. The two concepts, benefit and risk, are in a state of more or less constant trade-off.

This again requires us to make a subjective value judgment. For example, the risk of automobile accidents is quite high and car accidents occur frequently in daily life. Our sensitivity to this risk, however, is far weaker than our fear of harm from environmental hormones or from nuclear power stations. Presumably, one major reason for this is our positive sense that the benefits we can obtain from automobiles exceed the losses we might incur from automobile accidents. One could add here that the principle of distance, mentioned earlier, can be applied also to the benefit perception. We can accept the benefits of cars quite easily because they are directly visible in our daily life; whereas the benefits of electric power, even if these benefits are also part of our daily life, are not so directly visible (i.e., we do not usually care much about where and how the electric power is generated).

In addition to the risk-benefit balance, the psychological trade-off relationship also involves other factors. When we accept the idea of risk, we often put priority on distinguishing among many possible risks. In other words, risk perception involves priority setting among many risks. Risks accompanied by voluntary activities are far more acceptable than risks incurred by involuntary activities. Consequently, the risks of skiing or mountain climbing are usually less regarded than the risks of ingesting food preservatives on a daily basis.

Since risk perception alters from person to person, from group to group, and even from culture to culture, the next stage of safety management is to collect data on risk perception through sociological research. Much of this research shows current public concerns, as well as current public understanding of risk perception. This sociological research should be helpful to political decision makers who are responsible for reducing risks and hazards.

## 3. Risk Assessment

Once a risk is perceived as dangerous, particularly when probable outcomes are unacceptable to a person or to a group, the person or the group takes the next step in the safety management process in order to avoid these negative outcomes. That step is the assessment of risks.

The most important factor in this assessment is to understand the probability of a risk. When we compare one risk whose probability is extremely low to another whose probability is rather high, it would be natural and rational that the latter risk be taken more seriously than the former. And sometimes this occurs. But the problem is there are many other cases where this does not occur. The risk with high probability may be neglected—or not even perceived—whereas the risk with a low probability may be considered quite alarming.

In the area of risk assessment, in principle, there is no room for this kind of irrationality. The process of risk assessment includes several subcomponents, and the researches should ask a number of questions: i.e., where, how, in what manner, and how often could the risk materialize and cause harm.

Let us first deal with the last question. Here it is most appropriate to use mathematical and quantitative methods. There are, however, two different approaches: one is empirical and the other is theoretical.

One of the typical examples of risk assessment based on the empirical method is risk assessment of transport-related accidents. Statistics show that one is more likely to lose one's life through an air accident when one has traveled 2,000,000,000 kilometers by aircraft. A similar calculation can be made for the risk of automobile accidents. The result is that automobile accidents are more likely than aircraft accidents by a factor of ten: i.e., a person is more likely to die of a car accident after he or she has traveled 200,000,000 kilometers by car. As far as these calculations are concerned, when compared to each other, traveling by car is ten times riskier than traveling by aircraft. Of course, these figures are based on the distance traveled and there might be other ways to compare the two. For instance, one could compare the figures calculated on the basis of travel time. However, no credible theory would predict that a person will die after he or she had traveled 200,000,000 kilometers by car. Nor would such a prediction be possible for aircraft accidents. These figures are solely empirical. In that sense, this approach, even though it is quantitative, cannot be called scientific. This is in spite of the fact that these figures are generally considered to be reliable, particularly when decision makers place priority on one over another in risk management strategy.

These conclusions lead us to the field of medicine: for example, the idea of EBM (evidence based medicine) which is today being popularized in Japan. Evidence of EBM can sometimes be supported by medical, physiological, and biological theories. But not always. Many, or even most, of the evidence is of epidemiological nature, collected from trial and error, e.g., cases of successful and failed therapies. A therapy which has had a greater number of successes is recommended because it is supported by "evidence." A therapy with a smaller number of past successes is excluded from the so-called clinical (or critical) path, which is the set of standardized therapies recognized in EBM. This shows how our society relies on empirical data, particularly when the amount of collected data is regarded as sufficiently large. In the theory of probability, this reliability is rationalized by "the law of large numbers."

Another approach to risk assessment is what we can call a theory involved-approach. Let us take the risk assessment of "man-machine systems" as an example. A man-machine system consists of several parts; some parts are machines or hardware sections, and other parts are human beings. Usually, however, a risk assessment is done in the same way both to hardware sections and to human beings. In other words, human beings are considered only as parts of the system, and their abilities and disabilities are assessed in the same way as hardware parts.

This practice is generally supported by scientific theory. A hardware component consists of many parts, made of metals, plastics, gum, and many other materials. The theories of material engineering can provide predictions on the fatigue process in the aging of each material. Based on these predictions, we can calculate the probability of trouble, failure, or breakdown of that component section. In terms of the human being component, we can also predict the efficiency of the component, the fatigue curve in time, and the possibility of faults and errors, etc. through the theories of physiology, psychology and behavioral sciences, human engineering and so on.

In this man-machine model, one problem, one breakdown, one fault in a section may cause a series of failures in the rest of the system, and this failure or fault can occur in any section independent of other sections. In this situation, the probability of a failure of one component section is "independent probability." Yet "conditional probability" also plays an important role in risk assessment. A fault or failure taking place in section A may cause section B, next to section A, to experience a related failure. The probability of this failure at section B will differ from the probability of a similar failure in section B, unrelated to failure in section A. In other words, the probability of a failure in section B is an independent probability, when the failure takes place without any relation to section A, whereas the probability of the same failure at section B is a conditional probability when the failure takes place as a result of the occurrences in section A. The two probabilities are not necessarily identical.

Thus, to describe the behaviors of the whole system, we must have a set of possible flows of events, and must calculate probability for each. Of course, a man-machine system will have its own target outcome. If it is an anti-aircraft defense system, the target outcome should be an effective attack on enemy aircraft. In other words, among a great number of possible event flows, the flows which produce the expected target outcome as the final event should be considered as successful. The other event flows should be considered unsuccessful in one way or another. Unsuccessful event flows are risks in themselves because such event flows should be avoided from the viewpoint of system operators.

This type of risk assessment of a system is based on scientific theories. Risk assessment of this kind is sometimes called PRA, which stands for Probability Risk Assessment. For instance, this method is usually adopted today for risk assessment of nuclear power plants.

Of course we are not in a position to say that we can analyze all possible events and behaviors of each component section of a system. In other words, we cannot compile a full event chart, in which all possible events, and the behaviors of every component of a system, are exhaustively described. Consequently, the process of risk assessment can never be complete. There is always room for modification.

At this point we can consider one of the most crucial issues in risk management: information on failures, faults, accidents and breakdowns. As we saw above, we cannot identify in advance all possible events and behaviors of a component unit, whether hardware or human beings. Besides, the causal relations between the behavior of sections A and B are not linked by a Newtonian mechanics-like determinism, but by quantum mechanics-like probabilistic indeterminism. By this I mean that the prediction of risks, through the process of risk assessment, is in principle non-deterministic.

One of the reasons for this is that component units sometimes do what the theories do not predict or forecast. These unexpected and uncertain behaviors, which cannot be foreseen by existing theories or by past experience, are prone to take place especially at the human component level.

I would like to refer to a typical example here, which took place on a plane in 1982. The DC 8, which departed from Fukuoka with 174 passengers and crew members, was approaching Tokyo International Airport, when, just before landing, the aircraft suddenly stalled and fell into the sea. Twenty-four passengers died and many others were injured.

In this case, the sudden stall was caused by almost completely unforeseeable behavior of the chief pilot. At the moment just before landing the chief pilot pulled the lever for reversing the engines. As is well known, just after the touchdown the engines are reversed for braking. But nobody could anticipate that the chief pilot should do that *before* the point of touchdown. In the plane's voice recorder the copilot's shouting in the cockpit was clearly recorded: "What on earth are you doing, Captain?!"

This behavior of the chief pilot had been unforeseeable. Through this accident, however, the aviation industry learned that it should anticipate such irrational behavior. The information about what took place in this case was shared, and the designer responsible for the DC 8 modified the arrangement of levers in the cockpit panel so that fatal stalls might be prevented, even if another pilot should engage in similar irrational behavior.

The next example of component unit failure is actually more instructive. Again a DC 8 aircraft was involved. In the early 1970s a series of similar air accidents took place at several airports. For instance, a Canadian Airlines DC 8 suddenly stalled just before landing and crashed into the earth, costing over one hundred lives. Other similar accidents occurred at about the same time, and information on all these accidents was collected.

An analysis of the data indicated one identical cause of all those accidents. During a landing descent, pilots are required to do many things. Setting the aircraft's spoiler operation lever in the automatic position is one of these tasks. The spoiler, when it is activated, acts as a pneumatic brake, and is mostly used during the landing, though it can also be used during the flight. Thus, the lever for the spoiler operation can be set in two positions: one is automatic and the other is manual. When the lever is set in the automatic position, the brake does not work until the plane actually touches down. When the lever is set in the manual position, the spoiler activates immediately. Thus, we can understand why the manual position is used only when the plane is flying.

In addition, the spoiler operation at landing is usually done by copilots. The investigation of the accident data made it clear that in every accident of this kind the copilots set the spoiler operation lever in the manual position. In short, apparently, these accidents were caused simply by careless behavior of the copilots. But in this example, the process of risk management does not end with this simple conclusion that copilots were at fault. Why?

## 4. Risk Management

Risk management is based on the results of risk assessment, and through this process, we can create and manage various safety measures, in order to reduce the possibility of risks and minimize the possibility of harm from such risks. The risk management function can only be accomplished when the information on actual accidents, failures, and faults is sufficient in quality and quantity.

Let me go back to the example I referred to at the end of the last section. From a risk management perspective, it would not be enough to simply point out that the careless behavior of the copilots has caused the accidents. If this were so, the managers who are responsible for the crew might give the copilot a reprimand and make a ten percent cut of his salary for three months. And in this scenario, the same kind of accident will be repeated.

The point here is that measures will need to be taken to avoid future accidents caused by other copilots committing the same error. To search for effective preventive measures is one of the chief subcomponents of the risk management process. In this spoiler case, a solution was found to assure future safety. In the aircraft concerned, the two positions of the lever (for automatic and for manual) of spoiler operation were both situated along the same straight line. So when a copilot intended to set the lever in the automatic position, against his or her intention, the lever could easily be erroneously set in the manual position, because it is located in the same operating line as the automatic position. Of course, if the positioning was done carefully, this mistake could be avoided. But we cannot expect a human being to always be careful enough. Instead we should improve the design of the operating line for the spoiler lever.

Risk management analysis resulted in a request to the designer of the cockpit panels to improve the operating line of spoiler lever, so that copilots could set the lever in either of the two positions, automatic or manual, with no confusion. This improvement resulted in the end of this type of accident.

This example is quite instructive in understanding the risk management process of a man-machine system. In such a system, human beings are an integral part of the system. As far as the system hardware is concerned, the probability of a fault in a component unit can be calculated based on theories of science and engineering. Of course, even in that case, we cannot draw a completely comprehensive, deterministic chart, as discussed above. But still, to a considerable extent, even an incomplete chart will allow us to access the risks of the faults foreseeable to us.

When human beings are involved in a system, however, the situation changes drastically. Unforeseeable human behaviors are, by their definition, beyond the realm of our imagination. Nobody could imagine that a well-trained regular pilot should reverse the engines just before the point of touchdown. Similarly, it was difficult for anybody to imagine that a copilot should place the spoiler lever in the manual position during the landing process.

However, studying actual events can extend the reach of our imagination. In that sense, the whole body of data, on all the accidents that ever happened in the past, is a treasure box for risk management. That is one reason, for instance, why international laws and conventions allow a third organization to collect data on aviation accidents, independent of police investigations.

It is notable that, compared to other high-risk fields, the field of medicine is greatly behind in the practice and philosophy of risk management. Let me refer to the situation in Japan to illustrate what I mean. In 1999, a shocking medical accident was reported at a university hospital. At that hospital one patient with a lung disease and another patient with a heart disease were supposed to be operated upon on the same day and at the same time. When the two patients transferred to the operation rooms from their ward, a misfortune happened. Their stretchers were exchanged and delivered to the wrong room. The medical staff did not notice this, and in each room, the operations started. One patient had his healthy lung opened, and the other had his healthy heart opened. Only at that moment did the staff notice the misidentification.

In that hospital, it had previously been noticed that the accident most likely to happen would be misidentification of patients. In other words, people at this hospital were already aware of the high possibility of patient misidentification, and at the in-house conferences, the introduction of wristband name tags had been discussed several times. But strong opposition and criticism kept them from adopting the wristband identification method. Opponents argued that patients are not parcels, nor are they freight objects. Patients would not like to be treated like this. I think this argument is completely wrong, particularly when viewed from the perspective of risk management.

In the end, however, the medical profession learned from this case, and now many hospitals of a certain size have adopted the wristband nametag method. The practice of incident-accident reporting is just now being institutionalized in large hospitals.

In 2002, the first annual incident report edited by the risk manager of an influential national hospital included an article on pharmacy queries. The article shows the first statistical link between the number of queries made by the pharmacy section of the hospital and individual doctor's prescriptions. The statistics made it clear that the peak in pharmacy queries was in May, and researchers started to examine the reason for the May peak. The answer was rather simple: in April the hospital accepts many interns, and in May these interns begin their work in the hospital, including writing prescriptions.

We can derive one important lesson immediately from this finding: that is, new interns are not ready to act independently without the guidance of a supervisor. At the very least the prescription written by a new intern should be checked by his or her supervisor. Of course, in a few big hospitals this double-checking is institutionalized. But in the hospital in our example, this was the first time staff understood the real nature of the problem and how they should respond to this problem. This is a positive byproduct of incident reporting, but even such a simple and elementary statistical check method has only just began to be used in Japan's medical institutions.

There is still widespread resistance to the institutionalization of incident reporting. A section leader of a big hospital told me that as a leader he was obliged to gather data on the failures and faults, as well as negligence, of his team members. But since the section leader knew that almost every one in his team did his/her best under difficult conditions, he simply could not bear to inform on them. The leader was trying to take care of his team, but he overlooked the fact that the purpose of incident reports is not to blame anyone legally or ethically, but to learn from mistakes and to develop better practices in the future.

Another problem in the field of medicine is the general reluctance to accept the philosophy of risk management. Intrinsically, medical treatment itself includes the possibility of risk. Surgical operations and even medicine may hurt patients in one way or another. The fact that intact survival of patients is the ideal of modern medicine tells us that modern medicine does not assure patients are intact after the end of the treatment. As I already mentioned above, doctors select the therapeutic treatment which they regard as the best from among various alternatives, based on their experience and on epidemiological evidence.

In other words, the process of medical treatment itself forces practitioners to adopt risk management methods. However, doctors believe that they themselves are good risk managers because of the direct relationship between doctor and patient. Consequently, many doctors cannot extend their perspective to recognize that medicine as a whole is a social system, in which doctors, nurses, other co-medicals—and even patients—perform their respective roles. Only when the medical treatment process is understood in this way, will we be able to establish medical risk management as a social institution.

The U.S. Committee for Quality of Health Care has published several reports on building a safer health system. It is interesting to note that one report is titled: *To Err is Human* (NAS, 2000). This is the fundamental premise of risk management. Unfortunately, however, in the field of medicine this premise is not always shared by medical professionals. Consequently, misbehaviors, faults and accidents are very often regarded as simply discreditable, immoral, or something that should be concealed from the public. Besides, there is an assumption among medical professionals that details of professional medical practice should be concealed behind a curtain of professional secrecy. These assumptions have formed a closed atmosphere among medical professionals which is quite specific to them. This has kept the medical profession, as a whole, from institutionalizing the incident-accident report.

From the examples given above, we can safely conclude that foolproofing is a key concept in risk management. And to establish a foolproof system, it is crucial to collect detailed data on incidents, accidents, and failures. Within the data there will be many lessons that tell us just how "foolish" human beings can be.

Another aspect of collecting negative data is whistle-blowing. I would like to mention the QC circle movement here. The concept of QC (quality control) was imported from the U.S. into Japan after World War II, and was used with great success in Japan. Japanese workers on production lines were willing to point out the problems of the lines and to propose positive solutions. This success contributed to the formation among foreign countries of the myth of Japanese workers (high morale, firm loyalty, spontaneity, and diligence). This movement included a self-reporting system.

Unfortunately, this self-reporting system has not been further developed by the Japanese firms. On the contrary, it has produced a twisted result. We call it *naibu-kokuhatu* in Japanese. *Naibu* means "inside," and *kokuhatu*, if it is literally translated, means "impeachment" or "accusation," but more likely "information." This concept implies reporting the troubles or scandals of an organization, especially to the media. This activity is always done anonymously. Certainly it is a kind of whistle-blowing, but it does not incorporate the spirit of whistle-blowing.

Whistle-blowing inherently derives from a will to improve the organization, whereas *naibu-kokuhatu* is provoked by malice against the organization. In the Japanese society, in most cases, whistle-blowing takes the form of *naibu-kokuhatu*. Of course I am not arguing that this kind of whistle-blowing is definitely of no use. It is not only the medical profession that has a self-enclosed character, especially on scandalous internal matters. There are many cases where disclosure of an internal scandal by an inside informant through the mass media did result in social justice. But viewed from the perspective of risk management, *naibu-kokuhatu* is only an unfavorable result of the failure of risk management.

Genuine whistle-blowing, on the other hand, is a substantial part of risk management. It is worthwhile to refer here to the recent institutionalization of official whistle-blowing related to nuclear power in Japan. The safety management of nuclear industries in Japan is double-layered, under the supervision of the NSCJ (Nuclear Safety Commission of Japan), an affiliate of the Cabinet Office, and NISA (Nuclear and Industrial Safety Agency) of METI (Ministry of Economy, Trade Industry). NISA was formed three years ago, and related to this organization, a special whistle-blowing law was enacted. The law provides that NISA is obliged to accept any whistle-blowing report related to the nuclear industry.

The first whistle blowing case involved one of the inspectors who were commissioned to do regular examinations of a nuclear power plant belonging to the Tokyo Electric Power Co. (TEPCO). When the inspector read the report which was sent to TEPCO at the end of the examination, he noticed that some of the figures of the examination results were modified. He personally reported what he had found to NISA through the new channel provided by the law.

This case can help us to understand how important whistle-blowing is for risk management. Without the whistle blower's information, the examination of TEPCO's plant—and the plan for repair and maintenance based on this plan—would not have been sufficient and effective.

So far I have emphasized the significant role that information plays in risk management. Here I would like to sum up the discussions up to this point.

- Risk management of a system starts with risk assessment of each component part of the system.
- The assessment is basically done using the probability analysis.
- For the probability analysis two methods are adopted, one is empirical, and the other is theoretical. In a man-machine system, the latter is mainly applied to the hardware parts of the system, whereas the former is applied to human beings.
- For the empirical method, information on failure cases is most important and useful. Whistle-blowing is a valuable tool for that purpose.
- Based on the probability of risks at each component unit, and the estimated loss when the risk materializes as harm, we can set the priority of measures to diminish and reduce the risk and the loss.
- According to this prioritization, protective measures against risks and losses are designed and applied to individual component units and sections.
- Fatal collapse of the whole system takes place following the Swiss cheese model (see Fig. 1). Therefore a holistic perspective on the whole system should be added to the piecemeal method above mentioned, lest the Swiss cheese model should be realized.
- The whole risk management system relies on the feedback method. In other words, risk management is a continuous and never-ending process.

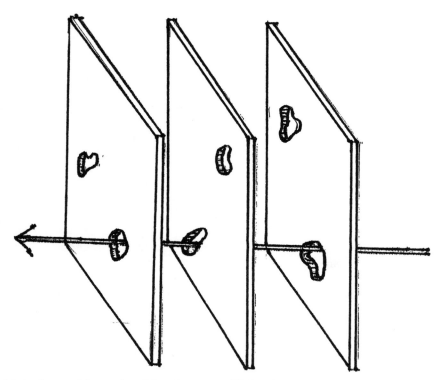

*Fig.1 Swiss cheese model; every slice of cheese has some small holes. The arrow can pass through only if the holes are located like the figure.*

## 5. *Anzen* and Safety

In the first section of the present paper, we discussed the delicate differences of meaning between safety and *anzen*. As far as risk management (or safety management) is concerned, however, those differences in meaning are negligibly small. Once we are back in our actual society, we notice that the success of risk management cannot always produce *anzen* among the public, although in terms of safety management, safety is sufficiently assured. Real problems lie here, I believe.

Let me take a nuclear power problem as a typical example. In 2003, Japan's NISA publicized the results of the probability calculations of several risks related to nuclear power plants. One of the results is related to the probability of a fatal reactor breakdown caused by aircraft accidents. This calculation was based on the following data: the locations of nuclear power plants; the flight routes of all aircrafts permitted by the regulations in Japan; accumulated flight periods of all planes per year; the probability they may be drawn into the crash; and so on.

The result was "$10^{-7}$/year." That is, this type of accident is expected to take place only once in ten million years. Another way of expressing this is to say that it may happen only once in the total history of human beings. Then does this assure us that, as far as the plane crash accident scenario is concerned, nuclear power plants are *anzen* enough? On a logical level, this seems to assure enough "safety." But this did not produce a public sense of *anzen* at all.

One problem here is the concept of probability itself. It is clear that to apply probability to a single event is senseless. Only when it is applied to an ensemble, does "probability" acquire a meaning. So, to assure safety in terms of probability does not produce a feeling of safety in particular individuals. Even if we are firmly assured that the probability of a particular risk is negligibly small, it does not mean that the occurrence of that risk is definitely denied. And as a consequence, we cannot help fearing that a bad thing may still happen to us. This psychology on probability is almost inescapable for us. Anxiety regarding *anzen* cannot be reduced by the introduction of scientific probability.

Another problem is an emotional bias among the public. For instance, an accident at a nuclear power site tends to create overreaction and over-anxiety in the public. It is easy for us to criticize such an overreaction as irrational and non-scientific. But we have to comprehend what actually takes place. Scientific assurance of safety by safety management experts is actually rather ineffective, when safety managers are faced with such "groundless" fear and anxiety. But still we should not give up pursuing not only safety, but also *anzen*.

To realize "*anzen*", what should we add to safety management? This is quite a challenging question, and I do not have a definite answer. All that I can do here is to make a few suggestions.

The first concerns our fear and anxiety. Epidemiological studies have revealed that as civilization advances, the disease structure of a society also changes. In less-developed civilizations, the main diseases suffered by members of that society are infectious diseases of the digestive system. In the second stage of development, the main diseases are infectious diseases of the respiratory system. When society advances to a third stage of civilization, the core diseases are adult diseases, or more accurately, lifestyle related diseases. At the final stage, members of the society suffer from a lack of adaptability to the society within which they themselves live. In short, people find it quite difficult to accommodate themselves to the social environment they live in.

WHO (World Health Organization) published some interesting statistics in 2002. This report records the percentage of patients that suffer from mental disorders among the total patient population of various continents. According to the study, in Europe and North America, the figure is 43 percent, whereas in Africa it is 18 percent. For the past five years in Japan, the number of suicides has increased steadily. At present, the fifth highest cause of death in Japan is accident, but we can extrapolate that accidents may be replaced by suicide in the near future as a major cause of death in Japan. If the main reason for suicide is mental disorder, the above hypothesis might become reality.

However, without any statistics, we could conclude that members of modern, contemporary society lose mental stability, calmness and peace. A major cause for this is desire. Modern society encourages its member to have desires. If one desire is fulfilled, the satisfaction produces another desire, and forms a vicious circle. Another cause for mental instability may be the fear of loss. Through the cycle of desire and satisfaction, people's various desires have been fulfilled. But this situation itself creates and re-creates a fear—a fear of losing what they have already had.

It is said that approximately 45 percent of suicides in Japan are men in their fifties. In most cases they were fired from their firm, and they are susceptible to select death because of their economic anxieties. But if one would select death, when one has economic anxieties, almost all Japanese should have selected death immediately after WWII. In those days, there were few who had regular jobs, and inflation was raging. Every one had economic anxieties, but nobody selected death. Presumably they had nothing to lose. Today, by contrast, people have plenty. And that is the cause of their anxiety.

It is interesting to note that at a recent regular meeting of the WHO, there was a hot discussion about a new definition of health. In the Charter of WHO, the definition reads as follows: "physical, mental and social well-being." At this meeting some member countries proposed adding "spiritual" and "dynamical" to the original three. In the context of *anzen*, we cannot help but be led into the religious world. In short, the concept of *anzen* might extend its semantic space to this spiritual wellness realm. If so, *anzen* studies should include theological considerations.

## References

Casey, S.M.; *Set Phasers on Stun*, 1993, Aegean Pub. Co.
Kohn, L.T. and others (eds.); *To Err is Human,* 2000, National Academy of Sciences
Lewis, H.W.; *Technological Risk,* 1990, W. W. Norton and Co.
Murakami, Y.; *Anzen-gaku (Anzenolgy)* in Japanese, 1998, Seido-sha
Slovic, P.; *The Perception of Risk,* 2000, Earthscan Pub. Ltd.
Stern, P.C. and Fineberg, H.V.; *Understanding Risk,* 1996, National Academy Press
Vincent, Ch., and others (eds.); *Medical Accidents.* 1993, Oxford University Press

# twelve

# Ideas of Public and Fundamental Happiness for the World of Diverging Convergence

## Yoshimichi Someya

## What Phase of the Human Evolution Are We in?

Theilhard de Chardin, the French paleontologist, stated that Homo sapiens sapiens left the so-called divergent path and began to walk the convergent one by utilizing higher technology in agriculture and animal husbandry in the era of the Neolithic Revolution,[1] which took place between the end of the Pleistocene period and the beginning of the Holocene period (de Chardin, T.,:121-123). De Chardin argued that "phyla under humans [read Homo sapiens sapiens after the Neolithic Revolution] did not show any fusion despite the fact that they were destined to live near one another in limited areas of the earth. Humans [read Homo sapiens sapiens before Neolithic Revolution] evolved under the sign of divergence"[2] (de Chardin, T.,: 111). And he explained, "Under the slow accumulation of racial propinquity and cultural exchange which were taking place in the end of the Pleistocene period decisive change took place in the bundle of Homo sapiens [sapiens]. They shouldered the forward hominization—significant proof exists that reveals sedentariness and collectivity in this era—from dispersed human societies [changed] into organized ones" (de Chardin, T.,: 121-122).

De Chardin claimed that culture based on the prominent technology had brought about the convergence,[3] and further that culture had been maintained and nurtured by the civilization[4] which itself had prospered on the basis of the advanced technologies. Through successive phases of technological development it seems that at last we have reached a stage of human evolution where all humans are interconnected to one another by an informational network (e.g., the internet); by a material network (e.g., money); and by a human network (e.g., individual interactions). Such global phenomena have been brought about through many kinds of technologies, especially the internal combustion engine, communication technology and information technology.

Thus, roughly speaking, human evolution may be divided into two phases: that of divergence and that of convergence. De Chardin explained these two phases metaphorically: a diverging loose process from South Pole to the Equator, and a converging compressed process from the Equator to the North Pole.

## The Era of the Equator

Theilhard de Chardin said that from the Neolithic Revolution until now humans have passed the Equator (de Chardin, T.,: 118-119). In other words, we have been living our lives in a mixture of divergence and convergence that can be expressed as diverging convergence or converging divergence.

What happens in this complicated situation? De Theilhard said, "We frequently ask why the unknown mixture of anxiety and hope around us agitates individuals and people. Can we find the ultimate cause of this anxiety in the change of turning where we pass suddenly from the universe of divergence where many lines are still dominant, to another type of universe of rapid confluence with time?" (de Chardin, T.,:148-149). The number of persons who experienced anxiety caused by a mixture of divergence and convergence has increased gradually, as the area affected by the Neolithic Revolution expanded over time. After the advent of more advanced civilizations this mixture of anxiety and hope became more strongly established, and after the Industrial Revolution the rate of change accelerated further. All of these dramatic technological revolutions after the Neolithic Revolution brought about profound change in human society.

We can see that not only convergence but also divergence is affected by technological advances, if we scrutinize the matter further. For instance, at the end of the fifteenth century, European colonialism affected people around the world, and can be considered a large-scale divergence of Europeans. There are also parallels with our own time; the same sort of divergence of world power seems to be intensifying now. We have many problems caused by the mixture of divergence and convergence, and we are forced to live under severe tensions as a result.

## *Empire*: a Contemporary Convergence?

After the fall of the USSR in 1991, the United States became the one and only superpower in the world. After 1991, the U.S. came to behave as if it were an empire which ruled the world. Many people around the world now fear that they will be forcibly coerced by the "American Empire." But I think U.S. hegemony will not last long, because the U.S. will encounter resistance from much of the world. I think this is an inevitable consequence of a regime that is operated by the logic of capitalism, and in which the powerful become more powerful and the weak become weaker. Thus the world is only temporarily under the influence of the one remaining superpower, the United States. This theory was first outlined by Michael Hardt and Antonio Negri.

According to Hardt and Negri, *empire* is "a decentered and deterritorializing apparatus of rule that progressively incorporates the entire global realm within its open, expanding frontiers" (Hardt & Negri: xii) or "a sovereignty—composed of a series of national and supranational organisms united under a single logic of rule" (Hardt & Negri: xii). Hardt and Negri argue that such an apparatus of rule is "materializing before our very eyes" (Hardt &

Negri: xi). The authors find that "Over the past several decades, as colonial regimes were overthrown and then precipitously after the Soviet barriers to the capitalist world market finally collapsed, we have witnessed an irresistible and irreversible globalization of economic and cultural exchanges. Along with the global market and global circuits of production has emerged a global order, a new logic and structure of rule—in short, a new form of sovereignty. 'Empire' is the political subject that effectively regulates these global exchanges, the sovereign power that governs the world" (Hardt & Negri: xi).

Within the structure of the new world order, all humans will converge physically. If we use Redfield's term "technical order," the order of the apparatus is defined as "order which results from mutual usefulness, from deliberate coercion, or from the mere utilization of the same means" (Redfield, R.: 21). Redfield adds, "in the technical order men are bound by things, or are themselves things. They are organized by necessity or expediency" (Redfield, R.: 21).

The rapid development of technology and the expansion of capitalism or globalization seem to drive convergence in the world. But this convergence is not what de Chardin referred to. De Chardin considered convergence as a "new environment of psychic attraction and interconnection gradually created in the biosphere by the rise of reflection" (de Chardin, T.,: 111). But this convergence of *empire* (Hardt & Negri's term) is forcibly organized by the new technical order. The convergence desired by de Chardin, however, must be constructed unanimously, based on the moral order of the whole world.

Technical order as defined by Redfield seems to be composed of laws and other social rules. But the principle controlling the technical order of Empire from the bottom up is the single logic of capitalism—which is indifferent to human morality. In *empire* profit is the supreme value and other values like truth, right, good, beauty and humanity are frequently sacrificed. In *empire* the technical order is so preponderant that the moral order seemingly cannot cope with it.

## Individual Involved in Capitalistic Convergence

Pathological phenomena can be witnessed everywhere in the world today. Terrorism, ferocious murders, and tragic suicides are increasing in many cultures. We see so many people who are obese in the United States, or so many people who suffer from depression and emptiness in Japan, and we know that people in the developed countries have serious psychosomatic problems. Under the oppression of capitalism, people are fragmented or over-individualized and personal bonds are cut off. The main cause of this emptiness in Japan is lack of personal bonds (Morotomi, 1997, Okano, 2000). People who suffer from emptiness are all victims of consumerism and individualism, the result of capitalism.

The issue of pursuit of individual happiness rather than communal happiness in contemporary Japanese society may be considered by looking at the usage of terms of happiness. In Japanese there are several terms that designate happiness, including *sachi*, *saiwai*, *shiawase* and *koufuku* or, simply, *kou* and *fuku*.

*Sachi* originally meant *mana* (i.e., power which was believed by stone age hunters to be attached to hunting tools such as arrows). Later the term also referred to the game which was killed by the hunting tools. This term connotes naturalness and supernaturalness rather than artificialness. *Sachi* was firmly related to animism.

The term *saiwai* was originally *sakiwai* meaning to flourish with divine aid (Sakakura et al. 652), or to develop outwardly as one reaches adulthood (Oono, et al. 546). As such it is true that the term implies naturalness and supernaturalness. But ancient people believed that they could cause *saiwai* themselves by uttering beautiful and vigorous words. It was Koda Rohan[5] who clearly pointed out the non-naturalness of the term *saiwai*. When he wrote "Without doubt people's *saiwai* was created by themselves" (Koda 1949:242), Koda Rohan insisted that *saiwai* is created by human efforts.

I think the difference between *sachi* and *saiwai* is related to the development of culture and civilization. Humans evolved from primates, and were molded with the assistance of culture which humans themselves created. Thus from the beginning human beings were firmly connected to artificialness. But I think it was after the agricultural revolution of 10,000 years ago—more particularly after the birth of civilization of 5,500 years ago—that increasingly developed technology enhanced the artificialness of human existence.

The original meaning of *shiawase* is "to encounter." It implies happening and consequences. And it also implies passivity, which is quite contrary to *saiwai*, which connotes constructive and generative forces. Originally *shiawase* meant to encounter both good luck and bad luck, but later it came to mean only encountering good luck. Both good luck and bad luck are natural consequences, which transcend human power. *Koufuku* is a combination of Chinese words *kou* and *fuku* that includes a broad range of meanings: *sachi*, *saiwai* and *shiawase*. This word is ambiguous, possibly because of this breadth of meaning. We can understand *saiwai* and *sachi* to mean the cause of happiness and *shiawase* to mean a good result. If we carefully read Koda's essays, we learn that he clearly distinguishes *saiwai* from *shiawase*. He uses *saiwai* when he refers to communal happiness (e.g., related to *hito-no-yo* (the human world) or *warera* (us)); he uses *shiawase* to refer to private happiness (e.g., *waga* or my happiness).

Recently Nagata, a Japanese poet, wrote "Now the word *shiawase* is popular. To be *shiawase* is believed to be happy. Today when we use *shiawase* frequently, we lose the consciousness of *saiwai*. Our image of happiness has changed" (Nagata 324-325). As Nagata pointed out, it seems that contemporary Japanese society is flooded with people who pursue their individual *shiawase* and do not care for communal *saiwai*, which is constructive and generative. The development of capitalism makes people egotistic seekers of happiness, although they find only emptiness because their desire is never satisfied. What people tend to lack is a spiritual relationship with others, with the surrounding natural environment, and with the cosmos. In this respect the public thoughts, which will be shown later, may contribute to help them get away from this tendency.

Within Hardt and Negri's *empire* we will be more and more over-individualized and more and more oppressed by capitalism as our freedom is further restricted. That is why Hardt and Negri emphasized the importance of the range of popular resistance to this oppression.

## How Can We Check the Outrunning of the Technical Order?

If the world today is controlled by the logic of capitalism, and if this phenomenon is "an irresistible and irreversible globalization," then the technical order of the world must be checked and controlled by a firm moral order in the world.

The moral order that could be expected to control the technical order of worldwide convergence must come from all cultures or civilizations, in the past and present, which have ever been in the world. The term "moral order" is used here in the same way as defined by Redfield. According to Redfield, moral order refers to "all the binding together of men through implicit convictions as to what is right, through explicit ideals, or through similarities of conscience" (Redfield, R., 20) and is "therefore always based on what is peculiarly human—sentiments, morality, conscience—and in the first place arises in the groups where people are intimately associated with one another" (Redfield, R., 20).

According to Redfield, the technical order tended to come before the moral order. And, as Redfield further points out, the purpose was often to break the traditional moral order and to remake it (Redfield, R., 74ff.). After the Scientific Revolution, secularization, a new paradigm of the technical order, started to take shape. It began first in Western Europe and later spread to other areas of the world. As is well known, this new paradigm of the technical order has broken the traditional moral order of the world. Many people abandoned traditional religions and moralities and came to pursue goals—not spiritual or related to moral order—but material goals related to the technical order.

In addition, we are dealing with capitalism, which inevitably widens the economic differences among people, and which makes the world more and more unstable. Now it is time for us to remake the traditional moral order, and to construct a new global moral order—by utilizing today's powerful technical order, an order with rapid means of transportation and widespread, highly developed communication and media infrastructures.

## From Differential Convergence to Harmonious Convergence

Culture—as a system of living created by humans themselves to enable their own survival—stands between the "outer nature," that is, the so-called natural environment, and the "inner nature," that is, humans as psychosomatic beings. Culture itself was created by humans, and became a part of human existence which then became essential for human survival. Without culture humans cannot live as humans. Thus humans consist of an inner nature and of a culture.

Culture, which stands between the inner nature and the outer nature, can function either to connect both natures or to divide them. Before the Neolithic Revolution humans used culture as a device to connect rather than to divide, since humans lived very close to the outer nature. However, since the Neolithic Revolution—when humans began to make use of the outer nature (to rule it by cultivating plants and domesticating animals) humans have been using culture as a device to divide.

The new technical order, that is, modern technology, chartered by a moral order of humanism—which considered nature as a mechanical extension (not as a living one) and discriminated against nature—brought about a vertical differentiation between humans and the natural environment. Nature has been considered as something which ought to be manipulated by humans. This process has become increasingly violent. Everywhere on earth we can see that the natural environment is being destroyed.

Humans began to apply this method of control to human society itself. Especially for these five hundred years after the Age of Exploration, men of Western Eurasia applied this method to the rest of the world in the form of capitalistic colonialism developed by successive innovations in technology. The non-European people involved in this process were considered as "natural" (i.e., lower order) by Europeans. Thus, the vertical differentiation discussed above also took place in human society. Capitalistic colonialism was chartered by a moral order which consisting of ethnocentric humanism. This moral order placed Europeans at the top of the hierarchy of all peoples. And the liberalism or individualism propounded by the European powers matched well with capitalistic colonialism, and guaranteed benefits to the powerful and the rich rule over the weak.

Capitalistic colonialism still dominates the developing countries. In such countries we can also see so-called domestic colonialism. In these countries, we can witness the phenomenon that the powerful become more powerful and the rich become richer while the weak become weaker. The divide between these groups is becoming wider. This causes now very serious political and social problems. In the towns of Indonesia, for instance, *becak* or trishaw drivers, who belong to the lowest-income class, cannot earn more than fifteen thousand Rupiah (or about $2) a day. These drivers can barely survive, and they cannot afford to give their children enough school education to find good jobs. The children themselves have no alternative, other than taking low-income jobs such as *becak* driving (Someya, 1988:304f). We can witness the dramatic social contrast with rich people in the street when the air-conditioned luxury cars pass beside the heavily sweating *becak* drivers.

At present, it seems that we are in a culmination stage of hierarchical divisions in the relationships between humans and nature, and among humans themselves. Humans who are crossing the Equator must change the hierarchical and antagonistic convergence (led by the modern technical order) into an egalitarian and pacific convergence (backed by moral order) which takes into consideration the natural environment, as well as all humans and future generations.

## Excavating Civilizations to Find Cultural and Civilizational Commonalities

Each civilization consists of elements of local culture, of so-called local civilizations, and of modern, global civilizations. These elements are stratified in layers from the bottom to the top. At the bottom we will find the most primitive and animistic cultures and at the top we will find modern civilization. In the middle we will find such local civilizations as Hindu, Buddhist, Confucian, Islamic, Christian and Native American ones. I regard modern civilization not as the local civilization of Europe, but as the world's new global civilization, which has already become detached from Europe and has been spreading throughout the world. The local civilization of Europe was constructed in Europe during the Renaissance, on the basis of Greco-Roman civilization, which had been re-introduced from the Islamic academic community who had preserved it throughout the Dark Ages. Greco-Roman civilization was once received by Islamic civilization where the culture was nurtured and then handed back to Europeans. Now European civilization has become the universal one, accepted by people throughout the world. During the course of history, civilizations have moved to different places and have flourished there before moving on again.

If we excavate throughout the layers of each civilization, we will understand that (along with other civilizations) each civilization shares a common primitive and animistic culture in the base. However, this primitive culture, which has been undervalued by modern civilization, must now be examined because its harmoniousness with nature should be reevaluated.

As mentioned before, primitive culture did not divide the inner nature and the outer nature. Rather it connected both natures. Our Stone Age ancestors considered any natural phenomenon to be a living entity and they could sense outer nature directly because they lived close to it. We must understand that each civilization today still contains such a primitive culture. For instance, we will find primitive cultural elements in familiar fairy tales, ghost stories, and folk religions. By recalling such elements—that can help people feel sensitive to lives that dwell in nature—we can relativize the modern concept of nature, which objectifies and regards nature as a mere mechanical extension. This relativistic view of the concept of nature must be considered today when we see that the natural environment is increasingly destroyed. But we must not confine these concepts only within fairy tales and folk religions. We must also revitalize the concept and put it back in human life itself.

In addition to its naturalism, the fundamentality and universality of the concept of primitive culture also must be emphasized—since if we find out there is the similar concept of nature at the base of all civilizations, without doubt, we would be able to understand each other more easily, and to develop the dialogue between civilizations more smoothly. The hidden concept of nature at the base of civilization must be disclosed.

Local civilizations also must be identified and examined, so we can compare them with each other in order to look for the common elements among them. In this respect I am thinking of a particular example. When I was conducting field research in Jogjakarta, an Indonesian Muslim drew a conical mountain like Mount Fuji and told me that anyone who believed in Islam or Hinduism or Buddhism or Christianity aimed to the common goal, although the ways each believer chose to attain the goal was different.

Indeed we can hear similar teachings in many religions. For instance, "Do unto others as you would have them do unto you" in Christianity almost coincides with the Islamic saying "No one of you is a believer until you desire for your neighbor that which you desire for yourself." These teachings are also similar to the Buddhist teaching "Treat all creatures as you would like to be treated," to the Hindu teaching "Do not do to others which if done to you would cause you pain," and to the Confucianist teaching "Do not do to the others what you do not want to be done." Though these verbal expressions are different, the concept is almost the same. In addition, we can find similar teachings like "Do not kill" in Christianity and *Ahimsah* (not to kill) in Hinduism and Buddhism.

I think that so far we have tended to focus on the differences between other civilizations and our own, possibly because the other civilizations are unfamiliar to us. From now on we must make efforts to look for commonalities rather than differences.

## Rohan Koda's Idea on Public Happiness

In the long tradition of Japanese civilization we can find a particular moral wisdom which is a composite of the local culture and Buddhist and Confucian civilization. Kenji Miyazawa's public and altruistic idea on happiness is an example of this. He argued in his essay *Nomin geijutu gairon youkou* (Outline of Introduction on Peasantry Art) "that individuals cannot be happy until the whole world becomes happy" (Miyazawa, K. 1967).

Another idea of public happiness was explored by Rohan Koda. In his essay on three ideas of happiness, Rohan Koda only used the term *fuku*. Perhaps the author intended to discuss the cause of happiness rather than the effect, but in any case he did not define *fuku* clearly. In his discussion of *fuku*, Koda quoted a vulgar understanding that *fuku* meant "riches, high social position and honor" (Koda, 1954:343). In another part of this essay, Koda stated that *fuku* means "things, affection and knowledge which should contribute to realization of the happiness (*koufuku*) of mankind" (Koda, 1954:367). We must pay special attention to this second definition, because Koda considered *fuku* to be the causal condition of happiness and, at the same time, to be its result. In my view, Koda focused on the former (cause of happiness) too much, and neglected to clarify the latter (result of happiness). The latter should be investigated more deeply, because I think supreme happiness will be found not in the psychosomatic satisfaction, but in finding one's true self, "working life in one-self" (Morotomi, 185f) or *aku* (Ki Ageng Suryomentaram, 1985:1-26, 1989:1-33, Someya 1997:258-270, 2001:1-17). I will discuss this matter later in the chapter.

Returning to Koda's essay, the author laid out what to do in order to become happy. His suggestion is *sekifuku* (save happiness), *bumpuku* (share happiness), and *shokufuku* (pro-liferate happiness). *Sekifuku* means to save *fuku* properly, i.e., not to exhaust it. Koda said that men of *sekifuku* were strangely blessed with more *fuku* than men of no *sekifuku*. He assumed the reason why men of *sekifuku* were blessed with more *fuku* was that their neigh-bors loved them, while men of no *sekifuku* were hated or regarded as public enemies (Koda, 1954:342-353). In other words, happiness should be created by good human relationships. In contrast, *bumpuku* means to share one's *fuku* with others. *Bumpuku* is the opposite of *sekifuku*. Koda regretted that in real life, men of *sekifuku* were not always men of *bumpuku* or vice versa. He added that men of low rank, who were not men of *sekifuku*, would not be able to become men of high rank, and men of no *bumpuku* would not be able to get help from others (Koda, 1954:354-365). Here again, good human relationships are themselves considered as causes of happiness. Finally, *shokufuku* means "to contribute things, affec-tion and knowledge to the realization of happiness of mankind" (Koda, 1954:367). Koda preferred *shokufuku* over *sekifuku* and *bumpuku*, because *shokufuku* could proliferate more *fuku*. Koda wrote "there is no way except proliferating *fuku* to get *fuku*" (Koda, 1954:370). "We can obtain happiness from our ancestors because of their *shokufuku*. Now we, who are blessed with previous generations' *shokufuku*, must proliferate *fuku* to leave it to our own offsprings"(Koda, 1954:371). Here again, affectionate human relationships between the generations is emphasized.

Koda's idea, one that emphasizes *shokufuku*, may be called an idea of production systems that encourage the proliferation of *fuku*. In other words, his idea emphasizes the production of happiness. This means that Koda's idea is not focused on *shiawase* and does not empha-size consumption. When we look at today's world from Rohan's viewpoint, we realize why we frequently emphasize *shiawase* rather than *saiwai*. In my view, we are all deeply affected by the consumer culture.

Though Koda did not define the concept of happiness, we must reassess the public nature of his idea of happiness. He used the term *bumpuku* to describe the happiness that is to be shared publicly and "horizontally," i.e., to the present world (*hito-no-yo*), and used *shokufuku* to describe the happiness to be shared publicly and "vertically" from the previous generation to the following generation. I think Koda's idea of public happiness cannot be emphasized too much, since people today, especially people in developed countries, tend to pursue their own happiness rather than caring for suffering people in developing countries, or conserving natural resources and the environment on behalf of the future generations.

## Ki Ageng Suryomentaram's Idea of Fundamental Happiness

A philosophy—called *Kawruh Jiwa* in Javanese or knowledge (science) of soul—was expounded by Ki Ageng Suryomentaram,[6] a prince from Jogjakarta, Indonesia. This phi-losophy is a creative set of principles, based on ideas from traditional Javanese civilization, which itself is based on an animistic culture with influences from India's Hindu-Buddhist civilization, the Arab world's Islamic civilization, Europe's Christianity and modern civilizations. Especially important here are the Hindu-Buddhist and Sufistic influence, for it seems to me that *atman* in Hinduism, the central stupa as a symbol of *Vairocana* (Hattori, 58-60) of the Buddhist temple of *Borobudur* in Central Java, and *haqq* (Arabic) which means the essence or god, (*ana al haqq* or I am God) in Sufism is very similar to *aku* (I, Javanese) of *Kawruh Jiwa.*

The most important value system which regulates the structure of Javanese civilization is, I am sure, the antipodes concepts of *alus*ness and *kasar*ness. These antipodes can be consistently observed in such religious or ideational aspects of Javanese civilization including *Kawruh Jiwa* (knowledge/science of the soul). It goes without saying that *aku* in *Kawruh Jiwa* is the innermost, profound and hidden part of a human being. These adjectives "innermost," "profound," "hidden," are represented collectively in the Javanese word *alus*. And this innermost, profound and hidden part is, according to *Kawruh Jiwa*, always calm or tranquil. The calmness is also called *alus*. One of the features of *aku* is this calmness (also called *tantrem* in Javanese)[7].

One of the points emphasized by Ki Ageng Suryomentaram in his lectures and speeches (later published in such books as *Kawruh Jiwa Wejanganipun Ki Ageng Suryomentaram* and *Ajaran Ajaran Ki Ageng Suryomentaram*) is that a person is composed of *aku* (his essential inner self that can communicate with the others' *aku*) and *karep* (his desires—also essential for a person to live, but involving contention [over property, status, and power] with others' *karep*). Both *aku* and *karep* are eternal. They were, are and always will be. They created, create and will create humans. The relationship between *aku* and *karep* is explained as follows: *aku* is a watcher who only watches, without feelings of like or dislike, without blaming and without hoping. *Aku* does not order, compel, love or guide its counterpart, *karep*. "I am a watcher of my desire (*aku kuwi tukang nyawang karep*)." *Aku* and *karep* have different natures: *aku* makes sense of human life and *karep* generates human conduct. *Aku* never takes action but *karep* generates human actions that seeks *semat* (material wealth), *drajat* (social position, prestige, social honor) and *kramat* (political power). Ki Ageng Suryomentaram asserted that, after separating these elements within oneself, one can afford to be happy by identifying self with *aku* and by experiencing others' feeling. This will be true even though one may feel sorrow and joy alternating through one's lifetime. According to Ki Ageng Suryomentaram, happiness is different from joy, and the true happiness lies in a calm feeling (in the soul). He also asserted that, by understanding this fact, humans can escape from fear.

Another point emphasized by Ki Ageng Suryomentaram is the importance of following the way of nature (*aturan alam* in Javanese). When I was in Indonesia, I noticed that people who mastered *Kawruh Jiwa* often used the same words when they told me their life histories: *sakepenake, sabutuhe, saperlune, sacukupe, samestine, sabenere* (as one pleases, as one needs, only for the purpose, to an adequate degree, and as it should be). Some of these people emphasized hard work. According to them, to work hard is a human activity which closely accords with the way of nature, i.e. *samestine* (as it should be).

In summary, the philosophy of Ki Ageng Suryomentaram has the following characteristics:

### (1) Generativity or creativity

*Kawruh Jiwa* regards a person (*kramadangsa*) as a being generated by *aku* and *karep*. It is said that Ki Ageng Suryomentaram once said "to imitate chooses not to imitate, because the imitated does not imitate." By these words Ki Ageng seemed to urge his friends to be creative or generative. *Kawruh Jiwa* proponents give *rasa* (feeling, soul) priority over *mikir* (thinking) since thinking or reason hamper one's liberal activity, and *rasa,* as original feeling (soul), generates every human thought and aspect of human conduct, with the cooperation of *karep.*

### (2) Non-authoritarianism, egalitarianism and universalism.

That *Kawruh Jiwa* considers *rasa* (feeling, soul) as important, also means that this philosophy has a core of non-authoritarianism or egalitarianism/universalism, because according to this philosophy, *rasa* (original feeling, soul) is shared by all people, even though *rasa,* as it comes to existence, is varying. *Kawruh Jiwa* explains that this is the reason why people are capable of communicating with each other.

### (3) Non-self assertiveness rather than self-concernedness, liberalism and democratic nature

That *rasa* (original feeling, soul) is shared by all people, relates also to commonality and demonstration of compassion. Essentially, *Kawruh Jiwa* is a philosophy which aims at personal salvation, which frees people from agony and fear, and through which social development and democratic improvement can be achieved.

### (4) Materialism-free

According to *Kawruh Jiwa* happiness does not lie in the satisfaction of material needs, but lies in the tranquil and peaceful soul.

So far we looked at both Japanese and Javanese ideas about happiness. These ideas both emphasize publicness. If we examine civilizations throughout the world, we will see many common ideas. Indeed, Yoshihiko Morotomi addresses this idea in his book. Morotomi advised readers to notice the true egos in themselves in order to be liberated from agony (Morotomi, 176f). He said, "in the process of seeking something, a person's ego that is mindful of the self dies, but working life is activated. And when the ego dies, one will come to know the true subject or working life in oneself. That is one's very self. One will realize that ego that so far has been considered as self, is only a part of self" (Morotomi, 187). In spite of a different mode of expression I think his idea is very similar to that of *Kawruh Jiwa.* Another similar concept will be found in the sentences "One who lives is not me. Christ lives in me" in The Epistle of Paul the Apostle to the Galatians, 2:20, as pointed out by Morotomi (Morotomi, 187).

## Conclusion

In the long history of human evolution, we are now at a particular stage. Using the terminology of Teilhard de Chardin, we are experiencing both the divergence and the convergence at the same time. These processes are enhanced by the technical order, which consists of advanced modern technology and the economic system of capitalism. Both the inner nature, i.e. the human body, and the outer nature, i.e. natural environment, are exposed directly to these influences and are destroyed. In the face of this crisis we must construct a firm moral order which aims to public and fundamental human happiness.

## Notes

1. This term was invented and defined by G. Childe, an English archeologist.
2. All species have adapted themselves to their environment in order to survive and have so become species different from their ancestors. This divergent process is called divergence and has been the general way of evolution.
3. According to Theilhard de Chardin convergence is "new environment of psychic attraction and interconnection gradually created in the biosphere by the rise of reflection" (de Chardin, T.:111) and refers to the "function to operate true organic synthesis on the continually potential species engendered by ramification of phyla" (de Chardin, T.:112).
4. In this paper I use the terms "culture" and "civilization." Civilization is a particular type of culture which appeared after the construction of cities. Civilizations were created by advanced technology. Civilizations tended to be controlled by technology or technical order, and thus to be checked by morality or moral order.
5. Koda Rohan was one of the most famous authors in modern Japan. He was born in Tokyo in 1867. He wrote many novels and essays, including the famous *Koufuku sansetsu* (Three Essays on Happiness), based on his wide knowledge of Chinese religion, philosophy and history. He died in 1947.
6. Ki Ageng Suryomentaram was born in 1892 in Jogjakarta, Indonesia. He led a happy life, but at heart he was not satisfied, as he saw economic, social and political disparities between the people—not only in Java, but throughout the world in the era of colonialism. Later in life he left the royal court and became a farmer. In 1927, Ki Ageng Suryomentaram discovered the reason for the dissatisfaction that had distressed him since his youth. In 1928, in the form of poetry, he wrote *Wejangan Kawruh Beja Sawetah* (Teachings of Science of True Happiness). Frequently he gave lectures to the people. He died in Jogjakarta in 1962.
7. For further details concerning the structure of Javanese culture and society, see Someya 1993 and 1999.

## References

Childe, G. 1967 *What Happened in History*.
de Chardin, Teilhard. 1956. *La Place de L'homme Dans la Nature*. Paris: Editions du Seuil.
Hardt, Michael & Negri, Antonio. 2000. *Empire*. Cambridge & London: Harvard University Press.
Hattori, Eiji. 1997. Nankai no Daijou Bukkyou no Michi: Borobudur to Angkor Bunmei wo Megutte (Maha-yana Buddhism Along the Maritime Silk Routes), *Journal for the Comparative Study of Civilizations*. No. 2, Center for the Comparative Study of Civilizations, Reitaku University, Japan.
Ki Ageng, Suryomentaram. 1985. *Ajaran Ajaran Ki Ageng Suryomentaram (Ki Ageng Suryomentaram's Teachings)*. Jakarta: Inti Idayu Press.
_____. 1989. *Wejanganipun Ki Ageng Suryomentaram (Ki Ageng Suryomentaram's Teachings)*. Jakarta: Inti Idayu Press.
Koda, Rohan. 1949. *Rohan Zenshu (Rohan's Collected Edition)* vol. 11. Tokyo: Iwanami Shoten.
_____. 1954. *Rohan Zenshu (Rohan's Collected Edition)* vol. 27. Tokyo: Iwanami Shoten.
Miyazawa, Kenji. 1967. *Miyazawa Kenji Zenshu (Miyazawa Kenji's Collected Edition)*. Tokyo: Chikuma Shobo.
Morotomi, Yoshihiko. 1997. *Munashisa no Shinrigaku (Psychology of Vanity)*. Tokyo: Kodansha.
Nagata, Hiroshi. 1997. *Shijin de Arukoto (To be a Poet)*. Tokyo: Iwanami Shoten.
Okano, Moriya. 2000. *Transpersonal Psychology*. Tokyo: Seidosha.
Oono, Susumu, et al. eds. 1982. *Iwanami Kogo Jiten (Iwanami Dicitionary of Ancient Words)*. Tokyo: Iwanami Shoten.

Redfield, Robert. 1953. *The Primitive World and Its Transformation*. Ithaca: Cornell University Press.

Sakakura, Atsuyoshi, et al. eds. 1984. *Kadokawa Kogo Daijiten (Kadokawa Dictionary of Ancient Words)*. Tokyo: Kadokawa Shoten.

Someya, Yoshimichi. 1988. *Bechahiki Kazoku no Monogatari (Life Histories of Becak Drivers' Family)*. Tokyo: Imura Bunka Jigyosha.

————. 1993. *Alus to Kasar: Gendai Jawa Bunmei no Kozo to Dotai (Alus and Kasar: the Structure and Change of the Modern Javanese Civilization)*. Tokyo: Daiichi Shobo.

————. 1997. Jawa niokeru Shokuminchi Shugi to Bunka-Ki Ageng Suryomentaram no shisou to koudou ni miru (Colonialism and Cultural Resistance in Java: as Seen in Ki Ageng Suryomentaram's Idea and Action), Yamashita, S., & Yamamoto, M., eds. *Colonialism and Culture*. Tokyo: Shinyosha.

————. 1999. Jawa Bunmei no Juusoukouzou (Stratifcation of Javanese Civilization), Yoneyama, T. & Yoshizawa, G., eds. *Kouza Hikaku Bunmei (Lecture of Comparative Civilizations)*. Tokyo: Asakura Shoten.

————. 2001. How Did the People Get Happiness through Learning a Philosophy of Ki Ageng Suryomentaram? Someya, Y., ed. *Psychosomatic Responses to Modernization and Invention of Cultures in Insular Southeast Asia*. Department of Cultural Anthropology, Shizuoka University.

## thirteen

# Understanding Peace, Security, and *Kyosei*: An Intercultural Communication Perspective

### Mary M. Meares

As humans, one of our most basic characteristics, one that some theorists claim makes us human (e.g., Fisher, 1987), is the ability and the need to communicate. While some see communication as a simplistic and linear process of message transmission, most scholars of human communication define communication as the process of creating meaning through human interaction via the exchange of symbols over time (Galvin & Wilkinson, 2003). This process may take place as individuals interact face-to-face or may be mediated through technology (e.g., electronic mail or telephones). The symbols used may be verbal (using language) or nonverbal (via facial expressions, gestures, clothing, use of space and time, or artifacts). Communication may be intentional or unintentional (Watzlawick, 1978). We communicate on an interpersonal level with other individuals, groups, other members of organizations, and co-workers. Our governments, nongovernmental organizations, and corporations have representatives who interact with their counterparts in other governments and organizations. On a local, regional, national, and international level, all of these interactions contribute to individual and collective perceptions of peace, security, and *kyosei* (conviviality or ability to live interdependently in harmony with others).

The purpose of this chapter is to examine how knowledge of the process of human communication, and specifically intercultural communication, can contribute to our understanding of how peace, security, and *kyosei* are created and maintained and, in contrast, how these conditions can be threatened or destroyed by conflict, insecurity, and insensitivity to others. Intercultural communication is the process of communication between two or more parties from different cultural backgrounds. Culture can be defined in many ways. Jenks (1993) and Stohl (2001) describe a number of different views of culture, including those seeing culture as a complex social pattern and a communicative practice. The view of culture as a complex social pattern reflects the perspective that culture is conditioning, and that we are conditioned to behave and communicate in certain ways. This view of culture focuses less on values or beliefs and more on behavior, making a space for criticism of the societal patterns based on power and status, and employing emic (within culture) as well as etic (across cultures) methods. The view of culture as a set of communicative practices reflects E. T. Hall's (1976) perspective that culture *is* communication. From this perspective, culture is constituted interactively through communication; values are not included as a separate element, but rather the focus is on the process. Thus, culture can be seen as both a product of communication and as a force that shapes communication, or as a cerebral and communicative practice. In this sense, communication is intrinsically connected to culture, both shaping it and being shaped by it. In the following section, the ways in which communication creates peace (and conflict) and security (and insecurity), and the ways in which communication is necessary for developing *kyosei* (the ability to live interdependently in harmony with other), will be examined with attention to the challenges of intercultural communication.

## Peace and Conflict

While peace can be described in various ways, its most salient characteristic is the absence of conflict. Conflict can be based on perceived goal incompatibilities, as well as procedural differences, value differences, affective differences, or cognitive differences (Martin & Nakayama, 2004). While conflict often occurs between people from the same culture, conflict is of special interest to intercultural communication researchers, because when parties from different cultural backgrounds interact, there is a high potential for misunderstanding and stress. Ting-Toomey and Oetzel (2001) identified a number of factors that contribute to potential conflict in intercultural interactions. These include the culture value patterns of each participant (e.g., individualism or collectivism), conflict norms (e.g., expectations of equity or hierarchy, directness or indirectness), facework behaviors (e.g., apologies), level of emotional expression (e.g., restrained or elaborated), and conflict interaction styles (e.g., competition or avoidance). While peaceful, harmonious communication may be more than simply avoiding conflict, analysis of conflict can often provide insight into salient issues that prevent peaceful interactions.

Through an analysis of conflict styles popular in different cultures, Ausberger (1992) described two very different cultural orientations toward conflict: conflict as opportunity and conflict as destructive. From the first perspective, conflict is seen as a normal process that provides an opportunity for individuals to negotiate changes in relationships, redistribute outcomes and resources, and resolve tension between two parties. For individuals who espouse this view, constructive conflict (while not always pleasant or easy) is a necessary part of human interaction and helps to develop stronger and healthier relationships (Canary, Cupach, & Messman, 1995). In fact, individuals are often taught explicitly how to engage in conflict in a way that keeps the interaction constructive, often through direct communication about the problem. An example of this perspective can be seen in the corporate policies of Intel, an American-based technology corporation. Two of Intel's core values are "risk taking" and "results orientation" (Intel Corporation, 2004). All Intel employees participate in a conflict-training seminar that teaches them to directly confront other employees with whom they have a conflict for the good of the organization as well as the individuals involved.

From the second perspective (Ausberger, 1992), conflict is destructive and disrupts or destroys peace. Based on this perspective, individuals should avoid conflict for the good of their group and society. Individuals should adapt to the situation, culture, and existing norms in order to avoid conflict and maintain healthy relationships. Also congruent with this view is the idea that those who deviate from the norms and cause conflict should be punished for that violation of trust. This perspective reflects a less individualistic view of the world and is typical of Asian countries, including Japan, where conflict is often avoided to prevent destructive results. In these cultures a third-party intermediary or other high-context techniques are used to avoid direct confrontation. When someone from this orientation interacts with those from the conflict-as-opportunity orientation, there is the potential for escalation in the conflict (and potentially alienation and withdrawal on the part of the party who tries to avoid conflict) as a result of these different expectations. An employee from a collective culture or espousing a view of conflict as destructive would be at a disadvantage in the Intel culture described above.

On a national and international level, peace and conflict between nations are influenced by the cultural backgrounds and expectations of the politicians and negotiators involved in developing agreements and guiding interactions. Intercultural mediators must take into account differences in orientations toward conflict, as well as differences in perceptions of outcomes and cultural norms. Many examples abound in diplomatic communities of gaffs that have resulted in a breakdown in communication between representatives of different nations (Hall, 2001). These varying views of conflicts can often influence not only the parties involved, but the security of their nations as well.

## Security and Insecurity

Security can be defined as "freedom from risk or danger," "freedom from doubt, anxiety, or fear," or "something that assures safety" (American Heritage Dictionary, 2001). This *perception* of safety is related to the presence or potential for active or underlying conflict as well as perceptions of others in the surrounding environment.[1] While there may always be some risk of danger due to natural or man-made phenomena, it is the action of others which most influences our sense of control over our environment and our corresponding sense of safety. Thus, this sense of security is not merely an individual perception, but is dependent upon our sense of constructive connection with others. From a Japanese perspective, feeling community acceptance is also an important part of experiencing a sense of security. For both American and Japanese citizens, acceptance and connection to local community may reduce uncertainty about potential dangers or about existing threats to security.

Uncertainty is something many humans attempt to avoid because it challenges our sense of security. As we interact (and communicate) with others, we attempt to gather information in order to reduce any uncertainty we feel. Initial interactions with individuals from a different culture may result in stress because of difficulty in understanding the behaviors of culturally-different others (Gudykunst, 1995). Two types of uncertainty are experienced in intercultural interactions: predictive uncertainty and explanatory uncertainty. Predictive uncertainty is the inability to anticipate the behavior of others because of a lack of knowledge of cultural norms and contextual expectations. For example, someone traveling into a new country or entering a new school or workplace may find that they do not know what to expect. An international student, although very accomplished academically, when starting an academic program in a foreign country may be anxious about attending class at first, as he or she does not know what behavior to expect from the professor or from other students.

The new student cannot predict the behaviors of others because he or she does not know the norms for behavior in the new environment.

Explanatory uncertainty is the inability to understand why people have acted in a certain way. To continue the example above, the individual in the new setting may find that as he or she interacts with others or observes others, the individual does not understand why members of the new culture have behaved in certain ways. An American going to Japan, for example, may not understand why a Japanese colleague who speaks excellent English continually apologies for his lack of ability to speak the language. Both predictive and explanatory uncertainty raise the stress levels of individuals, which may further reduce their ability to interact and adjust, decreasing their sense of security and increasing the potential for conflict.

The ambiguity that is inherent in intercultural communication is often a challenge to a sense of security (Casse, 1982). Because parties involved in an interaction come from different cultural frames of reference, interpreting another's verbal or nonverbal cues may be a challenge to their sense of security. Thus each party's ability to evaluate whether something represents a risk or danger may be inhibited, and anxieties may abound. Tolerance for this type of ambiguity is one personality characteristic necessary for competence in intercultural communication.

## *Kyosei*: Creating Interdependent Harmonious Relationships

*Kyosei* (conviviality, or the ability to live in symbiotic harmony with others) can be contrasted with actions or inactions that create a hostile or isolating environment characterized by incivility and discourtesy.[2] While *kyosei* requires more than just politeness, our judgments about the relative civility or incivility of an action (and their subsequent contribution to harmonious or disharmonious relationships) are based on the cultural norms within which we operate. These norms can include expected verbal and nonverbal behaviors, as well as interaction norms.

Behavior deviating from what is expected in a particular context is often judged to be discourteous, detracting from an environment of *kyosei*. Grice (1975) developed four axioms for verbal language appropriateness. He said that verbal communication should be appropriate in terms of quantity, quality, and relevance and that they should be performed appropriately—but that all verbal communications are judged based on the context and culture in which the interaction occurs. Our knowledge of the context is crucial to understanding meaning and to responding appropriately. An individual who talks excessively may be perceived as rude by others, yet the definition of excessive is dependent on both the setting and the culture. Cultures have been described as elaborate or restricted in style (Gudykunst & Ting-Toomey, 2003). The elaborate style uses a larger quantity of language, and language is used very expressively. In contrast, the restricted style makes greater use of direct, simple language and silence is encouraged, especially in situations that are ambiguous or where language is perceived to be unnecessary. Thus, an individual from a restricted-style culture may have very different expectations than one from an elaborate-style culture of the quantity of verbal communication; each may perceive the other as being rude or inappropriate, yet each is following culturally appropriate rules.

"Face" concerns are another area in which communication difference may contribute to a perceived lack of *kyosei*. Face is the degree to which an individual seeks to maintain his or her positive image and/or the positive image of another person. Hu (1944) originally described the Chinese concept of face, explaining that the Chinese language has two words that are translated as "face" in English. *Lien* is respect for someone of high moral character. *Mien-tzu* is the prestige and recognition gained through personal effort and success. Japanese has two similar concepts—*mentsu* and *taimen* (Morisaki & Gudykunst, 1994). The concept of face is important for understanding interpersonal communication in Asian cultures. However, face is not just an Asian concept. For example, Goffman (1959) wrote about the way people present themselves in daily life as a performance, in which each person is managing the impressions that other people have of them. Goffman described face as something that can be lost, saved, and protected as a way of managing one's own self-presentation. Face is not just a way of communicating, but also a motivation for communicating.

Brown and Levinson (1987) described the concept of politeness as a language universal. *Politeness* is the degree to which people use language and phrasing to manage face or public identity. Brown and Levinson described face as having two components. Negative face is the desire to have your actions unimpeded, and positive face is the desire for approval and connection with others. Brown and Levinson also described different "face super-strategies" for managing both positive and negative face including positive politeness, negative politeness, and off-record politeness. However, norms for the use of these strategies are very different in different cultures.

Ting-Toomey, in a description of her Face-Negotiation Theory[3] (Ting-Toomey, 1994; Ting-Toomey & Kurogi, 1998), defined face as "a claimed sense of favorable social self-worth that a person wants others to have of her or him" (Ting-Toomey & Kurogi, 1998, p. 187). Cultural variables, individual variables, and situational features all affect conflict management and face-management strategies. Face concerns can be managed through a number of different behaviors and strategies (Oetzel, Ting-Toomey, Masumoto, & Yokochi, 1999). Self-face can be maintained or enhanced by defending one's own perspective or using aggression to obtain one's own way. Other-face (the face of the other party) can be maintained or enhanced by obtaining help from a third party who can intervene in a conflict; by avoiding interacting with the other person or about the issue; by pretending that the conflict does not exist; by apologizing for one's own behavior; or by giving in to the other person. Mutual face can be maintained or enhanced by looking for ways to join together the different perspectives; by privately discussing the conflict; by considering the other and his or her perspective; and by showing a willingness to compromise with the other person. Competence in "facework" in a culture is being able to use face strategies that are perceived as appropriate and effective in order to maintain impressions in interpersonal communication. Strategies evaluated as appropriate and effective vary by culture. Competence also includes adaptability to the interaction.

Ting-Toomey described facework competence as different from individualistic and collectivist perspectives. Ting-Toomey and Kurogi (1998) noted that members of collectivistic cultures use a greater degree of indirect face strategies than do members from individualistic cultures. *Collectivistic cultures* are those in which members see themselves more as members of groups rather than individuals. *Individualistic cultures* are those in which members see themselves as separate from others. Ting-Toomey and Kurogi (1998) predicted that individuals from collectivistic cultures would use more avoiding and obliging facework in conflict. Individuals from individualistic cultures were predicted to use more dominating and controlling facework behaviors in conflict. A recent example helps to illustrate the difference. The author of this article, an American, and a Japanese friend both responded to the same email from a superior, but both gave very different responses due to different expectations of power distance and face. The Japanese respondent's email included phrases like "please," "thank you for your help," and "I'm sorry to cause problems," in order to max-imize the power distance and protect the face of the superior. The American respondent's email simply stated the difficulty in responding to the request and promised an answer as soon as possible, minimizing power distance and protecting self-face.

Competence in facework in a culture is being able to use face strategies that are perceived as appropriate and effective to maintain impressions in interpersonal communication. Strategies evaluated as appropriate and effective vary by culture. Competence also includes adaptability to a specific interaction. To create and maintain a sense of *kyosei*, an individual must be able to negotiate differences in face orientation and in facework norms. This ability to negotiate these differences also contributes to the potential for conflict and to the sense of security or insecurity that may be experienced in the process of communicating.

## Challenges of Power, History, and Privilege in Achieving Peace, Security, and *Kyosei*

While the discussion thus far has focused on differences between cultures in communi-cation style and norms related to peace, security, and *kyosei* (conviviality), there are a num-ber of other issues pertinent to this discussion that relate to power, history, and privilege. Intercultural communication takes place within the context created by the personal and cultural backgrounds of the individuals who are communicating, as well as the social and political background of the groups and nations to which they belong.

As children are learning the behavioral norms of the cultures in which they are raised, they also learn how to think about other groups based on their family's and community's views (Martin & Nakayama, 2004). The history of contact between groups, as well as the economic and political contact between them, can be positive or negative. A Palestinian child and an Israeli child are likely to be taught to fear each other's cultures and to expect conflict because of the continuing conflict their groups face. African American children may be taught to expect conflict or incivility when interacting with white Americans because of the history of slav-ery and civil rights in the United States. Members of different groups (or nationalities) may be taught very different histories of their conflicts (Fukumoto, 2003). Even conflicts which have already been resolved can influence current interactions, manifesting themselves in the form of expression and lack of expression available to certain groups (Meares, Oetzel, Torres, Derkacs, & Ginossar, 2004). Issues of privilege within a society often result in certain mem-bers having less access to venues for ensuring that their stories be heard, while others remain unaware of their own place of relative power in the interaction. While those whose voices are privileged may feel secure, those without a voice are likely to not feel as safe.

The language used in interactions between people from different cultural backgrounds is another important factor to consider. Language is an inherent part of our identities and the norms of the languages we speak shape how we portray ourselves and how we view the world (Whorf, 1956). Individuals from different cultures may both be fluent in (or even native speakers of) the same language, but if they are not both native speakers, then the native speaker has an advantage. The non-native speaker, depending on linguistic proficiency (as well as the topic and the context), may face more difficulty in articulating his or her ideas. And a non-native speaker with a strong accent may have more difficulty being understood by a native speaker. Even with native speakers, though, different cultural group memberships may mean different verbal and nonverbal versions of the common language, resulting in differences in meaning that may or may not be easily understood by outsiders (Hall, 2001). These differences, both linguistic and paralinguistic, also result in judgments being made by others about intelligence, ability, and competence, which can influence a communicator's sense of security and conviviality.

The *contact hypothesis* (Allport, 1954; Amir, 1969) is the prediction that the more interaction someone has with people from other cultures (given certain conditions), the less ethnocentric he or she will be. Unfortunately, contact can also serve to reinforce existing stereotypes and prejudice if the individuals do not share equal status and equal goals, and if they are not open to other viewpoints. Intercultural conflict is a result of cultures having different values, expectations, and communication styles, without the individuals involved having the ability to see the differences as acceptable or to develop ways of interacting with people from other cultures. *Ethnocentrism* is the degree to which someone is unable to shift frames of reference to see something from the perspective of another person. Ethnocentrism can cause intercultural conflict, especially when an individual feels his or her cultural perspective is threatened. Ethnocentrism influences the ability of an individual to view other face strategies and orientations as valid and appropriate.

## The Case of the *Ehime Maru*: A Conflict Challenging Security and Civility

While intercultural conflict can occur on many levels from interpersonal to international, a recent case of national-level intercultural conflict between Japan and the United States was the *Ehime Maru* incident. On February 9, 2001, nine Japanese citizens died as a result of a rapid-surfacing exercise carried out by the crew of the United States nuclear submarine *Greenville*. Due to failure of the submarine crew to ensure that the area was unoccupied, the submarine collided with a training ship, the *Ehime Maru* ("Students, Crew," 2001). The submarine was conducting a rapid-surfacing exercise for visiting oil company guests on a tour, whose presence may have distracted the crew from performing the required safety assessments ("Submarine Accident," 2001). Four of the dead were Japanese high school students studying to work in the fishing industry. What had previously been perceived to be a relatively safe environment (with potential danger mainly from natural events) resulted in a disaster due to human error, increasing a sense of insecurity and predictive uncertainty about the actions of the Americans and harming the potential for *kyosei*.

While this case presents many potential avenues for further evaluation, it exemplifies some of the differences in expectations for facework between the two countries, and also demonstrates some of the larger contextual issues related to conflict. The United States and Japan have an ongoing relationship within which this case is embedded. The United States defeated Japan in World War II, occupied the country after the war, and has maintained military bases in Japan since that time. During the subsequent period, there have been many incidents of conflict between U.S. military personnel and Japanese citizens, including disagreements over crimes committed, jurisdiction for investigations, time limits for land use, and potential environmental dangers (Morrison, 2000).

While the *Ehime Maru* incident was covered in detail in the media, coverage of the behavior of the captain of the *Greenville*, Commander Scott Waddle, provides one example of the differences in behavioral expectations between the Japanese public and the American public. A month after the incident, Waddle publicly apologized to the families of those who died in the incident ("Families of Missing," 2001). This was not accepted well by all of the Japanese family members; some commented publicly in the Japanese media on their perceptions that the apology was insincere because of the delay in it being offered. In contrast, many Americans described themselves as being surprised and touched at the sincerity of Waddle's apology when he appeared on U.S. television speaking about the incident, and he was described as a hero for accepting responsibility for the incident (Penn, 2001). Television host Larry King praised Waddle for accepting blame for the incident and apologizing promptly. These differences in perceptions between the Japanese and Americans reflect different ideas about appropriate facework behavior when responsible for tragedy, as well as differences in ideas about accountability and ethics (Dubnick, 2003). From a Japanese perspective and Grice's (1975) axioms for appropriateness in language use, the apology was not sufficient—it was not performed appropriately or in a timely manner, and it lacked substantiveness. From an American perspective, Waddle went above and beyond what would be expected from someone in that situation. In fact, from an American perspective, "excessive" use of apologies can be perceived as a sign of weakness or insecurity, so in an American context, Waddle should *not* have apologized more.

At the military court of inquiry, Waddle appeared in uniform with his wife at his side to defend himself and did not display a remorseful or apologetic persona (French, 2001). This was perceived as demonstrating a lack of sincerity or sensitivity by the Japanese public. From an American perspective, Waddle, while sensitive to Japanese public opinion (as demonstrated by his willingness to apologize), was appropriately managing his public appearance in order to repair the damage to his image (Goffman, 1959). Additional conflict emerged when Waddle received only a minor punishment for his role in the incident (Penn, 2001). Criticism came from the Japanese public, the media, and some government officials who, from their cultural point of view, felt that Waddle should have received greater punishment and taken greater responsibility ("Waddle Penalty," 2001; Ishii, 2001). Analysts also brought up examples of other times where the United States military actions had resulted in accidents to civilians, calling the U.S. lack of responsibility "a mockery of civil society's common sense" ("Waddle Penalty," 2001). While United States public opinion was undecided over the incident, more blame was focused on the Navy policies regarding the presence of visitors rather than on Waddle specifically and the recovery efforts provided a sense of closure (French, 2001).

While the United States government did pay reparations to the Japanese government and the families of the dead ("Last Two," 2003), this incident served to reinforce stereotypes of Americans as being unwilling to take responsibility for their actions. This example of conflict demonstrates how intercultural differences in communicating can increase conflict and insecurity, reducing the sense of *kyosei*. While Waddle was acting in a way judged appropriate in the American context for restoring a sense of harmony and positive feelings, from a Japanese perspective, his actions were lacking and failed to restore a positive relationship. Differing concepts of apology resulted in questioning of Waddle's sincerity and a disturbed sense of *kyosei*. If a similar incident had occurred with a Japanese submarine instead of an American one, the captain likely would have acted quite differently because the cultural expectations would call for different facework and appropriate contrition. Because of the cross-cultural nature of the incident, there was more potential for post-accident conflict and perceived inappropriate behavior, resulting in a further erosion of Japanese collective trust in the United States.

## Conclusion

The case of the *Ehime Maru* provides an example of how different cultural expectations for responsibility and apology make resolution and restoration of trust challenging when a conflict has occurred. While most examples are not as widely known as this, many of the same factors, including power and history, come into play as individuals interact in the workplace, in social relationships, or as representatives of their organizations and governments. More knowledge of intercultural differences is a potentially powerful cognitive resource for individuals experiencing conflict. In the *Ehime Maru* case, had the American been more familiar with Japanese culture and had the Japanese been more familiar with American cultural norms for apology and responsibility, there might have been less conflict and misunderstanding after the accident; though, the fact that it occurred at all would still be a grave challenge to *kyosei*. Living in harmony with others also implies being responsible for actions taken and an awareness of the effect of those actions on others.

The human desire for peace, security, and *kyosei* are strong, but in intercultural interactions, even when there is not a tragedy of the magnitude of the *Ehime Maru* incident, they can be challenging to obtain. Differences in communication norms and in expectations in different cultures can result not only in conflict, but in challenges to resolving that conflict, as individuals employ different facework strategies in order to restore harmony. On an individual level, knowledge of intercultural concepts and development of intercultural skills can help individuals to become more competent in interacting with those who are different from themselves. Better understanding of intercultural communication concepts and theories can help individuals to explain conflict, and potentially to reduce conflict, or help to resolve it. Increased understanding of intercultural conflict—as well as an increased understanding of differences in politeness and other behavioral norms—are challenging goals. But this increased understanding can contribute to a greater sense of security in intercultural interactions at a local, regional, nation, or global level. And this, in turn, can lead to an increase in *kyosei*.

## Notes

1. See the chapter in this volume by Cottam and Marenin for a more complete investigation of human security.
2. *Kyosei* is described in more detail from a Japanese perspective in several of the chapters in this volume, including those by Professors Murakami and Chiba.
3. Ting-Toomey initially described Face-Negotiation Theory in 1994 (Ting-Toomey, 1994). In 1998, a revised Face-Negotiation Theory was published with Kurogi (Ting-Toomey & Kurogi, 1998).

## References

Allport, G. W. (1954). *The nature of prejudice.* Cambridge, MA: Addison-Wesley.
Cupach, W. R., & Metts, S. (1994). *Facework.* Thousand Oaks, CA: Sage.
Amir, Y. (1969). Contact hypothesis in ethnic relations. *Psychological Bulletin, 71*, 319-341.
Augsburger, D. (1992). *Conflict mediation across cultures.* Louisville, KY: Westminster/John Knox Press.

Brown, P. & Levinson, S. (1987). *Politeness: Some universals in language usage.* Cambridge: Cambridge University Press.

Canary, D. J., Cupach, W. R., & Messman, S. J. (1995). *Relationship conflict.* Thousand Oaks, CA: Sage.

Casse, P. (1982). *Training for the multicultural manager: A practical and cross-cultural approach to the management of people.* Washington, D.C.: SIETAR.

Dubnick, M. J. (2003). Accountability and ethics: Reconsidering the relationships. *International Journal Of Organization Theory And Behavior, 6*(3), 405-441.

Families of missing have mixed feelings on captain's apology. (2001, March 9). *Japan Economic Newswire.* Retrieved August 18, 2004 from http://web.lexis-nexis.com.

Fisher, W.R. (1987). *Human communication as narration: Toward a philosophy of reason, value, and action.* Columbia, S.C.: University of South Carolina Press.

French, H. W. (2001, November 5). U.S. makes amends to Japan for sinking of ship. *The New York Times,* p. A6. Retrieved August 18, 2004 from http://web.lexis-nexis.com.

Fukumoto, A. (2003). *Transforming conflicts over memories of war into constructive dialogue: Exploring Japanese communication, national identities, and collective memories of World War II.* Unpublished doctoral dissertation, University of New Mexico, Albuquerque.

Galvin, K. M., & Wilkinson, C. A. (2003). The communication process. In K. M. Galvin and P. J. Cooper (Eds.), *Making connections* (pp. 4-10). Los Angeles: Roxbury.

Goffman, E. (1959). *The presentation of self in everyday life.* Garden City, NY: Doubleday.

Grice, H. P. (1975). Logic and conversation. In P. Cole and J. Morgan (Eds.), *Syntax and semantics: Vol. 3 Speech acts* (pp. 41-58). New York: Academic Press.

Gudykunst, W. B. (1995). Anxiety uncertainty management (AUM) theory: Current status. In R. L. Wiseman (Ed.), *Intercultural communication theory* (pp. 8-58). Newbury Park, CA: Sage.

Gudykunst, W. B., & Ting-Toomey, S. (2003). *Communicating with strangers: An approach to intercultural communication* (4th ed.). New York: McGraw-Hill.

Hall, B. J. (2001). *Among cultures: Communication challenges.* Wadsworth.

Hall, E. T. (1976). *Beyond Culture.* Garden City, NJ: Anchor Press.

Hofstede, G. (1991). *Cultures and organizations: Software of the mind.* New York: McGraw-Hill.

Hu, H. C. (1944). The Chinese concept of "face." *American Anthropologist, 46,* 45-64.

Intel Corporation (2004). *The workplace: Our values are at the heart of everything we do.* Retrieved August 20, 2004 from http://www.intel.com/jobs/workplace/values.htm.

Ishii, K. (2001, April 25). Waddle case reflects U.S. leniency. *The Daily Yomiuri,* p. 2. Retrieved August 18, 2004 from http://web.lexis-nexis.com.

Jenks, C. (1993). *Culture.* London: Routledge.

Kluckholn, F. R., & Strodtbeck, F. L. (1961). *Variations in values orientations.* Evanston, IL: Row, Peterson.

Last two families settle Ehime Maru case with U.S. Navy. (2003, February 1). *Asahi Shimbun Global News Wire.* Retrieved August 18, 2004 from http://web.lexis-nexis.com.

Martin, J. N., & Nakayama, T. K. (2004). *Intercultural communication in contexts.* New York: McGraw-Hill.

Meares, M. M., Oetzel, J. G., Torres, A. B., Derkacs, D., & Ginossar, T. (2004). A critical analysis of employee mistreatment and muted voices in the culturally diverse workplace. *Journal of Applied Communication Research, 32,* 4-27.

Morisaki, S., & Gudykunst, W.B. (1994). Face in Japan and the United States. In S. Ting-Toomey (Ed.), *The challenge of facework: Cross-cultural and interpersonal issues* (pp. 47-94). Albany, NY: State University of New York Press.

Morrison, C. E. (2000, July 21). Okinawans will remain unhappy. *International Herald Tribune,* p. 8. Retrieved August 18, 2004 from http://web.lexis-nexis.com.

Oetzel, J. G. (1998). Explaining individual communication processes in homogeneous and heterogeneous groups through individualism-collectivism and self-construal. *Human Communication Research, 25,* 202-224.

Oetzel, J. G., Meares, M. M., & Fukumoto, A. (2003). Cross-cultural and intercultural work group communication. In R. Hirokawa, R. Cathcart, L. Samovar & L. Henman (Eds.), *Small group communication: Theory and practice*, (8th ed., pp. 239-252). Los Angeles, CA: Roxbury.

Oetzel, J. G., Ting-Toomey, S., Masumoto, T., & Yokochi, Y. (1999). *Developing a cross-cultural typology of facework behaviors in interpersonal conflicts.* Paper presented at the annual meeting of the International Communication Association. San Francisco, CA.

Penn, W. (2001, May 3). Waddle saves face. *The Daily Yomiuri*, p. 10. Retrieved August 18, 2004 from http://web.lexis-nexis.com.

Stohl, C. (2000). Globalizing organizational communication. In F. M. Jablin & L. L. Putnam (Eds.), *The new handbook of organizational communication* (pp. 323-375). Thousand Oaks, CA: Sage.

Stephan, C., & Stephan, W. (1992). Reducing intercultural anxiety through intercultural contact. *International Journal of Intercultural Relations, 16*, 89-106.

Students, crew recall sub-accident experience. (2001, February 11). *The Daily Yomiuri*, p. 2. Retrieved August 18, 2004 from Lexis-Nexus.

Submarine accident shaking Japan-U.S. relations. (2001, May 1). *Journal of Japanese Trade & Industry.* Retrieved August 18, 2004 from http://web.lexis-nexis.com.

*The American Heritage Dictionary of the English Language* (4th ed.). (2000). New York: Houghton Mifflin Company. Retrieved August 11, 2004 from http://dictionary.reference.com/search?q=security.

Ting-Toomey, S. (Ed.) (1994). *The challenge of facework: Cross-cultural and interpersonal issues.* Albany, NY: State University of New York Press.

Ting-Toomey, S., & Kurogi, A. (1998). Facework competence in intercultural conflict: An updated face-negotiation theory. *International Journal of Intercultural Relations, 22*, 187-225.

Ting-Toomey, S. & Oetzel, J. G. (2001). *Managing intercultural conflict effectively.* Thousand Oaks, CA: Sage.

Triandis, H. C. (1995). *Individualism and collectivism.* Boulder, CO: Westview.

Waddle penalty a mockery of civil society's common sense. (2001, April 26). *Asahi News Service.* Retrieved August 18, 2004 from Lexis-Nexus.

Watzlawick, P. (1987). *The language of change.* New York: Norton.

Whorf, B. L. (1956). *Language, thought, and reality.* Cambridge, MA: MIT Press.

## fourteen

# Ethical and Religious Perspectives on *Kyosei* (Living Together)

### Michael W. Myers

This chapter advances three theses:

1. *Kyosei* (conviviality, or living together justly and peacefully) requires a moral backdrop or moral nature against which moral and intellectual virtues may be practiced.

2. Ethical reasoning is autonomous and cannot be superseded by simple divine commands.

3. Nevertheless, the religious imagination can feed the streams of our moral lives and can suggest new forms of moral relationship.

Peace, security and *kyosei* (conviviality): Like a Venn diagram of three overlapping circles, each term contains a unique semantic space. Each term also contains a semantic space shared with one of the other two terms; finally, a component of meaning is shared between all three terms. The shared space might usher in the following proposition: *kyosei* depends on secure and peaceful living arrangements; the goal of achieving peace, security and conviviality depends on fostering each in understanding and practice; and each term sheds light on another—indeed, the three seem to be interrelated notions.

This chapter will focus on *kyosei*, or living together justly and peacefully. It will bring to the topic a number of disciplinary perspectives, especially those of philosophy, ethics and religious studies. When a philosophical perspective is brought to bear on the problem of living together, an ancient discipline is renewed. This discipline is social ethics. In historical tradition, the emergence of a strong social ethic has been one of the authentic indicators of the birth of philosophy. One thinks of Socrates, Plato and Aristotle in Greece, or Confucius and Mencius in China. The philosophies of these thinkers were highly colored by social and ethical concerns. Although social ethics have not been emphasized recently, the need for a sound social ethic is greater than ever today.

One might ask, Why mix religion into the issue of *kyosei*? Are not the problems of living together great enough for social ethics without religion? The answer to the second question is both yes and no. The argument of this chapter will present the independence of ethical thinking as a rational, practical and universal enterprise. Yet in point of fact the religious question will not go away so easily. Religious traditions—both theistic and nontheistic—command us to behave in certain ways. These traditions attempt to inform our collective and individual consciences of the differences between right and wrong. They feed our creative imaginations with ideas strongly colored with ethical concepts. Therefore, we must examine the religious traditions in order to verify or confirm their right to command certain behaviors, structure our ideas, and feed our imaginations. We must acknowledge that religion can play an important and even indispensable role when it challenges the conventional morality of its day.[1] The concept of "living together" is at the intersection of ethics and religion. It is the task of this chapter to enter this area and try to provide some clarification. The discussion begins by specifying *kyosei* as living together in various forms of *moral relationship*.

## 1. Forms of Moral Relationship

We cannot define the forms of moral relationship so narrowly at the outset of this discussion that the restricted list of forms might inhibit the consideration of new and creative ways of living together. We can, however, look to ethical and religious traditions for some guidance and a *prima facie* list. The Confucian tradition, for example, offers five forms of moral relationship: emperor/minister, husband/wife, father/son, older brother/younger brother, and friend/friend. We can immediately see possibilities for new and creative relationships; in other words, we can see that these five relations may be widened in ways consistent with contemporary moral imagination. Parent/child, for example, allows for elaboration of roles and expectations in more ways than the traditional gender specific formulation of father/son. For us, father/son might be just one example of the larger parent/child (or even guardian/child) relation. Specificity in elaborating the father/son relation is necessary and valuable, but in today's world it is seen as only a part of a wider possibility for moral relationship between children and the adults who bring them up.

The contemporary legal and social controversy in the United States over gay marriage may serve as a second example. While the elaboration of roles and expectations for either side of the husband/wife relation continues to undergo transformation in the contemporary moral imagination, the widening of possibilities through wide spread acceptance of same sex partner relationships is profound. Both social conservatives and liberals have a stake in this American controversy, and both realize this possibility. The legal blessing of gay marriage opens up a new form of moral relationship. At stake is not just whether gay marriage is acceptable. At stake is the possibility of a new goodness.

Thus, it is easy to see that moral relationships have forms that are to some degree unpredictable, plastic and negotiable. These forms have a content or glue that binds them together. In ancient China, the following virtues were displayed by persons in relationship: *ren* (benevolence), *i* (justice or duty), *li* (propriety or ritual correctness), and *zhih* (wisdom). *Ren* formed the umbrella virtue that was truly the glue that held society together. The mere fulfillment of one's role is empty, according to Confucius, unless it is performed with a good heart. Thus Confucian ethics anticipated the Kantian and deontological ethics of duty performed with a good will. *I* is the virtue usually translated as justice or dutifulness.

It applies more to the action performed than to the agent performing the action. An act displays *i* insofar as it distributes justice toward the particular persons in relation to that action. *Li* was the archaic virtue of ritual correctness. It was transformed in Confucian philosophy (especially under Mencius) into an inner sense of deference and compliance. *Li* is clearly modeled in the parent/child relation as filial piety (*xiao*), but its meaning was already widened in ancient China to include the respect one owes one's elders. Finally, *zhih* is knowledge, including the knowledge of right and wrong. Here one may also find second order intellectual virtues such as rationality, practicality, and universality.

Mencius, Confucius' second generation disciple, called these virtues "shoots" or "germs." The organic metaphor was chosen advisedly, for according to Mencius, the virtues are as much a part of our human nature as shoots are to plants. He writes that if we practice these virtues, compassionate government will be as easy as rolling a ball around on the palm of the hand; conversely, if we neglect these virtues, we lose a part of our humanity in a very real sense:

> My reason for saying that no person is devoid of a heart sensitive to the suffering of others is this. Suppose a person were, all of a sudden, to see a young child on the verge of falling into a well. He would certainly be moved to compassion, not because he wanted to get in the good graces of the parents, nor because he wanted to win the praise of his fellow villagers or friends, nor yet because he disliked the cry of the child. From this it can be seen that whoever is devoid of the heart of compassion is not human, whoever is devoid of the heart of shame is not human, whoever is devoid of the heart of courtesy and modesty is not human, and whoever is devoid of the heart of right and wrong is not human. The heart of compassion is the germ of benevolence (*ren*); the heart of shame, of dutifulness (*i*); the heart of courtesy and modesty, of observance of the rites (*li*); the heart of right and wrong, of wisdom (*zhih*). Persons have these four germs just as they have four limbs.[2]

In this passage, Mencius not only lists the most important virtues, but also offers criteria to test them in action. The general test is the state of the heart/mind (*xin*). For Mencius, to do good works is not an additional requirement beyond our basic human nature, but is rather part of our definition as human. Mencius does not deny that we are capable of evil; rather he attempts to show (in this example and others) that the potential to do good works is part of our nature and can be cultivated and taught.

Thus, for Mencius, the forms of moral relationship and the virtues that bind them together can only take place if we as human beings are by nature moral beings. Elsewhere in the *Mencius,* Mencius' interlocutor Gaozi argues that human nature is indifferent and that morality is forced upon us and is external to us.[3] But Mencius refutes Gaozi in a series of famous analogies. For Mencius, only something good can go bad; only if we accept morality as part of our nature can we build a society of moral relationships. Mencius' position is consistent with religious traditions that argue their ethical positions on the basis of a moral human nature or a moral backdrop to human society. In this sense, the Confucian tradition is highly religious even though it is largely nontheistic.

## 2. The Independence of Ethical Reasoning

When conjoined, ethics and religion constitute a problem because of the putative claims of each over our lives. Peter Byrne, a contemporary British philosopher, sets out one form of the controversy between morality and theistic religion as follows:[4]

1.  Theistic thinkers contend that morality without religion is gravely deficient or even conceptually impossible.
2.  Atheistic thinkers claim that religion should have no influence upon morals and may even be a corrupter of morals.

Byrne argues that (1) and (2) rest on a false assumption. Morality is thought (wrongly) to consist primarily of a set of binding rules. The theist claims that the authority of the rules rests on a divine legislator; the atheist notes that if God is the rule-giver, the rules would be arbitrary and not universal. But without thinking of morality as a set of rules, the controversy weakens. Perhaps the function of religion in terms of morality is to feed the human imagination with new forms of moral relationship. Perhaps religion is more about creative imagination than the slavish following of rules. Perhaps even divine commands can be understood this way, as creative urges to "think outside the box."

The argument can proceed in two steps. First, Byrne's argument against morality as a mere set of rules allows for the questioning of the supposed incompatibility between morality and theistic religion. Second, divine commands might be alternatively interpreted as creative streams which feed the religious and ethical imagination.

The argument against morality as a mere set of rules is based on criticism of a commonly held belief about moral motivation: that is, that motivation is the hope of reward and fear of punishment that we commonly find in theistic religions. Such a motivation seems to assume that our nature is *not* moral and that morality must be imposed onto our non-moral (or even immoral) desires. Consistently with the view of Mencius, Byrne argues that desires and interests can naturally arise out of forms of moral relationship.[5] In a very real sense, we are rewarded by the satisfaction we gain from the moral activity itself. Heaven, if it exists, would also have to correspond to the ideal of moral completion and perfection. Thus, rather than merely a place to receive one's just rewards, heaven would be a place to form new and creative moral relationships.

Immanuel Kant holds a similar view of the autonomy of ethics and the necessarily moral nature of a postulated afterlife. For Kant, the highest good and the Holy Will require the postulation of an afterlife because we cannot achieve them in our finitude. Life and afterlife alike are aligned under a single moral backdrop. For Kant, "Practical reason contradicts itself if it abandons the idea that the world is under ultimate moral government."[6] Without heaven, without closure or a sense of final judgment and final determination, the secular moralist "leaves the pursuit of the good pointless if it has no answer to the problems raised by human finiteness and the world's evil."[7] Byrne argues, "The human order, considered without reference to a religiously sanctioned eschaton, always falls short of complete justice."[8] Such justice requires both the making of the world into a complete moral order and the postulation of an afterlife to perfect the process.

Agnostic or atheistic thinkers, however, may believe the solution to the justice problem cannot lie in the direction of theism, because theism is questionable on other grounds. The problem of evil, for example, raises questions for the theist. Can there be a just eschaton and an unjust world seemingly forever steeped in injustice? If there is a religious eschaton, it must complete the good in a way consistent with human justice and virtue. Here arises another point of argument for an independent ethics. Byrne argues against the renunciation of the world favored by some religious traditions (or one might say by sub-groups of most traditions). Religions ought not to become too otherworldly, for this leads to a social and political indifferentism.[9] Moral rules do benefit us by countering evil in the world (whether they come from a theistic or nontheistic source), and the world is in itself a worthy place.

But one may still ask, why be moral? Is the root of the religious objection to secular ethics that such ethics can offer the individual who respects morality no guarantee of anything other than a life of disappointment and self sacrifice?[10] Consistently with the view of Confucius, Byrne argues that there is inherent value in pursuing the goals and aims of virtue. At this point, Byrne completes the argument for the independence of a secular ethics. He does not think that moral theory must be committed to the existence of God in order to have a workable accounting of moral motivation. Byrne does not think that the truth and rationality of moral principles rely on the truth and rationality of belief in God. Yet he leaves open the possibility that a religious worldview might complete our moral lives. In the language we have adopted here, the religious imagination may feed the streams of moral life. And consistent with the view of Mencius, Byrne argues that the potential relevance of a religious worldview to ethical inquiry is established through a general account of human nature.

Byrne begins his discussion with a question: Can we say that certain types of actions are forbidden come what may? For example, a command might be given, "Do not murder," as a bar against killing the innocent. Byrne outlines four responses:[11]

1. The secular moralist may rely on an intuition that murder is wrong.
2. The secular moralist may accept a consequentialist theory: "Nothing is so bad that it cannot be well done in some circumstances."[12]
3. The religious moralist may rely on simple divine command theory. God says it is wrong, so it is wrong.
4. The religious moralist may defend the prohibition "on the basis of a metaphysic, some large-scale description of what human life is and how it relates to the natural world."[13]

Byrne prefers (4): "A complete ethics needs a substantive account of the human good and thus some connections with general thoughts about human nature."[14] Byrne wants to defend a secular account of morality on the basis of its seamless connection with epistemology and metaphysics. We have good reasons to act morally: for example, human kind flourishing in itself and the satisfaction of moral and rational good. We act morally in accordance with a larger nature. We need not ask the source of moral standards. Byrne's view is consistent with the dictum of Nietzsche: We take and ask not who it is that gives.

## 3. Divine Commands

In order to establish a relationship between morality and theistic religion, we begin with a question about divine commands. Does morality consist in a set of moral rules that flow from divine commands?[15] If so, the divine will would serve as the necessary and sufficient source of the truth and authority of moral rules. In simple divine command theory, what is right is that which is prescribed by divine will; what is wrong is that which is proscribed by divine will.

The refutation of simple divine command theory began in Greek tradition with the Socratic discussion of the Euthyphro dilemma.[16] In this dilemma, we are faced with two possibilities:

1. What is right is so simply because God commands it.
2. God commands what is right because it is right.

There are two good arguments against the first horn of the dilemma. First, we should have a moral reason for obeying God's commands. Second, we should be able to know right from wrong independently of knowing God's commands. But the second horn of the dilemma is also unattractive in at least two ways: it sets up a second standard; and it seems to make God's commands irrelevant to ethics.

Socrates' way of addressing the dilemma was to pose another question. He asked, How do we define justice or righteousness? Conventional Greek morality answered, "Justice is what is loved by the gods." In this case, justice is a property seen, led, produced, or carried. It is extrinsic to the nature of the thing to which the property is assigned. Justice has no power to account for why the gods love it, or in theistic language, why God prescribes it. It does not connect with the nature of first-order moral virtues like courage or generosity; neither is it incompatible with cowardice or meanness. Finally, it does not connect with second-order intellectual virtues like rationality, practicality, or universality. God's commands become in a real sense arbitrary. Morality is reduced to the rules of an exclusive group, a group that has awareness of a particular revelation. Religious ethics flowing from simple divine command theory thus violate the autonomy of moral agents.[17]

Socrates does not accept this view and thinks of justice rather as an intrinsic property of acts performed by people in relation to each other. Thus does it acquire explanatory power. Just acts are good for their own sake. Justice becomes connected with the nature of the act it qualifies—but at the cost of being independent of the divine will. Socrates opted for the second horn of the dilemma. In fact, he paid with his life in an Athenian court mired in conventional thinking.

Can divine command theory offer anything of value to contemporary people living in a community? Perhaps. Byrne offers a *modified* divine command theory where the commands are understood to be wider than just a set of rules. To see what bearing religion has upon morality in the context of religious faith, Byrne proposes looking at an analogy:[18]

God: people :: state: citizen

Byrne believes that the state/citizen relation has an extrinsic aspect that is useful to retain. The authority of the state depends on power *plus* a perceived legitimacy by the citizen. The state must have power *plus* the right to be obeyed, not mere might. And there is required a moral context behind the formation and enforcement of the state's laws and directives. The authority of the state requires goods and rights independent of state authority, and these goods and rights must be respected by state authority. Such goods include justice, internal and external security, and a measure of freedom.[19] The citizen is thus under the authority of and obligated to the moral background of justice, security and freedom; but the citizen also comes under the authority of the state itself, of its laws and directives.

Byrne next draws on an intrinsic definition of political obligation, in order to present an argument for both extrinsic and intrinsic bonds between citizen and state. He argues, "The obligation to the state emerges out of the identity between state and citizen when state power is legitimate."[20] It is not the case that the citizen grants authority only because of perceived good to be provided by the state; rather good further established as a consequence of education in citizenship.[21] Mores, customs, forms of living and social cooperation are fostered by the state.

In theological terms, extrinsic and intrinsic bonds can be called transcendent and immanent relations, respectively. In terms of the analogy, God is both over and above the people but also at the same time resides in the people's hearts and minds. St. Thomas

Aquinas expressed this analogy in terms of law. The divine law binds God to people while the human law binds state to citizen. Both divine law and human law share the backdrop of morality called *natural law*. The natural law is the rational human being's participation in God's eternal law. It forms the basis for positive human law while at the same time finding precepts in the sacred tradition as a reflection of eternal law.

If Aquinas' analogy is to work, God must be worthy of worship. Not just any commands by an omnipotent being will have the authority of moral law. Rather, authority depends on God's goodness and respect for moral requirements. This goodness and respect is independent of the precise content of God's decrees. If such a moral backdrop of goodness and respect for the moral law is indeed shared between God and people, if God is God and is worthy of worship, then we have an obligation to obey God. Analogously, law follows from society, but it also molds and directs a way of life proper in society. Law thus has both an intrinsic and an extrinsic aspect; it is not simply external command backed by sanction.[22] In the case of God's deliverance of the moral law, the intrinsic dimension is even more important than the extrinsic. Human law creates an imperfect order; divine law is "perfectly and directly creative."[23] For Aquinas, "[God's] will can thus be discerned not merely as external commands but also in the rational discovery of the rules and principles which must be followed if the human good is to be attained."[24]

Simple divine command theory is easy to refute because it deprives the God/person relationship of any moral background. Even so, Byrne argues that our relationship to God can be regarded as the foundation of ethics.[25] A summary of his reasons follows:

1. God's commands are a unique source of moral obligation in a natural world.
2. God's will in nature is the ground of human flourishing. In other words, human life and nature share a moral order through a common creation.
3. Our relation to God exemplifies the final human good of interrelationship.

For Byrne, then, the right is not primarily that which is commanded by God. Rather, the right is "that which embodies respect for the good that the divine order lays down as the best way in which a human life is to be lived."[26]

## 4. The Parable of the Good Samaritan

How might the divine order lay down guidelines for living a human life in the best way? How might a sacred tradition command? A sacred text might inform our moral relationships and help us to live together in new and creative ways. The parable of the Good Samaritan (Luke 10: 30-35) provides a test case:

> [Jesus said], A man was going down from Jerusalem to Jericho, and fell into the hands of robbers, who stripped him, beat him, and went away, leaving him half dead. Now by chance a priest was going down that road; and when he saw him, he passed by on the other side. So likewise a Levite, when he came to the place and saw him, passed by on the other side. But a Samaritan while traveling came near him; and when he saw him, he was moved with pity. He went to him and bandaged his wounds, having poured oil and wine on them. Then he put him on his own animal, brought him to an inn, and took care of him. The next day he took out two denarii, gave them to the innkeeper, and said, "Take care of him; and when I come back, I will repay whatever more you spend."[27]

Some additional background may be helpful here. The road from Jerusalem to Jericho was about thirty kilometers (eighteen miles) long, with a steep drop in elevation. The road was notoriously dangerous. The priest in the story is a Jewish priest. He represents "the highest religious leadership among the Jews."[28] The Levite represents a priest's right-hand man, a designated lay associate. The use of oil and wine is medicinal: "The oil served as a salve (see Isa 1.6) and the wine as an antiseptic."[29] Two denarii would pay for about two months of lodging in a first-century inn.[30]

All parables are purported words of Jesus to his disciples. A common (and sound) way of understanding these words is to view them as giving some sort of enlightenment or instruction about the kingdom of God, or as explaining the new way of living together that Jesus proposed to his listeners.

When interpreting a parable, it is useful to follow some guidelines. One first asks whether the parable can be found in any of the other gospels, because the internal evidence (comparing the context and the way the gospel writers cast the parables) can be highly instructive. Alas, the parable of the Good Samaritan can only be found in Luke.

A second interpretive strategy is to examine carefully the gospel writer's context. Luke places the parable of the Good Samaritan in the context of Jesus' response to a lawyer's question about eternal life. When the lawyer asks how one may gain eternal life, Jesus in turn asks him what is commanded in law. The lawyer responds with the dual commandment to love God and to love one's neighbor as well as oneself. Thus Luke places the parable in the context of a discussion of types of people who constitute one's neighbors. But the connection to eternal life is important, too. When the parable ends and a discussion about the Samaritan's mercy ensues, a connection is made between the half-dead man and his restoration to life by the Samaritan. To have mercy is to give life.[31] To be all-merciful is to have or to give a form of eternal life.

The most obvious interpretation of neighborliness in the parable is to identify with the Samaritan and to read the parable as a command to perform good acts toward strangers. We even have "Good Samaritan" laws in the United States that require us to help those in need. Televised situation comedies like *Seinfeld* test the social acceptance of Good Samaritan laws. Certainly, Luke wants us to read the parable as instruction to do good acts, for after telling the story, Luke writes that Jesus admonished the lawyer, "Go and do likewise."[32]

But another way to interpret the parable, and a third interpretive strategy for any parable, is to ask the question, How would the story be heard by Jesus' listeners? This is an interesting question for a number of reasons, not least of which is that it distinguishes between Jesus' audience and Luke's. There is some distance of time and space between the two audiences, and when we examine Jesus' audience, we are immediately thrown back into the Jewish world of the first century, with its competing sects, rabbis, and rabble-rousers.

The point is that the perspective we so easily take of the Samaritan—that is, to identify with him and to accept his heroic motivation to help a hurt person as he passes by—may have been quite impossible for Jesus' listeners to comprehend or act upon. Samaritans were the enemies of the Israelites. It thus seems that in this parable Jesus is asking his listeners not to identify with the hero, but rather with the victim.[33]

The victim in the story is not identified, but we can assume that he is Jewish. Of all the characters in the story, only the Samaritan is foreign; only he is identified by his nationality as a detested member of the neighboring kingdom. "He that eats the bread of the Samaritan is like to one what eats the flesh of swine."[35] Jesus' listeners, who interpret the Samaritan as a negative figure, naturally expect him to follow the behavior of the priest and Levite. But Jesus surprises them with the fact that it is the Samaritan who shows mercy to the half-dead man.

In fact, the appearance at all of the Samaritan is quite surprising. The triad expected by Jesus' listeners would have been priest, Levite and Israelite, and the listeners would have identified with the layperson Israelite. C. Montefiore has remarked that the parable's triad, i.e., priest, Levite and Samaritan, is no less odd and unexpected than "Priest, Deacon, and Frenchman" would be to us today.[35] Priest, Levite and Israelite, on the other hand, is a familiar description of the Jewish people. The turn in the story where the Samaritan becomes a hero thus jars the audience's expectations, and confronts the listener with the problem of with whom to identify.

If the audience cannot immediately identify with the Samaritan or with the apathetic priest and Levite, the only remaining option is to identify with the victim. As Bernard B. Scott puts it, "To remain in the story the hearer cannot play hero but must become a victim."[36]

> [T]he hearer's only possible course is to identify with the half-dead and be saved by a mortal enemy or else dismiss the narrative as not like real life. The hearer who expects an Israelite to come along and play hero finds that the Israelite is already half-dead and the only option is the Samaritan.[37]

Thus the parable overturns conventional expectations and morality. The Samaritan is not the enemy but the savior, and the listener is not able to play hero, but must enlarge his or her moral imagination, and take the point of view of the victim.

If the message of the parable is placed in the context of Jesus' other teachings about the kingdom of God, it becomes clear that the point of the parable is to break down the barriers between religious insider and outsider, and between friend and foreigner. The parable offers a new vision of what the new kingdom of God is supposed to be about. The new kingdom is about compassion, not purity, caste, or national restrictions. It is about a new kind of moral power. The parable "commands" by drawing our attention to a new kind of moral relationship, a relationship which expands our usual expectations about who the insiders and outsiders are in social life.

Now it is obvious that Jesus' story about the hurt Israelite and Mencius' story about the child about to fall into a well have striking similarities. What happens when we dare to interpret these stories across the boundaries of culture and time? Jesus' story helps us to understand Mencius in many ways. The priest and Levite that passed by, for example, are characters missing from Mencius' story. Mencius would not deny that not everyone will stop to help a child about to fall into a well. Rather, his point is that a person will naturally have a desire to help, because we all share a common humanity and moral nature with the child. Jesus' story also helps us to have empathy with the child and to see the child's point of view. Perhaps this was Mencius' point, too. In any case, he believed that the cultivation of the moral and intellectual virtues ought to be begun from childhood. For, as Mencius concludes, "[W]hen these [virtues] are fully developed, one can take under one's protection the whole kingdom within the Four Seas, but if one fails to develop them, one will not be able even to serve one's parents."[38] Mencius wants us to examine and enlarge our perspective as children toward our parents. He does not defend a supposed moral infallibility of parents toward children.

*Kyosei*—living together justly and peacefully—involves recognition that relationships can be moral. We can enlarge our relationships—that is, we can make them more universal, practical, and rational—by recognizing a moral backdrop, a moral nature common to all human beings. If we pay attention to the diverse religious traditions of the world—both theistic and nontheistic—we can feed the streams of moral imagination from the great wellsprings of religious storytelling. Human life—and afterlife, if we can so imagine it—is about forming new and creative forms of moral relationship and practicing them daily.

## Postscript: A Suggestion for Interreligious Dialogue

We have seen that an important aspect of *kyosei* is interreligious dialogue. Is the fruit of interreligious dialogue a philosophy of religious pluralism? Religious pluralism may be defined as the view that all of the world's religious traditions contain authentic paths toward ultimate meaning and beatitude. Pluralism can be compared with religious exclusivism, which holds that one's own religion is the unique way to salvation; and to religious inclusivism, which holds that one's own religion binds up and includes all the world in its saving grace.[39] Rather than simply offering arguments for pluralism in the face of counterarguments by religious exclusivists (however valuable that process might be), pluralists might apply *kyosei* as a criterion of peacemaking and moral development, to the real world of interreligious dialogue and see what results.

## Notes

1. This insight is due to Professor Anri Morimoto.
2. *Mencius* II A.6. I have substituted gender neutral pronouns.
3. *Mencius* VI A.1-4.
4. Peter Byrne, *The Philosophical and Theological Foundations of Ethics*, p. 129.
5. Byrne, p. 130.
6. Quoted in Byrne, p. 132.
7. Byrne, pp. 132-133.
8. Byrne, p. 134.
9. Byrne, p. 135.
10. Byrne, p. 135.
11. Byrne, p. 138.
12. Byrne, p. 138.
13. Byrne, p. 139.
14. Byrne, p. 139.
15. Byrne, p, 145.
16. Plato, *Euthyphro*.
17. Byrne, p. 147; from Nowell-Smith and Rachels.
18. Byrne, p. 148.
19. Byrne, pp. 148-149.
20. Byrne, p. 149.
21. Byrne, p. 149.
22. Byrne, p. 150.
23. Byrne, p. 151.
24. Byrne, p. 151.
25. Byrne, p. 151.
26. Byrne, p. 151.
27. Luke 10: 30-35 NRSV.
28. *New Oxford Annotated Bible*, marginal commentary, p. 118.
29. Marginal commentary, p. 118.
30. Marginal commentary, p. 118.

31. Bernard Brandon Scott, *Hear Then the Parable*, p. 191.
32. Luke 10:37b.
33. Scott, p. 200.
34. Quoted in Scott, p. 197.
35. Quoted in Scott, p. 198.
36. Scott, p. 200.
37. Scott, p. 201.
38. *Mencius* II A.6.
39. The typology is due to John Hick. See, for example, his "A Philosophy of Religious Pluralism" in *Classical and Contemporary Readings in the Philosophy of Religion*, chapter 30.

## References

Bible. English. New Revised Standard Version. *New Oxford Annotated Bible.* 3rd ed. Oxford: Oxford Univ. Press, 2001.

Byrne, Peter. *The Philosophical and Theological Foundations of Ethics: An Introduction to Moral Theory and Its Relation to Religious Belief.* 2d ed. New York: St. Martin's Press, 1999 (1992).

Confucius. *The Analects.* Trans. D. C. Lau. Harmondsworth, Eng.: Penguin, 1979.

*Divine Commands and Morality.* Ed. P. Helm. Oxford: Oxford Univ. Press, 1981.

Hick, John. *Classical and Contemporary Readings in the Philosophy of Religion.* 3d. ed. Englewood Cliffs, N.J.: Prentice Hall, 1990 (1964).

*Mencius.* Trans D. C. Lau. Harmondsworth, England: Penguin, 1970.

Nietzsche, Friedrich. *On the Genealogy of Morals.* Trans. Walter Kaufmann and R. J. Hollingdale. New York: Random House, 1967. See especially the First Essay.

Nowell-Smith, P. H. *Ethics.* Harmondsworth, Eng.: Penguin, 1954.

Plato. *Euthyphro. The Collected Dialogues.* Ed. Edith Hamilton & Huntington Cairns. New York: Pantheon Books, 1961 (1941).

Rachels, James. *The Right Thing To Do.* 2d. ed. Boston: McGraw Hill, 1999 (1989).

Scott, Bernard Brandon. *Hear Then the Parable: A Commentary on the Parables of Jesus.* Minneapolis: Fortress Press, 1989.

Thomas Aquinas. *Summa Theologiae.* vol. 18, 1a 2ae 18-21 & vol. 28, 1a 2ae 90-97. Tr. T.Gilby. London: Blackfriars, 1996.

## fifteen

# Understanding the People of Other Faiths: Conviviality among Religions

### Anri Morimoto

## 1. A Fly Crawling on a Goldfish Bowl

Is conviviality (*kyosei*) possible among different religions? There have always been a number of people who answer "no" to this question a priori. John Lennon was one. After the 9/11 terrorist attacks, people around the world heard his song "Imagine" played over and again: "Imagine there is no heaven, no hell below us, no country, no religion, nothing to kill or die for…" Religion in Lennon's imagination is one of the prime reasons why people hate each other and go to war. If religious conviction were intrinsically intolerant, and if believing in one religion meant rejecting other religions, then there would be little chance for us to live convivially (in the sense of *kyosei*) as long as there is religion. Those committed to Christianity, in particular, would be self-deceiving to say they were called to be peacemakers by Christ, the Prince of Peace.

Indeed, it seems to be the very nature of religious commitment to make exclusivist claims. Christians believe that Jesus Christ is the one and the only incarnation of the Word of God. A devout Jew would pray each morning with genuine thankfulness to God for not having been created a heathen. Muslims believe that the Qur'an is "God's final and unsurpassable revelation." According to Buddhist teachings, the Noble Eightfold Path is "the Only Way" to enlightenment. The Hindu *Veda* says "the almighty power of the Supreme Divinities is only One." My question concerns how to understand these claims. We certainly understand what they mean to us, but do we understand what they mean to the believers themselves?

Wilfred Cantwell Smith, who spent five years teaching Islamic and Indian history in Lahore and later took the directorship of Harvard's Center for the Study of World Religions, once said that we are sometimes like flies that crawl on the outside of a goldfish bowl. We make observations about the fish inside, measuring their scales and the like meticulously, but we never ask ourselves, and never find out, how it feels to be a goldfish.[1] Cantwell Smith was irritated when the logical positivists of his day dismissed religious statements as meaningless.[2] Using their criteria, for example, the ancient Egyptian statement that "the sky is a cow," might mean that the ancient Egyptians were unable to tell the difference between what we now call a cow and what we now call the sky. Cantwell Smith was not very pleased, either, to hear Christian missionaries of his day denounce the Hindu reverence of the cow as idolatry: "The Hindu reveres the cow that he sees, not the cow that we see."[3] Language usage is always embedded in social and personal contexts—religious statements even more so than others, for such statements are intended to convey personal sentiments and commitment.

Our task, then, is to understand intensely religious statements from the fish perspective. Here I would like to turn for help to Ernst Troeltsch, who, long before Cantwell Smith, made the plurality of religions and their absolute claims the focal subject of academic research. Indeed, says Troeltsch, "all religions are born absolute."[4] This observation applies both to the birth of a particular religion in history, and to the birth of a particular religious conviction in a person. If we see the logic of religious commitment from the fish perspective, we understand that the truth that believers adhere to is perceived as having complete validity. Otherwise it would not constitute a religious faith at all. Any authentic devotion, be it religious or not, is always expressed in the absolute. One cannot therefore expect, from the fly perspective, that those inside the fishbowl would say "any other faith would do or fare better." Calling to believers from the outside to abandon their absolutist claims will not achieve the intended effect, even through appeals to goodwill, mutual respect, or world peace. Troeltsch knew the force of this fundamental conviction—one which is operative at the very root of every profound religious perception. The claim of absoluteness is natural and universal to all forms of life and forms of inner conviction.

Such a claim of absoluteness, however, is not a result of a comparison with other systems. No one chooses a religion by comparing one with another and grading them like we do when we buy a car. We become involved in religion more like we fall in love. It "happens" to us one way or another as an event beyond our control or calculation. It is an "encounter" as Emil Brunner would explain, or it "happens" as part of *engi* (dependent co-arising) according to the Buddhist teaching. The Latin etymology of the word "absolute" (*ab-solutus*) suggests that it is "released from anything comparable," "peerless" or "unrivaled." Religious conviction is hence always expressed in the superlative, not in a comparative degree. An oft-quoted Hindu phrase has it right: The absolute Brahman is "the One without the Second." The object of Hindu devotion becomes the first object of such devotion, in an absolute (not relative) sense, and not in comparison with the second or the third. Saying "my God is supreme," therefore, does not necessarily mean that other ways are "secondary," let alone "mistaken" or "defective."[5] In other words, these concepts require different language games which outsiders have no ready way to evaluate.

Understanding people of other faiths begins with recognition of their genuine "otherness." Without this recognition, our understanding becomes domineering, especially when it means subsuming others in our own paradigm. Others have the right to refuse to be understood from the outside and remain "unintelligible." By recognizing religious claims as "absolute" in the above sense, we admit that religions are first of all "incommensurable." A religion does not compare, let alone compete, with another. On what basis do we compare them? By what standard do we evaluate them? This is precisely the point where contemporary Muslims feel alienated by our conversation. Whenever there is a talk on peace, democracy and human rights, the underlying presupposition is a liberal, Western, even American framework for understanding and evaluation. The discussion table is pre-arranged in favor of these groups.

Inter-religious dialogues can stagnate for the same reason. When Christians propose to have dialogues, they have a set agenda already in their minds. M. M. Thomas gives us an illuminating example: when a Hindu scholar was invited to a dialogue that was organized by Christian scholars, his first reaction was that the topic of the session, "creation and history," is totally alien to him, for the Hindu religion sees creation as a metaphysical evil to be overcome.[6] We might do well to give some thought to the possibility that the very idea of having inter-religious dialogues, or the necessity thereof, could be inexorably modern, Western and Christian. Our first step, therefore, should be to give proper recognition to the genuine "otherness" of others, by confessing our inability to understand or evaluate others from the outside.

## 2. The Internal Basis for Toleration

Recognition of our own "outsiderness" does not necessarily imply our ineptitude. In fact, if Troeltsch is right in his understanding of the "absoluteness" of religious conviction, we can say that those with a religious conviction are in a position to make an informed inference that people of other faiths may have similar conviction. Their own personal experience would resonate with those of others, even without the knowledge of the content of the others' faiths. A religiously committed person, precisely because he or she is committed to one religion, can understand that people of other faiths have the same kind of depth of feeling in their religious commitment. In our analogy, it is easier for a fish to guess what it is like to be a fish in another fishbowl. This recognition can be the basis of our conviviality.

In fact, this is not merely a possibility: religious conviction has been one of the most fundamental reasons for pursuing and securing toleration and religious freedom in human society.[7] A historical survey would reveal that there are multiple reasons for the rise and development of the idea of toleration and religious freedom. The irenic Renaissance humanism of Erasmus (1511) and Thomas More (1516) may have set the initial tone. Skepticism about human capacity for grasping the absolute truth also prompted this development, as we see in the works of Basnage de Bauval (1684) and Pierre Bayle (1697). The budding rationalism also played an important role, though its influence was limited to intellectuals. In a popular context, the growing weariness of rampant religious wars of seventeenth-century Europe bred indifference toward religion in general. Political wisdom was still another factor contributing to religious toleration, trying to avoid religious conflicts in the interest of practical benefits such as social stability and economic prosperity, as we see in Locke (1685) and Voltaire (1763). In this case, though, such toleration based on political expediency could easily be revoked by the ruler as conditions changed, as we see in the fate of the Edict of Nantes (1685). All these external factors must have reinforced the idea of toleration, but as a recent study argues, these factors alone would not have established a lasting peaceful coexistence of religions, unless the ideas of toleration had been internally supported by "a genuine belief in and commitment to toleration as something inherently good and valuable."[8]

One such internal rationale for religious toleration is provided by religion itself. Roger Williams, a "fiery puritan" of seventeenth-century New England, pursued the vision of a society completely free of religious coercion, not because he was an agnostic or a skeptic wishing to establish a secular nation, but because he firmly believed that it was the will of God. In his preface to *The Bloudy Tennent of Persecution* (1644), Williams writes that "it is the will and command of God, that a permission of the most Paganish, Jewish, Turkish, or Antichristian consciences and worships, bee granted to all men in all Nations and Countries." Williams was unwavering to his last days in his judgment that only the separation of the civil and the religious "can procure a firme and lasting peace," and that "true civility and Christianity may both flourish in a state of Kingdome, notwithstanding the permission of divers and contrary consciences, either of Iew or Gentile."[9] God does not require us to enforce the uniformity of religion, for each person's inner conscience is created to be free.

We see in Williams a classic example of religiously motivated toleration. Such a claim of religious freedom, unlike those derived from practical motivations, can persevere against prevailing notions to the contrary. The relationships between religious freedom and the development of a more generalized concept of human rights seems to be much broader than is commonly assumed by theorists of political studies, but I will not venture into this discussion here.

## 3. The Heresy of Believing

Roger Williams did not say that we should first examine the "content" of religion (or non-religion for that matter) before granting toleration. At stake here is our modern preoccupation with the intellectual aspect of religion. Cantwell Smith once sent a shock wave among modern theorists of religion by charging them with heresy. "A great modern heresy of the Church is the heresy of believing," he declared.[10] This heresy, according to Cantwell Smith, was so widespread (but also so insidious) that not only believers of religion, but also critics, skeptics and detractors of religion, are all equally trapped in the heresy without knowing it. Please note, this is *not* a heresy of unbelief, *nor* is it a heresy of believing this or that. It is a heresy of believing, period. What this means is that the view that "believing is religiously important" is a modern aberration. For centuries, believing had not been that important in the lives of religious people. But today, we all think that believing is what religious people primarily do. To be religious means to believe something, to give intellectual assent to some propositional truths. This is what Cantwell Smith calls "the heresy of believing."

As stupendous a claim as this may sound, Cantwell Smith offers ample evidence thereof, as he always does. The concept of "belief," first of all, does not appear in the Qur'an or in the Bible.[11] What surprises me is the fact that he counted the occurrences of the words, sometimes but not always with the limited help of pre-digital concordances, and that his investigations extended beyond the Qur'an and the Bible, to William Shakespeare, Francis Bacon, Thomas Hobbes, John Locke, David Hume and John Stuart Mill. The command of his textual corroboration is breathtaking, and I am presenting here what laboratory scientists would call a "follow-up experiment" of his findings, though my experiment was on a far more modest scale and with the help of computers.

By Cantwell Smith's count, the entire King James Version of 1611 uses "faith" 233 times, but "belief" only once.[12] My digital counting of the same words in the same original Authorized Version shows 231 occurrences of the word "faith" and only one of "belief." Given the difference in counting methods, the accuracy of Cantwell Smith's count is remarkable. The New Revised Standard Version of 1989 shows similar results: "faith" appears 245 times and "belief" appears only once.[13] It is now safe to reiterate Cantwell Smith's assertion that, compared to the overwhelming use of "faith," "belief" can technically be called "unscriptural." What is the difference here? Cantwell Smith explains that while "faith" is personal and trusting commitment, "belief" is intellectual assent to propositions. The inordinate emphasis we now lay on the second is what he calls "the heresy of believing." The transition is also perceptible in the history of the verb "believe." The statement "I believe in God" meant for many centuries "I pledge my heart to God and commit myself to live in loyalty to God." Today it means "I judge that God exists." Cantwell Smith demonstrates the shift, with an impressive array of quotations, in the object, subject and content of the sentences that use the verb "believe," but I refer readers to his book for further information.[14]

Actually, this distinction has long been known to theologians. Thomas Aquinas made the distinction between the intellectual *credere Deum* and *credere Deo* on one hand and the volitional *credere in Deum* on the other.[15] Martin Luther put weightier emphasis on *fiducia* in the *Augsburg Confession* of 1530,[16] but later Lutheran theologians from Philip Melanchthon (1559) to Johann Quenstedt (1676) made a more formal division, in fact following the footsteps of Aquinas to differentiate among *notitia, assensus,* and *fiducia*.[17] Protestant Orthodoxy theologians Martin Chemnitz (1591) and David Hollaz (1707) gave yet another set of terms to the same distinction, i.e., objective *fides quae creditur* and subjective *fides qua creditur,* though this time placing more emphasis on the intellectual side.[18] The same distinction between *fides quae* and *fides qua* appears in Reformed Orthodoxy as well.[19] Again, the priority is thereby transposed from *fiducia* to *notitia* and *assensus,* as we see in Johannes Wollebius (1626) and Petrus van Mastricht (1725), in a polemical effort to reject the Catholic notion of *fides implicita.*

The shift from "faith" to "belief"—from a trusting commitment to intellectual assent, from the personal to the propositional, from "believe in" to "believe that"—is so pervasive in modern culture that we have all fallen into the habit of thinking that religion is all about saying yes to this or that proposition. It was already a wrong turn when the Latin word *credo* was mistranslated as "I believe." It should have been translated as "I give my heart," for that is exactly what it means (cor = heart, do = give).[20] Now I can give my heart to God in a variety of forms. This giving may be expressed in myths and rituals, song and art, personal behavior and character, social norms and morals, institutions such as marriage or law, forming and reforming religious communities, and in intellectual formulations such as creeds or doctrines. In the past, however, "belief in doctrines," had not been the primary channel for articulating faith among these formulations. When this "belief" did become central, the division among different religious traditions became entrenched. Believing in one religion in this sense did, indeed, become rejection of other religions. By imposing our frame of understanding retrospectively, we tend to think that it has always been so throughout history. When St. Augustine wrote *De Vera Religione* in the year 391, however, he did not mean to write on Christianity as "the true religion" as opposed to other false religions. His real subject matter was simply "true piety." When Zwingli wrote his book *De Vera et Falsa Religione* in 1525, it was not about Christianity as "the true religion" in contrast to other "false religions": it was about "pious devotion" of Christians.[21]

## 4. Reclaiming Faith after Postcolonial Critique

Understandably, Cantwell Smith lamented the historical shift which we just traced. His implicit plea was that if we could restore the original meaning of the word "faith," we would be in a better position to understand people of other faiths. Among religions, creeds and doctrines are naturally different, sometimes even conflicting. If religion is all about giving assent to a divisive set of doctrines, there is little chance for us to understand each other. But if religion is primarily a matter of trust, piety, devotion, loyalty and commitment, then we can all somehow perceive what we have in common, regardless of religious tradition. The content of each faith may be different, but the quality is similar; and this awareness of similarity will hopefully cultivate within us a kind of empathy towards each other, leading us to a more convivial society.

It would be naïve, however, to think that all religions can live happily ever after in this innocent stage. Even Cantwell Smith was affected by this process. A noble-minded gentleman, he tried to pay the utmost respect to all the people he saw as different, and he gradually slid into a popular relativist paradigm. In later works, he insisted that "for Christians to think that Christianity is true, or final, or salvific, is a form of idolatry,"[22] and said that such an exclusivist claim "must be thrown off."[23] His indignation at the insensitivity of missionaries is certainly justified, but his indignation is misdirected. His assertions do not square well with his own perspective, for "faith," as he identified it, cannot be what it is without a degree of commitment. In other words, Cantwell Smith is now jumping out of the water and trying to be like a fly who observes the fish from the outside of the fishbowl. His call to "throw off" the conviction of faith might be welcome to the liberal Christian fish in Western water, but this position would, contrary to his good intentions, simply infuriate many in other fishbowls, especially in the Muslim world.

Proselytizing can certainly be insensitive and inappropriate, but we should take care that its critique does not fall into cultural positivism. In one of his earlier writings, Cantwell Smith remarked, "I personally do not expect many conversions from one tradition to another anywhere in the world in the coming hundred years."[24] He knew that as a result of increasing traffic and communication he would see a Muslim preacher from Cairo or a Japanese Buddhist in the United States, but he would never have imagined that Christian missionaries and teachers would come from the East to the West. Christianity for him, ultimately, remained a religion of and for the West. In his view, missionary efforts in the non-Western world should taper off, for these efforts were extremely imperialistic and paternalistic. This unspoken presupposition, put in crude terms, was that the non-Christian East should remain the way it has been, and missionaries should not delude naïve Asians into believing things that do not really belong to their cultural sphere. In this respect Cantwell Smith was a cultural romanticist, not unlike Claude Levi-Strauss, who came to see Japan and deplored the disappearance of the idyllic scenery of the Sumida River banks, wishing it had remained the way his favorite Ukiyoe artist, Hokusai, had painted the scene two hundred years previously.[25] No doubt Cantwell Smith was speaking from a sincere regret over past mistakes of Western Christianity, but he gave little thought, if any, to the development of Christianity in the East. In the twenty-first century—when Christians living in the non-Western world comprise, contrary to Cantwell Smith's projection, twice as many believers as those in the West—there must be a better way to face the plurality of religions. There must be a better way for both the East and the West to appreciate other people's values without losing allegiance to their own.

Here I think we can learn more from Troeltsch, for his analysis did not end where we left it. It is true that every religion is born absolute, Troeltsch says, but it is also true that every religion cannot retain that initial confidence. As is the case for all cultural activities involving the human spirit, one's religious conviction will encounter other claims of absoluteness. This is when comparisons begin. Adjustments are negotiated, and the first innocent confidence is gradually replaced by a guarded claim of absoluteness, sometimes clothed in the guise of academic or objective discussions. Doctrines and apologetics become the primary features of this stage. Yet, the claim of absoluteness "cannot be arrested"[26] at this second stage either, since after people realize the impossibility of proving the claim on historical grounds, the discussion returns to its original, albeit subjective, certitude. The deeper one ventures into theoretical effort to reach the unshakable foundation for the claim of absoluteness, the clearer the impossibility of this task. Inevitably, we see that the only sure foundation is in the original certitude of the dynamics of personal religious impulse. "If it is scientific study of history that has made this burden so onerous, it is also scientific study of history that frees men from this burden when it is thought through to the end."[27] The same applies as well, I should add, to those who take a non-religious or atheistic standpoint, for these options are not supported by any scientific foundation either.

Troeltsch's three-stage argument deserves recapitulation here, because it rationally places the claim of absoluteness beyond the reach of scientific corroboration. Thus, absoluteness is brought back to where it originally belonged, namely, to the subjective and personal conviction of religious dynamism, but this time the absoluteness has a rational and objective recognition that it can only be subjective. By the same token, however, this process reopens the way to appreciate comparable claims of other religions, for it is clear that they, too, must be subjective. By definition, all religious claims are subjective. And the same principle applies to those whose cognitive and behavioral principles are based on agnostic or atheistic beliefs, because these claims do require a degree of commitment if they are sincere and consistent—a commitment that stands on its own, beyond objectively demonstrable foundations.[28] We thus know that our worldviews, whether theistic or not, all stand equally in their subjective convictions.

## 5. "Idolatry" Redefined—In Its Original Sense

An explanation is due at this juncture with regard to the concept of "idolatry," for as long as Christians keep viewing other religions as "idolatry," there is not much room for conviviality. Cantwell Smith's proposal was to abandon this concept altogether, or to apply it to all religions equally, including Christianity. My proposal is different. I suggest looking carefully into the scripture to see what exactly is meant by the words "idols" and "idolatry."

The simple method I employ for this task is again based on the methods of Cantwell Smith, namely, counting word occurrences. In the New Revised Standard Version, the word "idol(s)" and its derivatives (idolatry, idolater, etc.), are used 127 times in the Old Testament and 33 times in the New. My findings are rather simple: Out of these 160 references, there is virtually no instance in which people of other faiths are directly accused of idolatry. The breakdown of my survey is given below.

The Old Testament references to the word "idol" can be roughly sorted into three categories. The first category, typical in the Pentateuch, includes injunctions to Israel against making, having or worshipping idols and carved images for themselves. The second category, as we see often in the Prophets (e.g., Isaiah and Ezekiel), warns the Israelites not to follow the foreign gods of other people, often by extolling Yahweh over other gods for his overwhelming power to save the people of Israel. The third category, by far the largest of the three, accuses Israel of disobeying these injunctions and warnings, and relates the ensuing wrath and jealousy of Yahweh toward them, as we see frequently in the historical books such as Kings and Chronicles. Out of the 127 references, I counted thirteen, thirty, and eighty instances respectively.[29] Please note, however, that in *all* of these instances, the point of reference is Israel. The Israelis are the ones addressed, warned and accused, not the people of other faiths.

We read, for example, in Deuteronomy that in the land of Egypt, "You have seen their detestable things, the filthy idols of wood and stone, of silver and gold, that were among them." (29:17) Here the deities of Egypt are called "idols," but the next verse explains why they are so called: "There is among you a man or woman, or a family or tribe, whose heart is already turning away from the Lord our God to serve the gods of those nations." (29:18) In other words, foreign gods become idols when the people of Israel are attracted to them. They become idols for those Israelis who waver and succumb in their hearts, not for the Egyptians who worship them in their own land. In the ancient people's imagination, the power of a nation incontestably corresponds to the power of the gods they serve. No doubt Israel knew how great the power of Egypt was, and hence the appeal of Egypt's gods must have been almost irresistible. That fascination makes the gods of Egypt "idols" for the Israelis. They are not idols *per se* for the Egyptians.

When we turn to the New Testament, the first thing we notice is the absence of the word in the Gospels. Jesus never used the word "idol," called nobody "idolater." His silence itself can be an audible statement, but I leave it to the reader's interpretation. In the Epistles, the reference is again predominantly focused on the moral, behavioral and ritual purity of the members of the Christian community who have already confessed their faith in Christ. The word is never directly applied to the people of other faiths outside of the Christian community.

I must add that there is one exception to this observation: St. Paul at Athens. There we read that "he was deeply distressed to see that the city was full of idols" (Ac. 17:16). The gods the Athenians revere are called "idols" here, and Paul is far from being attracted by them. This is practically the only instance modern missionaries could cite to justify their particular use of the word. But those who would insist on citing it should bear in mind that Paul's evangelism in the Areopagos was a complete failure. Interestingly enough, his attitude changes after this failure: he now limits the scope of the word "idolaters" to "anyone who bears the name of brother and sister" (I Cor. 5:9-11), that is, those within the Christian community, a usage which accords with the rest of the Old and New Testament usages.[30]

The accusation of "idolatry" is thus directed, both in the Old and New Testaments, almost exclusively at one's own people, not at other people with different faiths. Notwithstanding later developments in the concept of monotheism, an assumption common in the ancient Near-East was that each tribe had a deity or deities of their own.[31] It was not a question of right or wrong. Evangelism was not a mandate of the Old Testament. Idolatry becomes the subject of reference when it poses a danger to Israel's faith. When someone in his or her own community is lured away and drawn into worship of other deities, *that* is the occasion for other gods (which are otherwise not an issue) to emerge as "idols." The meaning of the term, central to the scriptural usage, then, lies in concern about the deviation of Israel's devotion. In principle, the term does not concern other people's worship in other people's lands. Even in the New Testament, where evangelism begins to take shape, the same primary concern dominates the use of the word. By counseling the members of the Christian community to avoid idolatry, Paul illumines the fact that idolatry is the sin for those who have committed themselves to Christ, yet have become perfidious.

It is therefore not scriptural at all for Christians to call other religions "idolatry."[32] If the word be used at all, it should be used according to the scripture, to show that the danger of idolatry resides with the user of the word, not with the ones called by that name.

## 6. Toleration, Security, and Identity

An important lesson to learn here is that our tradition-specific texts can be the basis for an internal critique of a religion. We have seen too many cases of canonical texts being co-opted for justifying prejudice and intolerance, but we should keep reminding ourselves that it was the renewed interest in the scripture that initiated and supported Luther's Reformation against the towering authority of the Church of the time. Jettisoning the ancient texts in the name of modernity would destroy such a vital means of self-criticism.

Religious identity, thus formed and reformed, is essential to the ambience of toleration in an increasingly pluralized world. Identity—and religious identity in particular—is the personal and communal basis upon which the character of toleration is developed. Conventional wisdom might tell that these two, identity and toleration, are antithetical to each other: that is, if a person is confident about his or her identity, the person would become intolerant of other views and values; and if the person is tolerant, he or she would be devoid of firm identity. Historical evidence, however, indicates the contrary: intolerance is a sign of insecurity. Those who feel secure in their identity can afford to be more tolerant than those who do not. When one's identity is threatened to the point where there is little margin left at its core, the person or the community is put on the defensive, and edges into the attitude of intolerance.

The rise of Christian fundamentalism in early twentieth-century America is a case in point. It was a reaction of conservative Christians against the spread of historical criticism regarding the scripture and the Darwinian theory of evolution. In response to this crisis of identity, conservative Christians upheld what seemed to them the indispensable tenets of Christianity, summarized in "Five Points" of doctrine. This is a classic example of the above-mentioned shift by which notional assent to a set of doctrines became the central concern of religion. One cannot fail to notice that these "Five Points" are precisely the points that were under attack by modern criticism. The fundamentalists inverted the challenged points, and staked their identity on them, making them into a shibboleth for their brand of faith. That is why the conservative Christians were excessively concerned with the infallibility of the scripture, for example, far more than they were concerned about the doctrine of the Trinity, which the Christian church has for centuries regarded to be fundamental. For this reason Heidelberg theologian Christoph Schwöbel calls fundamentalism "a phenomenon of misplaced fundamentality."[33] Islamic fundamentalism can also be construed as a product of the modernist and secularist challenge to this faith. The fanatical enforcement of veil-wearing on women and beard-growing on men, as we saw among the Afgan Talibans, is made into the "identity-marker" of Muslim faith in contrast to the Western cultural influences.

If the root of fundamentalist intolerance is in its "misplaced" fundamentality, as Schwöbel maintains, then its cure is to be found not in weakened, but in deepened religiosity, not in impoverished theology, but in improved theology that is consistently carried out within its critical mandate. It is the task of theologians, for example, to reassert that the scripture is not in and of itself divine. The authority of scripture rests not on the infallibility of the text, but solely on its role as the witness to and the means for transmitting the revelations in the text. Likewise, Muslim Mullahs can remind their fellow believers that the veil-wearing and beard-growing is not related to the traditional observance of "the Five Pillars" of Islam. When one's identity is challenged, one can dig deeper for an inner source of identity, as has been the case with all religions that have endured periods of tribulations in history. Religious intolerance can and should be corrected from within. Demanding toleration in the name of secular principles might be perceived as yet another threat to religious faith, and their sense of insecurity could result in further intolerance. To return again to Cantwell Smith's analogy, we should ask the fish to take care of the fish business. The simplistic liberalist slogan "celebration of difference" cannot be the basis of toleration, for it easily degenerates into "celebration of indifference" which does not encourage toleration.

Thus the solid foundation for conviviality can be found in a redefined confidence in respective traditions, a confidence that is attained only through a rigorous process of self-reflection. The future of each religious tradition depends on its capacity to allow such internal criticisms. The disciplined sense of security, thus achieved, would then itself help to spread security among different fishbowls as well. In short, a meaningful inter-religious dialogue presupposes a sustained and committed intra-religious dialogue.

## Notes

1.  *Meaning and End*, 7.
2.  *Believing*, 11-12.
3.  Wilfred Cantwell Smith, "Idolatry: In Comparative Perspective," Hick and Knitter, 53.
4.  Troeltsch, 138.
5.  John Hick's use of these words is therefore inappropriate. See his *The Rainbow of Faiths: Critical Dialogues on Religious Pluralism* (London: SCM Press, 1995), 67.
6.  M. M. Thomas, "A Christ-Centered Humanist Appoach to Other Religions in the Indian Pluralistic Context," D'Costa, 57.
7.  "Toleration" here means broadly "the condition of religious freedom." It is beyond the scope of the present article to discuss the difference between toleration, religious freedom and the more recent idea of "identity politics."
8.  Zagorin, 12.
9.  *The Complete Writings of Roger Williams*, vol. 3 (New York: Russell and Russell, 1963), 3, 4.
10. *Believing*, v.
11. Ibid., 39.
12. Ibid., 44.
13. In both counts, the occurences of "faithful" and "faithfulness" are not included.
14. *Believing*, 46-67.
15. *Summa Theologica*, II-2, 2, 2.
16. *Die Bekenntnisschriften der evangelisch-lutherischen Kirche*, 3 Aufl. (Göttingen: Vandenhoeck & Ruprecht, 1956), 53. See also his *Large Catechism* (ibid., 560).
17. Heinrich Schmid, *Doctrinal Theology of the Evangelical Lutheran Church*, translated by Charles A. Hay and Henry E. Jacobs (Minneapolis: Augsburg Publishing House, 1875; reprint, 1961), 414-415.
18. Horst Georg Pöhlmann, *Abriss der Dogmatik*, 3 Aufl. (Gütersloh: Gütersloher Verlagshaus Gerd Mohn, 1980), 79.
19. Heinrich Heppe, *Reformed Dogmatics: Set Out and Illustrated from the Sources*, edited by Ernst Bizer and translated by G. T. Thomson (Grand Rapids, Michigan: Baker Book House, 1978), 527-528.
20. *Believing*, 41.

21. *Meaning and End*, 29, 35-37. In both writings, though, the contrast of genuine and spurious ways of expressing this piety is described and debated.
22. "Idolatry," 59.
23. Ibid., 68, note 12.
24. Wilfred Cantwell Smith, *The Faith of Other Men* (New York: The New American Library, 1965), 12.
25. Claude Levi-Strauss, "Preface to the Japanese Edition," *Tristes Tropiques,* translated by Junzo Kawada (Tokyo: Chuokoron Shinsha, 2001), 5.
26. Troeltsch, 155.
27. Ibid., 160.
28. For a detailed critique of pluralism in the philosophy of religion, see my article "The (more or less) same light but from different lamps," 163-180.
29. Four cases (I Samuel 31:9, I Chronicles 10:9, II Samuel 5:21, and Daniel 11:8) are ambiguous, but they are descriptive rather than accusatory.
30. Another dubious instance is Acts 19:26 where St. Paul is accused by Ephesians of saying "gods made with hands are not gods."
31. The Old Testament scholarship makes a distinction between "monotheism" and "henotheism." See Gerhard von Rad, *Old Testament Theology,* vol. 1, translated by D. M. G. Stalker (Edinburgh: Oliver and Boyd, 1962), 210-211.
32. For this reason I cannot endorse Tom Driver's judgment on the use of the word "idolatry." See Tom F. Driver, "The Case for Pluralism," Hick and Knitter, 214.
33. Christoph Schwöbel, "Toleranz aus Glauben: Identität und Toleranz im Horizont religiöser Wahrheitsgewissheiten" (http://www.hmn.bun.kyoto-u.ac.jp/dialog/act5_schwoebel_d.html), viewed July 28, 2004.

## Suggested Reading

Gavin D'Costa, ed. *Christian Uniqueness Reconsidered: The Myth of Pluralistic Theology of Religions.* Maryknoll, New York: Orbis Books, 1990.

John Hick and Paul Knitter, eds. *The Myth of Christian Uniqueness: Toward a Pluralistic Theology of Religions.* Maryknoll, New York: Orbis Books, 1987.

Anri Morimoto. "The (more or less) same light but from different lamps: The post-pluralist understanding of religion from a Japanese perspective." *International Journal for Philosophy of Religion* 53 (2003): 163-180.

Wilfred Cantwell Smith. *The Meaning and End of Religion.* New York: Macmillan, 1963.

_____. *Believing: An Historical Perspective.* Charlottesville: The University Press of Virginia, 1977.

Ernst Troeltsch. *The Absoluteness of Christianity and the History of Religions,* translated by David Reid. London: SCM Press, 1971.

Perez Zagorin. *How The Idea of Religious Toleration Came to the West.* Princeton: Princeton University Press, 2003.

## sixteen

# The 21st Century U.S. Peace Movement

## T.V. Reed

No analysis of the prospects for peace, security and *kyosei* in the world today would be complete without an examination of the power represented by social movements. In particular, the movement against "corporate globalization" is a force to be reckoned with, a force making claims to be building new foundations for lasting social harmony. I will approach this "global justice (and peace) movement" through the lens I know best—the U.S. movement scene—but in doing so one of my key points will be that U.S. movements cannot be separated from wider transnational forces.

The contemporary peace movement in the United States is a complicated, multifaceted phenomenon, both because it is heir to many layers of historical precedent, and because in its current form, it is embedded in a larger, global movement structure. My approach to social movement analysis is interdisciplinary, drawing both on the social sciences and the humanities, and integrating elements from the political, economic, social and cultural realms.[1] At this preliminary stage of research, on a still evolving movement that has as yet met with only scattered scholarly analysis, my approach must of necessity be primarily descriptive. However, here and there throughout the essay I will venture a few speculative hypotheses, and suggest some possibly key lines of analytic inquiry. Most centrally, I want to suggest that to speak of a contemporary U.S. peace movement is to speak of two interrelated phenomena: an anti-war movement focused on U.S. intervention into Iraq; and a peace movement that is part of a worldwide set of forces arrayed against "neo-liberal globalization" policies and practices.

The parameters of any social movement are fluid, but designating the parameters of the current peace movement presents more than the usual difficulties. To chart the relationship between the movement against the Iraq war and occupation, on the one hand, and the movement against neo-liberal globalization on the other, let me posit an analytical (but not an empirical) distinction between "anti-war" movements and "peace" movements. I take anti-war movements to be aimed primarily at specific conflicts (Vietnam, Iraq, etc.); while peace movements, which continue and sometimes thrive even in the calm between wars, have a wider agenda—they seek not just to end a particular conflict but to establish conditions which will forestall future conflicts.

Peace movements, like anti-war movements, have varied immensely in scope and ideological focus, but generally they have understood that questions of peace cannot be divorced from questions of social justice and geopolitical power. The movement against corporate globalization can be seen as a peace movement in this wider sense.[2]

The anti-war movement directed against the U.S. invasion of Iraq is at once broader and narrower than the peace movement. It is broader because the range of positions opposed to this particular war and occupation force run the gamut from reactionary isolationists, to cautious conservatives, moderates and liberals opposed to unilateralism, and radical pacifists and leftists. Not all of these constituencies are inherently interested in "peace" as a lasting, long-term possibility resting on significant social change. Thus, I would argue that alongside this "big tent" breadth, there is narrowness to the anti-war movement when contrasted to a peace movement that grows out of a full analysis of global inequalities and the roots of war and insecurity. Yet at least some in each of the varied anti-war constituencies may contribute to a more sustained peace movement, and each is certainly important to the more immediate task of restraining preemptive U.S. power.

At its furthest reach, the peace movement is marked by a several-hundred-year legacy in the form of religious pacifists associated today with the twenty-first century peace movement. These pacifists can trace their roots back to the first European peace advocates on what would become U.S. soil, and to the seventeenth and eighteenth century peace churches (Quakers, Mennonites, and so on). Today we can also find representatives of liberal and radical strands of internationalism, with a lineage dating back at least to the anti-imperialist movement of the 1890s, as well as representatives of such groups as the Women's International League for Peace and Freedom, which were founded early in the twentieth century. Drawing on more recent history, the current movement includes representatives of each of the three main waves of peace movement activity in the U.S. since World War II—the test ban era of the 1950s, the anti-Vietnam War era of the 1960s and 1970s, and the nuclear freeze/anti-intervention movements of the 1980s. Historically, there have been three main strands of peace movement activism in the U.S. tradition— moral/religious pacifism, liberal internationalism, and radical anti-imperialism. Each of these strands is well represented, albeit in somewhat modified form, in the contemporary anti-war and peace movement(s). This historical depth, however, should not obscure the fact that, as has often been the case in the past, a very strong contingent of young activists, mostly growing out of the so-called anti-globalization movement, is a driving force in the peace movement today.

Using internationalism as a critique of nationalist warmongering has been a part of peace movement practice for many generations. But the current form of worldwide movement activity differs both in scale and in focus from most predecessor forms. To begin with, while earlier U.S. internationalisms tended to be driven either by small, elite cosmopolitan groups of middle class humanist peace advocates, or by tightly organized Marxist internationalists, the new phase (while including small numbers of representatives of both these older forms of internationalism) is much more varied in origins and characteristics, and is much more widely representative. Most significantly, the main internationalist impetus to the movement against corporate globalization has come largely from outside the U.S.

## From the Battle of Seattle to a Movement for Global Justice

While U.S. activists made a spectacular entry into the movement against neo-liberal corporate globalization via the "Battle of Seattle" in 1999, it was a late entry into a movement which had been developing for more than decade. While U.S. movement participants tend to exaggerate the importance of this particular event to the wider global movement, its importance to the current U.S. peace movement is hard to overestimate. Given the definition I proffered above, the movement against neo-liberal globalization has always been a peace movement, inside and outside the U.S., even before this movement became explicitly linked with peace in reaction to the U.S. intervention in Iraq. Thus, in tracing the history of that movement, I mean to outline what I believe to be some of the key political and economic roots of insecurity and war, and to show some of the key forces offering an alternative vision.

Tens of thousands of people, representing some 700 organizations worldwide, took part in the "Battle of Seattle" protests in late November 1999. Their immediate, and most visible target, was the World Trade Organization as it tried to hold its ministerial meeting in the "Emerald City." But the real targets were many, the grievances manifold, and the alternative vision that of a "democratic globalization," in contrast to the "corporate globalization" embodied in the WTO. The link between these hundreds of organizations was what they saw as a drastically unbalanced world economy in which the 200 richest corporations have twice the wealth of the pooled assets of 80 percent of the world's population, and in which fifty of the hundred wealthiest economies are not nations, but corporations.

The Seattle events represent both a moment of convergence for many U.S. social movements and a moment in which U.S. movements were de-centered in the context of a global struggle. While Seattle's mobilization was by no means the beginning of this new movement, for many in privileged seats in the United States, it was the first glimpse of how strong and varied were the forces arrayed against the global imbalances of wealth, power, rights and resources. As the *Washington Post* noted, "The WTO meeting was merely the place where these people burst onto the American public's radar. Social movements around the world had already linked into grass-roots networks, made possible by the astounding speed at which they can communicate in the Internet era."[3] The Seattle events at the close of the twentieth century were at once the culmination of the history of U.S. social movements in the second half of the twentieth century, and a transformation into something new for the twenty-first century. The Battle of Seattle was a culmination because the coalitional events bear the marks of virtually all the major progressive U.S. social movements of the previous century (ethnic rights, feminist, environmentalist, peace, labor, gay/lesbian, etc.). This event was a transformation in that it clarified a fact too little recognized about those earlier U.S. movements—that they were deeply interlinked, both nationally and internationally. Some analysts see Seattle as the site where various loosely linked anti-globalization movements began to transform into a single movement. Others argue that the impact was less dramatically unifying. But all observers agree that the actions in the "Emerald City" represented a significant turning point, where the forces arrayed against corporate globalization took on a new level of self-awareness and confidence. In particular, the forces were emboldened by the sense that the struggle had moved into "the belly of the [globalizing] beast."

In addition to being a successful direct action that postponed and significantly disrupted the ministerial convocation, the gathering in Seattle served as a kind of de facto summit meeting for hundreds of groups critical of the impact of the "neo-liberal" economic policies they saw devastating the planet and increasing the chasm between the rich and the poor. The citizens of the world assembled in the streets of Seattle included labor unionists and environmentalists, lumber workers and forest activists, students and teachers, farmers and cheese makers, Germans and Ukrainians, Africans and Asians, North Americans and Latin Americans, Johannesburgers and Seattleites, gays and straights, human rights activists and animal rights activists, AIDS activists and anti-nuclear activists, debt relief advocates and consumer advocates, feminists and "womanists," computer hackers and meat packers, children and elders, indigenous people and white urban professionals, Muslims and Jews, Christians and Buddhists, atheists and pantheists, anarchists and advocates of one world government. Some wore business suits, some overalls; some wore sea turtle costumes, some leather and piercings; and some wore almost nothing at all. By the time the tear gas clouds and pepper spray winds[4] had begun to clear in the late afternoon of November 30, 1999, the thousands who had gathered gradually learned the news that they had accomplished one of their central goals: they had shut down, for a time, the convention of one of the world's most powerful organizations. More important, the direct action and the accompanying mass counter-meeting reportedly emboldened delegates from the "developing world" in the ministerial meetings—and thus played a role in the eventual failure of the convention to gain support for a number of proposals thought to benefit only corporate and national interests in the "overdeveloped world."

To understand the kind of "peace through justice" position of this movement it is necessary to ask: What kind of "globalization" were these protesters protesting? Some degree of globalization, in both economic and cultural terms, has existed for at least the last 500 years (since Europeans set out on their colonial "adventures"). Because of this long history, critics disagree about the extent to which the most recent manifestation of globalization is wholly new, but most agree that over the last twenty-five years or so, certain novel features of a transnational political, economic and cultural system have emerged. Particularly when viewed in combination, these new features represent a significant change in global power relations. The key elements of today's globalization include: the increased role played by transnational organizations like the World Bank, the International Monetary Fund (IMF), and the World Trade Organization (WTO); a weakened role for national governments and parallel increase in the power of multi- or trans-national corporate entities; new economic practices that greatly intensify the segmenting of the labor force by distributing various parts of the production process around the globe rather than centralizing it in one nation; and new global communications networks. These various processes are then rationalized through a new version of free market political-economic ideology most commonly known as "neo-liberalism," and implemented in the less developed world through "structural adjustment programs" that promise future benefits in exchange for weakened environmental laws, fewer human rights and worker rights protections, and "austerity" measures that reduce or eliminate social services once provided by the state.

The mainstream press describes the movement as "anti-globalization," but relatively few activists express wholesale opposition to globalization. The activists are more likely to say that they oppose "corporate globalization," and that they advocate instead for "critical globalization," "democratic globalization," or "globalization from below." Each of these modifiers suggests key elements of the critique: that current forms of globalization are "uncritically" pro-corporate, that they are "undemocratic" in their lack of transparent representative institutions, and that they are imposed hierarchically from "above" rather than building up though local participation from "below." Most of the activists say they are not against a global economy, but against the damage to people and the environment done by this particular version of globalization—a version embodied in the current rules set down by the WTO and other representatives of transnational corporate capitalism, as mediated through (or in some cases around) the nation state.

The protesters believe there is another way to do this, or rather many other ways to do this, based on the principle that the millions of people currently excluded from decisions that dramatically affect their lives should have a say in what a global network of economies, governments and cultures should look like. These protesters argue that without economic democracy, political democracy, where it even exists, is severely undermined, but they do not propose a uniform (state-socialist, for example) solution. They argue for a pluralism of alternative economic and social forms as the necessary basis for peace, and that, far from bringing democracy with it as promised, "free trade" has more often undermined democracy in the developing world as governments use increasingly repressive measures to manage the social disruption caused by structural adjustment.

## Origin Stories

The complexity of the movement also means that it has many origins (and as many origin stories). As journalist-activist Naomi Klein quipped, "The movement began 500 years ago, or on November 30, 1999, depending on who you ask."[5] Most would say that its origins lie in a slow process of linking movement groups and non-governmental organizations (NGOs) into coalitions. Much of this array of social forces had been combining or "networking" in a variety of ways for over a decade, coming together in even larger coalitions after Seattle. Important large-scale, international grassroots movement activities that served as precedents included: the environmentally-focused but multi-issue Earth Summit in Rio in 1992; the broad coalition fighting in the early 1990s against the North American Free Trade Agreement (NAFTA); a massive wave of strikes and other worker actions directed against SAPs in Latin America and elsewhere throughout the 1990s; the "Fifty Years is Enough" protests at the World Bank's anniversary meeting in 1994; the International Women's conference in Beijing in 1995; the international support for the Zapatista struggles in Chiapas, Mexico and the "encuentro" convocations the indigenous activists hosted in 1996 and 1997; the 1998 campaign of environmentalists and consumer advocates that helped sink the Multilateral Agreement on Investment (MAI), a draft treaty that sought to loosen controls on international finance; and the global debt relief campaign coordinated by Jubilee 2000 (a coalition including many religious groups with strong representation from African American churches) that during the last half of the 1990s played a major role in bringing about a significant reduction of debt claims against developing nations.

Other key international organizing efforts in the 1990s that were important in building elements of the network include the global anti-sweatshop movement, with its U.S. base on college campuses, and the successful campaign to ban the use of landmines. Earlier groundwork had also been laid in the 1980s by the international movement against nuclear weapons, and by the transnational solidarity movements against South African apartheid and U.S. policy in Latin America.

Seattle and subsequent events turned a plethora of groups (focused on the environment, genetically engineered foods, human rights, consumer protections, women's rights, labor issues, poverty and debt relief) into a far more coherent force focused on a common enemy—neo-liberal policies underwriting disproportionate corporate and state power.

## Worldwide Webs of Movement

The organizational pattern in which the disparate groups and interests are linked in a larger global movement is essentially a network of networks. Writer Naomi Klein sees a parallel between that structure and new computer media: "What emerged on the streets of Seattle ... was an activist model that mirrors the organic, decentralized, interlinked pathways of the Internet—the Internet come to life."[6] Networks can be more or less formal, more or less permanent, but generally tend toward the informal and impermanent. As the net (or web) metaphor suggests, networks are organized horizontally, not vertically or hierarchically, and their points of connection, or lines of movement, can shift quickly from one path of connection to another. Klein, one of the most astute participant-observers and chroniclers of this network of movement(s), adds:

> Despite this common ground, these [anti-corporate globalization] campaigns have not coalesced into a single movement. Rather, they are intricately and tightly linked to one another, much as 'hotlinks' connect their websites on the Internet. This analogy is more than coincidental and is in fact the key to understanding the changing nature of political organizing. Although many have observed that the recent mass protests would have been impossible without the Internet, what has been overlooked is how the communication technology that facilitates these campaigns is shaping the movement in its own image. Thanks to the Net, mobilizations are able to unfold with sparse bureaucracy and minimal hierarchy; forced consensus and labored manifestoes are fading into the background, replaced instead by a culture of constant, loosely structured and sometimes compulsive information-swapping.[7]

Klein's analogy is useful, but perhaps a bit too tidy. It ignores, for example, the fact that a network pattern of organizing had been a tried and true structure for many direct action movement groups at least since the late 1970s.[8] It is also not a universally accepted structure by all components of this movement. Some worry that it is a structure that mirrors the chaos engendered by, and works to the benefit of, what the current system social theorist Manuel Castells calls "networked capitalism."[9] But Klein's analogy does point to a crucial cultural dimension of the movement, and the connection between the movement and new cyber-culture of the Internet is undeniable. Like the flow of information along the Internet, movement networks form and re-form in many different configurations, depending upon the need.

Klein's ancillary point, that the movement is not really a single movement, is also insightful. I would argue that what makes the global justice movement interesting and potentially quite powerful, is that it both is and is not a single movement. The non-hierarchical, networked character of the (non)movement means that it is not the kind of classic movement (with centralized authority and clearly delineated membership) that scholars of movements find easiest to study. That type of movement has been supplemented by more network style structures for a least thirty years, and what we have now is simply, or rather complexly, the global extension of an existing trend in movements.

Some anti-globalization activists suggest that the structure of the network is itself a prefigurative model of what "globalization from below" might look like. No one denies the great complexity of the global economy, but all these activists deny that management by corporate executives, state officials, and ministerial representatives is the only way to run the economy. For these activists, the organizational power of groups, able to reach various kinds of short and long-term agreements, suggests the capacity of ordinary citizens to manage global problems while maintaining local autonomy. Meanwhile, the "global culture" of the Internet does not replace local cultures, but does supplement them in ways that may prove crucial to the success of the movement.

Arguments will continue as to how far to take the movement/Internet analogy, but no one denies the importance of new media to the new movement. The movement in its current global form simply would not be possible without the low-cost, instantaneous communication and the rich research possibilities of the Net. Seattle was also a turning point in this use of the Internet and other "new media" as organizing and educational tools. Not only was the massive event largely organized via the worldwide web, but the Independent Media Centers (indy.media.com) that emerged during the Battle of Seattle have grown into a wide web of independent news centers around the world offering alternative views from those of what activists refer to as the "corporate media."

The Net provides groups with access to hundreds of corporate and governmental documents vital to understanding and strategizing against neo-liberal policy; and the Net is the only mass medium currently available without a built-in bias towards the status quo. Indeed, given the anti-corporate ethic of many computing subcultures, the Net may even have something of a bias against hegemony (though that is certainly not an inherently progressive bias, since terrorists and white supremacists have proved as adept as peace activists in using the new media). Moreover, few activists forget that, as Iain A. Boal puts it, the new media's "liberatory functioning as a tool for 'organizing from below' flourishes in the shade of its dominant use as essential support for the global transmission of administrative, military and commercial intelligence, and the enhanced surveillance of labor."[10] Most global justice activists are not among the naïve utopian technological determinists who see the Internet as the world's savior. Rather, they see it as a site of struggle where, with mobility, flexibility, imagination and daring, they may actually have some tactical advantages over their often stodgy, bureaucracy-bound opponents. "Hactivists," "camcorder commandoes," "data dancers," "code warriors," "digital deviants"—a new media culture of resistance has become a vital part of the movement.[11]

## Reformism(s) and Radicalism(s): Protests and Beyond

After Seattle, large-scale transnational movement actions continued apace in the early twenty-first century—in Washington, D.C. (April 16, 2000), Prague (September 26, 2000), Quebec City (April 20, 2001), and Genoa (July 18-22, 2001), among others—all involving thousands of protesters. Like the Seattle action, these were often met by police violence, but initially this only further emboldened the movement.

Testimony to the effectiveness of this series of actions has come from some unexpected sources, including the frank assessment of former World Bank economist and Nobel prize-winner for economics Joseph Stiglitz: "[I]t is the trade unionists, students, environmentalists—ordinary citizens—marching in the streets of Prague, Seattle, Washington, and Genoa who have put the need for reform on the agenda of the developed world."[12] Stiglitz makes clear that, whatever they may say publicly, the major world financial and trade organizations have been deeply shaken by the protests.

While these dramatic confrontations at "counter-summits" continue to receive the most press coverage (and continue to play a significant role), most activists most of the time work in their local corners of the world on the particular issues most immediately relevant to them—farmers on issues of genetically engineered crops; workers on labor rights; environmentalists on toxic waste issues; students on the problems of sweatshops that produce their college T-shirts; Palestinians, Israelis and Iraqis on peace issues in their region, and so on. Most agree that powerful large-scale demonstrations are important in invigorating the movement, and in giving activists worldwide a sense that they are part of something larger. But those actions are only the tip of the movement iceberg.

For example, Seattle's "festival of resistance," as activists dubbed it, was much broader than its best-known facet, the blockade of ministerial delegates. Protest events in Seattle began officially several days before the blockade, marked by prayers, meditation and education programs (sides of the action not much covered by the "corporate" media). Teach-ins on dozens of aspects of globalization and social justice (sponsored by groups like the International Forum on Globalization, Global Exchange, Indigenous Environmental Network, and Public Citizen) took place at city venues all week long. Local Seattle activists had created an interest in globalization issues in the city through a series of lectures, debates, workshops and public forums in the weeks and months preceding the ministerial meeting. Thus, local interest added to that of thousands of protesters made every event virtually a sold-out, standing-room-only affair. In contrast to *New York Times* critic Thomas Friedman's characterization of the protesters as know-nothing "flat earthers," this was a very well informed collection of people all hungry for further knowledge. Key movement intellectuals like Vandana Shiva and Warren Bello played an important role translating immensely complicated issues of global political economy into terms average citizens could grasp and debate.

The wide variety of movement constituencies are organized into two main components—non-governmental organizations (NGOs) and direct action-oriented movement groups. NGOs, as organizations originally growing out of the UN bureaucracy, are generally seen as tamer agents of change than direct action groups. But the name encompasses an extremely wide variety ideologically and in terms of focus, from environmental to human rights, to women's rights, health advocacy and so on. Some NGOs are more service oriented, others lobby to affect policy, and still others are virtually indistinguishable from direct action social movement groups in their resistance efforts. Direct actionists tend to see NGOs as more moderate and formal, if not bureaucratic, and NGOs tend to see direct actionists as disorganized and overly confrontational, but the borders between the two types of organizing are often porous.

In the general flow of the movement against corporate capitalist globalization, many NGOs form a mediating space between formal governments and the disruptive power of direct actionists. In an overall strategy, the two sectors often benefit each other, with NGOs proposing much-needed temporary reforms while the direct actionists push for deeper transformations. While this mutual benefit is not often felt or acknowledged by partisans of the respective modes of political activity, broad coalitions of these forces continue to work together on small and large-scale endeavors, including anti-war efforts.

## From Shadowing to Substance: the Forum Process

The creation of the World Social Forum was a key development in the global justice movement. The World Social Forum first met in 2001 in Porto Alegre, Brazil, partly as a symbolic challenge to the World Economic Forum of corporate leaders and trade ministers. In 2002, the second WSM meeting in Porto Alegre drew some 12,274 delegates representing close to 5,000 civil society organizations and movements, plus another 50,000 participant-observers. State political parties and military units—the two mainstays of the bureaucratic, nationalistic and militaristic forces the forum seeks to overturn—were excluded from participation in the forums.

The subsequent yearly world forums (most recently in Mumbai, India in January 2004), supplemented by many regional ones, have similarly expanded the numbers of participants. Mere "shadowing" of the WEF has been replaced by a proactive focus on the movement's alternative plans. Similarly, the currently favored descriptor, "the movement for global justice," suggests a move from the defensive to the offense, from reacting to globalization to designing and building alternatives.

The global justice summits are formed like the movement itself as a network of networks, not as a hierarchical organization. The WSF does not itself take positions (beyond its charter), but serves rather as a place for civil society groups to meet on an annual basis to educate, assess, strategize, network, and plan. The WSF charter reads in part:

> The alternatives proposed at the World Social Forum stand in opposition to a process of globalization commanded by the large multinational corporations and by the governments and international institutions at the service of those corporations' interests, with the complicity of national governments. They are designed to ensure that globalization in solidarity will prevail as a new stage in world history. This will respect universal human rights, and those of all citizens—men and women—of all nations and the environment and will rest on democratic international systems and institutions at the service of social justice, equality and the sovereignty of peoples.[13]

Within these broad principles, there is a wide array of ideological positions, from Anarchism to Zapatismo. Ideological certainty is largely anathema to the movement, both because of a predominant spirit of experimentalism, and because of a commitment to respect local conditions. The sheer complexity of ethnicities, positions, and ideas, makes it unlikely that any one faction could dominate, though sectarian efforts to do so will no doubt continue. The initial choice of Porto Alegre, site of a regionalist and localist challenge to Brazilian central state power, represents the WSF's continuing commitment to a diversity of solutions focused on particularities, even as it builds global networks. A variety of alternative economic and political systems have been suggested that can be hinted at by terms like bioregional social democracy, radically pluralist democracy, participatory democracy, economic democracy, decentralist socialism, regional egalitarian capitalism, and social anarchism. Some speak of "delinking" from the global capitalist system into national or regional economies, others of recreating global capitalism in less monomaniacally profit-centered forms, and still others of various combinations of economic forms growing from a variety of sources: communal farms to international fair trade networks. Many of the participating groups are directly involved in creating alternative economic networks, both for practical reasons and as models for alternative systems.

## Non-violence, Terrorisms and the Impact of 9/11

For at least thirty years, non-violent social movements have debated the question of whether or not property destruction constitutes violence, and that debate has continued with the global justice movement. At times, as in Seattle, great tension arose between "black bloc" members who argued that strategically targeted "vandalism" or "revolutionary destruction" undercuts the corporate equation of property and persons, and those who argue on principle that such tactics are outside the tradition of respectful non-violent civil disobedience, or that, regardless of the principle at stake, such actions trash the image of the movement and undermine its credibility with the wider populace. At other times, such as the action in Prague in 2000, a rapprochement was reached in which three separate contingents with differing tactics marched on the meeting from different directions—a Yellow group committed to traditional non-violence; a Pink/Silver contingent advancing through "tactical frivolity" (costumes, street theatre, dance etc.); and a Blue force seeking to engage police in "combat."

The context of these debates changed drastically, however, particularly in the U.S., after the attack on September 11, 2001. Movement journalist L.A. Kaufman, writing only days after the attack on the World Trade Center and the Pentagon, put into words what many activists were already feeling: "everything has changed," when two key icons of corporate world trade and U.S. military power were destroyed and quickly transformed into symbols of innocent victimhood. Kaufman wrote:

> [T]he September 11 attacks definitively interrupted the unfolding logic of the movements for global justice. The IMF/World Bank protests in D.C. were going to be simultaneously broader, more diverse, and more intense than any demonstrations in recent U.S. history. The AFL-CIO was pouring unprecedented resources into the events, mobilizing its membership on a massive scale, and faith-based and non-governmental organizations were activating thousands of people who had never come to a globalization protest before.... Our movements' vision of global justice is needed now more than ever; we will simply need to take great care in presenting that vision in a way people can hear.[14]

It is hard to imagine two groups more different than the Al Queda terrorists and the anti-globalization activists, but a conservative U.S. administration quickly pushed through Congress the badly misnamed "PATRIOT act," a measure so sweeping that it seemed to turn all dissent into a pretext for applying the terrorist label.

A particularly brutal suppression of demonstrators in Genoa, Italy in the summer of 2001, including at least three deaths and hundreds of injuries, had already put the European branch of the movement into a reassessment phase when 9/11 shocked the world. In February of 2002, the 60,000 activists from around the world who attended the second World Social Forum in Porto Alegre reaffirmed the movement's commitment to nonviolence. Soon thereafter, in March of 2002, close to two million people protested in Rome over labor issues, and in Barcelona 500,000 protested an international trade meeting. Both protests were without incident, and in Barcelona the two-day festival, involving more than twenty-five decentralized actions, playfully avoided all confrontations with police. These actions seemed to be solidify the current mood in the movement—a spirit uncompromisingly strong and imaginative enough to draw media attention, but relying on the weapon of serious humor rather than rocks to disarm authorities. This tactical reconsideration partly forced upon the movement by 9/11 allows the moderate, policy-oriented branch and the direct actionists to be in closer contact, a particularly important factor in keeping anti-war elements allied with the peace and justice forces in the U.S.

The other new situation emerging out of the 9/11 events was a resurgence of nationalism, particularly in the U.S. While analysts have glibly talked of the decline or death of the nation state, many nation states in recent years have in fact seen a growth in nationalism—either ethnically based (sometimes with the help of "cleansing") or, as in the U.S. case, driven by a sense of a common enemy. Any movement focusing on the global, even in mostly opposition, must deal seriously with neo-nationalist sentiments heightened by the effect of a "global" war on terrorism not notably respectful of the boundaries of other nations.

## Wars and Peaces

Despite the complexities offered by the post-9/11 situation in the U.S. and around the world, the movement for global justice has continued to grow in the twenty-first century, bringing with it the legacy of a half-century of extraordinary social movement action on behalf of economic, social and environmental justice. The U.S. branch of the movement gradually returned to life after 9/11; and between 75,000 and 200,000 people (estimates ranged widely, as always) protested peacefully in April 2002 in Washington D.C. against the IMF and World Bank. Corporate scandals in the U.S., centered around Enron, World-Com and a host of other companies, seemed to confirm what protesters had been saying about the hypocrisies of neo-liberal free trade. Though it seemed unlikely that "corporate terrorism" would be added to the list of targets in the "war on terror," it also seemed clear that the latter could not fully deflect attention from the former.

Alongside movement growth, however, came new forms of U.S. militarism in the guise of wars on terror, in Afghanistan and Iraq. The global justice movement was quick to respond to each of these "wars," and became the backbone of resistance to these actions in the U.S. The extensive network provided by the global justice movement (along with more specific anti-war discourses and networks arising from earlier opposition to Desert Storm) is the main reason for the unprecedented growth of a very large anti-war movement in the U.S. and around the world *prior to actual combat.*

The U.S. war on Iraq has generated what may well be the largest anti-war movement in the history of the world. Indeed, the *New York Times* went so far as to declare it the wider movement the world's second superpower.[15] On February 15, 2003, to cite one example, millions of people in 600 cities in more than sixty countries demonstrated across the globe against the then-impending war. This, the largest "focus group" (as G.W. Bush dismissively called it) ever assembled, rested to a great extent on the cyber- and face-to-face networks forged by the movement(s) for global justice. While there was initially some concern that an anti-war movement would distract from larger movement goals,[16] calls for resistance to the then-emerging war came quickly from the European Forum, and soon thereafter from the World Social Forum. One of the two key coalitions active in the U.S., United for Peace and Justice, bears in its very name (and likewise in its constituent groups) the mark of the globalization movement. More moderate "anti-war" coalitions included Win Without War, backed strongly by Internet powerhouse MoveOn.org. While stopping the war proved impossible in the face a U.S. president contemptuous of the views of anyone beyond his small circle, the sometimes tense coalescence of the anti-war and global peace movement has created a strong dynamic whose power has already greatly shaped the U.S. political landscape. Despite Bush's narrow (re)election in November of 2004, polls showed that by that time the majority of Americans, joining the rest of the world, believed the war on Iraq to have been a "mistake" (far too mild of a term, certainly, but a far cry from popular U.S. sentiment as the war began, and one measure of the movement's impact).

At the World Social Forum, in Mumbai, India in January 2004, a subgroup held a "General Assembly of the Global Anti-war Movement." As the organizational site that most fully legitimates a claim to a single global peace and justice movement, the formation of a separate anti-war assembly suggests that anti-war work is necessary but comprises only one part of the total movement. As activists embedded in a larger structure, these anti-war workers are among those most likely to bring to light the transnational intricacies of struggle in which the evolving movement(s) in the U.S. will play their particular role. The movement for global justice has the potential to become a rich alternative to the clash of fundamentalisms between the right-wing evangelical crusaders in the White House and the jihadist militants whose cause the right-wingers have done so much to foment.

## Notes

1. See T.V. Reed, *The Art of Protest* (Minneapolis: University of Minnesota Press, 2005). That book and its accompanying web site of the same title will include an annotated bibliography on the movement for global justice.
2. My distinction might well be compared to Johann Galtung's well known sense of the difference between "negative peace" (the absence of war) and "positive peace" (peace based upon sustainable justice).
3. Quoted in Jeremy Brecher, et al. *Globalization From Below: The Power of Solidarity* (Boston: South End Press, 2000), x.
4. In the wake of the "police riot" unleashed in Seattle, the city government has had to pay several hundred thousand dollars in damages to protesters.
5. Mike Prokosch, and Laura Raymond, eds. *The Global Activist's Manual: Local Ways to Change the World,* (New York: Thunder's Mouth Press, 2002), 1.
6. Naomi Klein, "The Vision Thing," *Nation* July 10, 2000 http://past.thenation.com/issue/000710/0710klein.shtml
7. Klein, "The Vision Thing."
8. See, for example, Noel Sturgeon, "Theorizing Movements: Direct Action and Direct Theory," in Darnovsky, et al., *Cultural Politics and Social Movements* (Philadelphia: Temple University Press, 1995).
9. See Castells, *The Information Age,* three volumes (London: Blackwell, 1999).
10. Yuen, et al., eds. *The Battle of Seattle: The New Challenge to Capitalist Globalization* (New York: Soft Skull Press, 2001), 379-80
11. Various perspectives on the developing use of the Internet in transnational grassroots organizing can be found in: G. Lins Ribiero, "Cybercultural Politics: Political Activism in a Transnational World," in Sonia Alvarez et al. eds., *Culture of Politics, Politics of Culture* (Boulder, CO: Westview Press, 1998): 325-52; Harry Cleaver, "The Zapatista Effect: The Internet and the Rise of Alternative Political Fabric," *Journal of International Affairs* 51(2): 621-40; and in "Social Justice Movements and the Internet," special issue of *Peace Review*, 13(3), Sept. 2001.
12. Stiglitz, *Globalization and Its Discontents*, 9.
13. World Social Forum charter: http://www.forumsocialmundial.org.br/eng/qcartas.asp.
14. Kauffman, "All Has Changed," *Free Radical #19* September 17, 2001. http://www.free-radical.org/.
15. Patrick Tyler, *NYT* February 17, 2003.
16. See Nacha Cattan, "Anti-Globalization Movement Split on War" *Forward* Oct. 12, 2001, 6.

## Suggested Reading

Appelbaum, R. P. and W. I. Robinson (2004). *Critical Globalization Studies*. New York, Routledge.
Aronowitz, S., H. Gautney, et al. (2003). *Implicating Empire: Globalization and Resistance in the 21st Century World Order*. New York, Basic Books.
Bandy, J. and J. Smith (2004). *Coalitions across Borders: Transnational Protest and the Neoliberal Order*. Lanham, Md., Rowman & Littlefield.

Buckman, G. (2004). *Globalization: Tame it or Scrap it?: Mapping the Alternatives of the Anti-globalization Movement.* New York, Zed Books.

Conway, J. M. (2004). *Identity, Place, Knowledge: Social Movements Contesting Globalization.* Halifax, N.S., Fernwood.

Fisher, W. F. and T. Ponniah (2003). *Another World Is Possible: Popular Alternatives to Globalization at the World Social Forum.* London; New York, Zed Books.

Goodman, J. (2002). *Protest and Globalization: Prospects for Transnational Solidarity.* Annandale, N.S.W., Pluto Press Australia.

Guidry, J. A., M. D. Kennedy, et al. (2000). *Globalizations and Social Movements: Culture, Power, and the Transnational Public Sphere.* Ann Arbor, University of Michigan Press.

Keet, D. and Institute for Global Dialogue. (2002). *The WTO-led System of Global Governance: Tactical Options and Strategic Debates amongst Civil Society Organizations Worldwide.* Braamfontein, Institute for Global Dialogue.

Lofland, J. (1993). *Polite Protesters: the American Peace Movement of the 1980s.* Syracuse, N.Y., Syracuse University Press.

Marullo, S. and J. Lofland (1990). *Peace Action in the Eighties: Social Science Perspectives.* New Brunswick N.J., Rutgers University Press.

Mertes, T. and W. F. Bello (2004). *A Movement of Movements: Is Another World Really Possible?* London; New York, Verso.

Opel, A. and D. Pompper (2003). *Representing Resistance: Media, Civil Disobedience, and the Global Justice Movement.* Westport, Conn., Praeger.

Peace, R. C. (1991). *A Just and Lasting Peace: the U.S. Peace Movement from the Cold War to Desert Storm.* Chicago, IL, Noble Press.

Piper, N. (2003). *Transnational Activism in Asia: Problems of Power and Democracy.* New York: Routlege.

Smith, J. G. and H. Johnston (2002). *Globalization and Resistance: Transnational Dimensions of Social Movements.* Lanham, Rowman & Littlefield.

Veltmeyer, H. (2004). *Globalization and Antiglobalization: Dynamics of Change in the New World Order.* Aldershot, Hants, UK; Burlington, VT., Ashgate.

## seventeen

# Achieving Peace and Security: A Transnational Feminist Environmentalist Perspective

## Noël Sturgeon

### Introduction: Transnational Feminist Environmentalism

What can a transnational feminist environmentalist analysis offer us in understanding the causes of war and terrorism today, or seen another way, as a guide to reach the elusive goals of peace and security? This paper explores a particular transnational feminist environmentalist analysis of contemporary militarism and its interconnections to the exploitation of women's labor and of the environment, briefly indicating along the way how the development of this perspective arose through the process of direct theorizing involved in a particular social movement history (Sturgeon 1995).

A transnational feminist environmentalist perspective takes gender as a primary category of analysis, while looking always to the relation between how women are treated and understood and how the environment is treated and understood. There are many varieties of feminist environmentalism (Sturgeon 1997), but the version I present here is materialist (in that it looks to the ways in which production and reproduction are organized to result in specific social relations that have particular consequences for women and for the environment); it is historically situated; and it is attentive to the material consequences of cultural contexts, symbols, and practices. As a transnational theory, it is deeply critical of the racism and sexism of most nationalisms, it puts its analysis always in a global context, and it attempts to decenter U.S. and First World ethnocentrisms. (Bacchetta 2004)

The challenge we will give to this kind of analysis is to provide something useful to say in understanding the present post-Cold War situation—a U.S. invasion of Iraq and Afghanistan, terrorist attacks around the world, and several, seemingly-intractable, violent flashpoints around the world (including the ongoing Israeli occupation of Palestine). I will argue that a transnational feminist environmentalist analysis can give us four useful analytical approaches: arguments against the inevitability of war; arguments for the effectiveness of nonviolent approaches to conflicts; arguments for the importance of a global environmental justice perspective for achieving peace; and an illuminating analysis of the relation between the globalization of capital, the exploitation of women and the environment, and the persistence of violence and militarism.

## Undermining the Nature of War

The first thing a transnational feminist environmentalist perspective can offer us is hope, because such a perspective rejects the popular assumption that war, violence, and exploitation are inevitable consequences of human nature. From a feminist viewpoint, arguments from nature are highly suspect, though they also have been used strategically for liberatory purposes (Sturgeon, forthcoming). Slavery was supported by arguments about natural racial inferiority; the exploitation of women sexually and as domestic laborers was (and is) legitimated by arguments about women's natural capacities; and imperialist endeavors by Europeans, and by the United States, have been justified by beliefs in the White Man's Burden and Manifest Destiny that propose white people to be naturally superior to darker, supposedly "uncivilized" Others. Given this legacy, arguments that assume that violence and war are natural parts of human instinctual make-up should be treated very critically from a feminist perspective. The way in which violence in many cultures has been problematically associated with strength, power and masculinity—and nonviolence with passivity, ineffectiveness and femininity—should lead us to reject, or at least question very deeply, any assumptions that violence is an inevitable part of human nature.

It is important to say this at the beginning of a paper exploring a transnational feminist environmentalist contribution to the study of how to achieve peace, because there has been a long history of feminist antimilitarism, of women's peace movements across the globe, and because some of the arguments used in these movements were arguments that promoted the idea that women were biologically attuned to peace, while war was naturally a man's business (Alonso 1993). But in the context of contemporary global anti-war movements, such as we have seen manifested by the worldwide opposition to the U.S. war on Iraq,[1] such arguments supposedly drawn from nature, about men's and women's propensities for war and peace, should be seen as ethnocentric, based as they are on ahistorical frameworks and unfounded cultural universalisms (Featherstone 2004). For while some men in some cultures, and some classes, are encouraged and rewarded for their propensity for violence, others are not; and while some women may be assumed to be nurturers, others are not nurturers (Mageo 2004). Rejecting the idea that men (and women!) are biologically prone to violence is a hopeful position, since it allows for the possibility of achieving nonviolent societies.

Today, feminist intellectual frameworks are shaped by two over-arching precepts: the idea that gender roles and gender difference (ideas of proper masculinity and femininity) are socially constructed, historically specific, and culturally variable; and the idea that gender is a category of analysis that can be usefully applied to almost every aspect of life. In fact, it is better to talk, from a feminist perspective, about masculinities and femininities in the plural, to allow one to distinguish the way gender roles are inflected by class, cultural, racial, or sexual social locations. It is not necessary to a feminist perspective to deny biological difference, but it is essential to deeply question the social meanings attached to those differences, approaching them as fluid and variable. Thus, while a transnational feminist environmentalist perspective would reject the notion that men are naturally violent, and women are naturally nonviolent, it would still allow us to account for what has been called "the gender gap" in men and women's support for war—that, given a few fluctuations, men are more likely to support war than women. Thus, military institutions can be seen as "masculinist"—that is, legitimated by ideologies of patriotism involving strength through violence, equating all three ideologies with a form of extreme masculinity that is misogynistic and homophobic—whether or not men or women are the ones being trained as soldiers (Feinman 2000). Gender divisions of labor that assign most caretaking work to women, and then underrate that work, may produce different value systems in men and women (but not necessarily uninflected by race, class, and cultural differences) that can explain the gender gap in men's and women's support for war.

## Feminist Nonviolent Solutions to Conflict

Concomitant to a position that rejects essentialist assumptions about a human propensity to war, transnational feminist environmentalism argues for nonviolent solutions to conflict, holding to an understanding of peace as a substantive concept, involving human security rather than national security. This is the second useful perspective a transnational feminist environmentalist analysis can offer. Peace, in this view, is not just the absence of war, nor is it the achievement of security for a few. Often, the dominant ideal of "security" assumes that many threats to health and safety are beyond solution, and that the most that can be done is to make some people secure from such threats. A transnational feminist environmentalist position understands that the threats we face today—to the global environment, to food security, to political equality, to human rights—are not threats to any one group of people, but are threats to us all. Militaristic and nationalist arguments for "security" usually arise from positions of privilege. Witness the reaction of the hegemonic U.S. cultural/political interpreters to the terrorist attacks of 9/11 in New York. The dominant perception that these were the first such attacks, and that people, especially Americans, had been "safe" before this moment, comes out of a privileged perspective that not only ignores previous incidents of politically-motivated violence in the U.S. as well as other countries, and redefines "terrorism" to exclude U.S.-supported violence (such as past U.S. support for Osama bin Laden); but also overlooks the extreme conditions of fear, insecurity and violence that many poor people in the U.S. live in daily (Bunch 2004). A transnational feminist environmentalist definition of peace would include substantive rights to food, health, political equality, environmental quality, and control of one's own body—but would also include freedom from fear of violence, whether that violence is state-sponsored, or generated by militant opposition to states, or is a widespread gender-specific form of personal violence, such as rape or battering of women.

The practice and philosophy of nonviolence offered by this transnational feminist environmentalist perspective is not a traditional Gandhian perspective. Rather, it is a modified version influenced particularly by activists such as Ella Baker and Barbara Deming, as well as by groups like the Women's International League for Peace and Freedom and Women in Black. It is a nonviolent practice that is not self-sacrificing, or dependent only on achieving a change of mind in individuals, or located in a specific religious tradition, but which is confrontative, diverse, strategic, persistent, humorous, and aimed at hegemonic structures of inequality and institutionalized violence. It is a theory of nonviolence that depends on a political theory of participatory consent, rather than passive consent, and citizen obligation to act against state-sponsored violence directly, rather than to accept coercive practices of the state, social institutions, or culture (Sturgeon 1995).

Part of the preference for this form of nonviolent practice, embedded in participatory democratic forms, comes from the knowledge that war, even war fought for what seems like moral purposes, deeply affects women in long-term ways. Women are likely to experience excruciating suffering as a result of war. The recent 2002 report commissioned by UNIFEM, *Women, War and Peace* (Rehn and Sirleaf 2002), details the kind of impact war has on women. This is not to say that war does not have an impact on men—most of the direct casualties in a war are male, and men are subject to torture and imprisonment at greater rates than women. But the prevailing belief that war is men's business assumes male casualties as a necessary part of the cost of war. The effect of war on women needs to be more deliberately examined.

As the UNIFEM report shows, women are killed in wars as combatants and, along with children and older men, as "collateral damage." And in our wars today, in contrast to past wars, a majority of the casualties can be non-combatants, so the toll on women's lives has been growing. But women are also more subject to gender-specific forms of violence. To quote from the UNIFEM report:

> Violence against women during conflict has reached epidemic proportions...[women's] bodies become a battleground over which opposing forces struggle. Women are raped as a way to humiliate the men they are related to, who are often forced to watch the assault. In societies where ethnicity is inherited through the male line, "enemy" women are raped and forced to bear children. Women who are already pregnant are forced to miscarry through violent attacks. Women are kidnapped and used as sexual slaves to service troops, as well as to cook for them and carry their loads from camp to camp. They are purposely infected with HIV/AIDS, a slow, painful murder. (UNIFEM 2002, 12)

The most conservative estimations are that over 250,000 women were raped in the Rwandan genocide (UNIFEM 2002, 11), and over 30,000 women were raped in the Bosnian conflict (Enloe 2000, 140). And the rape of designated "enemy" women does not just occur in active armed conflict, but has been a part of official government policy in a number of militarized security states, such as Chile, Argentina, and the Philippines in the 1970s and more recently, Guatemala, Iraq, Israel, India (in Kashmir), Haiti, Indonesia, Bhutan, Zaire, China and Turkey. (Enloe 2000, 123). Most recently, there have been reports of the prevalence of rape in the U.S. Air Force Academy, at U.S. military bases in the Philippines and Japan, and of U.S. female soldiers by U.S. male soldiers during the latest deployment in Iraq in 2003.

War and militarism also causes the displacement of people on a massive scale. UNIFEM estimated in 2002 that forty million people were displaced because of armed conflict and human rights violations, and that 80 percent of these were women and children. (UNIFEM 2002, 21) At present, these numbers are likely to be even higher; estimates of the number of refugees from the conflict in the Darfur region in Sudan alone are close to one million. Refugees need to find food, shelter, and health care, and women bear the brunt of this work because of their traditional responsibilities for childcare, cooking, and caring for the ill. Women who are displaced, and who are desperate to care for their families, are frequently forced to choose sex work, or they are enticed and sold into sexual slavery.

After active conflicts are supposedly over, women have to contend with a heavily militarized society, in which many men have guns and intra-male and domestic violence is rampant. One of the most disturbing aspects of their study, for the UNIFEM researchers, was the finding that UN peacekeepers and workers in international charity organizations were also involved in sexually exploiting and violating vulnerable and displaced women in refugee camps. Thus, the very presence of those persons meant to protect and help the refugees instead continued the exploitation of and violence towards women.

In addition, the cost of a military economy, as it sucks away money for social services, falls heavily on women. In the United States, women are the majority of those on public assistance, because they are more often the ones taking care of children. State budget crises—affecting health care, public education, and other programs desperately needed by the poor—are further exacerbating the situation of poor women and children in the United States and around the world.

The arguments I have used to make the connections between feminism and antimilitarism could be summarized, using common U.S. feminist antimilitarist slogans, as the "guns vs. butter" argument and the "take the toys away from the boys" argument. The guns vs. butter argument is that women suffer from war because the gender division of labor means they have the most responsibility for the social, health, and educational aspects of a society—all of which are underfunded by a militarist economy. And the "take the toys away from the boys" argument is that militarism (the idea that violence is effective, necessary, and honorable) is built upon a form of masculinism that promotes and depends upon violence against women.

These two feminist antimilitarist arguments have been made for a long time, but in the 1980s a worldwide movement developed that combined both of these arguments. This movement began as a protest against nuclear power, and then expanded its focus to make strong connections between feminism, environmentalism, and antimilitarism. This was an analytical framework, however, that did not come about without intensive internal struggle over a number of political issues, including what kind of culturally specific "masculinism" was the problem for feminist antimilitarists, and what attention needed to be paid to the structures and dynamics of global capitalism. Third World feminists, U.S. feminists of color, working class and poor feminists, all should be credited with changing the terms of the analysis being promoted by feminists in more dominant social locations. The locations for this struggle were feminist antimilitarist demonstrations, at U.N. women's conferences and meetings, and feminist policy institutions in many countries. The development, through this political struggle, of a more complex feminist antimilitarist analysis has greatly influenced the anti-corporate globalization movement, and, I would argue, underlies the reach of the present global antiwar mobilization.

## Environmental Justice and Antimilitarism

So far, I have been delineating a particular feminist antimilitarist perspective, but I have said nothing about the connections between this perspective and an environmentalist analysis. This is the third perspective a transnational feminist environmentalist position can offer us. Just looking for a moment at the two recent U.S. wars against Iraq, we can see the huge negative consequences war has for the environment. Those consequences can be thought of as occurring in three ways.

The first is direct damage to the environment from war (bombing, oil fires, oil spills in the Gulf, depleted uranium shells, land mines, disruption of sanitary and water distribution systems, draining of wetlands, destruction of animal habitat, etcetera).

The second kind of environmental consequence is the strong official turn away from alternative energy policies, a rejection of energy conservation, and a renewed emphasis on nonrenewable and environmentally destructive sources of energy: oil and nuclear power. As our sources for oil in the Middle East are seen as problematically out of U.S. control, the political will to search for more non-renewable energy sources on U.S. lands increases. The result will be oil drilling in presently protected areas, oil spills, increased global warming, and the continued pollution of indigenous people's lands with nuclear waste (LaDuke 1999). Joni Seager estimates that the military is one of three most environmentally destructive institutions (along with governments and corporations), and often the most devastating to the environment because of the cloak of secrecy and the assumption of necessity that military organizations enjoy (Seager 1993).

And the third environmental consequence of war is what might be called the broad indirect costs to a wider environmental agenda: for example, the contempt shown by the U.S. for international law; the U.S. refusal to cooperate with international treaties to deal with global warming and other environmental problems; and the public relations cover the war has provided the Bush Administration's outright attack on environmental efforts in this country. From declaring environmental protesters "ecoterrorists," to gutting the Clean Air Act, to diluting the organic label, to easing restrictions on toxic waste siting, to shrinking budgets for Superfund clean-up, the Bush Administration is involved in a very serious rollback of hard-fought environmental achievements.

How do environmentalists deal with this attack in the context of a war polity and a war economy? I think that what is needed is a clear alternative, a pragmatic political vision, integrating environmental issues with other social justice issues that can connect the dots for the general public, demonstrating the interrelationships between this attack on the environment and the Bush Administration's simultaneous attack on working poor people, on women, on people of color and on Third World peoples. In other words, a transnational feminist environmentalist approach emphasizes questions of environmental justice—an environmentalism that makes connections between social inequalities and the production and continuation of environmental problems. As mentioned earlier, a redefinition of national security to mean human security would include an understanding of the necessity to keep our air, water, and food clean and healthy, as well as the necessity to ensure that environmental costs were not unequally distributed.

As Vandana Shiva (1997) and many others in the now-worldwide environmental justice movement point out, the negative consequences of environmental pollution, over-exploitation of natural resources, and commodification of seeds and foodstuffs is overwhelmingly borne by those in the world who are less powerful; conversely, environmental catastrophe is overwhelmingly caused by dependence on an economic system built upon inequality and oppression. Environmentalists have a particular role to play in connecting the human and natural costs of war, and in researching and promoting alternative, decentralized energy and agricultural technologies. This is why we see environmentalist activism embedded in the broader alternative vision of the contemporary anti-war mobilization. In the U.S., this development did not emerge in the Seattle anti-globalization protests in 1999, as some seemed to think when expressing surprise at the visible coalition in Seattle between environmentalists, anti-corporate globalization activists, and labor organizers. Rather, these were connections which were forged through the 1980s: nonviolent direct action movements against nuclear power and nuclear weapons; and a movement against U.S. intervention in El Salvador and Nicaragua (which was itself a global, environmentalist, feminist, and anti-militarist movement, as that movement made common cause with Third World anti-corporate globalization activists).

## The Political Economy of Women's Work, Nature, and War

The cross-national interactions between these sites of activism produced analytic links between the politics of environmentalism, feminism, and antimilitarism. But what we see today in the present anti-war mobilization is a more self-consciously global movement, set firmly in the context of a critique of global corporate capitalism (Reed forthcoming). This kind of political economic analysis is the fourth aspect a transnational feminist environmentalist perspective can develop, an aspect which arose out of political struggles between First World and Third World feminists in the context of forging international feminist coalitions.

In an economy in which many large corporations have bigger budgets than entire countries (LaDuke 1999), extreme, unprecedented inequalities of wealth are both feeding and resulting from militarism. Early in the post-Fordist period that produced this economic situation, some Third World feminist and antimilitarist organizations demanded not just that budget priorities change, but that the military budgets of the industrialized countries be given over to women as reparations for their unpaid work.[2] Though this demand may seem unrealistic, it was meant to bring out the connection between the creation of gross, unequal maldistribution of wealth and the resulting necessity to have a national security state supported by exorbitant military spending. And, importantly, these increasing inequalities of wealth are on a global scale, not just a national scale, thus resulting in a potential for worldwide unrest that, to some, seems to require the U.S.'s position as massive military superpower, willing to use its military strength either preemptively (in the Bush Administration's view) or at the behest of small collection of powerful nations on the U.N. Security Council (the more internationalist view of the Kerry Presidential campaign in 2004) to maintain the structures which foster this inequality.

Of course, there are many checks, balances, complications, and nuances involved in global political economic structures that, on deeper analysis, complicate this picture considerably. But it is clear that extreme inequalities of wealth are driving global conflicts, and that the resulting militarization deprives poorer countries and international aid institutions of the resources, access, and cooperation that would allow solutions to worldwide crises of health, education, human rights, and environment.

As I have said, this "guns vs. butter" argument is an important feminist antimilitarist analysis. But many Third World feminists and U.S. feminists of color pushed this argument further—their argument was that the caring work that was done in most societies predominantly by women was *productive* work. In other words, this was work which produced value, and which as unpaid work, was crucial to creating the surplus value that was the foundation of the growing global inequalities of wealth, and thus enabled the capital accumulation that fuelled neo-colonialist endeavors and required militarism (whether large-scale state militarism or the support of death squads and the School of the Americas) to put down resistance to neo-conservatism and neo-colonialism. Thus, analyzing women's role as caring unpaid or underpaid workers was not just about creating preferences for butter over guns, but about understanding that this exploitation of women's labor, both underpaid and unpaid, was part and parcel of the structures of global capitalist accumulation that foments and requires militarism. Thus, "pay women, not the military," the 1983 slogan put forth by the London-based antimilitarist feminist of color organization, Wages for Housework, was a slogan meant to challenge basic structures of global capitalism. However, paying women for their work is not enough to correct the problem. What matters is how much and under what conditions women (or men!) are paid for this essential work.

The caring work that had been socially assigned to women in many cultures has been an externality in the capitalist economy, just as nature is an externality. Just as air, water, biodiversity, and ecosystem health are reified as externalities (so that the exploitation, pollution, and overuse of them as natural resources doesn't have to be paid for, or to be accounted for) so has the work assigned to women—the work of daily human maintenance, of feeding, cleaning, changing diapers, eldercare, cooking, loving, celebrating, teaching the young— been treated as an externality. Much of this work has been separated off from the economy as though it were not part of sustaining life, and exploited without recognition or proper recompense—because it was seen as women's natural skill and duty. Nature was expected to be all bountiful and usable, as women are expected to be all-nurturing and available. If women are devalued, if femininity is feared, then women's work, and often nature itself, is also devalued. A transnational feminist environmentalist analysis allows us to see these connections between the way women's labor and natural resources are treated.

Furthermore, Third World feminists and U.S. feminists of color argued that economically privileged women, despite their supposed socialization to be more caring individuals, were complicit in these economic structures. Global Women's Strike (an organization that grew out of Wages for Housework) wrote a letter to U.S. feminists which pointed out:

> Feminists in industrial countries (in the 1980s)…ditched welfare mothers fighting for survival, and this also meant ditching women of color with the least. They plumped instead for careers for a few and for integrating into the ruling class and the management class. The result is that women's wages, deprived of the floor that welfare provided, collapsed. (And men's followed, as they always do. This lowering of men's wages is what closed the gap between the sexes, giving the appearance of leveling). (Global Women's Strike 2003, 2)

I would add to this analysis that the growth of the service sector during this neo-conservative period was a way of commodifying women's work at low wages with poor or no benefits. One of the results of this trend was that working class women in the U.S. during this period welcomed integration into the U.S. military, partly as a means to overcome the devaluing of their "service" work and to move themselves out of the ranks of the working poor (Feinman 2000).

The dismantling of welfare and other social services, coupled with the fall of real wages, was one of the hallmarks of neo-conservatism, and the process accelerated in what was called the Reagan/Thatcherite era. The success of this neoconservatist reworking of the Keynesian welfare state was also buttressed by the success of neocolonialism, justified by the fear-mongering Reagan Administration tactics of the need to fight an "evil empire" which required a huge military build-up (an ideological move repeated now by the Bush Administration). What followed was a round of debt crisis for the Third World, the imposition of structural adjustment programs which gutted social supports, increased environmental devastation for poor rural peoples in particular, and rising unemployment, hunger, and desperation (Stiglitz 2002).

These economic patterns, which I am summarizing here very briefly, were and are gendered, that is, they have always had gender implications. Through these processes, men were often unemployed and unable to help provide adequate food for their families, and poor, often young, women became the means for their families' survival. How? They became low waged workers in maquiladoras and sweatshops for multinational corporations; they became prostitutes, dancers and entertainers in tourist industries; and they became domestics and nannies for First World women.

As wages fell in the industrialized countries, the "family wage," that is, the ability of some men in middle and upper class jobs to bring home enough money to support a family, became more and more rare. Almost all women now entered the wage economy, but at different class levels. The caring work that had been done by upper-class and middle-class women was now understaffed, as they moved into the workplace, because generally men did not take on these jobs within the home, and no social services were funded to replace them, especially in the U.S. Now almost all women faced the tough situation that poor and working class women have faced for centuries—they had a double shift on the job and at home, and their overall workload increased.

This situation created what has been called a "care deficit" in First World countries, and a corresponding "care drain" in Third World countries (Ehrenreich and Hochschild 2002). Poor Third World women have become one of the largest exports from their countries, as domestics, eldercare workers, and nannies for elite First World women. The remittances these Third World women send back to their countries are sometimes the largest source of foreign currency for indebted and cash-strapped Third World governments, and as these women leave their homes to take care of other families, their own families lose their caring work (Parreñas 2002).

But as Barbara Ehrenreich and Arlie Russell Hochschild point out:

> It would be a mistake to attribute the globalization of women's work to a simple synergy of needs among women…this formulation fails to account for the marked failure of First World governments to meet the needs created by the entry of its women into the workplace…[and] it omits the role of men [who refuse to do "women's work"]…So, strictly speaking, the presence of immigrant nannies does not enable affluent women to enter the workforce; it enables affluent men to continue avoiding the second shift. (Ehrenreich and Hochschild 2003, 8-9)

Yet affluent men feel threatened by the entry of elite women into formerly male domains. They feel the "care deficit" as well—the shift in control over women in their class. I speculate here that this is part of the underlying reason for the rise in sex tourism, sex trafficking, and mail-order brides, the third stream of the expanding flow of women forced to work in other countries. Some of these women may be working by choice in these jobs, if sex work is a better situation that other kinds of available work, but many of them are working in conditions of extreme coercion and sometimes outright slavery. Their clients are overwhelmingly rich men from industrialized countries.

A transnational feminist environmentalist perspective pays attention to these connections: this perspective looks at the way the World Bank's and the International Monetary Fund's control over the economic choices of indebted countries encourages the rapid export of natural resources from poor countries; and the way these economic choices lead to environmental devastation, as well as to the export of a country's women and the accompanying exploitation and suffering. And we need to look at the connection of these trends with the growing militarization within these countries and within our own, as well as the growth of cults of violent masculinity. Arguments from nature—which support aggression and violence as natural tendencies, especially for men—are based on a belief in violence as part of a set of genetically-programmed needs for attaining reproductive success. These are also the kind of arguments that define war as honorable, necessary, and a matter of pride, fueled by masculinist tropes such as "Bring It On." Sut Jhally argues instead that the appearance and promotion of a particular form of American masculinity in the 1980s—the image of the super-beefy, extra-violent Rambo male—was partly a backlash against feminism and rapid changes in gender relations, and partly a response to increasing unemployment for working class and poor men. Further, this "tough guise" drives U.S. support for violence at home and throughout the globe (Jhally1999, Mageo 2004).

Various versions of this form of extreme, violent masculinism are socially constructed, not natural, and are accessed differently by people in different gender, class, race, religious and national formations. For instance, what are the connections between the unemployment of men in Third World countries and the rise of Islamic militant fundamentalism? How, along with economic insecurity and resistance to U.S. dominance and support for Israel's occupation of Palestine, are the possibility of changing roles for Muslim women connected to the appeal for many young Muslim men of suicide bombing, guerrilla jihad, and the kidnapping and murder of hostages? How are similar forces (economic stress, racism at home, and changing gender roles) connected to the appeal for many young U.S. men of participating in militarist adventures?

We must move away from an earlier feminist position that militarist violence is something men do because they are men, and analyze the structural and economic forms of various forms of masculinism as well as other gendered trends driving present military conflicts around the globe. The increasing numbers of immigrant domestics and nannies are connected to the rise of sex trafficking and mail order brides, as well as to the existence of predominantly female sweatshop labor. And all of these are part of a specifically gendered set of global changes that underlie the World Bank/IMF structural policies, in which male unemployment and the lack of basic food, health, and reproductive services produce a pattern of global circulation and exploitation of Third World women by First World global city-dwellers on the one hand, and increasing desperation, fundamentalism, and militarization for Third World and poor First World men on the other. Although masculinist violence can be appropriated by women in order to gain the civic and nationalistic power it represents, what we see at present is a war between two forms of masculinist fundamentalism, the Bush Administration's Christian version, and an Islamic militant version, which are both deeply patriarchal, and are fuelled by different versions of masculinity in crisis. Unless these gendered aspects of this situation we face are recognized, real peace cannot be achieved. The Bush Administration's masculinist, violent response to 9/11, despite the veneer of politically expedient and insincere concern over Afghan women's rights, has not produced peace or justice. Instead, as is happening in Afghanistan and is likely to happen in Iraq, women who suffered under one form of violent, patriarchal regime will continue to suffer under another version of violent patriarchy (RAWA 2004). War is not an avenue to peace and equality, either in the U.S. or abroad.

## Seeking a Just and Full Peace

What are some answers to the problems we face? Should we be paying women for all the work they do, putting a price or an hourly wage on that work? That, in fact, has been what is happening, but it has been happening in an economy in which women and women's work are the least valued. Similarly, the externalities of natural resources have continued to be commodified, if only corporations can control and market them. This is what Bechtel tried to do with the water in Bolivia, until it was stopped by indigenous activists in the Cochabamba region (Brecher 2000).

If the commodification of what was previously thought of as free externalities is going to happen, then that caring work, and those natural resources, have to be valued much more and much differently than they are now. They would have to be valued as the most important work and the most precious resources we have. And if we start to pay fairly for "women's work" (not necessarily work done only by women!) and for natural resources, than we also need a simultaneous cap on profits and overvalued kinds of work, to enable us to value caring work and natural resources adequately.

The other aspect that needs to be stressed is insisting on women's participation in peace-making and nation-building. Recently, the U.N. passed Resolution 1325, requiring that women be part of these processes in significant rather than token ways (Abdela 2004). Here in the U.S., only 14 percent of our elected representatives are women (in the U.S. Congress), yet we present ourselves as having achieved political equality for women. In countries where that ratio is much higher, there are better social services and less economic inequality (Seager 2003). Particularly in areas that are presently or recently suffering from military conflict, there is a need to involve women, who have so much at stake in peace and war, in the political resolutions of the conflict. Focusing on the situation of the world's women—on their access to healthcare, to education, to civil rights, and to the control of their own bodies—is a means to reduce population, to raise the level of education for all, to ensure adequate health, and to achieve widespread well-being. Using the status of women as a benchmark will change priorities in radical and meaningful ways, bringing us closer to peace, a more just and full peace, than we have ever been before. Hopefully, full of hope, a transnational feminist environmentalist perspective can provide part of the means to see these connections and inspire the political will to make these changes.

## Notes

*An earlier, different version of this argument was given as a keynote speech and transcribed as "Feminism and Environmentalism in a Time of War," *Journal of Environmental Law and Litigation* 18 (Spring 2003): 209-222.

1. Between five to thirty million people marched in coordinated protests around the world the week of February 8 to 15, 2003. Despite disagreement on the numbers, sources agree these were the largest coordinated antiwar demonstrations ever seen (McFadden 2003; Frenkel 2003; Leupp 2003; Koch 2003).

2. In a longer version of this paper, I trace the relationship of the organization that made this particular demand, the London-base Wages for Housework, with the U.S. white antimilitarist organizations in the 1980s, showing the way in which the political economic analysis I summarize here as "pay women, not the military," developed (Brown 1983).

## References

Abdela, Leslie. 2004. "No Place for a Woman." In *Flanders* 2004: 258-262.

Alonso, Harriet. 1993. *Peace as a Women's Issue.* Syracuse University Press.

Bacchetta, Paola, Tina Campt, Inderpal Grewal, Caren Kaplan, Minoo Moallem, and Jennifer Terry. 2001. "Transnational Feminist Practices Against War." Circulated on the internet Sept/Oct 2001; reprinted in *Flanders* 2004:263-267.

Brecher, Jeremy, Tim Costello, and Brendan Smith. 2000. *Globalization from Below.* South End Press.

Bunch, Charlotte. 2002. "Whose Security?" *The Nation.* Oct. 23.

Brown, Wilmette. 1983. *Black Women and the Peace Movement.* Falling Wall Press.

Ehrenreich, Barbara and Arlie Russell Hochschild, eds. 2002. *Global Woman: Nannies, Maids, and Sex Workers in the New Economy,* Metropolitan Books

Enloe, Cynthia. 2000. *Maneuvers: The International Politics of Militarizing Women's Lives.* University of California Press.

Jhally, Sut. 1999. *Tough Guise: Violence, Media and the Crisis in Masculinity.* Media Education Foundation.

Koch, Connie, ed. 2003. *2/15.* HELLO and AK Press.

Featherstone, Liza. 2004. "Mighty in Pink." In *Flanders* 2004:244-249.

Feinman, Ilene. 2000. *Citizenship Rites: Feminist Soldiers and Feminist Antimilitarists.* NYU Press.

Flanders, Laura, ed. 2004. *The W Effect: Bush's War on Women.* The Feminist Press.

Frenkel, Glenn. 2003. "Millions Worldwide Protest Iraq War," *The Washington Post,* 2/16/03:A.01

LaDuke, Winona. 1999. *All Our Relations: Native Struggles for Land and Life.* South End Press.

Leupp, Gary. 2003. *Counterpunch.* Feb. 25. http://www.counterpunch.org/leupp02252003.html

Mageo, Jeannette. 2004. "Migratory Femininity in Cultural Fantasies, Male Gender Instability, and War," Paper presented at the Gendering Research Across the Campuses Conference, Washington State University.

McFadden, Robert D. 2003. "From New York to Melbourne, Cries for Peace," *NYT,* 2/16/03: 1.1.

Parreñas, Rhacel Salazar. 2002. "The Care Crisis in the Philippines: Children and Transnational Families in the New Global Economy." In Ehrenreich and Hochschild 2002:39-54.

RAWA. 2004. Website of Revolutionary Association of the Women of Afghanistan. http://rawa.fancymarketing.net/index.html

Reed, T.V. forthcoming. *The Art of Protest: From the Civil Rights Movement to the Battle of Seattle.* University of Minnisota (2005)

Rehn, Elisabeth and Ellen Johnson Sirleaf. 2002. *Women, War and Peace: Progress of the World's Women 2002.* Volume One. UNIFEM.

Seager, Joni. 1993. *Earth Follies: Coming to Feminist Terms with the Global Environmental Crisis.* Routledge, 2003. *State of Women in the World Atlas.* Penguin Books.

Shiva, Vandana. 1997. *Biopiracy: The Plunder of Nature and Knowledge.* South End Press.

Stiglitz, Joseph. 2002. *Globalization and Its Discontents.* W. W. Norton.

Sturgeon, Noël. 1995. "Theorizing Movements: Direct Action and Direct Theory." In Darnovsky, Marcy, Barbara Epstein and Richard Flacks, eds. *Cultural Politics and Social Movements.* Temple University: 35-51.

_____1997. *Ecofeminist Natures: Race, Gender, Feminist Theory and Political Action.* Routledge.

_____Forthcoming. *The Politics of the Natural.*

## eighteen

# War Memory and Peace: A Historian's Case Study of the Myths of Japan's Surrender

## Noriko Kawamura

This chapter will explore how history as a discipline can contribute to interdisciplinary comprehensive peace studies in an international and transnational context. It is an attempt to build a historical argument for peace by examining the role of war memory. The study will specifically focus on the memory of World War II in the Pacific as a case study.

Why do we need to look at war memory in peace studies? Ever since the time of Thucydides and the Peloponnesian War, human beings have not been able to shake off the thought that history might repeat itself, especially when they face potential manmade disasters, such as war. Thucydides produced his account of the Peloponnesian War with a view to warning future generations not to repeat the same mistake the ancient Greeks had made. In the complex society of the modern world, George Santayana's famous aphorism "Those who cannot remember the past are condemned to repeat it" haunts not only historians but also all of humankind. The twentieth century witnessed the two bloodiest worldwide wars in history and the creation of the ultimate weapon that threatens annihilation of the world.

In the realm of foreign policy that dictates international relations, Harvard diplomatic historian Ernest R. May demonstrates in his seminal book, *"Lessons" of the Past*, that national leaders are "often influenced by beliefs about what history teaches or portends." He suggests that policy-makers can and should use history, provided that they take a level-headed approach to history and avoid the danger of narrow-minded dependence on a single analogy or parallel.[1] Historians do not make it easy for political scientists and policy-makers to utilize history, as one State Department officer complained: "Historians refuse to generalize ... to give up detail and to give up shadings."[2] Despite this criticism, however, May's message is unmistakable and noteworthy: historians can play an important role by offering lessons from past experiences to policy-makers who must make decisions on the issues of war and peace.

Unlike specific use of the past in the making of foreign policy, people's collective memory of war touches diverse aspects of human community and has been a subject of study by scholars of various disciplines for various purposes; and historians and political scientists do not monopolize the field. It seems that, in search of peace preservation, historians can approach the issue of war memory in more than one way. Historians offer narratives, analyses, and interpretations of the past, thereby suggesting what readers should remember, as well as how readers should remember the past. Their narratives could become a powerful tool to promote or criticize certain attitudes towards war and peace. Historians can develop new perspectives on past events through studying new materials that were previously inaccessible. At the same time historians can also study interactions between historical narratives and collective memories of a state, society, and culture; can demonstrate how collective memory of the past can be reconstructed by historical narratives; and can show how individual and community memory, in turn, can shape community attitudes that influence future events.

Roger W. Smith, in his study of the Armenian genocide, eloquently explains broader ethical implications of memory of the past in the contemporary context:

> Recognition and remembrance involve more than regard for truth: they express compassion for those who have suffered, respect for their dignity as persons, and revolt against the injustice done to them. In the deepest sense, recognition and remembrance are related not only to what happened, but to questions of who *we* are, what *society* is, and how life and community can be protected against visions that would destroy both. To remember those who have come before us is an expression of ourselves—our care, our capacity to join in a community, our respect for other human beings. And through our capacities for memory and foresight, a community comes to include those who are living, who have died, and those yet to be born.[3]

Historians are an intrinsic part of this exercise whether they are conscious of the fact or not.

This study will examine the linkage between war memory and people's attitude toward peace by focusing primarily on a case study of Japan's memory and to some extent the United States' memory of how the Second World War in the Pacific theater was brought to an end. The chapter will especially examine whether the way the Japanese people remember the Showa Emperor's role at the close of the war influenced the way they remember the war and the way they came to embrace a peculiar pacifism after the war. Why focus on the emperor? The Showa Emperor is arguably the most controversial figure in the history of the Asia-Pacific War. He was sovereign of the state and commander-in-chief of the Japanese military, and above all the manifestation of divinity and a symbol of Japan's cultural and national identity. Nevertheless, the emperor escaped the war crimes trials, did not take responsibility for the war, and continued to reign for over four decades in postwar Japan; although his status was changed to "the symbol of the state and of the unity of the people" under the new constitution of Japan written by the Americans. The Showa Emperor closely mirrored both transformation and continuity from prewar imperial Japan to postwar pacifist Japan.

In the recent book *Senso-kan naki heiwaron* (Pacifism without a concept of war), Masayasu Hosaka, a journalist who has written extensively on the Pacific War, echoes the common criticism among Japanese liberal historians and intellectuals that the Japanese people's shallow pacifism is based on either superficial or inaccurate understanding of the causes and consequences of the Asia-Pacific War.[4] The majority of Japanese are against war in general, primarily because they have either remembered or have heard about the terrible personal sufferings the Japanese people endured during the Pacific War. According to a survey conducted in 1982 by the public broadcasting corporation of Japan (Nihon Hoso Kyokai), when Japanese talked about the Asia-Pacific War, the topic they discussed most frequently was the miseries and hardships they had experienced during the war; and the second most frequent subject was the atomic bombs dropped on Hiroshima and Nagasaki.[5] Numerous published oral histories in Japan are filled with emotional personal tales of material as well as psychological sacrifices, starvation, the Allied air raids on Japan which killed more than four hundred thousand civilians, and above all the atomic bombs. However, few Japanese articulate their opposition to war on the basis of what the Japanese government and its military machine had done to the peoples of other Asian countries or to the Allied powers during that war: between nine and fifteen million people lost their lives in China, and about four million perished in Vietnam. As many leftist historians point out, the invasion Japan started in China in 1931 is not even part of the Japanese public memory of the war.[6]

Some of the leading American historians of modern Japan share this criticism. As Carol Gluck points out, the issue among "the generations born since the war who now comprise some two-thirds" of the Japanese population "is not whether the Japanese remember the war, but how they do so, and to what contemporary effect." The postwar generations have grown up with what critics call the "sanitized" history textbooks that overwhelmingly reflect the so-called "Tokyo-war-crimes-trial view of history," which places the blame for the reckless aggressive war on the military, ultranationalists, and *zaibatsu* (industrial and financial conglomerates). These generations have learned the history of the Pacific War as "victims history" in the passive voice: in other words, "the China Incident was caused, Pearl Harbor was bombed, the atomic bomb was dropped," as though natural catastrophes had struck Japan.[7] John Dower discusses in his numerous works "victim consciousness" (*higaisha ishiki*) as a popular sentiment among the Japanese people regarding the Pacific War. He suggests that the atomic bombs dropped on Hiroshima and Nagasaki occupy a central place in this consciousness and states that "the trauma of nuclear devastation and unconditional surrender" reinforced "an abiding sense of Japan's peculiar vulnerability and victimization."[8]

If the perpetrators of the war were the military clique and big business, and if the Japanese civilians were victims, what was the emperor's role? John Dower offers a powerful narrative of how the Supreme Commander of the Allied Powers (SCAP), General Douglas MacArthur, played a critical role in exonerating the emperor from the war crimes trial and successfully preserved the imperial house in postwar Japan to facilitate the American reform agenda.[9] James Orr in *The Victim as Hero* demonstrates how SCAP as well as the Japanese government under U.S. occupation promoted the notion that both the Japanese emperor and his people were deceived by the military clique prior to and during the war, and therefore, were both victims of the war.[10]

Thus, what emerges from these studies are two familiar historical narratives: on the one hand, the widely held view among the Japanese people that the Japanese people themselves were the "victims" of the war, and on the other hand, the myth that the ever peace-loving Showa Emperor, who was powerless to prevent the military from starting the war, seized the opportunity to act as a peacemaker at the close of the war. In this version, the emperor put an end to the misery of his people and saved the nation of Japan from annihilation. The narrative of victimization and the myth of the emperor as a peacemaker have mutually reinforced each other's validity and forged what Carol Gluck calls a national "mythistory," which is comprised of "the stories" that a nation tells its people and teaches its children "in the name less of the past than of the present."[11] Ironically, the two most important catalysts that firmly connected these two narratives were the actions taken by the Americans: the atomic bomb and the Tokyo war crimes trials.

The rest of the chapter will examine two issues. First, it is necessary to examine whether the Showa Emperor's *seidan* (imperial decision) to accept the Potsdam Declaration and end the war, a manifestation of his role as a peacemaker, was really a myth. Was his divine intervention really crucial in ending the war? Second, how did the atomic bomb and the Tokyo Trial perpetuate the narratives of victimization and the myth of the emperor's *seidan*?

There is a rich historiography on the role the emperor played at the end of the war. Fifty years ago Robert J.C. Butow's definitive work, *Japan's Decision to Surrender*, set the standard for studies on this subject both in Japan and the United States.[12] Butow emphasizes the efforts by the peace party (from the Foreign Ministry and the Navy as well as the court) to overcome the opposition mainly from the Army, which insisted on fighting till the bitter end. Butow demonstrates that the emperor was definitely in favor of peace after June 9, 1945, and Butow shows that the emperor played a critical role only he himself could play (as emperor) and made the peace party's goal attainable. However, Butow's work also suggests that the decision-making process was a team effort: that is, the process was pluralistic and consensus-oriented. Neither the emperor alone nor the peace party (acting on its own without the emperor's support) could have brought an end to the war. In the summer of 1945, the situation was unusual in the sense that two major groups—the Japanese government and the military leaders—failed to produce a unanimous recommendation for the throne: the emperor was asked to offer his opinion as a tie-breaker. The emperor made this personal intervention because the prime minister and the lord keeper of the privy seal created the stage that allowed him to do so under extraordinary circumstances. Butow also portrays the use of the atomic bomb and the Soviet Union's entry into war against Japan as equally important factors that hastened Japan's surrender, but not as decisive factors. He best summarizes his position in the following words: "The atomic bombing of Hiroshima and Nagasaki and the Soviet Union's declaration of war did not produce Japan's decision to surrender, for that decision—in embryo—had long been taking shape. What these events did do was to create that unusual atmosphere in which the theretofore static factor of the Emperor could be made active in such an extraordinary way as to work what was virtually a political miracle."[13]

Since then, Butow's interpretation of the *seidan* has been both confirmed and challenged by various diplomatic and military historians who had access to new materials that were previously unavailable (except, of course, the emperor's own documents that are permanently sealed by the Imperial Household Agency). As many Japanese leftist historians (as well as American historians) point out, the claim that the emperor's *seidan* made it possible for Japan to accept the Potsdam Declaration certainly helped General MacArthur's efforts to spare the emperor from war crimes trial—even if the emperor was only spared for political expedience in order to carry out American reform policies in Japan. Consequently, both Japanese conservative historians and American historians who formally served SCAP in Tokyo contributed to perpetuating the orthodox interpretation of the Showa Emperor as peace-loving constitutional monarch who was against the war, but could not stop the military until its fighting machine was practically wiped out and the hawkish military leaders lost credibility by the summer of 1945.

However, the United States decision to exclude the emperor from the Tokyo Trial provided Japanese leftist historians with a basis for bringing out some of the most critical charges against the emperor, especially on the issue of the emperor's responsibility for war. After the Showa Emperor's death in 1989, two camps of historians in Japan—the "palace group" school and the "leftist" historians—intensified the debate over the issue of the emperor's involvement in war decisions. Japanese leftist historians have been partially successful in reversing the orthodox interpretation, by portraying the emperor as a more active commander-in-chief (*daigensui*) of the Japanese military who actively participated in the making of war decisions. Such critics of the emperor are eager to bring him to trial in the court of history. Some Japanese historians have even suggested that the emperor was responsible for delaying Japan's decision to surrender rather than for hastening it. Borrowing heavily from these Japanese historians works, Herbert Bix's Pulitzer prize winning book made this issue an international controversy.[14]

Historians, ever curious about factual accuracy, cannot help asking exactly what role the emperor played in Japan's decision to surrender. The so-called emperor's "monologue" (*Showa tenno dokuhakuroku*) which he dictated in the spring of 1946 indicates that the emperor was fairly well informed about the war situation in 1945, and that he was stunned by the poor conditions of the Japanese islands' defense in the wake of the defeat in Okinawa. Obviously, by mid June of 1945, the emperor recognized that Japan had no hope of winning a victory in a decisive battle—a battle that the supreme command had been insisting upon in order to gain a better bargaining position for a negotiated peace with the United States. Between June 9 and 22, 1945, the emperor made it clear to the general staffs as well as to the government leaders that he desired peace, and he suggested that Japan seek peace mediation through the Soviet Union.[15]

However, the emperor's privately expressed wish would, by itself, not lead his country towards peace. Nearly three months elapsed before the Japanese government publicly declared its acceptance of the Potsdam Declaration. During these months, the real movers were the ministers, generals, and admirals. The diaries, memoirs, and biographies of the major players within the peace party (such as Lord Keeper of the Privy Seal Koichi Kido, Prime Minister Kantaro Suzuki, Navy Minister Mitsumasa Yonai, and Foreign Minister Shigenori Togo) all indicate that these men realized that Japan must end the war and that they worked quietly to achieve that goal. The officials acted quietly because they were under the constant threat of assassination by the war factions in the military.

Depending on which sources they rely on most, historians can create various *interpretations* as to who played crucial roles on this road to peace. The pluralistic decision-making process—which was based on the nebulous, triangular power relationship of the court, the general staffs, and the government—certainly makes it extremely difficult for historians to reach a clear-cut conclusion. If, according to one source, the emperor personally attributed the ending of the war to the great courage (*taiyu*) of Prime Minister Kantaoro Suzuki and Navy Minister Mitsumasa Yonai, should we give them credit?[16] Or, if after the war the emperor revealed that he had initiated the final critical imperial conference on August 14, 1945—the conference that actually ended the war—should we give him credit?[17]

There are other possible explanations as well. Renowned Pacific War historian Kazutoshi Hando (*Japan's Longest Day* and *Seidan: tenno to Suzuki Kantaro* [The Imperial Decision, the Emperor and Kantaro Suzuki]) argues that some of the Big Six of the supreme war council who on the surface insisted on fighting until the bitter end, particularly the war minister, General Korechika Anami, were prepared to sacrifice their lives so that the Suzuki cabinet could successfully accept the Potsdam Declaration and surrender. The logic here is that if the cabinet decided to surrender, in order to prevent the government from signing a peace, hawkish army officers would force the war minister to resign and dissolve the cabinet; if the war minister had refused to resign, he might have been assassinated. General Anami was aware of this possibility; therefore, he held on to the die-hard position to fight till the bitter end on the surface and allowed the Suzuki to continue to pursue peace, fully aware that the emperor would break the tie in favor of ending the war at the imperial conference. Thus the general made it possible for the Suzuki cabinet to finalize the surrender decision without the army's interference. According to Prime Minister Suzuki and his chief secretary (Hisatsune Sakomizu), what made a difference in General Anami's thinking was the emperor's grave concern about the future survival of his country.[18] If this was the case, General Anami was a master of "*haragei*" (to accomplish his goal without telling his true intentions) and deserves credit for his efforts in realizing peace.

What these episodes tell us is that a delicate balance existed between the two factors: that is, the emperor's personal wish *did* matter to the highest ranking government and military leaders, but it was up to the leaders themselves to make policy decisions. On the issue of Japan's final decision to surrender, the crucial action seemed to be Prime Minister Suzuki's decision to ask for the emperor's "*seidan*." Without it, the emperor's opinion would not have become a national decision. The trick in pulling this off was that the prime minister had already known the emperor's wish ahead of time. Suzuki was playing "*haragei*" and took advantage of the traditional role that the emperor played in state rituals. In other words, the decision-making was still pluralistic and consensus-oriented. However, skeptics might also suggest that in view of the sense of urgency and determination on the part of the prime minister and the lord privy seal, the palace advisers would have extracted the emperor's *seidan* sooner or later, regardless of the emperor's personal opinion, just as the general staffs extracted the imperial sanction to commence the attack on Pearl Harbor. The question is which group had the strongest conviction and determination as well as the most effective means to persuade the emperor.

Unfortunately, however, this kind of factual analysis of complex circumstances interests only a few historians. It could be easily dismissed by the general public as trivial "details" or "shadings." People might even ask, if historians themselves cannot agree on what *really* happened, why they should bother to think about the past events. Here, it is important to go back to the earlier discussion on the constant interactions of the memory of the past, the creation and re-creation of narratives, and contemporary events and politics.

The rest of this chapter will look at how the two events—the use of the atomic bomb and the Tokyo Trial—contributed to perpetuating the Japanese victimization narrative and the myth of the emperor's *seidan*.

The heated controversy over the exhibition of the *Enola Gay* in the Smithsonian Institute in 1995 to commemorate the fiftieth anniversary of the end of World War II reminded many historians in the United States that the postwar international environment and contemporary domestic political expediencies could sanitize public memory of the past. Using the airplane that dropped the atomic bomb on Hiroshima as its central icon, the exhibition was supposed to examine not only "the bomb's creation, the decision to use it against Japanese cities," but also "the ground-level effects of atomic weaponry, the bomb's role in ending the war, and the new era it inaugurated." More important, the exhibition was supposed to be the occasion to examine "the ways in which decades of historical research and debate on these topics had altered and deepened our [Americans'] understanding of them."

However, the show was abandoned because of emotionally charged protests by military officials, veterans' lobbying groups, and conservative politicians, who did not want to display artifacts and images from ground zero in Hiroshima and Nagasaki which could remind us of the fact that hundreds of thousand of men, women, and children were incinerated and irradiated by the blasts. These critics accused the Smithsonian managers, curators, as well as the historians who served as museum advisers, of being "anti-American," "politically correct," advocating "countercultural values of the Vietnam era" and destroying the "keys" to American unity. The editors of *History Wars* warn that "the *Enola Gay* controversy tells us about the state of our nation." Americans are not free from "the snares of trivializing, sanitizing, and sanctifying the past."[19]

John Dower argues that the mainstream American counterpart to the victimization narrative shared by many Japanese is "a heroic or triumphal narrative, in which the atomic bombs represent the final blow against an aggressive, fanatical and savage foe." Opponents of the Smithsonian's original plans wanted to believe that the atomic bombs in Hiroshima and Nagasaki were "moral" and "humane" because they ended the "Good War" and saved American lives. This American triumphal heroic narrative ends where the Japanese victimization narrative begins. The opponents of the exhibition did not want to show small objects from ground zero such as a lunch-box containing carbonized rice and peas that belonged to a seventh-grade school-girl whose corpse was never found, because they were afraid that in the audience's memory what the *Enola Gay* symbolizes would be overshadowed by the memory of the school-girl's lunch box.[20]

A decade earlier in 1985, on the fortieth anniversary of the atomic bombing of Japan, Paul Boyer had criticized the United States failure "as a people to come to terms with Hiroshima and Nagasaki," saying that Hiroshima became "a kind of hole in human history." He wrote in the *New York Times*: "A few years ago I interviewed Ralph Lapp, the Manhattan Project physicist who later became a vigorous critic of the nuclear arms race. One of his comments was particularly striking: 'If the memory of things is to deter, where is that memory? Hiroshima … has been taken out of the American conscience, eviscerated, extirpated.'"[21] In 1995, the triumphant heroic narrative on the atomic bomb seemed to be still reigning as patriotic orthodoxy in the United States. Another decade has nearly passed: we will see what will unfold.

Despite diametrically opposite positions of the United State and Japan over the issues of the legitimacy and morality of the use of nuclear weapons, many Americans and Japanese accept the narratives of war that affirm their respective government's existing policies, and they are willing to go along with the foundational narratives to serve their own country's national interests. While the U.S. government maintains an official line that the atomic bomb was used to end the war quickly and to save American lives, many Japanese do not question the myth that in the wake of the atomic bombs, only the Showa Emperor's *seidan* enabled the badly divided Japanese government to bring about the decision to end the war.

It is important to note that the emperor's *seidan* for Japan's surrender took place at the convergent point of these two narratives. Yoshikuni Igarashi put these narratives together in the opening chapter of his book, *Bodies of Memory*, and argues that they have together become a twofold myth of both the atomic bomb and the Showa Emperor as peacemakers: that is, the most inhumane weapon and the emperor's divine intervention ended the bloodiest war in the Pacific.[22] However, on this issue, the line between myth and reality is not so obvious. To Sadao Asada, a leading Japanese scholar on U.S.-Japanese relations, the story is not a myth. In his award-winning 1998 article in *Pacific Historical Review*, Asada argues that the "external pressure" from the atomic bomb allowed the emperor to prevail over the military and bring about the decision to terminate the war. He suggests that conventional bombing alone would not have driven the emperor to say that Japan must surrender or would have allowed a proud army to accept his decision. In Asada's interpretation, the atomic bomb and the Showa Emperor were both catalysts for peace.[23] On the other hand, although most Japanese experts on the subject would not deny the fact that the use of the atomic bomb precipitated Japan's decision to surrender, these events would not emphasize the shock of the atomic bomb as much as Asada does. They equally emphasize the effect of the Soviet declaration of war on Japan, pointing out the fact that the Foreign Office had been trying to seek Moscow's mediation for peace with the U.S. since mid-May 1945.

Regardless of what happened, the emperor's first historic radio announcement to the Japanese people on August 15, 1945, imprinted this twofold myth in the memory of the Japanese people. The emperor declared: "… the enemy has begun to employ a new and most cruel bomb, the power of which to do damage is indeed incalculable, taking the toll of many innocent lives. Should We continue to fight, it would not only result in an ultimate collapse and obliteration of the Japanese nation, but also it would lead to the total extinction of human civilization." Therefore, the emperor told his subjects "to pave the way for a grand peace for all the generations to come by enduring the unendurable and suffering what is insufferable."[24] Prime Minister Suzuki's announcement quickly followed: "His Majesty made the sacred decision to end the war in order to save the people and contribute to the welfare and peace of mankind." This can be interpreted to mean that the "viciousness of the atomic bombs provided Japan's leaders with the opportunity to recast the emperor as the savior of the country."[25]

Coupled with the atomic bomb, the verdicts of the Tokyo war crimes trials sent a clear message to the Japanese people regarding who was responsible for the war. As described earlier, by excluding the emperor from the entire process of war crimes trials, SCAP and the postwar Japanese government created a history in which the emperor and his people were victims of a war which had been carried out by an aggressive and manipulative government dominated by the militarists. Because there was limited public discussion of the average Japanese person's responsibility for wartime acts, there was almost no pressure to force individual citizens to confront the issue of their own war responsibility. As a result, postwar generations feel little sense of responsibility for what their country did in Asia and the Pacific during the war. James Orr suggests that the emperor "as the preeminent and powerful symbol of both state and people, could have forced such confrontation by publicly asserting his own sense of responsibility and facing the consequences."[26]

As a matter of fact, available documents indicate that the emperor was personally willing to assume responsibility for the war at the time of Japan's surrender, and that he was prepared to abdicate if necessary, although the situation under the American occupation did not allow him to make his own choice one way or the other.[27] The unpublished emperor's apology which was drafted by Michiji Tajima, the head of the Imperial Household Agency between 1948 and 1953, indicates that the emperor personally felt "a deep responsibility" for the tragic outcome of the war and felt sorry for "his lack of virtue."[28] Whatever the emperor's true personal feelings were, however, there is no doubt that his hesitation and ultimate silence circumscribed open public discussion of his responsibility, and this, in turn, contributed to the anesthetizing of individual Japanese citizen's personal war guilt. A renowned film reviewer aptly commented in 1959: "Why didn't the Japanese people try to pursue the emperor's war responsibility? I think that the reason is that, for the vast majority of the people, the easiest way to exonerate themselves of war responsibility was to exonerate the emperor."[29]

Over four decades, the overwhelming majority of the Japanese people have either positively or tacitly accepted the Showa Emperor as the symbol of the new "pacifist" postwar Japan. According to a survey conducted among 3,080 Japanese voters by the *Yomiuri Shinbun* in August 1948, soon after the promulgation of the new constitution, over 90 percent of the respondents supported the continuation of the emperor system as defined under the new constitution. In the same survey, 68.5 percent answered that the Showa Emperor should stay on the throne, 18.4 percent preferred his abdication, and only 4 percent were in favor of the abolition of the emperor system.[30] When the era of Showa came to an end with the death of the emperor in 1989, the *Asahi shinbun*'s survey showed that "a full 83 percent of the population declared themselves content with the so-called symbolic emperor system" defined under the constitution.[31]

These surveys seem to confirm that the Japanese public is inclined to embrace the myth of the Showa Emperor as a peacemaker because doing so allows them to dissociate themselves from the issue of war responsibility.

As this study shows, the origins of the naïve and rather irresponsible pacifism in postwar Japan could be traced back to the Japanese people's memory of how the Asia-Pacific War came to an end and how their memory of the Showa Emperor's role in the war allowed them to dissociate themselves from the issue of war responsibility. It is important for historians to keep reminding the public of the danger of accepting myths and of ignoring the ways memories of past events can influence contemporary issues. Historians can offer narratives on crucial topics such as the Showa Emperor's role, the use of the atomic bomb, and the legacy of the Tokyo Trial to illuminate the rather unsettling causal relationship between war memory and people's attitude toward peace. And Japanese people badly need an accurate historical perspective on the Asia-Pacific War in order to engage constructively in the current debate over Japan's peace constitution, specifically over the clause on the renunciation of war in Article IX.

## Notes

1. Ernest R. May, *"Lessons" of the Past*, ix-xiv.
2. Ernest R. May, *"Lessons" of the Past*, 189.
3. Roger W. Smith, "The Armenian Genocide: Memory, Politics, and the Future," 14, in Richard G. Hovannisian, ed., *The Armenian Genocide: History, Politics, Ethics*.
4. Yasumasa Hosaka, *Senso-kan naki heiwaron*. Yutaka Yoshida, *Nihonjin ho senso-kan*.
5. Yutaka Yoshida, *Nihonjin no senso-kan*, 198.
6. There are numerous Japanese historians who treat Japan's military aggression in Asia and the Pacific as the so-called Fifteen Year War (e.g., Akira Fujiwara, Saburo Ienaga, Yutaka Yoshida, and Akira Yamada).
7. Carol Gluck, *Showa: The Japan of Hirohito*, 11-13.
8. John Dower, "The Bombed: Hiroshima and Nagasaki in Japanese Memory," 280-281.
9. John Dower, *Embracing Defeat*, chapter 11.
10. James J. Orr, *The Victim as Hero*, 14-31.
11. Carol Gluck, "The Idea of Showa," 1.
12. Robert J.C. Butow, *Japan's Decision to Surrender*.

13. Robert J.C. Butow, *Japan's Decision to Surrender*, 231.
14. Akira Yamada and Atsushi Koketsu, *Osusugita seidan*. Herbert Bix, *Hirohito and the Making of Modern Japan*.
15. Hidenari Terasaki and Mariko Terasaki Miller, *Showa tenno dokuhakuroku*, 115-120.
16. Michio Kinoshita, *Sokkin nisshi*, 229.
17. Hidenari Terasaki and Mariko Terasaki Miller, *Showa tenno dokuhakuroku*, 133.
18. Kazutoshi Hando, *Seidan*.
19. Edward T. Linenthal and Tom Engelhardt, eds., *History Wars*, Introduction by the editors.
20. John Dower, "Three Narratives of Our Humanity," in Edward T. Linenthal and Tom Engelhardt, eds., *History Wars*, 72, 87-90.
21. Paul Boyer, *Fallout*, 10.
22. Yoshikuni Igarashi, *Bodies of Memory*, chapter 1.
23. Sadao Asada, "The Shock of the Atomic Bomb and Japan's Decision to Surrender—A Reconsideration," *Pacific Historical Review*, 477-512.
24. Robert J.C. Butow, *Japan's Decision to Surrender*, 3-4.
25. Kenneth J. Ruoff, *The People's Emperor*, 128-129.
26. James J. Orr, *The Victim as Hero*, 34.
27. Hidenari Terasaki and Mariko Terasaki Miller, *Showa tenno dokuhakuroku*, 126. Michio Kinnoshita, *Sokkin nisshi*, 223, 228. Diary of Kido Koichi in the collection of Kido-ke bunsho (in microfilm), Japanese National Diet Library, August 29, 1945; October 17, 1951; November 28, 1951; April 4, 1952; May 2, 1952. Kentaro Awaya, et al., eds., *Kido Koichi jinmon chosho*, 559-562.
28. Kyoko Kato, *Showa tenno shazai shochoku soko no hakken*, 10.
29. Tadao Sato, "Hirohito no bisho (Hirohito's Smile)" *Chuo koron* (September 1959), cited in Kenneth J. Ruoff, *The People's Emperor*, 136.
30. Yutaka Yoshida, *Nihonjin no senso-kan*, 46.
31. *Asahi shinbun*, February 8, 1989, cited in Carol Gluck, "The Idea of Showa," 17.

## References

Asada, Sadao. "The Shock of the Atomic Bomb and Japan's Decision to Surrender—A Reconsideration." *Pacific Historical Review* 67 (November 1998): 477-512.

Awaya, Kentaro, et al., eds. *Kido Koichi jinmon chosho* (Protocol of the Interrogation of Kido Koichi). First edition. Tokyo: Otsuki shoten, 1987.

Bix, Herbert P. *Hirohito and the Making of Modern Japan*. New York: Herper Collins Publishers, 2000.

Boyer, Paul. *Fallout: A Historian Reflects on America's Half-Century Encounter with Nuclear Weapons*. Columbus: Ohio State University Press, 1998.

Butwo, Robert J. C. *Japan's Decision to Surrender*. Stanford: Stanford University Press, 1954.

Dower, John W. "The Bombed: Hiroshima and Nagasaki in Japanese Memory." *Diplomatic History* 19 (Spring 1995): 275-295.

————. *Embracing Defeat: Japan in the Wake of World War II*. New York: W.W. Norton and Company, 1999.

Gluck, Carol, and Stephen R. Graubard, eds. *Showa: The Japan of Hirohito*. New York: W.W. Norton and Company, 1992.

Hando, Kazutoshi. *Seidan: tenno to Suzuki Kantaro* (The imperial decision: the Emperor and Kantaro Suzuki). Tokyo: Bungei shunju, 1988.

Hosaka, Yasumasa. *Senso-kan naki heiwaron* (Pacifism without a concept of war). Tokyo: Chuokoron shinsha, 2003.

Igarashi, Yoshikuni. *Bodies of Memory: Narratives of War in Postwar Japanese Culture, 1945-1970*. Princeton: Princeton University Press, 2000.

Kato, Kyoko. *Showa tenno shazai shochoku soko no hakken* (The discovery of a draft of the Showa Emperor's apology). Tokyo: Bungei shunju, 2003.

Kinoshita, Michio. *Sokkin nisshi* (A chamberlain's diary). Tokyo: Bungei shunju, 1990.

Linenthal, Edward T., and Tom Engelhardt, eds. *History Wars: The Enola Gay and Other Battles for the American Past*. New York: Metropolitan Books, 1996.

Masumi, Junnosuke. *Showa tenno to sono jidai* (The Showa Emperor and his era). Tokyo: Yamakawa shuppan, 1998.

May, Ernest R. *"Lessons" of the Past: The Use and Misuse of History in American Foreign Policy*. New York: Oxford University Press, 1973.

Orr, James J. *The Victims as Hero: Ideologies of Peace and National Identity in Postwar Japan*. Honolulu: University of Hawai'i Press, 2001.

Smith, Roger W. "The Armenian Genocide: Memory, Politics, and the Future." Edited by Richard G. Hovannisian. *The Arminian Genocide: History, Politics, Ethics*. New York: St. Martin's Press, 1992.

Ruoff, Kenneth J. *The People's Emperor: Democracy and the Japanese Monarchy, 1945-1995*. Cambridge: Harvard University Press, 2001.

Terasaki, Hidenari, and Mariko Terasaki Miller. *Showa tenno dokuhakuroku: Terasaki Hidenari, goyo-gakari nikki* (The Showa Emperor monologue and the diary of an unattached court official, Hidenari Terasaki). Tokyo: Bungei shunju, 1991.

Yamada, Akira, and Atsushi Koketsu, *Ososugita seidan* (Delayed Imperial Decision). Tokyo: Showa shuppan, 1991.

Yoshida, Yutaka. *Nihonjin no senso-kan: sengoshi no nakano henyo* (Japanese views of the war): transformation in the postwar history). Tokyo: Iwanami shoten, 1995.

# nineteen

# A Reflection on the Pacifist Principle of the Japanese Constitution and on the Idea of Human Security

## Shin Chiba

## 1. Introduction: "Peace Constitution" and Postwar Pacifism

Japan's aggressive war activities, which had lasted fifteen years after the invasion of Manchuria, ended in the most devastating kind of defeat on August 15, 1945. In the intervening years, imperial Japan's military forces had attempted to conquer the neighboring countries of East and Southeast Asia and had attempted to defeat the Allies. As is widely known, the Japanese troops' invasion of neighboring and enemy countries caused disastrous consequences and horrible losses. The invasion is reported to have resulted in approximately twenty million casualties, including invaders and victims, soldiers and civilians.

After its defeat, Japan set forth on the task of rebuilding the nation anew out of the ashes and broken remains under the Allied Forces' occupation of the land. In 1947, Japan promised to entirely demilitarize the nation, and renounced war altogether, in line with the demands of the Potsdam Declaration. This resolution for the renouncement of war and the abdication of military forces was promulgated in 1947 in the so-called "Peace Constitution."

Thus, in its Preamble and in Article 9, the postwar Japanese Constitution is unique in its proclamation of the pacifist principle. Let me quote the second paragraph of the Preamble, and Article 9, as follows:

The Second Paragraph of the Preamble:
......We, the Japanese people, desire peace for all time and are deeply conscious of the high ideals controlling human relationship, and we have determined to preserve our security and existence, trusting in the justice and faith of the peace-loving peoples of the world. We desire to occupy an honored place in international society striving for the preservation of peace, and the banishment of tyranny and slavery, oppression and intoler-

ance for all time from the earth. We recognize that all peoples of the world have the right to live in peace, free from fear and want.

**Article 9:**

1. Aspiring sincerely to an international peace based on justice and order, the Japanese people forever renounce war as a sovereign right of the nation and the threat or use of force as a means of settling international disputes.
2. In order to accomplish the aim of the preceding paragraph, land, sea, and air forces, as well as other war potential, will never be maintained. The right of belligerency of the state will not be recognized.

For the last half-century or so, the constitutional principle of pacifism as one of three fundamental principles—the other two being popular sovereignty (democracy) and respect for fundamental human rights—despite changes and tensions under postwar politics, has managed to operate well enough as postwar Japan's public philosophy. Furthermore, it is important to note that the type of pacifism stipulated in the Constitution does *not* simply mean "anti-war-ism" or "war-opposition" in a broad sense of the term.[1] For this broad kind of pacifism only rejects the so-called aggressive war but supports a so-called just war or self-defense war. It is rather a radical kind of *pacifism—tettei heiwashugi*—heavily influenced by the Japanese experience and deep sense of shock and remorse for the war's calamity.

Japan's constitutional pacifism demands that all wars be considered illegal. This shows the historical lineage of Japanese constitutional pacifism. This pacifism goes back in international law history to a series of stipulations which suggest the "outlawry of war" in various historical documents: the Covenant of the League of Nations (1919), the Anti-war Treaty (1928), and the UN Charter (1945). In addition, Japanese constitutional pacifism took a step further both by rejecting as a principle military power settlements of international disputes and by aiming not to retain any potential to wage war.

However, when it comes to the conduct and policy of the Japanese government, the principle of constitutional pacifism was, in fact, consistently under threat from about 1949 onward. This was due to the beginning of the Cold War, which brought about a shift in U.S. East Asian policy. This in turn had a great impact on the postwar policies of Japan's conservative administration. The self-defense forces were created in 1952, with government explanations that this would not lead to development of the military or the war potential that the Constitution clearly prohibited. More recently, in December 2001 during the war in Afghanistan, Japanese self-defense forces were dispatched to the Indian Ocean and the Arabian Sea in order to provide logistic support to the U.S. and its allies. And in December 2003, the self-defense forces were sent to Samawa in Iraq for humanitarian and nation-rebuilding tasks. The great majority of constitutional law scholars in Japan regard these actions by the Japanese government as unconstitutional. The politics of Japan today has entered, as Masaya Kobayashi argues, the stage of "decisive unconstitutionality."[2] Never in the postwar period has such a clear violation been committed against the principles of Japan's constitutional pacifism.

There is no doubt, concerning the principle of *radical pacifism*, that the recent series of Japanese government actions mentioned above clearly mark a turning point in postwar Japanese politics. With regard to the principle of constitutional pacifism, the dispatching of self-defense forces overseas has weakened the Koizumi administration's legitimacy, due to the apparent unconstitutionality of these actions. At the same time, these actions of the Japanese government clearly imply that the tacit social contract between the Japanese people and the government concerning pacifism (as it was enacted in 1947 when the Constitution was ratified) was unilaterally breached by the government. We are now faced with a critical situation, witnessing a breach of the social contract regarding postwar Japan's pacifism, as something similar to what Robert N. Bellah referred to as a "broken covenant."[3] What is meant by a "broken covenant" here, then, is a situation in which the Japanese people's tacit social contract with the government (a social contract in which the principle of pacifism was accepted and upheld) has been made obsolete.

Today public opinion has also changed greatly. It was reported in the *Tokyo Newspaper* (February 15, 2004) and in the *Asahi Newspaper* (May 1, 2004) that about 70 percent of Diet members and 51 percent of the Japanese populace are considering the need for constitutional revision in one way or other. Constitutional revision of the Preamble and of Article 9 has been proposed both by the current ruling party—the Liberal Democratic Party (LDP)—and the prime opposition party—the Democratic Party of Japan (DPJ). And about 40 percent of the population now seems to agree to changing the actual statement of Article 9 to acknowledge the self-defense forces as the nation's proper military and to eliminate or change the "absolute-pacifistic" wordings of Article 9. Thus, in the post-Cold War period a number of politicians, bureaucrats, journalists, scholars and ordinary people in Japan began to question the feasibility of the pacifist principle of the Constitution: that is, to question the Constitution's *radical pacifism*. A steady and yet conspicuous turn to neo-conservatism took place in the Japan of the post-Cold War period. Today this neo-conservative bias can be observed in a number of areas—e.g., the Koizumi administration's national politics, its foreign policy, the sentiment and public opinion of the Japanese populace, and in the media treatment of peace, security and war. The same trend can also be witnessed in the emergence of neo-nationalism in discussions of diverse public issues—e.g., history textbooks, Japan's wartime and postwar responsibilities, including the problem of the so-called "wartime comfort women" and foreign policy toward North Korea.

The last point to consider is the characteristics of Japan's postwar pacifism. Postwar Japanese pacifism is deeply rooted in, and hence supported by, the miserable and tragic experiences of Japanese people who suffered great losses and human misery. As a prominent leader of citizens' movements in postwar Japan, Makoto Oda mentioned in a recent book that postwar Japanese pacifism is a "pacifism of immediate experiences" (*taiken teki heiwashugi*), rooted deeply in the strong feelings of ordinary people of Japan about the calamity and guilt of war.[4]

Japan's constitutional pacifism has implied a tacit social contract among the people themselves, as well as between the people and the government. As is true with every promulgation of a Constitution, the making of a Constitution is an act of social contact which enables the people to take ownership of the political regime to which they are committed.[5] Although a view is still held by a few observers that the Japanese Constitution was "imposed from the outside" because of its initial drafting by the U.S. authorities (GHQ) and hence was never genuinely an agreement of the people, the Constitution itself, and its pacifist principle in particular, were, in fact, welcomed and supported by the great majority of the Japanese people. This welcoming atmosphere of the people was documented by the public opinion surveys conducted by major newspapers at that time. The welcoming atmosphere meant that the making of the Constitution was based upon the tacit consent among the Japanese populace at that time.[6]

But this "pacifism of immediate experiences" had a fatal flaw in that it did not become a "pacifism of reflected experiences." To be sure, the "pacifism of immediate experiences" has its own strengths. This is evident in the fact that it was never an abstract ideal, dissociated with ordinary people's everyday feelings and experiences. Indeed, the call for pacifism was the natural cry of a people who had known a hellish experience—the human misery that comprised the sufferings of the Japanese people after the atomic bombs.[7] The Japanese people, at a rare moment in history, were allowed to have a glimpse of the ontological futility or impossibility of war in the age of nuclear weapons.

As it is often the case with life itself, the very strength of the Japanese populace—who learned the precious lesson of pacifism from their "immediate experiences" of calamities of war—turned into a weakness in itself. That is to say, the "immediate experiences" of the futility of war did not become incarnate in the national life in a way which could be shared by even the next generation. It meant that the passing away of the war generation, after a lapse of time, simply might signify the end of postwar Japanese constitutional pacifism. I am afraid that something like this is happening in the current Japanese discussion about war, nationalism, and constitutional alteration.

It is true that postwar Japanese pacifism was based on the people's weariness and abhorrence of war experiences. It was not an active kind of pacifism as seen in nonviolent pacifism, conscientious objection to war activities, and so forth. But this *ensen* (war weariness/abhorrence) pacifism was deeply rooted in the Japanese tradition. In his recent book on civil disobedience, Toshio Terajima, a Japanese political theorist, has attempted to make the rejection of conscription a category of pacifism which characterizes the genealogy of hidden pacifism in Japan.[8] For some people, however, *ensen* pacifism does not count as an authentic kind of pacifism, due to its passivity.

Despite these historical and ideological setbacks, however, I would like to emphasize here the significant and favorable role which constitutional pacifism has played in Japan's postwar history. For example, Japan's postwar pacifism, no matter how passive and vulnerable it has been, prevented the Japanese government from engaging in war activity until recently. The Japanese self-defense forces killed no one for five decades. Indeed, it was a great achievement or a non-achievement, one might say, especially in view of the losses of about twenty million lives during the Asia-Pacific War (also known as the Fifteen Years War). This contributed greatly to the maintenance of peace in East Asia. Peace, which was negative peace in the sense of the absence of war, was maintained for more than four decades in East Asia. Furthermore, the presence of Article 9 also helped generate a postwar civic culture of peace and democracy. Critical citizenry could use the provisions of Article 9 to criticize and contain the government's potentially militaristic activities within a permissible pacifism. Through education, the abhorrence of war and the demand for the prohibition of war have been inculcated in the hearts of Japan's young people for many years. Ordinary Japanese people today are not likely to believe in the *Realpolitik* of military operation.[9]

## 2. The Preamble and Its Declaration of the Right to Live in Peace

As previously mentioned, the postwar government made a series of "interpretive changes of Article 9"—*kaishaku kaiken*—and, based upon these changes, the government took a number of problematic steps such as the creation of self-defense forces, the conclusion of the U.S.-Japan Security Treaty, and so forth. In contrast to the positions taken by the government, the majority of scholars of the Japanese Constitution still hold to a strict interpretation of Article 9: that is, as meaning both the renunciation of war (including so-called self-defense war) and the non-possession of military forces. In recent years, constitutional or political theorists from a relatively younger generation—such as Asaho Mizushima, Akihiko Kimijima, Toshio Terajima, and myself—have advanced a "nonviolence-pacifist" interpretation of Article 9. This is somewhat different in its implication and nuances from the somewhat "non-resistance-pacifist" interpretation of the majority of the scholars of the relatively older generation. For, example, Terajima argues that the first clause of Article 9 expresses the principle of nonviolence and that its second clause is the manifestation of the principle of total disarmament.[10] However, these younger interpreters, who adhere to a nonviolent pacifist reading of Article 9, tend to make a distinction between the nation's right to self-defense war (*jus ad bellum*) and its right to self-defense or self-preservation: these scholars affirm the latter but reject the former. This distinction also enables them to argue as well that the Preamble and Article 9 do not prohibit Japanese citizens, in the case of emergency, from engaging in nonviolent defensive activities of various kinds such as "citizenry defense," "civil defense," "social defense," "general strikes," or "non-cooperation."[11] Again in recent years, such diverse advocates as Charles M. Overby, Masao Kunihiro, and Makoto Oda have argued that the Preamble and Article 9 are congenial with the idea of a pacifist Japan as the "conscientious objector nation."[12]

In 1962, constitutional law scholar Yasusaburo Hoshino wrote a celebrated article entitled "Heiwateki seizonken joron" (A Prolegomenon to the Right to Live in Peace). In this article, he proposed a view that the Preamble's declaration of peace should be strictly understood as a universal right—not only of the Japanese people but also of the people of the world. Since that time a number of constitutional law scholars have explored the meaning of the right to live in peace in many different ways. In 1973, the First Naganuma decision acknowledged for the first time that the right to live in peace is a human right. But what kind of right is the right to live in peace?

There has been discussion among scholars about the constitutional grounding of the right to live in peace, i.e., whether this right is grounded in the second paragraph of the Preamble alone, or in the Preamble and Article 9, or in the Preamble, Article 9 and Article 13. It is not so useful in the context of this article to enter into the details of the discussion. Suffice it to say here that this right to live in peace declared in the Preamble is not only grounded in Article 13 and other related human rights stipulations, but is also institutionally expressed and supported by Article 9.

The first point to establish is that the right to live in peace declared in the Preamble is grounded in Article 13, which stipulates the constitutional respect for the people's "right to life, liberty, and the pursuit of happiness." The right to peace does not make any sense unless the right to life is recognized. The right to live in peace is certainly part of the people's right to life, liberty and pursuit of happiness. And this right to peace is guaranteed unless it infringes on public welfare. The concept of public welfare also includes the contents of Article 9, i.e., the abdication of war and the non-possession of military forces.

The bearer of the right to peace is, according to the wordings of the Preamble, people in the world as well as the people in Japan. T. Fukase, T. Yamauchi and others maintain that this idea includes not only the Japanese nation and individuals belonging to it but also foreign residents in Japan and people around the world.[13] Thus, according to this view, the right to live in peace first and foremost implies that the Japanese people have a right to peace both as a nation, and as individuals vis-à-vis other states as well as their own state. But in addition, the right to live in peace means not only the right of all inhabitants in the land of Japan but also the right of all peoples and all individuals in the world to live in peace. Thus, possessors of this right are 1) the Japanese nation and individuals; 2) the residents in Japan; and 3) the people and individuals of the world (though not the states of the world). Likewise, the right of self-defense that was presumed in Article 9 must be the nation's right as well as the individuals' right but not the state's right.

What does the right to live in peace mean or include then? First of all, one should bear in mind that the Preamble's stipulation of the right to live in peace has a definite and concrete historical setting: a world threatened by war and militarism. So the concept of the right to live in peace is one that is closely related to the threat of the state power, militarism in particular. Therefore, *primary* and *narrow, definite* and *negative* meaning is a people's right to reject every sort of state demand for conscription or imposition related to war. The demand for the renouncement of war and the non-possession of war potential in Article 9 is a necessary institutional corollary of this right. So in my view, this *military-related characteristic* of the right to live in peace should never be forgotten. In other words, a unique feature of the right to live in peace as stipulated in the Preamble consists in the prevention of one's own state or military from either rejecting or violating people's or individuals' right to live in peace. Here can be detected a kind of pessimistic realism or skepticism in the Japanese Constitution that was born out of the people's painful experiences of the demonic war.

The implication or ramification of this *primary* and *negative* sense of the right to live in peace is rich and deep, indeed. I would like to indicate a historical linkage of some of the wordings of the Preamble to Franklin D. Roosevelt's "Four Freedoms," the last two in particular, i.e., "freedom from fear" and "freedom from want." The second paragraph of the Preamble speaks of the human condition "free from fear and want" as well as "the banishment of tyranny and slavery, oppression and intolerance for all time from the earth." Therefore, the *primary* and *negative* sense of the right to live in peace includes the right of individuals or people to be liberated from enslaving and dehumanizing power of every kind, whether it be fear, want, tyranny, slavery, oppression or intolerance. So the right to live in peace *negatively* guarantees that neither war nor one's own country's military—nor another country's military nor starvation nor terrorism nor anything else—can infringe, or threaten to infringe, one's own life, dignity and freedom.

Furthermore, this strict definition of the *negative* aspect of the right to live in peace can be combined with a *broader* and *positive* definition of it. In implication it is natural and appropriate to postulate that the right to live in peace *positively* means the right to act freely, to keep one's dignity, and to pursue one's own life in peace. Its *positive* meaning includes more comprehensively the pursuit of economic, spiritual, intellectual, and cultural activities in peace.[14]

## 3. The Idea of Human Security and the Right to Live in Peace

### (1) The Idea of Human Security

The idea of human security was officially proclaimed for the first time by the "Human Development Report" presented by the United Nations Development Programme (UNDP) in 1994.[15] The report spoke of the need for a wholesale reformulation of the idea of security, and proposed the need for a departure from state or national security by means of military power and nuclear weapons. The document also talked about the evolution from the narrow concept of the state or national security to the broader concept of human security. This is a postulation about the change from the notion of territory- and military-oriented security to the idea of human security through sustainable human development in the post-Cold War era. Although these proposals were not adopted in the Social Development Summit at Copenhagen 1994 (for which the Human Development Report 1994 had been prepared), the idea of human security was regarded—even outside the UN—as an indispensable concept for reshaping the international security policy at that time. The notion of human security under the current situation remains undetermined and fluid with its meaning still open to diverse interpretations.[16]

To be sure, since the late 1970s UN-related commissions have been proposing a departure from the paradigm of state or national security, to a broader conception of security such as common security. But the end of the Cold War was a decisive factor that promoted a radical alteration in the notion of security. Another concept to consider which supported the idea of human security was an earlier idea of "basic human needs" proposed by Johan Galtung and others. This earlier notion of "basic human needs" also paved the way for the emergence of the idea of "human security." At any rate, for the past few decades, a number of global problems have been clearly concentrated in the so-called third world: starvation, poverty, ecological disaster, the depletion of natural resources, population explosion and terrorism. Pivotal ideas like "human development," "basic human needs," "sustainable development" and "human security" were developed in order to cope with these global problems.

In terms of the substantive meaning of human security, cardinal values appear to include the ideas of "freedom from fear" and "freedom from want," again reminiscent of Franklin D. Roosevelt's "Four Freedoms" New Deal slogan of 1941. As was previously indicated, similar wording is observable in the Preamble of the Japanese Constitution. But in the latter, the negative concept of peace as the absence of war had already been overcome by the positive concept of it as the elimination of "fear" and "want," of "tyranny" and "slavery," of "oppression" and "intolerance." Therefore, the notion of human security is part of a somewhat idealistic lineage—not merely theoretical but also historical—of Franklin D. Roosevelt's New Deal philosophy and the Japanese Constitution, whose original draft was prepared by some New Dealers in the occupation forces.

From the mid-1990s, the idea of human security began to be adopted and elaborated as one of the central policies not only by the United Nation-related organization such as UNHCR, but also by governments of countries like Canada, Norway and Japan. The Japanese government began to pick up the idea of human security and established the Human Security Fund and continued to help financially so as to enhance and make concrete the policies of human development.

There is, however, an apprehension continually expressed by scholars in the fields of international law and international relations regarding the diffusion of the concept of security through such ideas as human security, democratic security and cooperative security.[17] Furthermore, questions are sometimes raised in this connection with regard to the relationship between the traditional idea of state (or national) security and the more recent concept of human security. There have been different understandings concerning whether priority should be accorded either to state security or to human security. My view is that unless the priority of human security over the state security is upheld, the notion of human security will be abused as a mere slogan or a façade, so that it may be coopted by the ideology of state security to justify its own existence. Thus, the idea of human security has to be coupled both with the principle of *nonviolence* in the sense of no use of military forces, and with the principle of *democratization* in the sense of empowering the socially vulnerable and the powerless. Johan Galtung, for example, is apprehensive about the actual function of human security. Recently he has stated that he preferred the notion of "basic human needs" to that of "human security." For Galtung argues that due to the usage of the very term "security," the notion of human *security* can easily pave the way for the militaristic operations of state *security*, either by a single sovereign state such as the United States or even by the United Nations. Thus, Galtung is afraid that it would be very likely for the notion of human security to be misused, either as a sort of camouflage or as an idealistic slogan by a sovereign state system (and by the United Nations) so as to strengthen and justify the state's militaristic security strategy.[18]

An important point to note, therefore, is the necessity to underscore that the means for achieving human security should be *nonviolence*, and that the goal of human security is the *democratic empowering* of a powerless people. The idea of human security aims at achieving the people's "basic human needs" such as food, health, shelter, employment, income, the protection of the natural environment, the elimination of crimes, conflict prevention, peace building and so forth. These problems cannot be handled without the cooperation of concerned citizens and people.[19]

### (2) Human Security and the Right to Live in Peace

When the "Human Development Report" of 1994 was first presented to the world, a number of Japanese scholars—of the Japanese Constitution, international politics and international relations—began to recognize a certain strong resemblance between the idea of the right to live in peace stipulated in the Preamble of the Japanese Constitution and the newly presented idea of human security.[20]

In the current conditions of international politics, the idea of human security, backed up by the right to live in peace, can be regarded as a counter-vision of a more humane world governance, as opposed to the financial globalization—neo-liberal global hegemony—of the "new world order." Furthermore, recent developments of the idea of human security by Kinhide Mushakoji and others tend to suggest that the idea can become the core of a counter proposal, to offset the monopolization of security strategy by the sovereign state system.[21]

Then, in order to retain the idea of human security as an alternative vision and strategy, in contrast to the current imperialistic, neo-liberal globalization of the "new world order," this vision must be grounded in, and combined with, ordinary people's moral and legal self-proclamations of the right to live in peace. The world today needs the painful realism and skepticism of the Japanese Constitution. This painful realism holds to the premise that the militaristic strategy of the sovereign state can easily lead to the destructive consequence of denying the lifeworld of ordinary people; that is, destroying their very life, peace, and security. The United Nations needs this sort of painful realism in order to use a strategy of human security in a wise and constructive manner. In this connection it is worth remembering that S. Ogata and A. Sen, the Chairs of the "Commission on Human Security" issued an aforementioned Commission Report in May 2003 called "Human Security Now." "... The state remains the fundamental purveyor of security. Yet it often fails to fulfill its security obligations—and at times has even become a source of threat to its own people. That is why attention must now shift from the security of the state to the security of the people—to human security."[22] The Japanese government's current adherence to the idea of human security has serious defects due to Japan's strong commitment to the global hegemony of the "new world order." Unless Japan's main strategy is altered by the government, in line with the postulates of the right to live in peace, the Japanese government's slogan on human security sounds very weak and even hypocritical.[23]

## 4. Conclusion: A New Politics of Survival at the Threshold of the 21st Century

Despite the recent upsurge of terrorism in some parts of the world and despite the neo-imperialistic slogan of "anti-terrorist war" that permeates the world today, I would like to argue that the threshold of the twenty-first century will demand a paradigm shift in the politics of survival, from the modern Hobbesian scheme to a post-Hobbesian one. A post-Hobbesian orientation in the politics of survival has to be informed and sustained by such ideas as ecological justice, human security, and the right to live in peace. These ideas will alone be capable of doing justice to the needs and aspirations of the people living in this age.

Where does the Japanese politics of constitutional pacifism start to express itself? What is the right step for Japan to take at the beginning of the twenty-first century in order to promote peace, reconciliation, and nonviolence in a world afflicted with suffering, misery, and fear of terrorism and war? I have two suggestions in mind.

First, I would like to propose that the first thing that the Japanese government should do is to officially proclaim its war responsibilities and guilt for its aggressions during World War II. The government should offer reparations for the victimized nations. One might think that because more than half a century has passed since the end of World War II, it would be too late to perform such an act of war responsibility and guilt. But in my view, it is never too late to do the right thing, and especially to correct past neglect to do what should have been done.

The postwar Japanese government never made an official governmental apology to, or provided financial compensation for, the victimized nations. Its official position was that the postwar government's compliance with the Potsdam Declaration, and its participation in the Tokyo Tribunal, had once and for all settled the issue of Japan's war responsibility. Therefore, the argument goes, such contemporary issues as compensation for the wartime comfort women from neighboring countries mobilized into imperial Japan's war activities should be made not by the Japanese government, but by initiatives of Japanese private organizations, groups, and individuals. However, this official government view is not sufficient, especially when one considers the atrocious nature of Japan's Fifteen Years War.

The second proposal for the Japanese government (in a ten to twenty year time frame) is to establish, if possible, an East Asian collective security agreement based upon reconciliation and friendship among East Asian countries such as Taiwan, South Korea, North Korea, the Philippines, and China. In the context of twenty-first century politics in East Asia, it is an imperative to establish the collective security regime. Japan can participate in this collective security regime by undertaking and fulfilling non-militaristic roles. In the Pacific region, the U.S.-Japan Security Treaty should be reorganized as a Pacific security treaty among all the Pacific Rim countries. Meanwhile, in view of a future world of peace that might be coming a century from now, Japan should try its best to encourage the establishment of a decentralized and world-federal UN police and military forces only to disarm every state in the world at one and the same time. The UN police and military forces are needed, for example, to cope with the terrorist activities around the world.

Prince Shotoku, who lived in the end of the seventh and the beginning of the eighth centuries, promulgated the famous Constitution of 17 Articles (604). This document was the first "Peace Constitution" ever written in Japan that clearly stated in Article 1: "Let peace be respected among you." (*wa o motte totoshi to nasu.*) Prince Shotoku also spoke of the words taken from *Rongo* (The Analects of Confucius): "Let us have peace but not become the same." (*wa shite do sezu.*). His pacifist idea of *wa* is the same positive peace which Galtung and others spoke of: an attitude mutually possessing the core of peace, benevolence and forgiveness which even covers and extends to one's own enemy. *Wa* is for Prince Shotoku the peaceable attitude which overcomes group egoism and self-centeredness. Unfortunately his notion of *wa* is often misunderstood and misrepresented in Japan. In his case *wa* is never *do*, or sameness. *Wa*, on the contrary, can be said to be Prince Shotoku's own idea of *kyosei*. For to the Prince, *wa* basically means an attitude of seeking commonality by affirming the other's difference and the heterogeneity. This is something similar to Ivan Illich's notion of "conviviality." Kyoji Watanabe, a Japanese translator of Illich's book *Tools for Conviviality* (1973) rendered the term "conviviality" *jiritsu-kyosei* which means something like "the condition of living together with respect for the mutual sense of independence."[24] Prince Shotoku's idea of *wa* has rich theoretical potentials in its implication and application. Thus, it seems to possess radical relevance to our contemporary discussion of peace, security, and *kyosei*.

## Notes

1.  Cf., Teichman (1986), 1-12.
2.  E.g., Kobayashi (2004), 4-8. Chiba (2004), 42-43.
3.  Bellah (1975).
4.  Oda (2001), 12-14.
5.  E.g., Arendt (1976), 166-178. Cf., Chiba (1996), 121-158.
6.  It does not necessarily mean that there have not existed some historical or ideological shortcomings in the promulgation of the Japanese Constitution of 1947. The following are among the examples: the survival of the emperor-system as "symbolic emperor-system" as a compensation for the near-to-tal disarmament of the mainland of Japan, the thorough going militarization of Okinawa in lieu of the adoption of Article 9, and the continuous disregard for the voice of the victimized neighboring Asian countries and of the Asian residents in Japan. E.g., Koseki (2002), v-x, 1-50, 105-107, 275. Mizushima (1997), 153-156. Kan (1995), 7-9, 102-105, 112-113, 156-161.
7.  According to John W. Dower, some difficult years immediately after Japan's defeat proved to be the years of "miracle" when the Japanese, while "embracing defeat," began to search for a new way of living. Despite the most miserable and fatal kind of the defeat of war, strangely enough a kind of idealism began to catch hold of the people's heart and became a national reality during the short period immediately after the war. Cf., Dower (2001), xiii-xv. Dower (1999), 24-25.
8.  Terajima (2004), 188-191, 200-212. Cf., Fukase (1987), 89-91, 131-135.
9.  E.g., Ota (1990), 92-93. Okudaira (2003), 34-35. Sugihara (1998), 121-122. Yamauchi (2003), 252-255.
10. Terajima (2004), 260-267.
11. E.g., ibid., 185-318. Sharp (1990). Randle (1994). Mizushima (1997). Kimijima (2004), 79-84. Chiba (2003), 209-211.
12. E.g., Overby (1997), 30-31, 109, 130-134. Oda (2003).
13. E.g., Fukase (1987), 227. Yamauchi (1992), 282-287.

14. E.g., Fukase (1987), 198-285, 290-291. Yamauchi (1992), 278, 287-292. Yamauchi (2004), 98-100, 262.
15. UNDP Human Development Report (1994), 22-46. Kokuren Kaihatsu Keikaku (UNDP) (1995), 22-40.
16. Cf., Kurusu (2001), 115-122.
17. E.g., Ueki (2004), 85-86.
18. This view was expressed at the following international symposium. Johan Galtung, "Keynote Speech: Human Security—Promotion of Justice and Peace," at The 23rd International Symposium, Cosponsored by ISSJ, Sophia University and SSRI, ICU (December 14, 2003).
19. Yamauchi (2004), 283-285. Cf., Mushakoji (1998), 170-174. Cf., Mushakoji (2003), 117-124,185-186.
20. K. Mushakoji, an eminent peace researcher, for instance, wrote an important article entitled "Heiwateki seizonken to ningen no anzenhosho" [The Right to Live in Peace and Human Security] in 1998. For Mushakoji it is an imperative to combine the notion of human security and that of the right to live in peace, because the former as a *policy goal* can give the latter as a *human right* a much needed historical orientation, while the latter provides the former with the legal basis. Cf., Mushakoji (1998), 166-193.
21. Cf., Mushakoji (2003), 19, 31-38, 185.
22. Ogata and Sen (2003), 2. Cf., Ningen no anzenhosho iinkai report (2003), 10-11.
23. Cf., Urabe (2004), 64-65.
24. Cf., Illich (1989), xv-xvii, 16-85, 160, 212-213. 218-220.

# References

Hannah Arendt, *On Revolution* (New York: Penguin Books, 1976).
Robert N. Bellah, *The Broken Covenant: American Civil Religion* (New York: Seabury Press, 1975).
Shin Chiba, *Arendt to Gendai* [Arendt and the Present Age] (Tokyo: Iwanami Shoten Publishers, 1996).
Shin Chiba, "Sengo nihon no shakaikeiyaku wa haki saretanoka" [Was the Social Covenant of Postwar Japan Broken?] in *Senso hihan no kokyo tetsugaku* [Critical Public Philosophy against War], ed. M. Kobayashi (Tokyo: Keiso Shobo Publishers, 2003).
Shin Chiba, "Rikkenshugi no kiki to shimin seiji no shorai" [The Crisis of Constitutionalism and the Future of Citizens' Politics], *Horitsu Jiho* [Law Journal], Vol. 76. No. 7 (June 2004).
John W. Dower, *Embracing Defeat: Japan in the Wake of World War II* (New York: W. W. Norton & Company, Inc., 1999).
John W. Dower, "Nihon no dokusha ni" [For Japanese Readers], in *Haiboku o dakishimete* [Embracing Defeat], Vol. 1. trans. Y. Miura et al. (Tokyo: Iwanami Shoten Publishers, 2001).
Tadakazu Fukase, *Senso hoki to heiwateki seizonken* [War Renouncement and the Right to Live in Peace] (Tokyo: Iwanami Shoten Publishers, 1987).
Dale M. Hellegers, *We, the Japanese People* (Stanford: Stanford University Press, 2002).
Glenn D. Hook and Gavan McCormack, *Japan's Contested Constitution* (London: Routledge, 2001).
Ivan Illich, *Conviviality notameno dogu* [Tools for Conviviality], trans. K. Watanabe et al. (Tokyo: Nihon Editors School Shuppanbu Publishers, 1989).
Kyoko Inoue, *MacArthur's Japanese Constitution* (Chicago: Chicago University Press, 1991).
Sunjun Kan, *Futatsu no sengo to nihon* [Two Postwar Periods and Japan] (Tokyo: San Ichi Shobo Publishers, 1995).
Akihiko Kimijima, "Buryoku nonai heiwa: koso to jissen" [Peace without Military Forces: Ideas and Practice], *Horitsu jiho* [Law Journal], Vol. 76. No. 7 (June 2004).
Masaya Kobayashi, "Risoshugiteki genjitsushugi toshiteno hisen kenpo kaishaku" [A Pacifist Interpretation of the Constitution as Idealistic Realism], *Chiba University Law Journal*, Vol. 18. Nos. 3 & 4 (February 2004).
Kokuren Kaihatsu Keikaku (UNDP), *Ningen kaihatsu hokokusho 1994* [Human Development Report 1994] (Tokyo: Kokusai Kyoryoku Shuppankai Publishers, 1995).

Shoichi Koseki, *Heiwa kokka nihon no saikento* [Re-examining the Pacifist State Japan] (Tokyo: Iwanami Shoten Publishers, 2002).

Kaoru Kurusu, "Ningen no anzenhosho" [Human Security] in T. Akaneya and K. Ochiai, eds., *Atarashii anzenhoshoron no shiza* [The Perspective of A New Theory of Security] (Tokyo: Aki Shobo Publishers, 2001).

Percy R. Luney, Jr. and Kazuyuki Takahashi, eds., *Japanese Constitutional Law* (Tokyo: University of Tokyo Press, 1993).

Asaho Mizushima, *Buryokunaki heiwa* [Peace without Military Power] (Tokyo: Iwanami Shoten Publishers, 1997).

Kinhide Mushakoji, "Heiwateki seizonken to ningen anzenhosho" [The Right to Live in Peace and Human Security] in T. Fukase et al. eds., *Kokyu sekaiheiwa notameni* [For Perpetual World Peace] (Tokyo: Keiso Shobo Publishers, 1998).

Kinhide Mushakoji, *Ningen anzenhoshoron josetsu* [A Prolegomenon to the Theory of Human Security] (Tokyo: Kokusai Shoin Publishers, 2003).

Ningen no anzenhosho iinkai report: "Anzen hosho no konnichiteki kadai" [The Committee of Human Security Report: "Human Security Now"] (Tokyo: Asahi Shinbun Publishers, 2003).

Makoto Oda, "Heiwa kenpo o motsu nihon to chikyu shimin no rentai" [Japan which Has Peace Constitution and Solidarity with Global Citizens], in *Chikyu shiminshakai to daigaku kyoiku no ikashikata* [Global Civil Society and the Way to Revitalize University Education], eds. ICU SSRI & Sophia University ISSJ (Tokyo: Gendai Jinbunsha Publishers, 2001).

Makoto Oda, *Ryoshinteki senso kyohi kokka* [The Conscientious Objection State] (Tokyo: Kodansha Publishers, 2003).

Sadako Ogata, Amartia Sen et al., "The Commission on Human Security Report: Human Security Now" (May 2003).

Yasuhiro Okudaira, *Kenpo no sozoryoku* [Imaginative Power of the Constitution] (Tokyo: Nihon Hyoronsha Publishers, 2003).

Kazuo Ota, "Kenryoku hibuso to nihonkoku kenpo" [Disarmament of Power and the Japanese Constitution], in *Heiwa to kokusaikyocho no kenpogaku* [Constitutional Studies of Peace and International Cooperation], eds. Y. Sugihara et al. (Tokyo: Keiso Shobo Publishers, 1990).

Charles M. Overby, *A Call for Peace: The Implications of Japan's War-Renouncing Constitution* (Tokyo: Kodansha International, 1997).

Michael Randle, *Civil Resistance* (London: Fontana Press, 1994).

Gene Sharp, *Civilian-based Defense: A Post-military Weapons System* (Princeton: Princeton University Press, 1990).

Yasuo Sugihara, "Kenpo dai 9 jo no Gendaiteki Igi" [The Contemporary Significance of the Constitution's Article 9] in T. Fukase et al. eds., *Kokyu sekaiheiwa notameni* [For Perpetual World Peace] (Tokyo: Keiso Shobo Publishers, 1998).

Jenny Teichman, *Pacifism and the Just War* (Oxford: Basil Blackwell, 1986).

Toshio Terajima, *Shiminteki fufukujyu* [Civil Disobedience] (Tokyo: Fukosha Publishers, 2004).

Toshiya Ueki, "9 Jo to anzenhosho taisei" [Article 9 and the Security System], *Jurist*, No. 1260 (January 1 & 15, 2004).

Noriho Urabe, "Kenpo 9 jo to ningen no anzenhosho" [The Article 9 of the Constitution and Human Security], *Horitsu jiho* [Law Journal], Vol. 76. No. 7 (June 2004).

Toshihiro Yamauchi, *Heiwa kenpo no riron* [The Theory of Peace Constitution] (Tokyo: Nihon Hyoronsha Publishers, 1992).

Toshihiro Yamauchi, *Jinken, shuken, heiwa* [Human Rights, Sovereignty, Peace] (Tokyo: Nihon Hyoronsha Publishers, 2003).

# Contributors

**Chiba, Shin**
Professor of Political Theory in the Division of Social Sciences and Dean of the Graduate School at International Christian University.

**Cottam, Martha**
Professor of Political Science in the Department of Political Science/Criminal Justice Program at Washington State University.

**Fujita, Hidenori**
Professor of Sociology of Education in the Division of Education at International Christian University.

**Hooks, Gregory**
Professor of Sociology and Chair of the Department of Sociology at Washington State University.

**Hallagan, William S.**
Associate Professor in the Department of Economics at Washington State University.

**He, Yijin**
Assistant Professor in the Department of Economics at Washington State University.

**Inaba, Frederick S.**
Associate Professor in the Department of Economics at Washington State University.

**Kawamura, Noriko**
Associate Professor in the Department of History and Director of the Asia Program at Washington State University.

**Kunugi, Tatsuro**
Formerly United Nations Assistant Secretary-General and Minister at the Permanent Mission of Japan in Geneva, and Professor of International Relations at International Christian University. Currently Center of Excellence Visiting Professor at International Christian University, and Visiting Professor at United Nations University.

**Marenin, Otwin**
Professor of Criminal Justice in the Department of Political Science/Criminal Justice Program at Washington State University.

**Matsuda, Noriyuki**
Professor and Chair of the Department of Quantitative Finance and Management in the Graduate School of Systems and Information Engineering at the University of Tsukuba.

**Meares, Mary M.**
Assistant Professor of Communication in the Edward R. Murrow School of Communication at Washington State University.

**Morimoto, Anri**
Professor of Theology in the Division of Humanities at International Christian University.

**Morshed, AKM Mahbub**
Professor in the Department of Economics at Southern Illinois University.

**Murakami, Yoichiro**
Professor Emeritus of the University of Tokyo, currently Othmer Distinguished Professor in the Division of Humanities and Graduate School Professor at International Christian University.

**Myers, Michael W.**
Professor in the Department of Philosophy at Washington State University.

**Nziramasanga, Mudziviri**
Associate Professor in the Department of Economics at Washington State University.

**Parks, Craig D.**
Associate Professor in the Department of Psychology at Washington State University.

**Rackham, David W.**
Professor of Psychology in the Division of Education at International Christian University.

**Reed, T. V.**
Professor of English and Director of American Studies at Washington State University.

**Rosa, Eugene A.**
Professor of Sociology in the Department of Sociology, Edward R. Meyer Professor of Natural Resources and Environmental Policy, Affiliated Professor of Environmental Science, and Affiliated Professor of Fine Arts at Washington State University.

**Someya, Yoshimichi**
Professor of Anthropology in the Division of Social Sciences at International Christian University.

**Stehr, Steven**
Associate Professor of Political Science and Chair of the Department of Political Science/Criminal Justice Program at Washington State University.

**Stone, Asako**
Ph.D. Candidate in the Department of Psychology at Washington State University.

**Sturgeon, Noël**
Associate Professor of Women's Studies and Chair of the Department of Women's Studies at Washington State University.

**Weber, Edward P.**
Associate Professor of Political Science in the Department of Political Science/Criminal Justice Program, Affiliated Professor of Environmental Science, and Director of the Thomas S. Foley Institute for Public Policy and Public Service at Washington State University.